HUMAN RIGHTS
IN SOUTHERN AFRICA

Edited by
Isaac MUTELO

HUMAN RIGHTS
IN SOUTHERN AFRICA

Theory and Practice

Preface by
Professor Therese Sacco

Domuni-Press

2024

THIS BOOK IS PUBLISHED
BY DOMUNI-PRESS
RESEARCH COLLECTION

Law

ISSN: 2999-2508
ISBN: 978-2-36648-213-3
© DOMUNI-PRESS, January 2024

Contents

Acknowledgements... 7
Preface.. 9
Notes on Contributors... 11
Introduction to Human Rights in Southern Africa.. 17

PART I: EDUCATION, MEDIA AND ICTs... 33

Douglas Musebenzi
A Critical Interrogation of the Realisation of the Right to
Free Basic Education in Zimbabwe, Zambia and South Africa 35

Dzavo Joseph
Human Rights Crisis in Zimbabwe: What is the Role of the School? 51

Tapiwa Musasa
Youths Rights to Quality Education in Rural Areas with Reference to
Gokwe North District, Zimbabwe: Challenges and Opportunities................................. 67

Wellington Gadzikwa and Pedzisai Ruhanya
Social Media and Communication Rights in Zimbabwe... 77

Isaac Mutelo and Steven Lishandi
The Role of Print and Online Newspapers in Protecting and
Promoting Human Rights in Southern Africa: The Case of Zimbabwe.......................... 91

Elisha Mupaikwa
The Nexus between National ICT Policies and the Right to Information Access:
An Analysis of ICT Policies in Selected Southern African Countries............................ 99

PART II: CHILD RIGHTS, PRISONER'S RIGHTS AND LABOUR RIGHTS...... 117

Witness Chikoko
Birth Registration among Street Children of the Harare Central
Business District, Zimbabwe: Challenges and Opportunities 119

Witness Chikoko and Kudzai Mwapaura
Substance Abuse and Sexual Behaviour among Street Children with Reference to
the Child Agency Theory: The Case of Harare Central Business District, Zimbabwe 129

Isaac Mutelo and Oswald Mgaya
The Confluence of Child Rights, Duties and Parentage: The Case of Southern Africa 139

Dorcas Tatenda Chitiyo
An Analysis of the Tenets of a Social Contract in Relation to the Blanket
Disenfranchisement of Pretrial Detainees and Prisoners in Zimbabwe 149

Peter Chikondi Matsimbe, Reuben Chifundo Nazombe and Isaac Mutelo
Competing Images of the Girl Child and Ending Child Marriages in Malawi 167

Thandekile Phulu
Labour Rights as Human Rights: A South African Perspective 185

PART III: HUMAN RIGHTS, DEMOCRACY AND THE ENVIRONMENT 201

Daglous Makumbe
Has Democracy Lost its Aura? Elections, Military Coups,
and Human Rights: Selected Cases from Southern Africa 203

Mundende James
Leadership Crisis, Democracy and Human Rights 223

Mazuruse Irony
The impact of the shrinking of Democratic Space in Zimbabwe on National
Development: A Case of the Second Republic of Zimbabwe 231

Thandekile Phulu
Intersecting Human Rights and Environmental Rights in South Africa.......................249

Lele Dominic Dummene
Karl Marx Justice in Environmental Discourse in South Africa 265

PART IV: HUMAN RIGHTS, RELIGION AND CULTURE.....................................281

Tendayi Dzinoreva, Francis Machingura and *Pearl Gambiza*
Divergent` or Convergent: The Battle of Culture, Religion and Human Rights..........283

Deliah Nyaradzo Jeranyama
Influence of African Traditional Religion on the Protection of Women
and Children's Rights in Blended Families within Shona Societies 295

Tauya Chinama, Edward Muzondo and *Isaac Mutelo*
Critical analysis of the Freedom of Thought, Conscience and Religion:
A case of Zimbabwe 309

Taruvinga Muzingili, Muzondo Edward, Kudzai Mwapaura and *Noel Garikai Muridzo*
Ritual Killings: Desire for Prosperity, Cultural Falsity and
Implications on Creeping Human Rights Laws in Southern Africa 319

Aubrey Tshepo Manthwa
Towards the Development of a Human Rights Script that Oscillates with Indigenous
Knowledge System: Emergence of Post—Decolonial Human Rights Discourse.........333

Muzondo Edward, Taruvinga Muzingili and Tauya Chinama
Domestication of Disability Rights in Southern Africa:
Lessons from a Zimbabwean Experience..345

Acknowledgements

The effort of over 28 contributors, including scholars, researchers, lecturers, teachers, social scientists, legal practitioners, philosophers, social workers and humanitarians, is unreservedly acknowledged. Special gratitude to Prof Anthony Chennells, Dr David Kaulem, Ms Tsitsi Wakatama, Prof Bernard Matolino, Mr Francis Zangairai, Fr Laurien Nyiribakwe, Dr Heidi Matisonn and Dr Immanuel Phiri for providing editorial assistance. I also wish to express my appreciation to Prof Therese Sacco, President of St Augustine College of South Africa, for providing a beautiful preface for this voluminous work. Other colleagues within the Dominican family, Mutelo family, Arrupe Jesuit University, University of Zimbabwe and Domuni Universitas supported the project.

Preface

This is a must have book for several reasons. First, Human Rights in Southern Africa, edited by Isaac Mutelo, is inclusive. It is inclusive of multiple disciplines. This is testament to the notion that we can no longer think, contemplate, write, and act in narrow silos of singular movements, and professional and academic disciplines. The scourge of violence and abuse requires that we all work together from our various positions. Second, it inheres the drive towards decoloniality through including and embracing voices of Southern African Africans; voices of women and men within the global south; voices of activists, practitioners, lecturers, and academics steeped in the praxis of human rights; and voices that move the discourse from focusing on individual human rights to concentrating on communal, societal, regional, and continental rights.

This is an essential reader for those who desire to sharpen, magnify, elevate, and embrace contributions to the discourse and practice of human rights by Pan African scholars and practitioners. It is a primer for those in the global south who study, confront, teach, and write about human rights as it fundamentally challenges systems that function as gatekeepers against voices that are not those of white men to preserve their status and power. Historically, and contemporarily, the cognitive empire delegitimates the empirical value of African and Indigenous voices, methods, and traditions. The nexus comes together where women's contributions are limited and reverberates with the silencing of African and Indigenous knowledges where histories, identities and experiences are either scanted or vandalised.

It is a key text as the knowledge generated is relevant to learning, teaching, and acting in the human rights arena in Southern Africa as it confronts conditions and problems in Africa articulated by Africans. It contributes to pertinent curriculum, pedagogies, research and learning and teaching in an African context.

It inspires young Africans to confidence, building respect, dignity and pride thereby encouraging generations of our young to study and engage in the essential study and practice of human rights within Southern Africa.

I feel privileged to be invited into this community of scholars, practitioners, and activists.

Prof Therese Sacco
(President, St Augustine College of South Africa)

Notes on Contributors

Aubrey Tshepo Manthwa (PhD) is Chair of the Department of Public Constitutional and International Law and Senior Lecturer at the University of South Africa. She has completed LLB, LLM and LLD with the University of South Africa. Her LLD focused on the interplay between giving African law its space in South Africa as a primary legal system. Her research interests include administrative law, constitutional law, family law, human rights law and customary law.

Daglous Makumbe (PhD) is a Research Associate in the Faculty of Economic and Management Sciences at the University of the Western Cape. His research interests include international criminal law, international relations, democracy and human rights, and international conflict management. He has published books, book chapters, and journal articles and presented at local, regional, and international conferences.

Deliah Nyaradzo Jeranyama (MA) is pursuing a Doctor of Philosophy with the Catholic University of Zimbabwe. She holds a Master's degree in Peace and Governance and an honours degree in Humanities and Social Sciences from Africa University. She is currently a Lecturer at Africa University with almost 10 years of teaching and research experience. She has conducted several commissioned and non-commissioned researches in the field of peace and her interests are in the areas of African traditional religion, negotiation and mediation, human-wildlife conflicts, development-induced conflicts and cultural identities. Deliah has also conducted some research on human rights in the context of African Traditional Religion as well as conflict dynamics that surround both women and children.

Dorcas Tatenda Chitiyo (LLM) is a registered legal practitioner practicing in Zimbabwe and a PhD student at the University of South Africa. She currently lectures at the Bindura University of Science Education under the Faculty of Commerce in the Department of Intelligence and Security. Dorcas is a gender, sexual health rights and policy specialist, queer rights advocate, social justice advocate, legal researcher and criminal law litigator.

Dzavo Joseph (PhD) holds a Diploma in Education from the University of Zimbabwe, a Bachelor of Education Primary with a Specialization in Social Studies from Great Zimbabwe University, a Master of Education in Philosophy of Education from Midlands State University in Zimbabwe, and a Ph.D from the University of Fort Hare. He is a lecturer at Madziwa Teachers' College and previously worked as a Part-time Lecturer at Ezekiel Guti University in Zimbabwe. He has presented at international conferences and published several articles and book chapters.

Douglas Musebenzi (LLM) is a Lecturer at Herbert Chitepo Law School, Great Zimbabwe University, Zimbabwe. He holds a Master of Laws Degree from Midlands State University, an LLB from UNISA, a Bachelor of Science Degree in Psychology, and a Diploma in Education from the University of Zimbabwe. He is an Associate Member of the Institute of Chartered Secretaries and Administrators of

Zimbabwe and a Fellow Member of the Institute of Administration and Commerce. His areas of research include child rights, women's rights, rights of persons with disabilities, international human rights law, legal ethics and accounting for legal practice.

Elisha Mupaikwa (PhD) is a lecturer in the Department of Library and Information Science at the National University of Science and Technology. His lecturing career began in 1999 when he was employed as a lecturer in the Information Technology department at the Bulawayo Polytechnic College. In 2012, he joined the Department of Library and Information Science as a Lecturer. In this department, he has actively participated in curriculum development, recommending courses that are in line with technological developments globally. This has been both at undergraduate and postgraduate levels. His major areas of research have been in the disciplines of information systems and development communication. Elisha holds a Higher National Diploma in Computer Studies, Bachelor of Science degree in Computer Studies, Diploma in Technical and Vocational Education, a Master of Science in Library and Information Science, and PhD in Library and Information Science.

Edward Muzondo (MSW) holds a Bachelor of Science Honours Degree in Social Work and Master of Science in Social Work from the University of Zimbabwe. He is a licensed clinical social worker with expert knowledge in behavior modification using various Motivational Enhancement and Interviewing Techniques. His research interests include mental health, disability, sexual and reproductive health rights, drug and substance use and social protection. He is currently serving as a Lecturer at the Eswatini Medical Christian University's Department of Social Work.

Francis Machingura (PhD) is the Director of the University of Zimbabwe Centre for Postgraduate Studies. He is an Associate Professor at the University of Zimbabwe, Arts and Languages Education Department, under the Faculty of Education. He is a specialist in biblical studies. His areas of special interest are: interaction of religion and gender, religion and politics, religion and health, religion and inclusivity, religion and sexuality and Pentecostal Christianity in Africa. He has published several books, articles and book chapters.

Isaac Mutelo (PhD) is an Associate Lecturer at Domuni Universitas (Toulouse, France) and Lecturer and Director of Quality Assurance (including Research, Innovation and Publication) at Arrupe Jesuit University in Harare, Zimbabwe. He is also a religious Catholic Priest belonging to the Order of Preachers, commonly known as Dominicans. He is a graduate in Theology, Philosophy, Education and Human Rights Law, and acquired his MA and PhD degrees in Philosophy with a specialisation in religion and politics from the University of KwaZulu Natal in South Africa. He is currently pursuing his Master of Laws (LLM) in Human Rights Law and Constitutionalism with Cavendish University Zambia (CUZ). His areas of research include religion and politics, human rights law, environmental law, interreligious dialogue (Muslim-Christian relations), and ethics. He is author of *Muslim Organizations in South Africa: Political Role Post-1948.*

Kudzai Mwapaura (MSW) Holds a Masters and Bachelor Degree in Social Work from University of Zimbabwe. He is a registered Social Worker, Lecturer and

Researcher. His major research interests include disability, child protection and community development. Currently, he works as a lecturer at Women's University in Africa.

Lele Dominic Dummene (PhD) is a Social Scientist; his primary area of research is social sciences/humanities; particularly sociology, education and development, environmental education, and qualitative research methodology. He lectures sociology, climate change and development, politics, community development, ethics, theories of development, and other social science/humanity courses. He is a consultant on environmental justice, environmental education, and environmental social movement organizations.

Mazuruse Irony (MA) is a Lecturer at Zimbabwe Ezekiel Guti University (ZEGU), Part-Time Lecturer at Zimbabwe Open University (ZOU) since 2010 and The Institute of Water and Sanitation Development (IWSD). His areas of research include Human rights, Disaster Management, Poverty alleviation and Politics. He holds a Master's Degree in Development Studies (MSU), Honours Degree in History and Development Studies (MSU), Post-Graduate Diploma in Education (ZOU), The Diploma in Humanitarian Aid and Project Management (Development Capacity Building Centre for Africa (CBCA). He is currently pursuing his doctoral studies in Disaster Management with the University of South Africa (UNISA).

Mundende James (BA Hons) is an author, researcher and a teacher. He published a book in 2020 entitled 'Why Poverty in Africa?' His research interests include economic history, international relations, ethics, philosophy and religious studies. He is also working on a plethora of research papers focusing on citizens' participation in democratic processes, gender issues as well as peace building among others. He holds a Dual Honors Degree in History and Geography from Catholic University of Zimbabwe. He is currently studying an MPhil (History of African Poverty) at the Catholic University of Zimbabwe.

Noel Garikai Muridzo (PhD) is an African registered social worker with over 20 years of experience in practice and academia. His research interests include child protection, climate justice, corporate social responsibility, and international social work. Noel is currently Regional President of the International Federation of Social Workers (IFSW) Africa Region and a past Vice President of (IFSW). He has also served as the President of the National Association of Social Workers Zimbabwe (NASWZ). He is the current Director of the School of Social Work at Midlands State University in Zimbabwe.

Oswald Alois Mgaya (BA) is a priest from the Catholic Diocese of Njombe in Tanzania. He holds an Advanced Diploma in Philosophy, Diploma in Theology, Diploma in Ignatian Spirituality, and a Bachelor of Arts in Theology. In August 2018, he was appointed assistant parish priest at Manga Catholic Parish and in September 2019, he was appointed a Parish Priest of the same parish. He is currently pursuing Master's Degree in Philosophy at Arrupe Jesuit University in Zimbabwe. His research interests include child protection, moral philosophy, education and formation.

Peter Chikondi Matsimbe (LLB Hons) is a Malawian lawyer, admitted to the Malawi Bar in 2018. He first worked at *Nyirenda & Msisha* under the supervision of Senior Counsel Modecai Msisha for three years. He later joined *Masumbu & Company* where he currently works. He has taken special interest in commercial law, labour law, intellectual property, human rights and personal injury. His interest in child rights research and advocacy stems back from his time in law school at Chancellor College - the University of Malawi through the Child Rights Clinic. He desires to make a meaningful positive impact through research and action in ensuring protection and advocacy of child rights in Malawi and the world at large.

Pearl Gambiza (MA) is a Programs Officer at Young Achievement Sports for Development (YASD). She holds a BSc Honours Degree in Politics and Public Management and a Masters (MA) in Development Studies from the Midlands State University, and a Master of Science in Child Sensitive Social Policies from Women's University in Africa. Her research interests include gender equality and women's empowerment, child protection, LGBTQIA+ discourse and sports for development and peace (SDP).

Pedzisai Ruhanya (PhD) is the Director of the Zimbabwe Democracy Institute and former senior lecturer at the University of Zimbabwe's Journalism and Media Studies. He holds degrees from Zimbabwe, the United Kingdom, and Post-graduate fellowships from the USA and South Africa. His degrees include a Bachelor of Law degree from the University of Zimbabwe. His research interests include media and democracy, political economy, human rights law, transition politics and politics in transition.

Reuben Chifundo Nazombe (MA) holds a Bachelor of Laws (LLB) Degree from the University of Malawi and a Master of Arts in Philosophy from Arrupe Jesuit University. He was admitted to the Malawi Bar in 2016 and briefly worked as Law Consultant at M & M Global Law Consultants in Blantyre. He currently works as a Deputy Director of the Jesuit Centre for Ecology and Development in Lilongwe, Malawi. He has a general interest in social justice research. His interest in child rights research goes back to the Child Rights Clinic at Chancellor College, which exposed him to the plight of the rights of children and how the societal attitude towards children is very critical in bringing solutions to the many problems faced by children in the world today.

Steven Lishandi (MA) is a Humanitarian from Zimbabwe and he currently resides in the United Kingdom. He holds a Bachelor of Arts Honours Degree in Philosophy and Humanities and a Master`s Degree in Philosophy with specialisation in Social Philosophy, both from the Arrupe Jesuit University. He is service oriented and seeks the common good. He has keen interests on Human Rights, Justice and Peace. He is a youth advocate and he also advocates for the child and vulnerable adults protection.

Tapiwa Musasa (PhD) holds a PhD in Development Studies from the Catholic University of Zimbabwe, MSc in Development Studies from Women's University in Africa, BSc in Social Sciences from Great Zimbabwe University, Diploma in Education from Gweru Teachers' College, and a Diploma in Personnel Management from the Institute of Personnel Management in Zimbabwe (IPMZ). She is a senior Lecturer at the Catholic University of Zimbabwe. Tapiwa's areas of research interest include child rights, gender and development, indigenous knowledge systems, human rights, food security, and disaster management among others.

Tauya Chinama (MA) is a youth advocate and holder of Diploma in Philosophy and Religious Studies from St Bonaventure University in Lusaka, BA in Philosophy from Pontifia Universita Antonianum in Rome, Post-Graduate Diploma in Education from the Catholic University of Zimbabwe, and Masters in Philosophy from Great Zimbabwe University. He is also a doctoral student at the Catholic University of Zimbabwe and a member of the Students and Youth Working on Health Action Team (SAYWHAT) research fellowship programme. His areas of research include religion, human rights and humanism.

Tendayi Dzinoreva (MA) is a PhD Scholar at the University of Johannesburg in the Ali Mazrui Centre for Higher Education studies. She holds a Bachelor of Education and a Master of Education from the University of Zimbabwe. Her PhD research focuses on teacher education and ICT integration within the curriculum. Her research interests include higher education, curriculum studies, technology integration, social media and *Unhu/Ubuntu*.

Thandekile Phulu (LLM) is a Law Lecturer and Principal for the School of Humanities and Law at Triumphant College in Namibia. She is currently completing a Doctor of Laws Degree (LLD) at the University of Pretoria. She completed both her LLM and LLB at the University of South Africa. She also graduated with a Bachelor of Arts at the University of Zimbabwe. Her research interests include human rights, the impact of technology and artificial intelligence on the employment relationship with particular focus on the conflict between employer and employee rights.

Taruvinga Muzingili (MSW) is a Lecturer at Midlands State University in Zimbabwe. He holds a Bachelor of Science in Social Work, Master of Science in Social Work from the University of Zimbabwe, Bachelor of Science (Special Honours) in Monitoring and Evaluation and a Master of Monitoring and Evaluation from Lupane State University. His research interests include child protection, green social work and social policy.

Wellington Gadzikwa (PhD) is a Senior Lecturer in Journalism and Media Studies at Africa University (AU) in Mutare, Zimbabwe. He previously held the same position at the University of Zimbabwe (UZ). His research interests include journalism standards and practice, media framing, tabloids and tabloidization.

Witness Chikoko (PhD) is a Senior Lecturer in the Department of Social Work at the University of Zimbabwe. He is also a Research Fellow in the Department of Social Work, University of Johannesburg, South Africa. He holds D. Phil in Social Studies, Master of Social Work, Post Graduate Diploma in Project Planning and Management, Bachelor of Science (Honours) Degree in Social Work all from the University of Zimbabwe. His research interests include childhood studies, social protection and disaster management.

Introduction to Human Rights in Southern Africa

Isaac Mutelo

Introduction

The notion of human rights refers to the norms, basic rights and freedoms that safeguard people from political, economic, legal, and social abuses or unjustified infringements. They are essential rights to which one is entitled by virtue of being human regardless of one's age, ethnicity, nationality, tribe, religion, gender or any other status (Sepulveda et al 2004; United Nations 2024; Nickel 2010). The awareness of fundamental rights such as freedom of religion, right to life, freedom of expression and opinion and right to education helps to prevent social, legal and political abuses (Nickel 2010). Although the idea of human rights is arguably a recent phenomenon in Africa, what constitutes them and how they can be guaranteed have become key issues.

The discourse, which has shaped our ideas about human rights in Africa, was initially formed in the Universal Declaration of Human Rights and subsequently adopted by the African Union mainly through the African Charter on Human and Peoples' Rights. Thus, the development of the human rights system in Southern Africa can be partly credited to the United Nations, international law and the African Union that have historically influenced the betterment of the human rights situation in some parts of Africa. In Southern Africa, the history of human rights has also been shaped by cultural values, the colonial legacy and the ongoing attempts to strengthen legal frameworks. In theory, all signatories to key human rights instruments in Southern Africa endorsed the rights and freedoms of their citizens. However, scholarly literature and media reports show that extensive human rights abuses and violations continue to occur in Southern Africa (Chigora 2015; Human Rights Watch 2023).

Historical Overview of Human Rights

The belief that human life is sacred has roots in several ancient traditions, religions and cultures while the notion of human rights can be traced to as early as 539 BC when Cyrus the Great freed slaves. After Cyrus and his troops had conquered Babylon, he granted everyone the right to choose his or her own religion and encouraged racial equality. Such decrees and "other principles were recorded on a baked-clay cylinder known as the Cyrus Cylinder, whose provisions served as inspiration for the first four Articles of the Universal Declaration of Human Rights" (United for Human Rights 2023). Other milestones that followed include the Magna Carta (1215) which defined rights and liberties of all persons and introduced the concept of 'rule of law'. This was followed by the Petition of Right which was drafted in 1628 by the English Parliament (House of Commons) to King Charles I proclaiming fundamental rights that protected citizens from arbitrary imprisonment and illegal taxation (Britannica 2023).

The Petition of Right was followed by the English Bill of Rights (1689) signed into law by William III and Mary II as co-rulers in England. The Bill "established the principles of frequent parliaments, free elections and freedom of speech within Parliament" including "the right of petition and just treatment of people by courts" (UK Parliament 2023). Thus, the Magna Carta (1215), the Petition of Right (1628), and the Bill of Rights (1689) became key legal documents in the United Kingdom by the end of the seventeenth century. The three legal instruments, especially the English Bill of Rights, inspired the promulgation of the United States Constitution that was drafted during the Constitutional Convention (also known as Philadelphia Convention) in 1787. Two years later, the French National Constituent Assembly adopted another human rights instrument, the French Declaration of the Rights of Man and of the Citizen (1789). In 1791, the new United States of America ratified the Bill of Rights stipulating specific fundamental rights of citizens and guaranteeing "freedom of religion, speech, and the press, and the rights of peaceful assembly and petition" (Library of Congress 2023).

By 1830, the notion of 'human rights' had already been introduced. For example, writing in 1831, William Lloyd Garrison referred to 'human rights' and in 1849, Henry David Thoreau included an extensive description of 'human rights' in his treatise *On the Duty of Civil Disobedience*. In 1867, Justice David Davis of the United States Supreme Court wrote: "By the protection of the law, human rights are secured; withdraw that protection and they are at the mercy of wicked rulers or the clamor of an excited people" (Lauren 2013:56). In 1891, Pope Leo XIII promulgated an Apostolic Exhortation *Rerum Novarum* highlighting fundamental rights such as property rights, citizens' rights, workers' rights and property rights.

One of the major milestones between World War I and World War II was the formation of the League of Nations which apart from promoting a common cause for human rights, became the first worldwide intergovernmental organisation to promote unity, peace and solidarity among nations. Another important development regards the Geneva Conventions which came into being between 1864 and 1949 and became prominent after World War II when they were revisited and subsequently readopted by the international community.

Towards the end of World War II in 1945, representatives of at least 50 countries gathered for the United Nations Conference on *International Organization* that resulted in the formation of the United Nations. Three years later, the United Nations adopted the Universal Declaration of Human Rights (UDHR), which continues to be a landmark document in the history of human rights. Since then, there have been several international and regional human right instruments including the International Convention on the Elimination of All Forms of Racial Discrimination (1965), International Covenant on Civil and Political Rights (1966), Convention on the Elimination of All Forms of Discrimination Against Women (1979), Convention Against Torture and Other Cruel, Inhumane or Degrading Treatment and Punishment

(1984), International Convention for the Protection of All Persons From Enforced Disappearances (2006) and the African Charter on Human and Peoples' Rights which was adopted in 1981 and entered into force in 1986.

Understanding the State of Human rights in Southern Africa

The history of human rights in Africa can be traced back to the pre-colonial era. Although the notion of human rights in its contemporary form did not exist in Africa by the eighteenth century, African societies such as Ancient Egypt (circa 3100 BCE - 30 BCE), Great Zimbabwe (circa 11th century - 15th century), Kingdom of Ghana (circa 4th century - 11th century) and Kingdom of Mali (circa 13th century CE - 16th century) had well-established systems and mechanisms that protected the dignity, rights and well-being of individuals based on social, moral, religious and cultural norms and values. Ancient Egypt had a well-established legal system which acknowledged several rights and freedoms, including the rights of women:

> The ancient Egyptians saw men and women, as well as people from all social classes but slaves, as basically equal under the law, and even the poorest peasant was allowed to request the vizier (The vizier was the main official in Ancient Egypt to assist the king), and his court for redress. Men and women had the right to own and sell property, create contracts, get married and divorce, collect inheritance, and pursue legal arguments in court. Married couples could own property equally and defend themselves from divorce by approving marriage contracts, which specified the financial commitments of the husband to his wife and children, should the marriage end. Women such as Hatshepsut and Cleopatra even became pharaohs, while others manipulated power as Divine wives of Amun (Easy to Learn 2023).

During the colonial era, the relationship between colonialism and human rights related to the "scope of imperial power and its transformative impact on rights" and the "political and social struggles" (Ibhawoh 2018:90). Most countries in Southern Africa experienced several human rights abuses and violations including land dispossession, forced labour and limited access to legal representation, health and education. In some cases, indigenous populations were racially segregated, forcibly removed from their traditional land, detained without trial and barred from voting during elections and having access to certain 'whites-only' institutions and residences (Mutelo 2023; Mamdani 1996).

In response to colonial oppression, several resistance and liberation movements advocating for freedom and the protection of human rights emerged in most countries in the region. These included the Zimbabwe African National Union (ZANU), the African National Congress (ANC) in South Africa, the United National Independence Party in Zambia, and the South West Africa People's Organization in Namibia. Most liberation movements in Southern Africa emerged during colonialism to establish justice, democracy, racial equality, rule of law and respect of human rights (Chigora 2015; Southall 2013). The eventual dismantling of colonialism paved the way for inclusivity, equality, respect for human rights, self-governing and democracy. In the post-colonial era, most countries in Southern Africa became signatories to several international and regional human rights instruments such as the Universal Declaration of Human Rights (UDHR) and the African Charter on Human and Peoples' Rights. National constitutions also clearly outline the rights and freedoms of citizens under the 'Bill of Rights' also known as the 'Charter of Rights' or 'Declaration of Rights'.

Regional bodies such as the Southern African Development Community (SADC), the Open Society Initiative for Southern Africa (OSISA), the United Nations Regional Office for Southern Africa (ROSA) and the Media Institute of Southern Africa (MISA) remain important actors in the promotion of human rights. Despite the end of colonialism and the presence of comprehensive legal frameworks for the promotion and protection of human rights, several abuses and violations continue to occur. The rights are often ignored in the ways in which states and the major organs – executives, legislatures, and judiciaries – relate to their citizens. For example, Human Rights Watch's 2022 Human Rights Report (Zimbabwe) noted that significant human rights issues included credible reports of:

> unlawful or arbitrary killings, including an extrajudicial killing; torture and cases of cruel, inhuman, or degrading treatment or punishment by the government; harsh and life-threatening prison conditions; arbitrary detention; political prisoners; arbitrary or unlawful interference with privacy; serious problems with the independence of the judiciary; serious government restrictions on free expression and media, including violence, threats of violence, and unjustified arrests or prosecutions against journalists, censorship, and arrests for libel; substantial interference with the rights of peaceful assembly and freedom of association; restrictions on freedom of movement; serious and unreasonable restrictions on political participation; serious government corruption; serious government restrictions on or harassment of domestic and international human rights organizations; deficient investigations of and accountability for gender-based violence, including crimes involving violence or threats of violence against women and girls; trafficking in persons; laws criminalizing consensual same-sex sexual conduct between adults, although generally not enforced; significant restrictions on workers' freedom of association; and existence of the worst forms of child labor (Human Rights Watch 2023).

In a context of extreme human rights abuse and violations, the effectiveness of regional bodies, human rights defenders and non-governmental organisations and institutions in promoting human rights is limited. The high levels of poverty, unemployment, inequality, cases of xenophobia and lack of good governance have also worsened the situation (Human Rights Watch 2023; Huntington 1991). In some cases, it is evident that colonial states created a legacy that continues to limit human rights in Southern Africa. The main objective of this book, therefore, is to deepen the understanding of human rights from both theoretical and practical perspectives in order to unpack the extent to which human rights are promoted and protected in the region. Several countries in Southern Africa are cited as case studies when exploring the state of human rights.

Part I: Education, Media and ICTs

Education, media and ITCs are important to the democratisation process and socio-political transformation of Southern Africa. Although several countries in Southern Africa face various human rights challenges with reference to education, media and ICTs, there are opportunities for the advancement of such rights. Countries such as South Africa, Zambia, and Namibia in the region have embarked on rigorous efforts to foster media freedom, improve access to ICTs and education through various policies, initiatives and programmes (Mlambo 2022).

Following this introductory chapter, the second chapter by Douglas Musebenzi interrogates the implementation of the right to free and compulsory basic education for children in Zimbabwe. The Zimbabwean government has repeatedly promised to provide free and compulsory basic education although the implementation of this right seems to be a mammoth task (Mapako & Mareva 2013:2; Mwanza & Silukuni 2020:321). Based on the question 'Is the right to free and compulsory basic education a paper tiger?' Musebenzi offers an examination on whether or not Zimbabwe is consistent with the international, regional and national standards while focussing on its practical implementation in Zimbabwe. Finally, a comparative analysis of Zimbabwe's implementation of the right to free and compulsory basic education is compared with other jurisdictions in the SADC region.

The third chapter by Dzavo Joseph explores the role of schools with reference to the human rights crisis in Zimbabwe. Having discussed human rights desecrations from pre-colonial, colonial, and post-colonial perspectives, the chapter analyses the role of education in addressing human rights challenges and subsequently addresses the democratic space in Zimbabwe. Schools are entrusted with the responsibility to promote human rights and democratic values among learners (Mwamwenda 2014; Flecknoe 2005). Democratic values ensure justice, unity, tolerance, peace, stability, and the prosperity of a country. The efficacy of the school is reflected through observations of democratic rights across the Zimbabwean communities. The main argument advanced by this chapter is that the success of the schools should see a reduction in the violation of human rights by all, especially around election time, and respect for democratic values and principles.

In the fourth chapter, Tapiwa Musasa examines the challenges and opportunities youths from rural areas in third world countries like Zimbabwe face towards achieving quality education, in line with the fourth goal of the Sustainable Development Goals. The chapter argues that rural areas in Zimbabwe have differential access to opportunities and facilities for quality education as compared to urban areas, thus presenting challenges and reducing chances of achieving the goal by 2030, which is also a violation of the rights of young people in Southern Africa and Zimbabwe in particular. Using Gokwe North (a rural area in the Midlands province of Zimbabwe) as a case study, the chapter highlights that learners are deterred from achieving the highest educational qualifications and to reach their maximum potential in education due to a number of challenges. These include the long distances between schools, which promote high rates of school dropouts, and the general shortage of Advanced Level schools in Gokwe North as compared to the large young population. In addition, institutions of higher learning like Vocational Training Colleges and Universities are scarce in Gokwe North and the Midlands Province at large which reduces the number of highly qualified personnel. The chapter recommends an increase in the number of primary and secondary schools in Gokwe North, as well as institutions of higher learning, through Government and Private sector initiatives.

The fifth chapter by Wellington Gadzikwa and Pedzisai Ruhanya analyses social media and communication rights in Zimbabwe. They argue that post-Mugabe Zimbabwe has been marked by continued intense political struggles between the government and various agents of social change pressing for democratic space, accountability and reforms on improved state-society relations using social media platforms such as Twitter and Facebook to make the government accountable. Through various ways such as internet shutdowns, overt and covert censorship, the Zimbabwean government is bent on discouraging the use of social media as communication rights' expressive platforms (Mustvairo 2021). The chapter notes that communication rights are critical for citizen's participation in governance issues. Citizens use digital platforms to mobilise protests against social and political ills. A broadened understanding of the public sphere that embodies the use of social media platforms as spaces to advance communication rights is used as an analytic framework for the chapter. The chapter concludes that social media platforms are critical in keeping the government in check and promote the right to enjoyment of communication rights in Zimbabwe.

In the sixth chapter, Isaac Mutelo and Steven Lishandi explore the role of print and online newspapers in the protection and promotion of human rights in Zimbabwe. The chapter argues that print and online newspapers are crucial in safeguarding human rights due to their ability to inform and influence citizens and their opinions, judgements and choices. Newspapers can be used to raise awareness, disseminate information about human rights abuses and violations, and to promote accountability and transparency through investigative journalism and electoral monitoring.

The seventh chapter by Elisha Mupaikwa discusses how national ICT policies for Southern African countries have integrated the internet in development communication and rural communication to enhance communities' right of access to governance and developmental information. This is achieved through a comparative analysis of national ICT policies for at least eight Southern African countries; namely, Botswana, Malawi, Mauritius, South Africa, Seychelles, Tanzania, Zambia and Zimbabwe. This chapter is important because the right to information is often recognized as a basic human right that when enacted, promotes citizen participation in governance and development initiatives that seek to improve the citizen's livelihoods. The right to information access creates the development of an information and knowledge society, which both are critical for the sustainable development of communities in the developing world (Marchant and Stremlau 2019; Chari 2009). While the United Nations and the African Union have often expressed their unflinching support for human right and basic freedoms such as the right to information access, some rural communities in Southern Africa still lag in accessing developmental and governance information. This is despite these nations having national ICT policies that recognize the importance of the internet in facilitating access to developmental and governance information. Over the past three decades, the internet has proven to be an effective tool for information access. Most governments have acknowledged the role played by digital technologies, particularly the internet, in facilitating access to developmental and governance information and have enshrined in their constitutions the right to developmental and governance information for their populations. The chapter, therefore, attempts to determine whether the internet has been recognized as a tool that nations have to use to support citizens' rights to governance and development information.

Part II: Child Rights, Prisoners' Rights and Labour Rights

While being marked by cultural diversity and historical complexities, the protection and promotion of child rights, prisoner's rights, and labour rights remain important in Southern Africa. Authors in this second part of the book explore the state of these rights from the perspective of both progress and persistent challenges. The eighth chapter by Witness Chikoko problematises birth registration processes among street children of the Harare Central Business District of Zimbabwe. Using a child rights perspective, Chikoko notes that the challenges associated with birth registration among street children are multiple and varied. Some of them include stigma and discrimination from the Registry's office, inaccessibility and/or lack of birth records, lower levels of literacy among parents, limited expertise by probation officers/social workers, inaccessibility of Registry's offices, shortage of money and the stringent Birth and Registration Act, among others. The challenges associated with the acquisition of birth certificates among street children of the Harare Central Business District demonstrates huge child rights abuse and violations. The chapter recommends full implementation of child rights, laws, policies and programmes so as to ensure that street children acquire birth registration.

In the ninth chapter, Witness Chikoko and Kudzai Mwapaura discusses substance abuse and sexual behaviour among street children of Harare Central Business District of Zimbabwe. The chapter notes that like other children, street children are abusing drugs for multiple reasons which increases their vulnerability. The chapter proposes the child agency theory as relevant or useful in terms of understanding sexual behaviours and substance abuse among the street children of the Harare Central Business District, Zimbabwe. The chapter also notes a number of weaknesses associated with the child agency theory such as the vagueness of agency, over emphasis on individual capabilities, agency also perceived as negative, problematic and challenging, among others (Tisdall and Punch 2012; Vanderbeck 2008).

In the tenth chapter, Oswald Mgaya and Isaac Mutelo discuss the confluence of child rights, duties and parentage in Southern Africa. The chapter argues that balancing child rights with the responsibilities of parents and/or guardians and children themselves is crucial for the well-being and holistic development of children in the region. Chapter eleven by Dorcas Tatenda Chitiyo offers an analysis of the tenets of a social contract in relation to the blanket disenfranchisement of pretrial detainees and prisoners in Zimbabwe. The chapter notes that the right to vote is a fundamental political right to participate in one's government. It is included in the principles of good governance which bind the state and constitute a component of a good electoral system as indicated by the founding values of the Constitution of Zimbabwe. Although the Constitution provides for the right to vote for every eligible adult citizen, no special measures have been made by the government to accommodate the enjoyment of the political right by citizens in prison or on remand. On that basis, the chapter considers whether prisoners and pre-trial detainees have the right to vote in light of the provisions of the Zimbabwean Constitution. The absence of provisions in the Electoral Act as the primary legislation (or regulations) from the Zimbabwe Electoral Commission (ZEC) as the key institution that could enfranchise pre-trial detainees and prisoners are analysed to establish if the limitation of the right to vote which is expressly guaranteed to every adult citizen in Zimbabwe is justifiable in an open democratic society. The chapter also explores the current position of disenfranchisement because of incarceration, an aspect that is canvassed to scrutinise whether any justification exists for this disenfranchisement. Thus, the chapter attempts to establish whether the current structure of the electoral legislation, which leaves Zimbabweans, disenfranchises pre-trial detainees and prisoners in a state of de-facto disenfranchisement, can withstand constitutional scrutiny.

In the twelfth chapter, Peter Chikondi Matsimbe, Reuben Chifundo Nazombe and Isaac Mutelo analyses the competing images of the girl child with reference to attempts being made to end child marriages in Malawi. Under the international human rights instruments, a child is viewed as a rights holder. In the context of child marriages, such marriages are seen as a violation of the child's rights. In the Malawian context, this image of the child is in competition with other images that condone child marriages, which in the end frustrate efforts to end child marriages. Therefore, the chapter concludes that ending child marriages is more of a conceptual issue because it is when the issues around the conceptual image of the girl child are properly addressed that legislation can work efficiently in tackling child marriages.

Chapter thirteen by Thandekile Phulu discusses the need for labour rights to be regarded as human rights in South Africa. At a domestic level, the Constitution of the Republic of South Africa (108 of 1996), the Labour Relations Act (66 of 1995), the Basic Conditions of Employment Act (77 of 1996), the Employment Equity Act (55 of 1998), and the Skills Development Act (97 of 1998) ushered in new labour legislation trends. These pieces of legislation combine international treaty provisions into domestic law. Several employee rights are given legal standing as a result of these pieces of legislation. On that basis, the chapter discusses numerous labour rights from both historical and contemporary perspectives in order to demonstrate the growth and development of South African labour rights. The chapter also examines how international law, regional law, and national law interact to give effect to these rights. Furthermore, because of advances in technology and changes in legislation, such as the legalisation of private cannabis use, there is a shift in employee's right to disconnect from the workplace. This facet is highlighted in the chapter, as are the deficiencies that are present in enforcing employees' off duty rights.

Part III: Democracy, Political Leadership and the Environment

The need to nurture democracy and good political leadership and safeguard the environment remains crucial in Southern Africa. While there has been significant progress on safeguarding the tenants of democracy and the rights of the environment, several challenges persist. Political leadership has somehow played a crucial role in shaping the region's democratic landscape, especially through economic growth and sustainability, political stability, civil society engagement, and free and fair elections (Statista 2023). There has also been progress regarding climate change, natural resource management and environmental awareness. However, several challenges such as corruption, poor political leadership and income inequality and disparities continue to undermine democracy, human rights and environmental protection efforts (Mbiatem 2018; Lanz and Gasser 2013).

Based on the question 'Has Democracy Lost its Aura?,' chapter fourteen by Daglous Makumbe dissects the changing democratic patterns that Southern Africa is currently experiencing based on countries such as Namibia, Madagascar, the Democratic Republic of Congo and Zimbabwe. The role of the regional bloc, the Southern African Development Community, is considered to evaluate its efforts in maintaining and enforcing democratic values in its member states. The chapter notes that democracy is losing its sensation in Southern Africa as some states have seemingly degenerated into authoritarian rule, militarism and dictatorship. It has transmogrified as many elections in the region have been highly controversial and allegedly manipulated. Southern Africa has also experienced a high incidence of military coups, primarily caused by constitutional and electoral manipulations. Archaic and anachronistic political transitions of the 19th century have resurfaced in Southern Africa, making the region experience different decades but with the same problems. Such undemocratic political transitions, sometimes initiated with modifications but tragic consequences, have caused retrogressive effects on the region's nascent democracy. Thus, a discussion of the extent to which democratic values are seemingly dwindling and losing their impression forms the backbone of the chapter. The chapter concludes that democracy has seemingly lost its quality as autocratic tendencies seem to be gaining more prominence unfettered.

The fifteenth chapter by Mundende James explores the intricacies of leadership, democracy and human rights. It notes that Western democracy presupposes that the state has an irreducible duty to uphold the wills of the people and the masses have inherent rights to question its modus operandi for transparency and accountability's sake. Political rights and freedoms are those which claim attention from civic organizations and international bodies as those that are highly abused, but there are a host of other rights that are under the subjection of infringements either by the state, employers or individuals. Some governments often accuse one another of abusing sovereign rights. Because of such anarchical and immoral situations due to constant pursuit of self-interests by countries on the international arena, the same is transpiring at local level as the internal issues are a microcosm of the macrocosm, 'small of the big'. On that basis, the chapter argues that the behaviour of nations towards one another is that which is reflected when the government interacts with its citizens so as the individuals in general. Further, a reflection of Pan-Africanist writings of scholars such as Rodney (1982); Lumumba (2016) and Nhemachena (2023) has demonstrated that, Western democracy has with its own complexities that are incongruous in as much as localities are concerned.

In chapter sixteen, Mazuruse Irony analyses the impact of the shrinking democratic space in the Second Republic of Zimbabwe on national development. The chapter notes that despite the demise of Mugabe, and numerous development initiatives, the Second Republic of Zimbabwe remains largely underdeveloped. Although democracy is a necessary ingredient for the development of a country, some countries are still struggling to achieve or introduce it in their development policies (Keane 2009; Huntington 1991). It is against this background that this chapter intends to demonstrate the effects of shrinking democracy on national development employing a case study of the Second Republic of Zimbabwe. The chapter further demonstrates an intrinsic relationship between human rights and democracy which is necessary for development. The non-compliance by the Second Republic of Zimbabwe to human rights and democracy can explain the country's low levels of economic development as evidenced by the nation being sanctioned, faces global isolation, foreign investors have shunned the open for business mantra, and brain drain continues to be rampant. This has resulted in the country reaching an economic meltdown.

In chapter seventeen, Thandekile Phulu discusses the intersecting human rights and environmental rights in South Africa. The United Nations General Assembly (UNGA) passed a resolution on 8 October 2021 recognising the human right to a clean, healthy, and sustainable environment as a basic human right. Notwithstanding the fact that this right is already recognised in several national jurisdictions, the global recognition of this right opens the way to its effective absorption into international law and improved domestic implementation. The environmental right is also enshrined in section 24 of the Constitution of the Republic of South Africa. The provision includes the right to clean air, since air pollution has a negative impact on human health. Air pollution also has an impact on land and water systems, as well as agricultural production.

In chapter eighteen, Lele Dominic Dummene discusses environmental justice and social justice from the perspective of Karl Marx's view of justice (economic justice) to address environmental injustices. In doing this, the chapter highlights the significance of Marx in contemporary discussions of environmental issues; thus, showing the importance of economic justice in environmental discourse. Karl Marx's view of justice (economic justice) is elusive and sometimes neglected in environmental discourse especially when addressing environmental issues in society (Agyeman 1978; Masters and Kisiangani 2010). Exploitation, inequalities and injustice dominates the distribution of environmental resources in communities and among some individuals. These inequalities and injustices in the distribution of environmental resources include exploitation of natural resources from indigenous land occupants, environmental racism and accumulation of surplus profits from the sales of natural resources. Hence, these inequalities and injustices call for justice in the environmental sector and in the distribution of environmental resources. When addressing justice in environmental discourse, environmental justice and social justice are the dominant forms of justices that are often employed to address environmental disputes and injustices.

Part IV: Human Rights, Religion and Culture

In Southern Africa, human rights, religion and culture are complex and interconnected issues that have continued to evolve. Regardless of the historical struggles and challenges, the region's complex tapestry of human rights, religion and culture indicates ongoing efforts to create a more inclusive and equitable society based on the values and principles of democracy. In chapter nineteen, Tendayi Dzinoreva, Francis Machingura and Pearl Gambiza explore the tension between cultures and religions which often influence human rights perspectives. They argue that the battle for supremacy between religion, culture and human rights is evident in the constant global contestations around what is right and acceptable. The most challenging and confusing aspect of this debate is when to apply or evoke culture, religion or human rights as a justification or defence for certain behaviour. Culture, religion and human rights define one's identity and socialisation. How one defines life is shaped by these concepts. Thus, the chapter posits that while there may appear to be contestations among the three, the binding values remain similar for culture, religion and human rights. Some arguments around peace, violence, development, violations and abuse are emphasized from the perspective of human rights. Using a systems thinking approach, the chapter attempts to answer the question of whether culture, religion and human rights are divergent or convergent aspects. Understanding the interrelatedness of these three elements is vital to shaping a generation of global citizens that is tolerant, inclusive, humane and respectful of one another (Teerikangas & Hawk, 2002; Fortman, 2011). Culture, religion and human rights are interdependent and should therefore be viewed as complementary rather than contrasting systems of human life. However, the chapter does not dispute the position that there are those who maintain that they are contradictory. Acknowledging the interwoven nature of cultural, religious and human rights systems could be the basis for unity, love, respect and Ubuntu thereby reducing instances of violation and abuse.

In the twentieth chapter, Deliah Nyaradzo Jeranyama discusses African Traditional Religion (ATR) and its influence on the protection of women and children rights in blended families in Zimbabwe. The chapter observes that African traditional religious beliefs, practices and values continue to have an influence on the lives of the Zimbabwean family unit. This comes from the reality that, although Christianity has been widely embraced, ATR principles do still shape how life in general and the family unit are approached. Amongst the many ATR beliefs is the belief in the existence of a spiritual world in which ancestors are believed to reside while having a significant control on the lives of the living beings. Further, this remains a part of the Zimbabwean people so much that behaviours, attitudes, perceptions and family decisions are closely aligned to ATR principles. Thus, the chapter begins with an analysis of how blended families are conceptualised within ATR and how ATR principles have a bearing on how women and children in these blended families are perceived. Further, attention is given to how these perceptions have violated or limited enjoyment of economic, social and cultural rights and benefits by women and children in blended families. This is followed by an analysis of the nature of the rights of women and children that are violated by ATR beliefs, practices and values as they are informed by the belief in the existence of a spiritual world. The last part of the chapter makes suggestions on harmonising the national frameworks for the promotion of the rights of women and children with African Traditional Religion so as to come up with a model that on one hand, harnesses the principles of ART and on the other protects women and children in blended families.

In chapter twenty one, Tauya Chinama, Edward Muzondo and Isaac Mutelo offer an analysis of the freedom of thought, conscience and religion as instituted in the Universal Declaration of Human Rights with specific reference to Zimbabwe. A key conclusion of this chapter is that religious intolerance often leads to human rights abuses, homophobia and fragmentation of society. Chapter twenty two by Taruvinga Muzingili, Muzondo Edward, Kudzai Mwapaura and Noel Garikai Muridzo explore the challenge of ritual killings from the perspectives of desire for prosperity, cultural falsity and implications on creeping human rights laws in Southern Africa. It may seem paradoxical to discuss the issue of ritual killing within the human rights arena due to ambiguity, confusion and fear associated with such acts. However, the chapter notes that ritual killings (murders) do not only constitute a serious violence to humanity, but breach to fundamental human rights of life and freedom. Several Southern African countries have been implicated against ritual killings which include Zimbabwe, South Africa, Zambia, Tanzania, Swaziland, Lesotho and Botswana. The authors claim that ritual killing as a narcissistic act in Southern Africa is driven by two major factors. The first driver of ritual killing has been motivated by insatiable desire for prosperity which include motives for quick riches, maintenance of business empires and power (Dombo, 201; Hall, 2011; Kasooha, 2009). The second factor is that ritual killing has been driven by cultural falsity where individuals sought to appease avenging spirits. Thus, the practice of ritual killing has been motivated by cultural beliefs, excessive love for wealth, power and greed. From societal response, current practices in ending ritual killings have been confined within the margins of courts and imprisonment of culprits, which is more reactive than preventative. Thus, this chapter demonstrates that laws in Southern African countries are creeping as they lack specific reference to ritual killings. To protect citizens from the scourge of ritual killings, the chapter contends that using legal instruments (laws and courts) alone provide limited monolithic lenses. Therefore, the chapter advises the adoption of socio-economic legal perspective to holistically end ritual killings in Southern Africa. The acts of ritual murder, regardless of the motive, whether for self-enrichment or to appease the ancestors for spiritual protection, require pedagogical community conscientisation which goes beyond the legal arena. The chapter concludes by noting that ritual killing as a human right issue in Southern Africa mirrors society's ideological and material concerns.

Chapter twenty three by Aubrey Tshepo Manthwa proposes the need to develop a human rights script that oscillates with indigenous knowledge system. The chapter posits that South Africa has adopted a Eurocentric understanding of human rights that does not serve the rights of the indigenous people of its country and their culture. The South African human right script is from international law and is similarly used by other countries in the world. Thus, the script is not neutral but a mirror of Eurocentric values, particularly the West. The equality jurisprudence applied in South Africa is based on Kantian ideology of individualism. It divorces the individual from the group he or she belongs. The ideological values of the international or universal human right script relied on in South Africa are foreign to South Africa in relation to their intersection with indigenous knowledge systems. By continuing to subject and inject these values in their western setting, state institutions in South Africa are further colonizing indigenous value systems. Attempts are often not made in most judicial pronouncements to interpret foreign constitutional values such as the right to equality and dignity in ways that can fit the South African indigenous knowledge system context. Courts and other state institutions expect that indigenous communities will merely change their daily lives and buy into foreign values. Decisions such as the one upheld in *Shilubana vs Nwamitwa* are celebrated because they achieved a measure of gender equality by allowing a female to succeed to traditional leadership. This is nonetheless compromised by the heavy reliance on Western conceptions of gender equality and failure to afford customary law an opportunity to achieve the same end. Thus, the chapter highlights the need for departure from the universal claim to human rights, and morality to a legal and knowledge system that is pluriversal which will allow other cultures and human rights systems to participate in forming and shaping law and morality. It also notes the need for a development or amendment of the values underpinning the Constitution to be based on the indigenous value system such as ubuntu or African communalism.

In the twenty fourth chapter, Muzondo Edward, Tauya Chinama and Taruvinga Muzingili discuss the domestication of disability rights in Southern Africa with specific reference to the Zimbabwean experience. They argue that disability rights are designed to promote, protect and safeguard the welfare of persons with disabilities globally. Disability rights are codified in international, regional and national legislations. Zimbabwe has ratified and domesticated a number of international and regional laws that promote the rights and welfare of persons with disabilities. These include the Universal Declaration of Human Rights, United Nations Convention on the Rights of Persons with Disabilities, and African Charter on the Rights of Persons with Disabilities as well as the SADC Protocol on Health among others. However, despite the existence of laws that enforce the enjoyment of disability rights in the region, the chapter notes that persons with disabilities are continuously living in subjugated circumstances. Key among them being difficulties in accessing the physical environment and information platforms, attitudinal barriers in social circles and discrimination in political and economic spheres of life. Thus, the chapter examines the extent to which the Government of Zimbabwe domesticates international and regional human rights laws into its own institutional and legislation frameworks on disability. This is discussed in relation to three categories of disability rights; that is, protection, provision and participation. The chapter also considers the history of disability rights from global, regional and national perspectives. This involves an exploration into the domestication process of broader human rights legislations in disability affairs in Zimbabwe. The chapter concludes by highlighting the prospects that social workers and other helping professionals should consider in order to ensure the maximum realization of disability rights in Zimbabwe and within the region.

References

AFỌLAYAN, F. S., 2004. *Culture and Customs of South Africa.* London: Greenwood Press.

AGYEMAN, J., (1978) Black People in a White Landscape: Social and Environmental Justice. *Built Environment,* 16(3), 232-236.

BRITANNICA, (2023) *Petition of Right: British history [1628].* [Online]. Available from: https://www.britannica.com/topic/petition-of-right-English-law

CHIGORA, P., (2015) Revisiting the Liberation Struggles in Southern Africa: The Zimbabwean Case. *Journal of Pan African Studies,* 8(1), 50-70.

CHARI, T., (2009) *Information and Communication Policy Formulation and the Divide in Zimbabwe.* [Online]. Available from: https://www.researchgate.net/publication/ 267269113_Information_and_Communication_Policy_Formulation_and_the_Informatio n_Divide_in_Zimbabwe#fullTextFileContent

DOMBO, V., (2011) Community Presented Unity Front against Ritual Killing. *Limpopo Times, 1-2.*

Easy to Learn. (2013) *Ancient Egypt.* [Online]. Available from: http://easytolearnancientegypt.weebly.com/rights-and-freedoms.html

FLECKNOE, M., (2005) *What can one school tell us about democracy.* [Online]. Available from: http://www.leeds.ac.uk/edcool/documents.

FORTMAN, B. D. G., (2011) *Religion and Human Rights: A Dialectical Relationship.* [Online]. Available from: https://www.e-ir.info/2011/12/05/religion-and-human-rights-a-dialectical-relationship/

HALL, E., (2011). *Murders Inquiry Highlights Trade in body Parts.* San Diego, Academic Press.

HUNTINGTON, S. P., (1991) *The Third Wave: Democratization in the Late Twentieth Century.* Oklahoma: University of Oklahoma Press.

Human Rights Watch, (2023) *Africa: Conflicts, Violence Threaten Rights: Improve Civilian Protection, Accountability for Abuses.* [Online]. Available from https://www.hrw.org/news/2023/01/12/africa-conflicts-violence-threaten-rights

Human Rights Watch, (2023) *2022 Human Rights Report (Zimbabwe).* [Online]. Available from: https://www.state.gov/wp-content/uploads/2023/02/415610_ZIMBABWE-2022-HUMAN-RIGHTS-REPORT.pdf

IBHAWOH, B., (2018) *Human Rights in Africa.* Cambridge, Cambridge University Press.

KASOOHA. I., (2009) Girl beheaded in Ritual Murder. *New Vision,* 16, 52-59.

KEANE, J., (2010) *'The Life and Death of Democracy'* on Fora TV. [Online]. Available from: http://fora.tv/2010/08/07/John_Keane_The_Life_and_Death_of_Democracy

LAUREN, G. P., (2023) *The Evolution of International Human Rights: Visions Seen.* Pennsylvania: University of Pennsylvania Press.

LUMUMBA, P. O., (2016) *Fighting Corruption in Africa: The Case for an African Association of Anti-Corruption Authorities.* [Online]. Available from: https://www.igg.go.ug/static/ files/publications/Presentation_by_PLO_Lumumba_Conference_-_CASE_FOR_AN_ AFRICAN_ASSOCIATION

LANZ, D. and GASSER, R., (2013) *A Crowded Field: Competition and Coordination in International Peace Mediation.* Centre for Mediation in Africa.

Library of Congress. (2023) *Today in History.* [Online]. Available from: https://www.loc.gov/item/today-in-history/december-15/#:~:text=On%20December%2015%2C%201791%2C%20the,of%20peaceful%20assembly%20and%20petition.

MASTERS, L. and KISIANGANI, E., (2010). *Natural Resources Governance in Southern Africa.* Braamfontein, African Institute of South Africa.

MARCHANT, E. and STREMLAU, N., (2019) *Africa's Internet shutdowns.* Oxford: The University of Oxford.

MAMDANI, M., (1996) *Citizen and Subject: Contemporary Africa and the Legacy of Late Colonialism.* Princeton, Princeton University Press.

MBIATEM, A., (2018). Presidential Term Limit Divide in the Democratic Republic of Congo: Another Security Threat in the Great Lakes Region? *The Journal of Political Science,* 2(1), 1–3.

MLAMBO, C., (2022) The Nexus between Information Communication Technology and Human Rights in Southern Africa. *Information* 13(8).

MWANZA, C. and SILUKUNI, D., (2020) Implementation of the free education policy in primary schools in Kafue District: Is it a compromise on quality of education in Zambia? *European Journal of Education Studies,* 7, 320-330.

MAPAKO, F. P. and MAREVA, R. (2013) The Concept of Free Primary School Education in Zimbabwe: Myth or Reality. *Educational Research International,* 1, 1-2.

MWAMWENDA, T. S., (2014) *Educational psychology an African perspective.* Sandton, Heinemann Higher and Further Education.

MUTSVAIRO, B., (2021) *Why social media activists face an uphill struggle in Zimbabwe.* [Online]. Available from: https://democracyinafrica.org/social-media-activists-face-an-uphill-struggle-in-zimbabwe/

NHEMACHENA, A., (2023). Kukumirwa Semombe Dzamavhu: When Voices Begin to Erupt from Bottoms, African Anthropology Becomes Colonial. *Journal of African American Studies,* 26, 436-455.

NICKEL, J., (2010) *Human Rights.* [Online]. Available from: https://plato.stanford.edu/entries/rights-human/

RODNEY, W., (1982) *How Europe Underdeveloped Africa.* Washington DC, Howard University Press.

ROGER, S., (2013) *Liberation Movements in Power: Party & State in Southern Africa.* Woodbridge, James Currey Limited.

STATISTA, (2023) *Democracy Index in Sub-Saharan Africa in 2021 by Country.* [Online]. Available from: https://www.statista.com/statistics/1204750/democracy-index-in-sub-saharan-africa-by-country/

SEPULVEDA, M., et al (2004) *Human Rights Reference Handbook.* San José, University for Peace.

TEERIKANGAS, S & HAWK, D., (2002). *Approaching Cultural Diversity through the Lenses OF Systems Thinking and Complexity Theory.* [Online]. Available from: https://www.researchgate.net/publication/228568739_Approaching_Cultural_Diversity_through_the_lenses_of_Systems_thinking_and_Complexity_Theory

TISDALL, E. K. M and PUNCH, S., (2012) Not so 'new'? Looking critically at Childhood Studies. *Children's Geographies* 10(3), 249-264.

United Nations, (2014) *What are Human Rights?* Office of the High Commissioner of Human Rights.

United for Human Rights, (2023) *A Brief History of Human Rights.* [Online]. Available from: https://www.humanrights.com/what-are-human-rights/brief-history/#:~:text= The%20Cyrus%20Cylinder%20(539%20B.C.)&text=He%20freed%20the%20slaves%2 C%20declared,Akkadian%20language%20with%20cuneiform%20script.

United Kingdom Parliament, (2023) *Bill of Rights 1689.* [Online]. Available from: https:// www.parliament.uk/about/living-heritage/evolutionofparliament/parliamentaryauthority/ revolution/collections1/collections-glorious-revolution/billofrights/#:~:text=It%20is%20an %20original%20Act,known%20today%20as%20Parliamentary%20Privilege.

VANDERBECK, R., (2008) Reaching Critical Mass? Theory, Politics and the Culture of Debate in Children's Geographies. *Area* 40(3), 393-400.

PART I:

EDUCATION, MEDIA AND ICTs

A Critical Interrogation of the Realisation of the Right to Free Basic Education in Zimbabwe, Zambia and South Africa

Douglas Musebenzi

Introduction

The promulgation of the 2013 Constitution in Zimbabwe was a watershed moment which brought a new era to basic education. Section 27 1(a) of the Zimbabwean Constitution espouses the national objective to education in terms of where concrete processes to promote free basic education should be taken by the state. The legal status of the national objective remains questionable as they are not part of the justiciable Declaration of Rights in Chapter 4 (Moyo 2019:148). The realisation of the right to free basic education in Zimbabwean schools seems to be inconsistent with some international legal instruments as schools charge parents fees in one form or the other. It is therefore important to interrogate whether Zimbabwe, Zambia and South Africa's national legislation have the minimum content of the right to free basic education and the extent to which the accomplishment of the right to free basic education is achieved in Southern Africa. The Zimbabwean Constitution provides for state-funded basic education. Most international legal instruments regulating the right to free basic education do not explicit reference to basic state funded education. The Zimbabwean Constitution seem inconsistent with the international legal framework on the right to basic education. This chapter will interrogate whether Section 75 (1) a of the Constitution of Zimbabwe provides the minimum core component of the right to free basic education as propounded by international law.

Human rights are protected in international conventions, national constitutions and statutes though they find little transformation into reality (Monageng, 2014:1). It is one thing to have a pulsating legal framework and another to realise an effective legal order. The Zimbabwe School Examinations Council (ZIMSEC) introduced examination fees for Grade 7 (Majome 2023). The request for fee payments for basic education has resulted in about 75% of children being unable to pay school fees nationwide (Mbanje 2023). The request for fee payments contradicts the fulfilment of the right to free basic education. The right to free basic education is critical for the existence and growth of a democratic society. Education is vital in the economic, social and cultural development of a nation. Against this background the chapter explores the realisation of free basic education in Southern Africa where Zimbabwe, Zambia and South Africa will be case studies. Reference is made to the international and regional legal framework on the right to free basic education. The national legal frameworks for Zimbabwe, Zambia and South Africa will also be examined with a comparative spectacle.

International Frameworks on the Right to Free Basic Education

The Universal Declaration of Human Rights (UDHR, 1948) was the first international instrument to explicitly emphasise the right to education. The UDHR informs internationally the realisation of the right to basic education. A number of international human rights instruments contain intricate principles set out in the UDHR including those that regulate the right to free basic education. Education is free in the basic levels in terms of Article 26 of the UDHR. The right to basic education was a priority during the declaration of human rights because it was viewed as critical in the lives of human beings. Quality in education was also considered by the UDHR in terms of Article 26. Another important document is the Convention against Discrimination in Education (CDE) which was the first international agreement to be accepted regarding education and provided for standards and a quality of education in terms of article 4. Education involves all types and levels of formal education, including fundamental features like accessibility, availability and quality of education. In terms Article 4(a) of CDE, state parties are to promote equality of opportunities in the matter of education and to make primary education free. Whereas the right to primary education was included in the UDHR as a mere aspiration, the CDE was the first international instrument to include an obligation on states parties to provide free and compulsory primary education (Arendse 2011:99).

Furthermore, the International Covenant on Economic, Social and Cultural Rights (ICESCR) is another important instrument which deals with the right to education. For example, article 13 (2) (a) of the ICESCR specifies that primary education shall be available and free to all. General Comment No. 13 of the ICESCR highlights the most inclusive and all-encompassing description of the right to basic education in international law. Education must be available and non-discriminative in terms paragraph 31 of ICESCR General Comment No. 13 on 'The Right to Education.' Basic education must be available and accessible for it to be non-discriminatory. Article 2 of the ICESCR provides that state parties should undertake ways, individually and through international assistance and co-operation with a view to attaining gradually the full recognition of the fundamental human rights. It instructs state parties to provide quality education based on availability, accessibility, acceptability and adaptability (Ramcharam 2005:19). The ICESCR provides that cost-free education means that the government should desist from imposing fees such that direct and indirect costs such as levies on parents be eradicated. ICESCR also identifies that fees are restrictive to the gratification of the right to education and therefore threaten its full realisation. The ICESCR where Zimbabwe, Zambia and South Africa are state parties, underscores the need for the full realisation of the right to free basic education.

Basic education is a range of educational activities that aim to meet basic learning needs and comprises both formal schooling primary and sometimes lower secondary and informal (Chürr 2015:2410). The notion of minimum core obligations suggests that there are certain minimum levels of fulfilment that takes priority on the general realisation of the right. The minimum core concept was castigated by General Comment 3 of CESCR while the minimum core approach was developed with the aim of providing clarity on the normative content of socio-economic rights (Moyo

2019:175). Minimum core obligations apply irrespective of the availability of resources of the country. State parties of ICESCR are under an immediate obligation to satisfy minimum essential levels of the rights recognised by the Covenant. The developing jurisprudence of CESCR stipulates that resource scarcity does not relieve states of the minimum obligations in respect of the implementation of economic, social and cultural rights (Scchuter 2019:591). The minimum core obligations apply at all times to developing and developed states and are considered as baseline that states should reach in the fulfilment of human rights. Primary education includes elements of availability, accessibility, acceptability and adaptability which are common to education in all its forms (Ramchanran, 2005:196).

Basic education should be seen wider than only primary education but should include secondary education. Availability means that education has to be accessible in appropriate quantities. The success of any right to education is dependent on the availability of that education. Accessibility means that education must be accessible to all without discrimination whilst acceptability entails that the state has the duty to ensure that the form and substance of education, including curricula and teaching methods, are acceptable, relevant, culturally appropriate and of high quality to children (Chürr 2015:2414). Adaptability is when the education system has to be flexible and expandable in order to adapt to the needs of changing societies and communities. Despite the minimum core obligations, the state is indebted to adopt legislative mechanisms to gradually realise the full scale of the socio-economic rights (Moyo. 2019: 175). The accomplishment of the right to basic education is holistic, including access and quality to education.

The Convention of the Rights of the Child (CRC) is another principal international treaty that addresses children's rights at international level. In terms of Article 28 (1) (a) of CRC), state parties are obliged to undertake all appropriate legislative, administrative and other measures for the implementation of the rights recognised in the convention (Ekundayo 2018: 113). The core objective of the CRC is to safeguard the rights of the child. The purpose of education must be to guarantee that children grow to their full potential. The CRC identifies the right to education for children, and that primary education be available and free to all. Furthermore, the CRC Committee in General Comment 7 acknowledged with appreciation that some states were planning to make preschool education available and free for all children. General Comment Number 7 also highlights that primary education must be made free and compulsory. According to General Comment 11 of the Convention on the Rights of the Child, accessibility entails the elimination of direct costs in ensuring children acquire education (Nhundu 1992:78).

Regional Instruments on the Right to Free Basic Education

The African Charter on Human and Peoples Rights (ACHPR) is the principal instrument in the promotion and protection of human rights in Africa. It creates a structure for the advancement and protection of human rights in Africa (Mutangi 2019:262). The ACHPR promotes a number of human rights inclusive of the right to basic education. Article 17 (1) of the ACHPR states that every person has a right to education. The ACHPR draws explanatory guidance from ICESCR which has comprehensive clarifications in Article 13 on the right to basic education. Similarly, the African Charter on the Rights and Welfare of the Child (ACRWC) epitomizes one of the sectorial mechanisms concentrating exclusively on children (Mutangi 2019:265). The ACRWC mandates states to guarantee full gratification of the rights of children by protecting and promoting their rights and welfare. The ACRWC which is binding on Zimbabwe makes the provision of basic education compulsory and free. Article 11 (3) of the ACRWC expounds that states should take appropriate measures to achieve the full recognition of the right to education.

The Southern African Development Community Protocol on Education and Training is another important document which acknowledges that education has the capacity to equip member states adequately for the 21st century. The Protocol recognises education as one of the key drivers for the sustainable socioeconomic and political development. It is expected that education systems bring about a change of behaviour that will create environmental integrity, economic viability and justice. Article 5 of the Protocol on Education and Training highlights the need for quality education and for disadvantaged children to be granted special admission. The Protocol has also identified the areas of cooperation in basic education in the region.

Zimbabwe's Legal Framework on the Right to Free Basic Education

The right to education is one of the critical socio-economic rights that should be available to every child without discrimination. Section 75 of the Constitution of Zimbabwe states that every citizen and permanent resident has a right to a basic state-funded education which the state, through reasonable legislative and other measures, must make progressively available and accessible (Mhandu & Dambudzo 2016:123). The right to basic state-funded education by the Zimbabwean Constitution is inconsistent with the international legal instruments in making basic education accessible as the international legal frameworks do not mention state-funded basic education. It is unclear why the Zimbabwean Constitution decided to drop the phraseology of free basic education to state-funded basic education. It is widespread to see school drop-outs even though the government is required to offer state-funded education (Mhandu & Dambudzo 2016:123).

Manyonganise (2013:478) maintains that there has been a negative impact on the accessibility of education to orphans and vulnerable children whose parents and guardians could not even afford the required fees. On that basis, free basic education becomes a myth and not a reality for children in Zimbabwe. Free basic education is to imply that the financial responsibility is shifted from a parent or guardian to some other entity (Mapako & Mareva 2013:2). So, can the notion of free basic education still be sustained in Zimbabwe? Zimbabwe, like most states in Africa, took it upon itself to provide free education as a fundamental human right. It is admitted that education is a basic human right, which is essential in fighting illiteracy, disease and poverty. The Section 75(1) (a) of the Constitution of Zimbabwe provides for basic education but does not include words like 'access,' 'progressive realisation' or 'within available resources.' The deliberate omission of the word access is similar to the South Africa *Juma Musjid Primary School case* that the government must provide education immediately and not through progressive realisation. Section 75 (1) (a) of the Constitution of Zimbabwe does not depend on the availability of resources but on state-funded education. On that basis, one cannot raise the argument that the country has inadequate resources to provide free basic education since the textual interpretation of Section 75 (1) (a) does not suggest that conclusion.

Moreover, the Education Act [Chapter 25:04] remains the major legal document which offer explicit pronouncements about the right to education for children in Zimbabwe. Basic education means education from early childhood up to the fourth form as provided by Section 2 of the Education Amendment Act of 2020. The Education Act further provides that primary education for every child of school-going age shall be compulsory. Compulsory primary education stresses the necessary education which is to be provided to all children without discrimination. Contrary to international law, the Zimbabwean Constitution provides for basic state-funded education and the Education Act imposes the liability to pay school fees including fees in terms of section 6 of the Education Act. Enforcement of socio-economic rights require a sound institutional framework. At the international level, most human rights instruments prescribe that states must institute domestic mechanisms or measures to protect and promote human rights (Kondo 2017:76). Any fee imposed can be viewed as an impediment which threatens the satisfaction of the right to basic education. Compulsory primary education in Zimbabwe is inconsistent with international and regional instruments as the Education Act provides for the lowest possible fees (Mapuva & Mapuva 2016:53).

Although the Education Amendment Act of 2020 emphasise the need to protect and respect the right to education, the education system is faced with challenges that include dilapidated buildings, inaccessible educational materials and the unavailability of teachers. The state has the responsibility to provide learners with adequate resources and facilities to enhance the learning process. The right to education therefore is subject to availability of state resources. Section 5 (1) of the Education Amendment Act of 2020 states that attending state-funded education is compulsory though it does not define explicitly how this would be realised in schools. However, the Act does not abolish school fees but stipulates that the Education Minister will continue to set school fees at state schools. Charging fees or levies in basic education compromises the right to free basic education. Any fees charged by the Education Amendment Act can therefore be regarded as an impediment to the gratification of the right to free education protected in international law.

While the Zimbabwean Constitution does not provide basic state-funded education to every child, the Education Amendment Act of 2020 castigates that every child is eligible to compulsory basic state-funded education. This discourse between the Constitution of Zimbabwe and the Amended Education Act of 2020 brings doubt on whether there is free basic education in Zimbabwe for all. The reading that citizens and residents are to get state-funded basic education seems to be discriminatory and inconsistent with the Education Amendment Act of 2020 which provides basic education to all children. The Children's Act [Chapter 5:06] does not cover the matter of children's right to education as specified by both UNCRC and ACRWC (Bhaiseni 2016:5). Since Children's Act of Zimbabwe does not have a provision for the children's right to free basic education, it is doubtful how the right to free basic education in Zimbabwe can be realised when essential legislation like the Children's Act does not have a provision for the right to free basic education (Bhaiseni 2016:5). The Children's Act must therefore have a provision to protect and promote the right to free basic education.

Regarding the policy framework in Zimbabwe, the Basic Educational Assistance Module (BEAM) programme was introduced to focus on access to education and to increase educational opportunities for disadvantaged learners. The primary objective of the BEAM programme was to reduce the dropout rates and reach out to children who have never been to school due to economic hardships (Maushe 2019:2). Since its inception in 2001, BEAM has managed to reduce the number of children who drop out of school due to failure to pay fees. A number of children drop out of school because parents and guardians fail to provide school fees and as pass rates slump, they are demotivated to pay fees for repeating students. BEAM is facing a myriad of challenges such as late arrival and unavailability of funding (Masuka, 2014:34). The BEAM programme has focussed on susceptible children and catered for their fees. Apparently, the BEAM programme has been instrumental in alleviating the continued hardships of economically disadvantaged families. However, its effective implementation is shrouded in complications due to a lack of adequate funding and massive corruption in the selection process.

Zambia's Legal Framework on the Right to Free Education

In Zambia, the government's obligation to education has been vibrant since it passed the 1964 Education Act governing the management of education (Mambo & Banja 2012:3). Zambia has ratified and accepted several international treaties and protocols that protect the right to education though financial challenges have remained a stumbling block in the implementation process. Initially, Zambia entered reservations to the commitment to provide free basic education. The 1991 Constitution of Zambia does not protect the right to education, however it is under review with the expectation that the right to education would be included in the revised constitution. It is disheartening to note that Zambia's Constitution does not have a provision on the right to free basic education, yet education is a bedrock for development of society. Zambia has followed the free education policy and adhered to the call by world organizations on 'Education for All.' The Zambian government through the Ministry of Education, on 15 March 2002, proclaimed the 'Free Education Policy,' which applied to grades 1 to 7 in primary school (Mwanza & Silukuni 2020:318). The Free Basic Education Policy in Zambia advocates the right of all children to universal basic education. Free Basic Education was buttressed by Zambia's 2002 Poverty Reduction Strategy Paper, which called for the elimination of fees for basic education. The 2003-2007 Strategic Plan for Education in Zambia called for the abolition of school fees. Zambia introduced free basic education as a policy statement made by the National Assembly.

Section 14(1) of the Education Act (2011) of Zambia states that every person has a right to basic education while section 15 states that a child has the right to free basic education which is government funded. This is similar to the Zimbabwean Constitution which states that every citizen and permanent resident has a right to basic state-funded education. Zambia provides free primary education from grades one to seven funded by the government through grants to schools. However, the government grants to schools have been inadequate. The budget allocation to education in Zambia is the lowest in the sub-region. However, Zambia has continued to improve in terms of access to basic education especially through the enactment of policies and programmes such as free primary education (Mwanza & Silukuni 2020:318). Free primary education is important in ensuring that everyone has access to education.

In spite of improvements in parity following the abolition of fees, disparities persist in Zambia. Charging of fees in schools is an impediment to the recognition of the right to free basic education. Many countries which include Zimbabwe, Zambia and South Africa have challenges in the implementation of free primary education policy due to poor funding and lack of school infrastructure. The Free Primary Education Policy enhanced access to education provision leading to an increase in the enrolment of pupils while bringing about a decline in the quality of education in Zambia (Mwanza & Silukuni 2020:321). This is partly because the implementation of the Free Primary Education Policy was characterized by inadequate funding from the government. Lack of funding of basic education in Zambia remains a stumbling block in the realisation of the right to free basic education.

South Africa's Legal Framework on the Right to Free Basic Education

The realisation of the right to basic education as stipulated under section 29 of the South African Constitution is not subject to resource availability and is a right that has to be directly and immediately realised (Murungi 2015:3162). The right to basic education constructs a positive right that basic education be delivered to each and every person. Section 29 of the Constitution of South Africa emphasises a strong belief that education is one of the core pillars for economic development and social transformation. However, the South Africa's basic education system has high incidences of school dropouts due to the high cost of school fees. South Africa has made considerable progress in terms of the enhancement of access to basic education through legislation, policy documents and interventions that are envisioned for access to education for all children. The South African government encourages all children in the compulsory school phase to attend school in terms of South African Schools Act 84 of 1996. Nevertheless, some children turn away from schools because of their parents' inability to pay school fees (Arendse 2011:120). This is unacceptable in view of the fact that South Africa has an international obligation to provide free primary education (Arendse 2011:120).

Section 3 (1) of South Africa Schools Act84 of 1996 safeguards that all learners have the right to access quality education and makes schooling compulsory for children aged seven–fourteen years. The Act stipulates that the state is mandated to fund public schools from the public revenue on an impartial basis. The School Fee Exemption Policy and No Fee School Policy are envisioned to disproportionately distribute state funds to low socio-economic schools. The South African Constitutional Court, in the *Government of the Republic of South Africa and Others v Grootboom and Others,* established a model of reasonableness review for adjudicating the enforcement of socio-economic rights (Moyo 2019:335). The Court declared that to implement socio-economic rights the standards foreseen by the Constitution depended on the reasonableness of the identified measures. However, the reasonableness approach fails to define the content of socio-economic rights. One may question its ability to protect individuals who are undergoing severe denial of the minimum levels of basic socio-economic rights. The realisation of the right to basic education cannot be subjected to the reasonable approach as it is to realise immediately without any qualifications.

Access to Basic Education

Access to education signifies approaches in which institutions ensure that students have equal chances to acquire knowledge and skills without compromising their status socially, economically or physically (Owuor 2018:174). For instance, when the government of Zimbabwe made basic education accessible through policies of free and compulsory education, the assurance of education principles is to guarantee that all learners have equal access to a high-quality education (Mwiinde & Muzingili 2020:106-107). Zimbabwe has enormous challenges in enhancing the accessibility of free and compulsory basic education as there are no clear guidelines on how compulsory basic education would be achieved. In terms of section 56 of the Zimbabwean Constitution, all persons are equal before the law and have equal protection and benefit of the law. Nevertheless, the Constitution of Zimbabwe seem is discriminatory in the provision of basic education which is for citizens and permanent residents. All citizens and permanent residents of Zimbabwe have a right to basic state-funded education in terms of Section 75 (1) (a) of the Zimbabwean Constitution. The Constitution of Zimbabwe does not provide state-funded basic education to children who are not citizens and residents of Zimbabwe although international instruments such as the UDHR, ICESCR, CRC and the ACRWC guarantees every child the right to free basic education.

The distance between the residences of children and the nearest public primary school is noticeable making it unbearable for children to access the schools, especially in rural areas. There are very few secondary schools in rural areas in comparison to primary schools such that secondary school pupils walk long distances to access education and in extreme cases pupils leave as early as 4 am and arrive back home around 6pm (Moyo, Ncube & Khupe 2016:860). The long distance from home to school in many rural schools of Zimbabwe compromise the quality of education and the accessibility of free basic education. Access to education in rural areas compared to urban areas in Zimbabwe compromises the right to free basic education in rural areas. Distance becomes an enormous challenge for children in the basic education sector as they are still young, tender and susceptible to long distances when compared to secondary school students. Insufficient and operational deficiencies point to a visible factor which is lack of resources (Mapolisa & Tshabalala 2013:2264)

In South Africa, it has been stated that a lot of children from underprivileged homes are deliberately barred from access to education. In the *Tripartite Steering Committee and Another v Minister of Basic Education and Others,* it was held that the right to education was worthless without transport to school. This indicates that accessibility to basic education is paramount in the realisation of basic education. Schools which are inaccessible are an impediment to the full recognition of the right to basic education. The Constitution of South Africa contains a concrete foundation for the enforcement of socio-economic rights (Akingbehin, 2021:79). Section 29(1) of the South African Constitution stipulates that the government must take the necessary steps to ensure that education is available and accessible to all. Though the Free Primary Education Policy was introduced with the good objective of increasing access to education, countries such as Zambia and Zimbabwe have historically experienced problems in terms of financing the programme (Mwanza & Silukuni 2020:321). Financial support in the provision of basic education in Southern Africa is limited due to budgetary constraints as most countries in the region have poor economies to sustain the availability and accessibility of education.

The Quality of Basic Education and Shortage of Teachers

The United Nations Educational, Scientific and Cultural Organization (UNESCO) has consistently emphasized that quality of education has been declining in most of the countries. The quality of learning resources such as textbooks and ICTs remain crucial. In Southern Africa, education embraces dimensions that include financial, material and human resources (Mafa & Tarusikirwa, 2013:3). For educational institutions to ensure that students are kept in schools, attention to the quality of education must be taken into consideration. The notion of free basic education has resulted in large enrolments subsequently compromising the quality of basic education. Scarcity of material resources contributes to ineffective teaching. The lack of quality of education is a hindrance to the fully recognition of the right to free basic education in Southern Africa (Moloi, & Mhlanga, 2021:4).

Another challenge in the implementation of the right free and compulsory basic education in Southern Africa concerns the shortage of teachers. The increase in the number of pupils enrolled at every level of basic education has surpassed teacher pupil-ratio in most Southern African countries (Mafa & Tarusikirwa 2013:2481). For example, the teacher-pupil ratio in Zimbabwe's primary education system is 1:40 and most classes have between forty and fifty pupils, way above the recommended teacher-pupil ratio of 1:27 (Mafa & Tarusikirwa, 2013:2485). To enhance quality basic education, the student–teacher ratio should be reduced drastically. Public education in Zimbabwe continues to be beleaguered by inadequate infrastructure and teacher shortages. In South African schools, class sizes are equally high. Zambia's average class size is between 46-50 pupils and the pupil-teacher ratio moved from 49:1 to 57:1 in 2005 (Mobela 2016:51). Seemingly, the teacher-pupil ratio is huge in Southern Africa and this greatly affects the quality of basic education.

Funding of Basic Education and Physical and Teaching/Learning Materials

Funding and resources are crucial to effective implementation of quality basic education since the goal of expanding equitable accessible education is inseparably linked to educational finance. The principle of equality and non-discrimination may help guide fiscal policies (Akande et al, 2020:284). Article 2(1) of ICESCR stipulates that maximum available resources may be obtained through requesting international cooperation and assistance. Inadequate funding to meet the ever-increasing demand of educational support has compromised the quality of education in countries such as Zambia. The government of Zambia should increase the funding to basic education so as to meet the requirements of the primary schools (Phiri & Marvin 2016:341). The decrease in the budget allocation of the education sector affects the running of primary schools with inadequate finances. This compromises the free basic education program, leading to poor quality of education. It challenging for countries such as Zimbabwe and Zambia to continue with the policy of free primary education despite the lack of adequate funding (Mwanza & Silukuni 2020:318). UNICEF on Basic Education Budget Brief for South Africa highlighted that government policy on basic education had not been implemented effectively (Venter 2020:1).

Another key challenge remains the lack of teaching or learning resources and facilities. The absence of the resources like reading material and apparatus for experiments cause teachers to fail to convey quality lessons (Dhlomo & Mawere 2020:108). Infrastructure such as classrooms, laboratories, workshops and libraries are congested, creating unfavourable learning environments, which adversely affect the teaching and learning processes (Mafa & Tarusikirwa 2013:2486). The lack of learning and teaching contributes significantly to limited realisation of the right to basic education. The Ministry of Education Statistical Bulletin reports that the education sector in Zambia experiences deficits in terms of learning material and infrastructure such that the pupil-textbook ratio rose to 18:1 in 2005 (Mobela 2016:51. This indicates that Southern African countries have serious challenges in the provision of teaching and learning materials which compromise the realisation of the right to free basic education.

Crafting Appropriate Remedies to the Challenges

South Africa has a statute on basic education and would be best practice for Zimbabwe and Zambia to have such a separate act which specifically caters for basic education. The enactment of a specific Basic Education Act would augment the scope of the right to free and basic education in Zimbabwe and Zambia. According section 29(1) of the Basic Education Act of South Africa, no public school shall charge or cause any parent or guardian to pay tuition fees for or on behalf of any pupil in the school. Zimbabwe and Zambia should also have a Basic Education Act to cater specifically for basic education. Having a dedicated statute on basic education will go a long way in realising the right to free basic education. The Children's Act should also provide for children's rights to education as it is one of the most central legal documents on children's rights (Bhaiseni 2016:5). The Act should align with the provisions of both the UNCRC and ACRWC on the right to education.

Secondly, all children of schooling age should have access to free quality education (Dakwa, Chiome & Chabaya 2014:233*)*. The Basic Education Act of South Africa creates the Education Standards Quality Assurance Council (ESQAC) with the mandate of guaranteeing that standards and quality in schools of basic education are preserved. Quality in the provision of basic education should be prioritized in Southern Africa so as to realise the right to free and compulsory basic education. Zimbabwe and Zambia should have a quality assurance council like the one in South Africa to monitor the quality of basic education in schools. Moreover, the Education International (EI) (2001) states that quality public education is a cornerstone of a democratic society and has the task of providing equality of educational opportunities for all learners (Mahere 2015:311). In Zimbabwe, financial constraints in the central government have resulted in decline of access to and quality of education services (Tshabalala 2013:2257). The government of Zimbabwe should provide quality basic education which is foundational to learning at the basic level. The government has a responsibility to provide basic education which would change lives and societies. The Education Act therefore must make available the curriculum, qualifications of the persons, the teaching methods and the assessment methods in basic education to ensure quality.

Thirdly there is need for the promotion of external partners and collaboration in free basic education. Several Non-Governmental Organizations (NGOs) like Save the Children and Oxfam International support education in Southern Africa. They support quality education for the most disadvantaged children and play a crucial role in the improvement mechanisms of basic education. The effect of donor aid in promoting access to education in developing countries cannot be ignored as it enables the flow of resources for education resulting in improved educational provision in Zambia since the 1990s. Thus, countries in Southern Africa should promote donor participation to support free basic education. In most cases, NGOs are instrumental in assisting the government to effectively implement the right to free and compulsory basic education in Southern Africa.

Finally, there is an emerging trend in public interest litigation which identify the lack of adequate facilities at schools as a violation of the learners' right to a basic education (McConnachie & McConnachie 2012:556). In the *Randolph County Board of Education v. Adams* case, it was held that charging parents fees for textbooks was unconstitutional. The court understood freedom to include items that were indispensable to basic education. The court concentrated on the use of textbooks, as a fundamental part of free basic education. Similarly, in the *Bond v. Ann Arbor School District* case it was held that textbooks were a critical component of free basic education. Textbooks and other learning materials shall be free of charge. The right to a basic education obliges the state to offer sufficient education in order for the right to be fulfilled. Parents and guardians are being prejudiced by the failure of the government to provide free and compulsory basic education.

Conclusion

This chapter comprehensively expounded the basic tenets to implementation of the right to free basic education in Zimbabwe, Zambia and South Africa. It explored international and regional legal instruments as well as national legal and policy frameworks on the right to free basic education. While grappling with implementation of the right to free basic education, it is evident that efforts have been made by the three countries to uphold this fundamental right. The realisation of the right to free basic education is in its various stages of implementation and is shrouded with enormous challenges. Education is the centrepiece of the satisfaction of the other fundamental rights. The minimum core obligation of the right to basic education imposes a duty on the state parties (Zimbabwe, Zambia and South Africa) to ICESCR to fulfil. In the *Mudzuru & Another v The Minister of Justice, Legal and Parliamentary Affairs & 2 Others,* it was held that rights cannot be fulfilled without consideration to the commitments undertaken by Zimbabwe under international law. It is imperative for Zimbabwe and other Southern African countries to comply with international law on the regulation of free basic education. A state which does not offer the minimum core obligation of the right to education is in breach of ICESCR. Basic education is an unqualified right and should be considered as the minimum core obligation.

Learning and teaching materials should be sufficiently provided by governments in order to ensure the full realisation of the right to basic education. It is therefore prudent for the governments in Southern Africa to take the necessary mechanisms to ensure that the right to free basic education is fully realised. If education is free children are able to go to school hence it is possible to make it compulsory for any children of school-going age (Mapuva and Mapuva 2016:53). For example, the BEAM programme in Zimbabwe should not only pay fees but also provide school uniforms and books. Most citizens in Zambia, Zimbabwe and South Africa fail to access the right to free basic education due to poverty and unemployment. It is imperative that the respective governments continue to increase substantial funding to basic education and also engage NGOs to assist in the provision of free and compulsory basic education. Enactment of the Basic Education Act in Zimbabwe and Zambia specifically dedicated to basic education will be a milestone in the protection and promotion of the right to basic education. Public interest litigation can also be carried out in Southern African countries so as to encourage governments to fulfil their obligation to provide the right to free basic education.

References

AFRICAN UNION, (1981) *African Charter on Human and Peoples' Rights.* [Online]. Available from: https://au.int/sites/default/files/treaties/36390-treaty-0011_-_african_charter_on _human_and_peoples_rights_e.pdf

AFRICAN UNION, (1990) African Charter on the Rights and Welfare of the Child. {Online]. Available from: https://www.acerwc.africa/en/page/about-the-charter#:~:text=Of% 20The%20Child-

AKANDE, D., (2020) *Human Rights & 21ˢᵗ Century Challenges, Poverty, Conflict and Environment*. Oxford, Oxford University Press.

ARENDSE, L., (2011) The obligation to provide free basic education in South Africa: An International Perspective. *Potchefstroom Electronic Law Journal, 6,* 97-127.

ARENDSE, L., (2020) Slowly but surely: The substantive approach to the right to basic education of the South African courts post-Juma Musjid. *African Human Rights Law Journal, 20,* 285-314.

BHAISENI, B., (2016) Zimbabwe Children's Act Alignment with International and Domestic Legal Instruments: Unravelling the Gaps. *African Journal of Social Work, 6 (1) 3-6.*

CASE TEXT, (1970) *Bond v. Ann Arbor School District, 383 Mich. 693.* [Online]. Available online from: https://casetext.com/case/bond-v-ann-arbor-school-district.

CASE TEXT (1995) *Randolph Co. Bd. of Educ. v. Adams, 467 S.E.2d 150 (W. Va. 1995).* [Online]. Available from: https://casetext.com/case/randolph-county-bd-of-educ-v-adams.

CESCR, (1999) *General Comment No 13 The Right Education.* [Online]. Available from: https://www.ohchr.org/en/resources/educators/human-rights-education-training/d-general-comment-no-13-right-education-article-13-1999.

CESCR, (1999) *General Comment No. 11: Plans of Action for Primary Education.* [Online]. Available from: https://www.ohchr.org/en/resources/educators/human-rights-education-training/c-general-comment-no-11-plans-action-primary-education -article-14-1999.

CESCR, (1999) *General Comment No. 3:The Nature of States Parties Obligations.* [Online]. Available from: https://www.ohchr.org/en/resources/educators/human-rights-education-training/general-comment-no-3-nature-states-parties-obligations-article-2-para-1-1990.

CHÜRR, C., (2015) Realisation of a Child's Right to a Basic Education in the South African School System: Some Lessons from Germany. *PELJ,* 18(7) 2405-2455.

DAKWA, F. E., CHIOME, C. and CHABAYA, R. A., (2014) Poverty-Related causes of School Dropout- Dilemma of the Girl Child in Rural Zimbabwe. *International Journal of Academic Research in Progressive Education and Development,* 3(3) 248-258.

DHLOMO, T. and MAWERE, P., (2020) Curriculum reform in Zimbabwe: An analysis of early childhood development centers' state of readiness to embrace the new curriculum. *Journal of African Studies and Development,* 12, 104-114.

EKUNDAYO, S. O., (2018) The Right to Free and Compulsory Primary Education in Ghana: Lessons for Other African Countries. *Journal of Law, Policy and Globalization,* 69, 106-116.

KONDO, T., (2014) Socio-economic rights in Zimbabwe: Trends and emerging jurisprudence. *African Human Rights Law Journal,* 1, 163-193.

MAFA, O. and TARUSIKIRWA M. C., (2013) The Impact of Basic Education on the Quality of Secondary Schools in Zimbabwe's Secondary Schools. *International Journal of Asian Social Science,* 3(12), 2477-2489.

MAHERE, S., (2015) A Study of the Right of Learners and Teachers to Quality Public Education in Zimbabwe *Zimbabwe Educational Journal of Educational Research,* 27(2) 307-331.

MANYONGANISE, M., (2013) Education for All: Myth or Reality for Orphaned and Vulnerable Children in Zimbabwe? *International Journal. Soc. Sci. & Education,* 3 (2) 476-485.

MAPAKO, F. P. and MAREVA, R., (2013) The Concept of Free Primary School Education in Zimbabwe: Myth or Reality. *Educational Research International,* 1(1) 135-145.

MAPOLISA, T. and TSHABALALA, T., (2013) The Impact of the Economic Meltdown on the Education System of Zimbabwe. *International Journal of Asian Social Science*, 3(11) 2257.

MAPUVA, L. and MAPUVA, J., (2016) *The Dilemma of Children's Rights to Education in the era of Fast Track Land Reform in Zimbabwe Revisited* -Cambridge Schools Publishing.

MASUKA, T., (2014) The New Constitution of Zimbabwe and its Implications for Social Workers. *Journal of Social Welfare and Human Rights*, 2(1) 29-40.

MAUSHE, F., (2019) In Search for the Right to Education: The Role of the Basic Education Assistance Module (BEAM) in Promoting Access to Education in Zimbabwe. *Journal of Development Administration*, 4, 1-6.

MAJOME, M. T., (2023). *The right to free education; Fact or Fiction?* [Online]. Available from: http:// www.newsday.co.zw/2019/0//th- right-to-free-education-fact-or-fiction.

MAWERE, D., (2013) Evaluation of the Nziramasanga Report of Inquiry into Education in Zimbabwe, 1999: The Case of Gender Equity in Education. *International Journal of Asian Social Science*, 3(5), 1077-1088.

MHANDU, R. and DAMBUDZO, I., (2016) An Examination of the Contribution of Private Colleges to Education in Zimbabwe: A Case Study of Ten Private Colleges in Harare Province European. *Journal of Education Studies*, 2(1), 119-172.

MBANJE, P., (2023). *75% Likely to be Unable to Pay School Fees.* [Online]. Available from: https://www.newsday.co.zw/2015

MOBELA, C., (2016) Impact of free primary education: A case study of government schools in Kabwe Urban District *International Journal of Multidisciplinary Research and Development*, 3(9) 48-60.

MONAGENG, M., (2014) *Using the Courts to Protect Vulnerable People: Perspectives from the Judiciary and Legal Profession in Botswana, Malawi and Zambia.* Johannesburg, Southern Africa Litigation Centre.

MOYO, S., NCUBE, D. and KHUPE, M., (2016) An Assessment of Factors Contributing to High Secondary School Pupils Dropout Rates in Zimbabwe. A Case Study of Bulilima District. *Global Journal of Advanced Research*, 3(9), 855-863.

MOYO, A., (2019) The Legal Status of Children's Rights in Zimbabwe. In Moyo A. (ed.) *Selected Aspects of the 2013 Zimbabwean Constitution and the Declaration of Rights.* Raoul Wallenberg Institute of Human Rights and Humanitarian Law pp. 126-162.

MOYO, A., (2019) Socio-Economic Rights under the 2013 Zimbabwean Constitution. In: MOYO, A. (ed.) *Selected Aspects of the 2013 Zimbabwean Constitution and the Declaration of Rights.* Raoul Wallenberg Institute of Human Rights and Humanitarian Law pp. 163-181.

MURUNGI, L. N., (2015) Inclusive Basic Education in South Africa: Issues in its Conceptualisation and Implementation *PELJ*, 18(1), 3160-3195.

MUTANGI, T., (2019) An Overview of the African Human Rights System. In: MOYO A., (ed.) *Selected Aspects of the 2013 Zimbabwean Constitution and the Declaration of Rights.* Raoul Wallenberg Institute of Human Rights and Humanitarian Law pp. 261-279.

MWANZA, C. and DARIOUS, S. D., (2020) Implementation of the Free Education Policy in Primary Schools in Kafue District: Is it a Compromise on Quality of Education in Zambia? *European Journal of Education Studies*, 7(9) 317-333.

NCUBE, W., (1998) *Law, Culture, Tradition and Children's Rights in Eastern and Southern Africa.* Ashgate.

NHUNDU, T. J., (1992) A Decade of Educational Expansion in Zimbabwe: Causes, Consequences, and Policy Contradictions. *The Journal of Negro Education,* 61(1), 78-98.

OWUOR, F. O., (2018) Policy Implementation and Determinant of Access to Education for Disable Learners in Siaya and Kisumu Counties-Kenya: A Phenomenological Study. *Journal of Public Administration and Governance,* 8(2), 174-226.

Office of the United Nations High Commissioner for Human Rights, (1989). *Convention on the Rights of the Child.* [Online]. Available from: https://www.ohchr.org/en/instruments-mechanisms/instruments/convention-rights-child

Office of the United Nations High Commissioner for Human Rights, (1966) *International Covenant on Economic, Social and Cultural Rights.* [Online]. Available from: https://www.ohchr.org/en/instruments-mechanisms/instruments/international-covenant-economic-social-and-cultural-rights

Office of the United Nations High Commissioner for Human Rights, (1948) *Universal Declaration of Human Rights.* [Online]. Available from: https://www.ohchr.org/sites/default/files/UDHR/Documents/UDHR_Translations/.

PHIRI, G. G. and MARVIN, K., (2016) The impact of free primary education in Zambia (A case study of Chipata district). *International Journal of Multidisciplinary Research and Development,* 3(8), 341-355.

RAMCHARAM, B. G., (2005) *Judicial Protection of Economic Social and Cultural Rights.* Leiden, Nijhoff Publishers.

SAFLII, (2019) *Centre for Child Law & others v Government of the Eastern Cape Province & others (ECB) case no 504/10.* [Online]. Available from: from http://www.saflii.org/za/ca ses/ZAECGHC/2019/126.html.

SAFLII, (2015) *Tripartite Steering Committee & Anor v. Minister of Basic Education and Ors. [1830/2015] [2015] (5) SA 107.* [Online]. Available from: http://www.saflii.org/za/cases/ ZAECGHC/2015/67.html.

SAFLII, (2011) *Governing Body of the Juma Musjid Primary School & Others v Essay N.O. and Others (CCT 29/10) [2011].* [Online]. Available from http://www.saflii.org.za/za/case s/ZACC/2011/13.html.

Southern African Development Community, (1997) *SADC Protocol on Education and Training.* [Online]. Available from: https://www.sadc.int/document/protocol-education-training-1997

Southern African Development Community, (1996) *South African Education Act of 1996.* [Online]. Available from: https://www.gov.za/documents/south-african-schools-act#

UNITED NATIONS, (2023) *United Nations Educational, Scientific and Cultural Organisation.* [Online]. Available from: https://www.un.org/youthenvoy/2013/08/unesco-united-nations-educational-scientific-and-cultural-organization/

VERITAS, (2015) *Mudzuru & Another v. Minister of Justice & Or CCZ 12/2015.* [Online]. Available from: https://veritaszim.net/node/1559

VERITAS, (2023) *Children's Act [Chapter 5:06] Amended.* [Online]. Available from: https://www.veritaszim.net/node/145

VERITAS, (2023) Constitution of Zimbabwe Amendment (No. 20) Act of 2013. [Online]. Available from: https://www.veritaszim.net/node/315

Human Rights Crisis in Zimbabwe: What is the Role of the School?

Dzavo Joseph

Introduction

Zimbabwe is often in the spotlight during election time, due to conflicts and violence. The current education system can be attributed to having less impact in minimizing the democratic crisis. A meaningful education system should be able to address the issue of democratic space, the right to liberty, justice and equality in practice. Schools should play a critical role to ensure nurturing of rights is developed as early as the primary school level. The education system should not just serve as a tool for employment for those who pursue it but sustain employment through democratic practices that support investment, property rights and production. In order to help in the understanding of democratic rights of justice, liberty and equality which are core, the chapter discusses their relevance to peace initiatives in Zimbabwe. The chapter further explores the history of infringements of rights and what schools could do to minimize the current human rights crisis in the country.

Understanding Key Concepts

The core democratic values and rights which should be emphasized are justice, equality and liberty. Bafaneli and Setibi (2015:17) view democratic rights as fundamental principles and standards that direct actions and enable citizens to live democratically. Fundamental principles or standards portray democratic rights as critical social needs. Democratic rights can also be understood as values that a community expects from its members where an individual acts as a member of the community (Botha, Joubert & Hugo 2016:2). Rights which are expected by the community as serving a common good by all are regarded as democratic. These are rights that should allow justice to prevail and individuals to exercise their liberty without hindrance.

That being the case, societies concerned with the future or continual survival should be seen to be taking critical steps to deliberately plan and include the development of democratic rights in the education system. Democratic rights are, therefore, understood as those beliefs and principles that allow for harmonious participation in citizenship activities in given institutions.

Dzavo, Luggya & Tanga (2022:31) define justice as a concept of fairness. Fairness considers the equality of individuals in the partaking of activities that accrue economic or social benefits. In education, the fair treatment or accordance of

51

educational benefits fairly to learners and results in the development of the same virtues in learners as attributes to be lived by when they become adults living in communities (Mwamwenda 2014; Dzavo et al 2022:31). Justice can also be regarded as a character set of principles for assigning basic rights and duties and for determining what they take to be the proper distribution of the benefits and burdens of social cooperation (Rawls 1999:3). Justice is realized when no arbitrary distinctions are made between persons in the assigning of basic rights and duties and when the rules determine a proper balance between competing claims to the advantages of social life.

The distinctive role of justice is to specify basic rights and duties and to determine the appropriate distributive shares; the way in which a conception does this is bound to affect the problems of efficiency, coordination and stability. Justice is also used to refer to laws, institutions, social systems, decisions, judgments, imputations, attitudes and dispositions of persons as well as persons themselves. This portray justice as the most important virtue of institutions. Justice is fairness and human beings agree to avail themselves of accidents of nature and social circumstances only when doing so is for the common benefit. Rawls (1999:3) sees justice as a critical value in an institution in order to bring about stability or efficiency to institutions and society at large. The practice of these rights is not optional, but a priority if the development of democratic rights is to be realized at a significant level. Thus, justice is a practice of equal consideration in participation and decision-making in the activities involving members forming a community. Liberty is linked to justice since it concerns right to think, act or behave without any interference from our government (Dzavo et al 2022:31). Liberty involves personal, political and economic freedoms, which points to the absence of unjustified restrictions. In education, this entails the creation of friendly environments where all stakeholders freely participate in educational activities as guided by democratic rights.

Rawls (1999:176) posits that liberty can also be discussed in connection with constitutional and legal restrictions. In these cases, liberty is a certain structure of institutions, a certain system of public rules defining rights and duties. On that basis, persons are at liberty to do something when they are free from certain constraints either to do it or not to do it, and when they are doing it or not doing it are protected from unwarranted interference by other persons. Liberty in schools can be taught and practiced through the daily routines of the institutions as part of the development of democratic rights. The key features of liberty are equality and justice, which calls for regulations, not restrictions based on human equality and the need for fairness to all or a just environment. Thus, non-interferences in lawful activities that are viewed as bringing about happiness or satisfaction to the individual participating in the activities of an organization or institution of choice.

The Michigan Department of Education (2009:2) considers equality as an environment where everyone should get the same treatment regardless of status or origin. Equality, on that basis, goes beyond a person's affiliation in society. In schools and communities, the development of democratic rights should be nurtured effectively in democratic environments. Post (2006:24) regards equality as a situation where the state accords all citizens equal freedom of participation in public discourse.

Citizens are entitled to be treated fairly with regard to the forms of conduct that constitute autonomous democratic participation. These forms of conduct are given to the citizens socially and historically and different forms will imply different forms of democratic equality. For example, equality in the context of voting will be different from equality in public discourse. Equality, therefore, levels all social, cultural and economic differences inconsistent with the moral equality of all citizens. In the development of democratic rights, members in a school or class operate as citizens whose rights to participate in school activities are bound by their affiliation to the school (Dzavo 2020). This, therefore, is then expected to extend to the immediate communities from which the learners come. The understanding focus on equal treatment on the basis of belonging to the same environment or institution of life.

Zimbabwe's History of Infringements of Rights

Historical Zimbabwean Kingdoms such as the Kingdom of Mutapa had their own challenges in terms of infringements of democratic rights. They had their own internal conflicts based on how they shared power and resources though they remained united, finding each other through their own African epistemology and pedagogy. Dzavo (2020:89) notes this historical fact by stating that during the pre-colonial era, the abuse of democratic rights was mostly driven and inspired by the struggle for land, resources and chieftainship. In the colonial era, abuses, however, were mostly centered on the struggle for land and ethnic recognition. In the post-colonial era, the abuse of democratic rights became much more pronounced and mostly centered on the struggle for political hegemony. In the same vein, conflicts and violence can be traced to early Shona states in Zimbabwe. The period can be traced to the 15th Century when the Torwa Dynasty moved into other areas around the country in search of resources. The successive Shona states coincided with the coming in of the Portuguese and later the groups set up by Mfecane from the South.

The subsequent periods were characterized by raids and strife between the royal dynasty and the *mwari* cult. In the 1830s, the Changamires state was engulfed by factions moving away in different directions across the country. The main cause of conflicts was centered on resources and the desire for power. Resources ranged from minerals, livestock and grain. Labour for the construction and strengthening of states was also a source of abuse as the strongest states needed subjects (*Varanda*) or slaves to work for them for production and for defense (Dzavo 2020:89; Beach 1974:633; Sibanda 1990; Dzavo 2020:89). In the 1890s, the coming of the British settlers shifted the infringements of democratic rights into another form. The now most powerful white colonist brought in an indiscriminate expropriation of African resources like land. In 1894, the settlers used a legal instrument, the first constitution of the country to justify the abuse of democratic rights (Beach 1974; Sibanda, 1990; Dzavo 2020:89).

The period resulted in the abandonment of community ownership of resources to individualism or a competition-oriented approach to life. The channel to resources would be possible through the new education system. Success in the new school system would lead to the acquisition of resources. This would also mirror the school pedagogy of the day. The coming in of the settlers demonstrates how the school from that period contributed to a large extent to the human rights crisis today through competition. In pre-colonial education, a King or Queen remained accountable to his or her society (*Mambo ndi Mambo ne vanhu*) because of the existence of other people hence he or she remained accountable and responsible to subjects. There were checks and balances, spiritual, social, physical and natural that responded to the king or citizens' behaviour when it threatened peace and stability in some African societies. Pests, natural disasters, diseases and deaths of people were all punishments that were met in the kingdom when blood was shed unnecessarily and self-centeredness was observed in the kingdoms. This was in a way a school system based on *Unhu/Ubuntu* philosophy addressing the democratic rights in Zimbabwean Kingdoms (Dzavo, Choto & Mutimukulu 2022:22). *Unhu/Ubuntu* philosophy in education gives learners the primacy to humanness and adopts a more holistic view of learners instead of reducing their abilities or potential. The teacher provides equal and respective education to all learners no matter their background or circumstances (Mahaye 2018). The development of democratic rights ensures the reduction or elimination of political violence in society by eliminating individualism or self-centeredness associated with the school today.

The traditional courts as part of the school system in the precolonial era, played a critical role in ensuring order and peace prevailed in society whenever there was a threat of any sort. Every member of the Kingdom was a watch person for any wrongdoing of a member of the community if it had a possibility of changing the living patterns of the society. So how was this done? There were reporting structures and systems in communities that would ensure that a problem is brought to the attention of the community authorities for consideration. The environment itself had its own natural checks and balances that would call for individual responsibilities. Any misbehaviour threatening the peace or sustenance of the community was debated by the community and solutions were found for all to live in self-contained peace (Dzavo, Choto & Mutimukulu 2022:22).

At independence in 1980, Prime Minister Robert Mugabe's reconciliation statement set the tone for the promotion of human rights. The statement was inclusive of all citizens despite the myriad differences. There was a coalition of the Zimbabwe African National Union – Patriotic Front (ZANU-PF) and the Patriotic Front-Zimbabwe African People's Union (PF-ZAPU) in government. The Prime Minister's speech also included non-interference of property rights of individuals that include the land. Mugabe further urged Zimbabweans to trample upon racism, tribalism and regionalism which can be viewed as ingredients of violation of human rights (Gusha 2019:2-6). A Challenge to the Prime Minister's Statement of Reconciliation took a negative turn on 6 August 1980. This was when Edgar Tekere was arrested for killing a white farmer and got acquitted in November the same year. The murder and court outcome showed that there was still animosity between some whites and Africans. In November 1980, fighting erupted in Bulawayo between the forces of the Zimbabwe People's Revolutionary Army (ZIPRA) and the Zimbabwe African National Liberation Army (ZANILA). As these events happened Joshua Nkomo and Robert Mugabe accused each other of sabotaging the country's peace initiatives. By January

1981 Joshua Nkomo was demoted from the post of Home Affairs to the portfolio of Public Affairs.

The preceding action did not please PF-ZAPU members who felt unfairly treated. Mugabe further demoted Nkomo to a Minister without portfolio. The same year in February another fight broke out in Bulawayo among national army members in which around 300 soldiers died. Ethnicity was the cause of such fights. Matters got worse when two senior army generals Lookout Masuku and Dumiso Dabengwa were arrested on accusations of keeping an arms cache in the ZIPRA farms. In 1983 Joshua Nkomo and all PF-ZAPU ministers were fired from the cabinet on the accusation of destabilising the new government. The reaction of former ZIPRA forces was to go back to the bush and operate as dissidents. Zimbabwe had to go through another dark phase in the next 6 years in the form of Gukurahundi. In January 1983 the Korean-trained Fifth Brigade was deployed in the Matabeleland and Midlands Provinces and the massacre of people began within a few days. People were murdered, mutilated and women raped (Gusha 2019:6). In 1986 the unity talks to stop the violation of human rights were initiated, which saw the signing of the Unity Accord on 22 December 1987 by Joshua Nkomo and Robert Mugabe. There was stability for some time till around the year 2000 when the Movement of Democratic Change (MDC) with the help of civil organisations successfully campaigned for a no-vote in a referendum to change the constitution. This angered the ZANU-PF government and that resulted in a violation of human rights through the land reform programme. Violence was used to reclaim farms from whites and in the process, people lost life and others injured. It was from this period onwards that periods before, during, and after elections became characterised by infringements of human rights (Mpofu 2021:40).

Other Countries Experiences of the Role of Schools on Teaching Democratic Rights

Globally, waves of contraventions of democratic rights have been extensively reported. Reference is made to the First (1914-1918) and Second (1939-1945) World Wars, in particular when political violence was witnessed. Even so, one cannot ignore global conflicts in recent decades where most parts of the world were engulfed in devastating infringements of democratic rights. There are displacements and maiming of thousands of harmless civilian populations by other civilians in some cases, or government security forces exerting the same on their citizens. Some of these horrific activities encompass ethnic, racial and xenophobic attacks (Dodo, Nsenduluka & Kasanda 2014:208).

From the foregoing, infringements of democratic rights appear to be a result of schools inadequately developing democratic rights in learners across the globe. The role of schools is not only to prepare the youth for the working place but to also prepare them to be democratic citizens who one day will support democratic values (Botha, Joubert & Hugo 2016:7). According to Subba (2014:37), the Republic of India places greater value on schools as places where democratic rights of equity, freedom and justice among others should be developed. The understanding is that for democracy to strive, learners should be taught democratic rights as a way of life. Teaching democratic rights means preparing children to become citizens who preserve and shape democracy in the future. In order to achieve this, Subba (2014:37) indicates that the government came up with the National Curriculum Framework (NCF, 2005) which strongly advocates values like cooperation, respect for human rights, tolerance, justice, responsible citizenship, diversity, reverence towards democracy and peaceful conflict resolution. Earlier on, the National Policy of Education (NPE, 1986) had also emphasised the teaching of democratic rights to eliminate intolerance, violence and superstition, to make India a democratic and progressive nation taking pride in its cultural heritage. The Indian experience is in line with Chinoda's (1986) views which indicate that teaching democratic values prepares learners for the tackling of civic issues adequately. The critical aspect of the Indian experience is a supportive policy framework to guide the development of democratic rights in schools.

The Indian experience buttresses the notion that schools indeed should have a role in growing democratic rights in learners. If schools have this role, one wonders then at what age this should start. Some countries like Zambia put much emphasis on the development of democratic values at secondary schools, while others like Kenya focus much on adults to address the phenomenon of the abuse of the democratic rights of its citizens, which continues to haunt the states (Adebayo & Zimba 2014:426; Onyulo 2017). The focus on secondary-school-going learners is motivated by Lawrence Kohlberg's (American psychologist) conventional reasoning and negates the pre-conventional reasoning found in primary-school-going learners. The second stage which is instrumental relativism forms the base for fairness of behaviour in learners which is the core of democratic rights. This latter stage is mostly concentrated in primary school-going children (Mwamwenda 2014). This is a critical age in which any nation should strive to invest its future in. The democratic future is not in the hands of the adults or political parties but in the young ranging from zero to fourteen years. It is to these that the rights to justice, liberty and equality should be quickly exposed. The school therefore should play this critical role in the survival of society.

In Europe, Croatia came up with a National framework, introduced in 2010, on the teaching of human rights. In the period between 2012 and 2014, the Ministry of Science, Education, and Sports worked on a programme on the implementation of human rights (Tibbitts 2015:34). Public discussions were organised by the Croatian Ministry of Education before and after the period of experimental implementation as well as during the development of the cross-curricular implementation (Tibbitts 2015:34). This demonstrates the level of commitment by the Croatian government to effectively addressing issues of democratic rights. The engagement in public discussions also shows the need for public support to enable effective curriculum implementation in schools as the public becomes aware of the value of what their children learn in schools, which is also critical for society. This is in line with the views of Murphy (1999) who indicates that in an ideal state, democratic values are clearly understood and shared by all and form part of the education system. It also agrees with Rogan and Grayson's (2003:1171) construct of capacity to support innovation and support from outside agencies. Other stakeholders like the community and policymakers are critical in the effective curriculum implementation, in this case, the development of democratic rights as shown by the Croatian state.

The Michigan Department of Education (2009) highlights that core democratic rights are the fundamental beliefs and constitutional principles of American society which unite all Americans. The rights are expressed in the Declaration of Independence, the United States Constitution, and other significant documents, speeches and writings of the nation. Moreover, learners are provided with a booklet on the teaching of core democratic rights in the schools. In addition, social studies as a subject was also used in conjunction with the booklet on democratic rights. Bahmueller (1992) and Giannini (1992) highlight that CIVITAS, a Framework for Civic Education, and a series of social studies bulletins, are critical publications designed to guide teachers in the understanding and development of democratic rights in schools. In the same vein, the Michigan Department of Education produces materials for the teaching of core democratic rights in the form of a module catering for different age groups (Michigan Department of Education 2009).

The situation in the United States of America (USA) is in line with Babarinde (1994:225) who claims that education should be practical and should be able to prepare a child to live in the community. The approach in the USA, littered in most cases with supportive activities, is conducive to the development of democratic values in learners. This action of providing a framework and some bulletins on how to guide implementation helps bridge the epistemological gap between the intentions of policymakers and the end user. The supportive stance makes social reform possible in any given society. This is so because social reconstruction is made possible when the state, teachers, community and learners are ready for curriculum implementation, in this case, for the sensitive content covering democratic rights (Ferreira & Schulze 2014:1; Lynch 2016; Rogan & Grayson 2003:1171). This gives confidence to teachers to effectively articulate and practise the development of democratic rights in schools.

The abuse of democratic rights in Kenya remains a critical phenomenon to date. According to Hansen (2009:2), the abuse of democratic values has played out in different ways throughout Kenya's history. It dates back to 1888 when Waiyaki wa Kenya, a Kikuyu Chief, was abducted and killed by the British after burning down the Fort of British East Company. British colonial policy in Kenya was founded upon the effective 'divide-and-rule' strategy which relied on building alliances with certain ethnic groups thereby escalating tensions between selected and other ethnic groups. Therefore, besides its immediate relationship with the abuse of democratic rights, colonialism, through divide-and-rule policies, brought about or escalated inter-community conflicts whose effects still determine the prevalence of the abuse of democratic rights. Onyulo (2017) and Hansen (2009:2) concur that after independence in 1963, the ruling party in Kenya was seen as serving the interests of the ethnic Kikuyu and that provided a rich environment for the abuse of democratic rights by other disgruntled ethnic groups who felt they were being left out in the distribution of the economic gains in the country.

Onyulo (2017) further highlights that intra-party violence is also common in Kenya, citing the abuse of democratic rights that characterised the ruling party politics during party primaries in preparation for the August 2017 General Elections. In spite of decades of violence in Kenya, the government has done very little to address the inadequate development of democratic rights through education. Jwan & Kisaka (2017:1) note that though the government made reference to the teaching of democratic rights through the National Goals of Education (Republic of Kenya, 1964:21-25), very little attention has been paid to the practice in schools. Hansen (2009:2), however, suggests legal and institutional reforms as a means of solving this catastrophic problem in Kenya. In the same vein, Onyulo (2017) notes that in 2013, the Kenyan Government enacted a series of measures like early warning systems that aimed at group interventions in disputes before they escalated. These strategies, however, target adults, most of whom are already involved in political violence, leaving schools that are supposed to shape the new world order through the development of democratic rights in learners.

A nation that concentrates on legal and institutional reforms which excludes educational reforms may only enjoy short-term moments of peace. Such reforms are likely to be superficial and may not endure as they may slightly address the market forces which are based on the spontaneous practice of democratic rights as part and parcel of a people's culture. Sustainable democracy and peace can only be realised when addressed through education at an early age, hence, education is not an option but a priority if justice, liberty and equality are to be realised (Mwamwenda 2014; Thornberg & Elvstrand 2012).

Having attained its independence in 1966, three years later in 1969 the Government of Botswana introduced the teaching of democratic values in primary schools (Mhlauli 2011:143). In 1975 the Government of Botswana convened a National Commission on Education and the Commission presented a report that was approved by the National Assembly in August 1977. The Commission attached significance to the teaching of democratic values as an overriding principle that should be promoted in the school system. It was against this principle that Social Studies was used as the channel to teach democratic values in primary schools in Botswana (Bafaneli & Setibi 2015:17). However, Mhlauli (2011:143) notes that youths in Botswana displayed behaviour that was not in tandem with democratic values. Further, the National Commission on Education also documented in 1993 an outcry from the Botswana public on the lack of democratic values in youths.

The outcry highlighted in Botswana shows cracks in curriculum implementation which in turn work against an effective development of democratic rights. Mhlauli (2011) assert that in Botswana that there was a need to empower schools and teachers to use suitable pedagogies and proper democratic practices to address the problem. Mhlauli,'s study fits well into the Rogan and Grayson (2003:1171) theory which highlights the roles of teachers, schools and other outside-school stakeholders in supporting or working against effective curriculum implementation. This negative situation as implied in Botswana contradicts the philosophy of reconstructionism, which regards the school as the pivot for the development of democratic rights (Conrad 2016). Though Botswana is generally viewed as a shining democracy in Africa, common trends should be drawn between Botswana and Zimbabwe on the teaching of democratic rights in schools.

South Africa, a multicultural society or a rainbow state coming out of the apartheid period, has major challenges in addressing issues of democratic values. In the last two decades, South Africa has witnessed some of the most gruesome xenophobic attacks. In these attacks, thousands of foreigners were displaced, some had their shops looted and set ablaze while some immigrants were hacked to death (BBC 2015; CNN 2015). Despite these violent activities, the South African Government has put strategies in place and displays commitment and a clear-cut vision to effectively address the issue of developing democratic rights in schools. According to Waghid (2014), the development of democratic values in South Africa has been informed and guided mainly by three primary considerations: first, to encourage people not to repeat the racist, repressive, and authoritarian apartheid past; secondly, to engender public deliberation to ensure that all are engaged with, situated in, and connected to the democratic aspirations of others, and; thirdly, to recognize the rights and responsibility of all citizens, uphold the rule of law, develop respect for the other as persons through our human interdependence (*Ubuntu*) and contribute towards building an equitable and just society on the basis of reconciliation with and mutual recognition of the other.

The Department of Basic Education (DoBE) document, drafted in (2011) provided a practical guide for teachers which is believed to promote the development of democratic rights enshrined in the South African Constitution. The practical guide provides examples of how democratic rights can be incorporated into schools and classroom management. The guide also gives teachers practical examples across a number of learning areas on how to develop a variety of lessons around democratic values in a democracy. The DoBE document (2011) sees as its main function the development of programmes that facilitate and promote the integration of democratic values in schools. The DoBE, therefore, lists the following documents as critical in the enhancement and implementation of democratic rights in schools: Values, Education, and Democracy (2000); Manifesto on Values, Education Democracy (2001); Integration Guide Book for Principals and Teachers (2004); Values and Human Rights in the curriculum (2005); The National School Pledge (2008); and Youth of South Africa (2008).

The Department of Education (2003) indicates that the manifesto emphasises democratic values which the education system should actively promote, among them tolerance, social justice, equality, respect and the rule of law. The manifesto further explores how democratic rights can be taught as part of the curriculum. Botha, Joubert and Hugo (2016) argue that learners in primary schools in South Africa are aware of democratic values and expect their peers and adults to practise them. This could actually serve as evidence of the efforts made by the South African Government to have democratic rights developed in schools.

The impact of these efforts to develop democratic rights by the South African Government may be difficult to assess considering the highlighted xenophobic incidents. This could possibly be explained by Rogan and Grayson's (2003:1171) profile of implementation which highlights the impact of the differences that occur among teachers in terms of the implementation of democratic values as a possible contributory factor to the discrepancies noted in South Africa. This is also supported by Ferreira and Schulze's (2014:1) study which revealed that certain South African schools showed gaps between the policymakers' intentions on democratic rights and their interpretation. The intentions need face-to-face epistemological support despite the available policy documents. The efforts, nevertheless, show great commitment by the South African Government towards addressing forms of violence in the republic through the inclusion of the development of democratic rights in the curriculum.

The Expected Role of the School in Zimbabwe

The practice of democratic education in schools makes learners appreciate the importance of democratic rights. In addition, scholars such as Haralambos & Holborn (2013), Mwamwenda (2014), and Suba (2014:37) indicate that the school as a major socialisation agent plays a major role in developing democratic rights in learners and, by extension, society. Additionally, Freire (2000) considers the classroom as a community in which democratic rights can be acquired through the structuring of the school on the basis of democratic principles. In this way, schools can cultivate an appreciation of democratic values in pupils. For example, studies carried out in Leeds and Scottish primary schools established that schools play a big role in instilling democratic rights in learners (Flecknoe 2009). Results from those studies show that the schools were able to play their role, hence learners were able to value other people's views and contributions. Learners were also able to respect different beliefs and participate effectively in an inclusive culture (Flecknoe 2009).

At independence in 1980, the Zimbabwean Government made radical curriculum changes from colonial education which seemed to neglect the teaching of democratic rights. Among the many subjects that were introduced was Social Studies (Zvobgo 1996). According to Chinoda (1986), Social Studies is a powerful subject that can enhance the development of democratic values in primary schools. The old Social Studies (1982) and new Heritage and Social Studies (2015-2022 syllabi) reflect democratic rights in their content. In the same vein, the 2013 Zimbabwean Constitution reflects quite a lot on democratic rights. The Preamble, for example, highlights that:

> We people of Zimbabwe, United in our Diversity by our common desire for freedom, justice, and equality and our heroic resistance to colonialism, racism, and all forms of domination and oppression... recognize the need to entrench democracy, good, transparent, and accountable governance and rule of law...reaffirming our commitment to upholding and defending fundamental rights and freedoms...cherishing freedom, equality, peace, justice, tolerance, prosperity....

Chapter 2:11 propounds that the state must take all practical measures to protect fundamental rights and freedoms enshrined in Chapter 4 of the Constitution and promote their full realisation and fulfilment. There is no indication, however, of how the state should fulfil that important obligation. Chapter 4 part 2:49(b) provides that every person has the right to personal liberty, which includes the right not to be deprived of their liberty arbitrarily or without cause. In addition, under the same Chapter, part 2:52(a) says that every person has a right to bodily and psychological integrity, which includes freedom from all forms of abuse of democratic rights from public and private sources. Section 53 is in line with 52(a) and highlights that no individual may be subjected to physical or psychological torture or to cruel, inhuman, or degrading treatment or punishment. Lastly, Chapter 4, part 1:46(1) (b) stipulates that a court, tribunal, forum, or body must promote the values and principles that underlie a democratic society based on openness, justice, human dignity, equality, and freedom. These chapters and sections, however, do not highlight the need for the inclusion of these democratic rights in education; neither do they make democratic rights mandatory in education. Chapter 2:27 makes basic education free and compulsory in primary schools.

The 1987 Education Act [Chapter 25:04] Part 2 Section 4 appears to be more on the protective side of the learner in terms of being allowed to attend school under prescribed conditions:

Fundamental Rights and Objectives of Education in Zimbabwe.
Section 4(1) subsection (2) (a) (b) states:
Notwithstanding anything to the contrary contained in any other enactment, but subject to this Act, every child in Zimbabwe shall have the right to school education.
Subject to subsection (5), no child in Zimbabwe shall
    (a)   be refused admission to any school; or
    (b)   Be discriminated against by the imposition of onerous terms and conditions in regard to his admission to any school;
On the grounds of his race, tribe, place of birth, national or ethnic, political opinions, colour, creed or gender
Subsection 3 (a) (b) reads:
For the purposes of subsection (2), a term or condition shall be deemed to be onerous if it requires the child upon whom it is imposed or the child's parent----
    (a)   To do anything; or
    (b)   To possess some quality, attribute, asset, or property;
which is not required to be done or possessed by children or parents, as the case may be of a different race, tribe, place of origin, national or ethnic, origin, political opinion, colour, creed, or gender,

A closer examination of the act show underlying principles of democratic rights such as justice, equality and liberty. Whenever policies and Acts are open to different interpretations, it can be an unfortunate recipe for deferential application by teachers. This in addition creates an epistemological gap in the intentions of policymakers and those of implementers of the curriculum (Ferreira & Schulze 2014). The Secretary's Circular Number 3 of 2002, Ref: D/111/1, published on 28 January 2002 has aspects that can be used to guide the development of democratic rights in primary schools. Part of the circular's introduction says:

The relevance of the curriculum is based on the extent to which it meets the needs of the individual learner…, society at large, and the future challenges of the country…The focus is on the individual's development of sound national values…, responsible citizenship.

Further, goal number 2 (2.3) (2.4) (2.8) reads:

(2.3) Producing citizens, who understand, appreciate, and accept their civic and moral responsibilities within society;
(2.4) promoting national identity, pride, unity, cultural norms, and values so as to preserve the Zimbabwe heritage through the teaching and learning of the appropriate humanities and indigenous languages;
(2.8) promoting the practice of inclusive education through flexible accommodation of special needs among learners.

Goal number 2, (2.3) (2.4) (2.8) of the circular highlights the need to produce citizens who understand, appreciate and accept their civic and moral responsibility within society. The circular further indicates that the education system expects pupils to develop skills and competencies in ethics and responsible citizenship. In that particular circular, ethics, and citizenship are supposed to be taught under Social Studies and Religious and Moral Education. This is part of what Zimbabwe has which can be used in reinforcing the teaching of democratic rights in schools. There are, however, no other known frameworks that guide the teaching of democratic rights in schools as an entity. This gap in frameworks that can guide teachers in the development of democratic rights may leave room for teachers or schools to apply democratic rights differently depending on their political and social environments. This could be in line with Kerr's (2000) observation that many countries lack interest in involving young people in public and political life. Such exclusions lead to the inability to deal with democratic issues like pluralism, multiculturalism, ethnic and cultural diversity, tolerance, social cohesion, and collective and individual rights. Responsibilities, social justice and freedom among others also suffer heavily yet they are crucial to societies.

The Nziramasanga Commission (1999) observed that democratic rights were not being adequately taught in schools in Zimbabwe. The Commission emphasised that education should be used as an essential tool for the development of these values in learners. The commission highlighted that vandalism, violence and indiscipline in our schools and society are a result of the lack of democratic values which should be developed through the formal education process. The Commission lamented the ongoing situation where democratic rights are covered under a few topics in Social Studies. The same problem was noted in the Heritage and Social Studies Syllabus 2015-2022 (Dzavo 2020:233). However, the lack of appreciation of democratic rights as demonstrated by violent reactions and intolerance to opposing democratic views in Zimbabwe, in general, including by the educated, makes one wonder whether schools in Zimbabwe really play their role as agents of socialisation of learners into democratic rights.

Conclusion

The chapter advocated for the formulation of a direct legal instrument that clearly directs the teaching of democratic rights. A policy document protects the implementers and forces curriculum implementers to act on this need as shown in the experiences from other countries. There is also a need to come up with a framework that guides teachers on the implementation of democratic rights in schools starting with primary schools. The primary schools were selected because the period of starting to develop a civic citizen is between the ages of 0-12, which fits well into the primary school-going age. Good habits and principles are easier to instil in children than in adults (Mwamwenda 2014). Furthermore, democratic rights are critical for sustainable development. The way young ones are brought up today shapes their adulthood behaviour and character. A person's character, to some extent, lies in the tradition in which he she was brought up and the experiences the person has undergone. The patterns of thinking and acting that have been instilled into us as children are fundamental to our instinctive patterns of behaviour in adulthood (Dzavo 2020; Dzavo et al 2022:31). The observation calls for intense contribution by the school and the community to develop in learners the much-needed virtues if Zimbabwe is to experience the most needed political change. It is not sound to attend to a failing or an undemocratic adult through various legal instruments if the democratic culture is not part of the adult individuals, through the school as one of the major socialising agents.

References

BABARINDE, K., (1994) Can Schools Teach Democracy. *Zimbabwe Journal of Educational Research*, 6(3), 225-238.

BAFANELI, S. and SETIBI, G., (2015) Promotion of Democratic Values by Junior Secondary School Teachers. *International Journal of Novel Research in Humanity and Social Sciences*, 2 (6), 17-30.

BAHMUELLER, C. F., (1992) *The Core Ideals of Civitas: A Framework for Civic Education.* Bloomington, Eric Digest.

BEACH, D. N., (1974) Ndebele Raiders and Shona Power. *Journal of African History*, 15, 633-651.

BOTHA, A., JOUBERT, I. and HUGO, A. (2016) Children's perceptions of democratic values: Implications for democratic citizen education. *South African Journal of Childhood Education*, 6(1), 1-8.

CHINODA, A. M., (1986) *Social Studies*. Harare, College Press.

DODO, O., NSENDULUKA, E. and KASANDA, S., (2016) Political Bases as the Epicenter of Violence: Cases of Mazowe and Shamva, Zimbabwe. *Journal of Applied Security Research*, 11(2), 208-219.

DZAVO, J., CHOTO, F. and MUTIMUKULU, N., (2022) *Ubuntuistic Approach to Peace Education. A Handbook for transformative pedagogy for institutional reform, reconciliation and Indigenisation for a Sustainable Peace for Teachers' Colleges in Zimbabwe.* Gweru, Midlands State University.

DZAVO, J., (2020) *The Role of Primary Schools in Promoting Democratic Values of Justice, Equality, and Liberty in Pupils: A Study of Shamva District, Zimbabwe.* Alice, University of Fort Hare.

DZAVO, J., LUGGYA, S. K. and TANGA, M. N., (2022) An analysis of the role of the School in Teaching democratic values: A Case of three Selected Primary Schools in Shamva District, Zimbabwe. *The Dyke Journal*, 15(2), 30-42

FERREIRA, C. and SCHULZE, S., (2014) Teachers' Experience of the Implementation of Values in Education in Schools: Mind the Gap. *South African Journal of Education*, 34(1), 1-7.

FLECKNOE, M., (2005) *What can One School Tell Us about Democracy.* [Online]. Available from: http://www.leeds.ac.uk/edcool/documents. (Accessed March 10, 2009).

FREIRE, P., (2000) *Pedagogy of the Oppressed.* New York, Continuum.

GIANNINI, R., (1992) CIVITAS: a Framework for Civic Education. *Organization of American Historians Magazine of History.* 7(1), 67.

GUSHA, I., (2019) Memories of Gukurahundi Massacre and the Challenge of Reconciliation. *Studia Historiae Ecclesiasticae*, 45(1), 2-14.

HANSEN, T. O., (2009) *Political Violence in Kenya. A Study of Causes, Responses, and A Framework for Preventative Action.* Pretoria, Institute for Security Studies.

HARALAMBOS, M. and HOLBORN, M., (2013) *Sociology: Themes and Perspectives.* London, Harper Collins.

JWAN, J. O. and KISAKA S. T., (2017) Democracy Ethics and Sound Justice: Implications for Secondary School Leadership in Kenya. *South African Journal of Education,* 37(3), 1-8.

LYNCH, M., (2016) *Philosophies of Education: Three Types of Student-Centred Philosophies.* [Online]. Available from: http://www.theedavocate.org/philosophiesineducation-3-types-student-centred-philosophies/

MAHAYE, N. M. E., (2018) *The Philosophy of Ubuntu in Education.* Scottsville, University of KwaZulu-Natal.

MHLAULI, M. B., (2011) Teaching Controversial Issues in Primary Schools in Botswana: Reality or Illusion. *British Journal of Arts and Social Sciences*, 2(2), 143-154.

Michigan Department of Education, (2009) *Our Core Democratic Values.* [Online]. Available from: http://www.michigan.gov/documents/10-02-core-democratic-values-48832-7.pdf.

MPOFU, W. J., (2021) Gukurahundi in Zimbabwe: An Epistemicide and Genocide. *Journal of Literary Studies*, 37(2), 40-55.

MWAMWENDA, T. S., (2014) *Educational Psychology an African Perspective.* Sandton, Heinemann Higher and Further Education.

NZIRAMASANGA, C. T., (1999) *Zimbabwe Report of the Presidential Commission of Inquiry into Education and Training.* Harare, Government of Zimbabwe.

ONYULO, T., (2017) *In Restless Kenya, 70% Worry about Another Round of Heavy Bloodshed with Presidential Elections.* [Online]. Available from: *https://www.washingtontimes.com/news/kenya-elections-renew-violence-fears*

POST, R., (2006) Democracy and Eequality. The Annals of the American Academy of olitical and Social Science, Law Society and Democracy: Comparative Perspective. *Sage Journals,* 603(1), 24-36.

RAWLS, J., (1999) A *Theory of Justice (Revised Ed.).* Massachusetts, Harvard University Press.

ROGAN, J. M. and GRAYSON, D. J., (2003) Towards the Theory of Curriculum Implementation with Particular Reference to Science Education in Developing Countries. *International Journal of Science Education,* 25(10), 1171-1206.

SIBANDA, M. J., (1990) *Turmoil and Tenacity Zimbabwe 1890-1990.* Harare, College Press.

SUBBA, D., (2014) Democratic values and democratic approach in teaching. *Journal of Educational Research,* 2(12), 37-40.

Government of Zimbabwe, (2013) *The Constitution of Zimbabwe.* [Online]. Available from: https://www.dpcorp.co.zw/assets/constitution-of-zimbabwe.pdf

THORNBERG, R. and ELVSTRAND, H., (2012) *Children's Experiences of Democracy, Participation and Trust in School* [Online]. Available from: https://www.researchgate.net/publication/235331447_Children%27s_experiences_of_democracy_participation_and_trust_in_school

TIBBITTS, F., (2015) *Curriculum Development and Review for Democratic Citizenship and Human Rights Education.* Paris, UNESCO.

UNITED NATIONS, (2016) *Seventeen Sustainable Development* Goals. [Online]. Available from: www.unric.or/en latest buzz/29844 sustainable-goals-are-and welcomed.

WAGHID, Y., (2014) *African Philosophy of Education Reconsidered on Being Human.* New York, Routledge.

ZVOBGO, R. J., (1996) *Transforming Education. The Zimbabwean Experience.* Harare, College Press Publishers.

Youths Rights to Quality Education in Rural Areas with Reference to Gokwe North District, Zimbabwe: Challenges and Opportunities

Tapiwa Musasa

Introduction

Education is a basic human right that has been identified as one of the most important strategies to promote sustainable development in the world, as evidenced by the inclusion of goal number four by the international community in the 17 Sustainable Development Goals propounded by the United Nations in 2015 (Rieckman 2017). Several other policies have also prioritised education as a pillar in achieving sustainable development at all levels. For example, the introduction of the Education for Sustainable Development (ESD) clause during the Earth Summit in Rio (1992), and chapter 36 of Agenda 21 consolidated international discussions on the critical role of education. In 2002, the announcement of the decade of education during the World Summit on Sustainable Development at the Johannesburg Plan of Implementation is also an indication that the international community has often recognized education as a pillar to achieving all SDGs (Kioupi and Vouvoulis 2019). Other important legal instruments include article 26 enshrined in the Universal Declaration of Human rights of 1948, article 28 in the Convention on the Rights of the Child(CRC), and article 11 in the African Charter on the Rights and Welfare of the Child. Similarly, objective 27, and section 75 enshrined in chapter 2 and Chapter 4 respectively of the Zimbabwean constitution of 2013 all emphasise the right to education for children, the youth and adults.

When the young people get an education, they get opportunities to learn life skills and grow their intellectual capacities to lead communities and nations in future. Through education, young people learn to research and innovate, thereby bringing out the best ideas learnt through sharing, observation and creativity. In addition, the juveniles get a chance to develop before they can engage into adulthood and start their own families as well as getting a chance to enjoy their youth. It is therefore very important to keep all children in school as long as possible, paying particular attention to the girl child.

Delaying marriage for the girl child has an impact on reduced child marriages and reduced fertility rates, thus quipping her with the necessary skills to be a competent equal partner in all academic fields alongside her male counterpart. The chapter explore the challenges people in rural areas encounter in their attempts to achieve quality education for the adult and young population, as well as examining the opportunities that can be utilised and maximised to the best advantage of the rural

67

population in terms of higher education attainment. Gokwe North district is found in the remote areas of the Midlands province and the district has been lagging behind for a long time in terms of development (Chiguye 2016). According to Brazer (2022), Gokwe North had the highest proportion of people using surface water in a study carried out in 2022, indicating shortages of clean water. This is an indication that there are underlying factors in the district that deter some young girls from attending school or achieving better grades because of the long distances they travel to look for water. In Gokwe North, hundreds of children are out of school because of pregnancy or early marriage, a situation which is threatening the achievement of SDG4 if the conditions are not improved (Katova (2022). This chapter also discuss the efforts being made by the Government of Zimbabwe if any, in terms of improving the quality and rates of access to education in Gokwe North. The paper also explore the factors, opportunities and challenges in Gokwe North towards achieving SDG 4, giving an insight on how the right to education for the youths in the district is being affected.

Quality Education in Rural Areas

The Sustainable Development Goals (SDGs) are a product of the international community in 2015 with the intention to give guidelines to member states on what to prioritise as they plan and implement development programs (Lawrence et al 2020). The national plans are supposed to be compatible with the international plans (Mostaque 2016). From the list of the SDGs, education is the most important for human development. According to Rieckman (2017:3), target 4.7 of SDG 4 state that authorities should ensure that by 2030 all learners acquire knowledge and skills needed to promote sustainable development including among others, sustainable development and lifestyles, human rights, gender equality, promotion of a culture of non-violence, global citizenship and appreciation of cultural diversity. This target clearly shows that education is the key to achieving all the 17 Sustainable Development Goals (SDGs). People have to be able to read and write for them to be able to participate effectively in planning and implementation of all development programs (Kurtcu 2019). Without education, learners of all ages may find it difficult even to understand the requirements of the SDG framework, thus each country should prioritise inclusive education and development of educational infrastructure across all regions-rural and urban.and of culture's contribution to sustainable development.

The process emphasises the need for Sustainable Livelihoods Approach (SLA), which is a way of thinking, planning, implementing, and monitoring development strategies targeting the needs of the vulnerable poor people (Serat 2017). The approach seeks pragmatic priorities, views, and interests of the concerned, searching for livelihood strategies that link the people with enabling environments and referring to their skills, social networks, physical and financial resources as well as the ability to influence core institutions. The Sustainable Livelihoods Approach taps from the following types of capital: human, financial, natural, physical and social capital. According to Kuzwayo (2016), human capital involves the skills and good health that enable people to work, while natural capital involves available natural resources like land, water, vegetation, and conservation strategies. Financial capital means financial resources people have and physical capital refers to the infrastructure at hand, which includes roads, secure shelter, adequate water supply, sanitation, and clean affordable energy.

Lastly, social capital refers to the networks and connectedness in society that enable people to trust each other and work together towards the common good of the community (Serat 2017 & Kuzwayo 2016). This will lead to the formulation of development policies that are people-centred and inclusive of the recipients of the development programs, in a bid to identify and reduce vulnerabilities of the poor. The benefits of education includes reduction of violence, enabling children to reach their highest potential, protecting children from trafficking and promoting environmental protection activities since educated people participate more in environment conservation clubs (White (2020). Education is able to reduce the high poverty levels, thus benefiting more than 420 million people around the world and contributing to the achievement of SDG1. On that basis, education can be regarded as a sustainable development approach, an investment, and a basic human right that improves skills and expands opportunities.

In addition, closing the education gender gap reduces child marriages as girls spend more time in schools, giving them a chance to grow and mature physically and mentally. Education also reduces child labour since children will be attending school instead of working in mines, plantations and houses. Other benefits of education to nations and communities include an improvement in maternal health, reproductive health and sexual health as knowledge is gained through interaction with others. John (2017) avers that a child born to a literate mother has 50% more chances of survival than one born to an illiterate mother. The economy is also boosted if the people are running businesses with information which leads to higher standards and advanced operational procedures. Inclusive education is also a benefit to disabled children and girls which ensures that no one is left behind in the spirit of equity and human rights. In concurrence, Kayani (2017) notes that education is the most important investment for humans because it promotes skills, knowledge and capabilities which in turn saves lives, lowers fertility and offers improved condition of sanitation as people gain more exposure through reading and training sessions. Interaction of groups promotes information flow, creativity and innovation thus uplifting the quality of life. Education also increases networking for people, increasing opportunities for the future and improving public health (Patrinos 2016; Kayani et al 2017). The job market awaits educated people with contemporary skills that befits the 21st century development initiatives, thus the need for quality education (Kumaralev & Suresh 2017). As such, education should be always available and easily accessible to all students from urban and rural areas.

According to Chakanika (2012), education is a basic human right documented in most policies in Sub-Saharan Africa. However, challenges remain outstanding and such that about 30 million children are not receiving any formal education in Sub-Saharan Africa, while 40% children are not meeting basic targets in literacy (Featherstone 2017). Denying young girls the right to education shuts them out and denies them a chance to participate in the economy as young, competent people alongside their male counterparts. In some cases, education in rural areas still needs to be improved because there are more schools in the urban areas as compared to the rural areas, despite the larger population of the youths in rural areas (Kapur 2018). This scenario is common in most developing areas, leading to a violation of the right to education for the youths in rural areas. Another key challenge regards the teacher-pupil ratio is uneven. A key informant who works in one of the remote schools in Gokwe North as a teacher noted that:

> I have 54 students in my class and it is very difficult to give attention to each and every one of them. It affects their performance in class and the education targets of literacy and numeracy cannot be compared with schools where the ratio is 1:25 or less. More should be done for rural areas in order to meet SDG4.

According to Mohamed (2020), South Africa still has a long way to go in achieving equal opportunities to access education. Economic, racial and gender inequalities continue to threaten the education sector even after apartheid because schools in rural areas and high-density residential areas are still lacking infrastructure like basic sanitation and water. While students in some schools still walk for more than one hour to attend the nearest school, students in the top 200 schools mainly located in urban areas get more distinctions than students in more than 6600 rural schools combined, indicating some gross inequality in accessing quality physical and human resources, technology and income (Mohamed 2020). John (2017) posits that there are social, cultural , health, geographical, religious and economic factors which hinder the success of education programs in most rural areas in the world. Remoteness and marginalisation are geographical factors that disadvantage those in rural areas from accessing quality education, unless deliberate efforts are made to improve infrastructure in the remote areas and reduce inequalities, which is a rare phenomenon in most developing countries. For example, the schools in Gokwe North are not well furnished and lack adequate inclusive facilities for all students. Asked to comment on the furniture and sanitation in the schools in Gokwe North noted that:

> In terms of toilets, a ratio of 1:20 per hole is recommended for boys, while a 1: 15 ratio is recommended for girls. Unfortunately, most schools are overcrowded and the student enrolments far exceed the recommended ratios. Even the furniture is old and unsuitable, while some of the buildings are dilapidated especially in very remote areas like Chomuuyu, Gandavaroyi and Tsungai. More needs to be done for our students to enjoy schools and match the pass rates in urban areas. The results of students here cannot be compared with those from urban areas because of the inequality and differential access to educational resources and infrastructure.

These factors need to be examined in order to make the quality of education relevant to the nations. In addition, Aleed (2016) avers that there are more barriers to achieving quality education in rural areas than urban areas because of the urban bias. More facilities, infrastructure and qualified teachers are found in urban areas. While it is the most important investment for the 21st century (Chakanika et al 2012), barriers remain especially in rural areas where teachers are frustrated due to isolation, poor salaries despite high level of education, lack of health and recreational facilities. Lack of access to technology due to the higher cost as well as gender discrimination are other factors, disadvantaging students from the rural areas (Shikalepo 2020). Asked to comment on access to technology and ICT equipment in Gokwe North, a key informant highlighted that:

> Our school was fortunate enough to get some computers from the presidential programs some years back. However, there is no computer laboratory in the school, and we had challenges of where to place them. They had to be lifted to different classes every time and sometimes they become accessible to teachers only and exclude the students who should be the rightfully intended beneficiaries. Right now, some of computers distributed by the former president are outdated and malfunctioning.

According to Chakanika (2012), rural areas are often neglected in terms of social and economic services, thus denying the rural citizens access to quality education. Without basic technology and up to standard teaching methods, then one questions the quality and relevance of the education received (Featherstone 2017), if it is enough to give the learners equal competence on a global perspective as compared to their urban counterparts or those from more developed nations.

According to Shava, Tlon, Shonhiwa and Hleza (2021), Zimbabwe experiences several challenges in providing quality education, which include inequality in access and outcomes along lines of gender, ethnic groups and geographical coverage. The country is also affected by its inability to retain qualified staff leading to skills shortage due to brain drain. Curricula in the education system tend to be disoriented from the economy leading to so many unemployed graduates. Less than 30% students enrol in the agricultural sector, engineering sector and other health sciences, while students enrolling for Masters, and PhD programs are very few (Shava et al 2021). Zimbabwean rural areas like Binga are excluded from accessing quality education because of inexperienced teachers, poor infrastructures, lack of stationery among other factors (Mutale 2015). This shows that exclusion is found due to remoteness, thus rural areas are often at a disadvantage. According to ZIMSTATS (2012), about 67% of the population in Zimbabwe resides in rural areas while 33% is in urban areas, and more facilities should be readily available to them since they are the majority.

The distance between primary, secondary and high schools is too long (between 15 and 25 kilometres) to promote enrolments and completion of education courses in Gokwe North district. There are only nine (9) Advanced Level schools in the whole Gokwe North District, which are far away from each other. One of the key informants noted that:

> We travel long distances to monitor and assess performance in the schools. Young children below 8 years travel for more than twenty kilometres one way to get to the nearest school. Only Nyamuroro and Nembudziya Government High School are less than 10 kilometres away from each other. Most of the schools are between 15 and 25 kilometres away from each other making it difficult for children to travel every day and perform well. These distances are also risky in terms of child abuse since perpetrators can follow the child from school any time. The distances also promote higher rates of school dropouts. Only 9 secondary schools namely: Nyamuroro Secondary school, Chinyenyetu Secondary School, Svibe Secondary School, Nembudziya Government

Secondary School, Chomuuyu Secondary School, Chireya Secondary, Zhomba Secondary School, Gumunyu Secondary School, and Tsungai High School have Advanced Level studies. This is very discouraging and most students just terminate their studies after Ordinary level, thus affecting lifelong opportunities for all as stated by target 4.7 of SDG 4.,

Challenges and Opportunities

The distance between schools in Gokwe North District is the worst enemy to achieving SDG4. Children as young as four years, who are in the first grade or in the Early Childhood Development (ECD) classes travel long distances of above 15 kilometres to get to the nearest school. Unlike other districts in Zimbabwe, to mention some parts of Masvingo as an example, where schools are found within a arrange of 5 kilometres, children in the Midlands province and Gokwe North in particular find it difficult to get to schools because schools are found in distances between 15 and 20 kilometres or more from each other (Mutale 2015). Such distances are among the greatest causes of school dropouts besides early pregnancies and child marriages. The pregnancies are usually a result of the long distances where children travel for so long distances without interference or interruption from neighbours and parents. Some pregnancies are also a result of rape, because perpetrators of rape can easily violate the young girls without anyone noticing because of the distances involved (Shikalepo 2020).

Rural areas in Gokwe North are full of forests and thickets which child abusers always take advantage of when committing such crimes. These are the major contributors to the 40% of children in Sub-Saharan Africa not attending school (Chakanika 2012). On the contrary, children in urban areas travel for less than 5 kilometres to get to the nearest school. If the distance is more than that, either the children are driven to school by their parents or they use public transport, which is either unavailable or unaffordable to rural learners. This is what Aleed (2016) called 'urban bias,' where rural areas are neglected in terms of infrastructure which support education, leading to poor grades, school dropouts, lack of enrolments especially for girls, and a general negative attitude towards education. Urban bias is also the reason why most of the youths will never return to their rural communities to work or invest in preference to urban areas or neighbouring countries so that they escape from the poor environments and lack of basic service provision like water, electricity, well-furnished schools and proper sanitary facilities.

Gokwe North District do not have access to inclusive and equitable quality education, which then affect their lifelong opportunities. Learners in Gokwe North Rural District also lack of institutions of higher learning like vocational training centres, colleges and universities. If there were more colleges and universities in the district, more people, particularly the youths, could enrol to further their education and the literacy rates, levels and standards of education in the district could improve. Some Universities like the Catholic University of Zimbabwe (CUZ) and Zimbabwe Open University (ZOU) have centres at Gokwe town centre, which is also far from

Gokwe North and still has limited programs to cater for the wide range of the young population in Gokwe North.

Poor infrastructure in Gokwe North also negatively affects the provision of quality education. The distances involved from the major urban centres as described in the relevant section in this chapter negatively impact enrollment of better qualified. More investment is needed in terms of classroom improvement, water and sanitation upgrading to avoid diseases and improvement of hygienic conditions in the school, which promotes the morale of the students and the teachers. High teacher -pupil ratios also demoralise the teachers and disadvantages the students, especially the slow learners, thus more classrooms and more teachers should be enrolled in Gokwe North to enable lower teacher-pupil ratios, high student and teacher morale, culminating to higher achievement of targets for SDG4. Some respondents clearly indicated that their children are demoralised by the whole education objectives since they rarely see one of their own coming back to the district to work there permanently. It is a clear fact that when people achieve academically, they go away into neighbouring towns and countries to look for better opportunities. Some students end up thinking there are no role models from the district to emulate, the reason why it is important to ensure parliamentarians, headmasters, doctors, and so on are encouraged to serve their home areas to boost youth morale in education. However, this can only be achieved when rural development, industrialization, rural electrification among others, are deliberately put on the development agendas, with effective planning, implementation, monitoring and evaluation, because no one wants to come back to a poorly serviced rural area. For SDG4 to be achieved by 2030, other SDGs should also be prioritised, although there is a great realisation that it is education, which will fuel the broader sustainable development framework. According to Patrinos (2016) and John (2017), there are many benefits of education, which include working in prominent companies, being a successful businessperson, and other benefits for child survival. Children born to educated mothers have 50% more chances of survival than those born to illiterate parents, thus there is always an advantage somehow for achieving quality education throughout life (Patrinos 2016; Aleed 2016; Riechman 2017; White 2020).

Gokwe North also has some opportunities that can be taken advantage of by stakeholders to promote SDG4 and uphold the rights of the youth to education. The vast pieces of land alluded to by Chiguye (2016) can be taken advantage of to construct more schools, more rural industries and health facilities close to every school, since there are also minerals, especially gold mines and coal reserves at Sengwa Colliery (Makoni et al 2015). A large young population can be taken advantage of to enrol into schools and work in industries after completing their education if stakeholders capitalise on the existence of the capital, physical and human assets emphasised by the Sustainable Livelihood Approach (SLA). Education is one such asset in the SLA, which promotes the effective implementation of all programs, thus even adult literacy classes for those adults who are still interested in education, or those who lost opportunities due to early marriage can be introduced in rural areas like Gokwe District where they once worked effectively. In view of the preceding discussion, the following recommendations should be considered:

- The Government should build more schools in Gokwe North to reduce the distance travelled by young learners to school in a bid to promote longer learning periods for boys and girls.
- The Government should put in place enhancement policies and systems for development partners and curricula development so that policies are strictly implemented to the advantage of youths and children in rural areas.
- More tertiary institutions should be introduced in Gokwe District to enable its residents to access tertiary education. Universities can be approached so that they establish learning centres Gokwe District.
- Stiffer penalties should be put in place for perpetrators of child rapes and child marriages.
- More rural development programs like rural electrification, clean water reticulation, industrial development, health and sanitation facilities should target more rural areas.so that the young and the youth are retained in their home areas for community development.
- Incentives like tax exemptions can be given for investing in remote rural areas.
- More teachers should be enrolled for rural areas as well as more classrooms to enable viable teacher pupil ratios, but this should be matched with an increase and improvement in educational facilities in the district.
- The private sector can be encouraged to repair the roads they use in their day-to-day business operations, in partnership with the Government so that rural areas can attract better teachers and other related resources for quality education and employment creation for the school-leaving youths.

Conclusion

Like many other rural areas, Gokwe North District encounter several challenges which negatively affect the achievement of SDG4. Major challenges include the long distances between schools, lack of institutions of higher learning in the district, poor accessibility of the district due to poor roads and high teacher-pupil ratios, which compromise the degree of quality education. The right of youth and children to education is being violated by such challenges and conditions, which need to be improved to increase the rate of access to education for children below 18 years and the youth in general. In addition, poor technological facilities, lack of role models to be emulated by the youth among others, are deterrents that promote school dropouts due to early pregnancies, early marriages or the simple challenge of travelling for such long distances are affecting the achievement of SDG4 by 2030 in Zimbabwean rural areas like Gokwe North. Urban bias is another factor leading the underdevelopment of rural areas, despite the fact that the rural areas have high percentages of youth and children as compared to cities or urban areas in general.

References

ALEED, Y., (2016) *Effects of Education in Developing Countries. Journal of Construction in Developing Countries*. [Online]. Available from: https://www.researchgate.net/publication/311607929_Effects_of_Education_in_Developing_Countries

BRAZER, A., (2022) *Gokwe Food System Study*. [Online]. Available from: https://www.researchgate.net/publication/364071242

CHAKANIKA, W. W, et al., (2012) *The Challenges of Rural Education in Africa*. [Online]. Available from: https://www.researchgate.net/publication/336676604_The_challenges_of_rural_education_in_Africa

CHIGUYE, L. T., (2016) *Flood Risk Prediction Using Remotely Sensed Data in the Sanyati Catchment Area: A Case of Gokwe North District*. [Online]. Available from: r.msu.ac.zw:8080/jspui/bitstream/11408/2124/1/R125036J.pdf

JOHN, E. S., (2017) *Female Education in Developing Countries*. [Online]. Available from: https://www.researchgate.net/publication/323497891.

FEATHERSTONE, S., (2017) *The Promise and Challenges of Education in Sub-Saharan Africa*. [Online]. Available from: https://www.wise-qatar.org/promise-challenges-education-ssa-scott-featherston-david-ferreira/

KAPUR, R., (2018) *Education in Rural Areas*. [Online]. Available from: https://www.researchgate.net/profile/Radhika-Kapur-2/publication/329059160_Education_in_Rural_Areas/links/5bf3bedca6fdcc3a8de379d1/Education-in-Rural-Areas

KATOVA, L., (2022) *Population Distribution by Districts and Wards*. [Online]. Available from: https://www.zimstat.co.zw/wp-content/uploads/Demography/Census/2022_Population_Distribution_by_District_Ward_SexandHouseholds_23012023.pdf

KAYANI, M. M, et al., (2017) *Analysis of Socio-Economic Benefits of Education in Developing Countries: An Example of Pakistan*. [Online]. Available from: https://www.zimstat.co.zw/wp-content/uploads/Demography/Census/2022_Population_Distribution_by_District_Ward_Sex andHouseholds_23012023.pdf

KIOUPI, V. and VOUVOULIS, N., (2019) *Education for Sustainable Development: A Systematic Framework for Connecting SDGs to Educational Outcomes*. Available on-line [Online]. Available from: https://pdfs.semanticscholar.org/61c1/18d77443c6fe.

KUMARALEVU, A. and SURESH, E. S. M., (2017) *The Quality of Education and its Challenges in the Developing Countries*. [Online]. Available from: https://www.researchgate.net/publication/335972264_The_Quality_of_Education_and_its_Challenges_in_Developing_Countries.

KURTCU, E., (2019) *Initiatives and Obstacles to Reaching SDG4*. [Online]. Available from: ocisdg.com/en/blog/initiatives-and-obstacles-to-reaching-sdg4.

LAWRENCE, A. W., IHEBUZOR, N., and LAWRENCE, D. O., (2020) *Some Challenges Militating Against Developing Countries Achieving SDGH 4 on Targets: Nigeria as Case Study*. [Online]. Available from: https://www.researchgate.net/publication/343073808_Some_Challenges_Militating_against_Developing_Countries_Achieving_SDG_4_on_T argets_Nigeria_as_Case_Study.

MAKONI, A. C. et al, (2015) *Rubella outbreak Investigation, Gokwe North District, Midlands Province Zimbabwe 2014: A Case Control Study*. [Online]. Available from: https://www.ncbi.nlm.nih.gov/pmc/articles/PMC4725663.

MOHAMED, S., (2020) *South Africa: Broken and Unequal Education Perpetuating Poverty and Inequality.* [Online]. Available from: https://www.amnesty.org/en/latest/news/2020/02/south-africa-broken-and-unequal-education-perpetuating-poverty-and-inequality.

MOSTAQUE, L., (2016) *Moving Forward with the SDGs: Implementation Challenges in Developing Countries.* [Online]. Available from: https://www.researchgate.net/publication/333032841_Moving_forward_with_the_SDGs_Implementation_challenges_in_developing_countries

MUTALE, Q. (2015) *Challenges Facing School Children in Rural Zimbabwe: A Case of Tyunga and Luunga Wards of Binga District.* [Online]. Available from: https://www.iiste.org/Journals/index.php/RHSS/article/download/22098/23232

NORMAN, A. S. and King, N. A. (2015) *The Challenges of Quality Education in Africa: Some Hints and Tips.* [Online]. Available from: https://www.researchgate.net/publication/313293519_The_Challenges_of_Quality_Education_in_Africa_Some_Hints_and_Tips.

NWOGU, G. A. I., (2015) Barriers of Access to Educational Opportunity in Nigeria: A Philosophical Perspective. *Journal of Education and Practice,* 4(6), 148-177.

PATRINOS, H. A. and PSACHASROPOULOS, G. (2010) *Returns to Education in Developing Countries.* [Online]. Available from: https://doi.org/10.1016/B978-0-08-044894-7.01216-1.

PATRINOS, H. A., (2016) *Why Education Matters for Economic Development.* World Bank Blogs. [Online]. Available from: https://blogs.worldbank.org/education/why

RIECHMAN, M. (2017) Education for Sustainable Development Goals (SDGs). [Online]. Available from https://www.researchgate.net/publication/319306756_Education_for_Sustainable_Development_Goals_SDGs.

SERAT, O. (2017) *The Sustainable Livelihoods Approach.* [Online]. Available from: https://www.researchgate.net/publication/318018970

SHAVA, G. N, et al., (2021) Quality and Education for Sustainable Development Challenges towards a Transition in Zimbabwean Higher Education. *Indiana Journal of Humanities and Social Sciences,* 2(11), 17-28.

SHIKALEYO, E. E., (2020) *Challenges Facing Teaching at Rural Schools: A Review of Related Literature.* [Online]. Available from: https://www.researchgate.net/publication/341787476_Challenges_Facing_Teaching_at_Rural_Schools_A_Review_of_Related_Literature

WHITE, H., (2020) *Ten Benefits of Education in Developing Countries.* [Online]. Available from: https://borgenproject.org/10-benefits-of-education

Zimbabwe National Statistical Agency, (2012) *Provincial Report Midland: Population 2012.* [Online]. Available from: https://www.zimstat.co.zw/.../population/Midlands.pdf

Zimbabwe National Statistical Agency, (2022) *Gokwe North District, Population Statistics, Charts and Maps.* [Online]. Available from: https://www.citypopulation.de/en/zimbabwe/admin/midlands/702__gokwe_north

Social Media and Communication Rights in Zimbabwe

Wellington Gadzikwa and Pedzisai Ruhanya

Introduction

The fall of former President Robert Mugabe in November 2017 did not end the Zimbabwean crisis. The post-Mugabe Zimbabwe is marked by continued intense political struggles between the government and various agents of social change pressing for democratic space, accountability and reforms on improved state/society relations using social media platforms such as Twitter and Facebook to make the government accountable. The new dispensation led by President Emmerson Mnangagwa promised a new era with reforms in the media and communication being an integral part. The chapter argues that social media platforms are critical communicative platforms in Africa, mainly as citizens seek to broaden the public sphere through digital platforms. Through various ways such as internet shutdowns, overt and covert censorship, the Zimbabwean government, like other African states, are bent on discouraging the use of social media as communication rights expressive platforms. Communication rights are critical for citizens' participation in governance issues. Citizens use digital platforms to mobilise protests against social and political ills. A broadened understanding of the public sphere should embody the use of social media platforms as strategies to advance communication rights. The chapter argues that social media platforms are critical to keeping the government in check and promoting the right to enjoyment of communication rights in Zimbabwe, albeit in a constrictive socio-political environment.

Communication Rights in Perspective

Social media platforms are instrumental in the exercise of communication rights of citizens. Communication rights are a fundamental feature of humanity (McLeod 2018). The ability to communicate, receive, process, share and produce messages is central to human interaction and participation. To understand and to be understood not only enables the expression of basic needs and wants but also enables interaction and participation at a family, community, national and global level (McLeod 2018). Communication rights are captured in several international conventions and declarations. Communication rights are a fundamental human right (McEwin & Santow 2018). This is made explicit in article 19 of the Universal Declaration of Human Rights, which goes beyond the right for people to communicate and communicate effectively within their dominant culture. This right is unrestricted by any criteria such as age, status, ability or communicative capacity, people have a right to receive and convey messages, to hold opinions, and express themselves. What is more fundamental about the rights of communication is that every person should uphold other's right to communicate as they interact with people in daily life in order to enhance equality, justice and human dignity, addressing both freedom of opinion and expression and rights and freedoms without distinction of such issues as language among others (United Nations 1945). The right to communicate is also captured in various international conventions and declarations such as articles 19 and 25 of the International Covenant on Civil and Political Rights (United Nations 1966a), articles 5 and 15 of the Convention on Rights of the Child (United Nations 1989) and article 21 of the Convention of the Rights of Persons with Disabilities (United Nations 2006). The rights of communication are also wide and include the rights of communicating in one's own language including article 5 of the Universal Declaration on Cultural Diversity (United Nations 2007a).

As McLeod (2018) observes, the importance of communication rights is obvious since these rights are included in almost every convention, declaration and covenant of the United Nations with just a few exceptions. Communication rights are also included in the UNESCO conventions and declarations; however, the importance of communication rights goes beyond just enabling freedom of opinions, expression and language. Once these rights are realised, people are more readily able to realise other human rights. Another important dimension is that communication rights are easily becoming important in the 21st century where the survival of the fittest relies on communicative abilities rather than manual labour skills (Ruben 2000). In addition, people with difficulties in communicating may be vulnerable to human rights abuses (World Health Organisation and World Bank2011; Marshal & Barrett 2017).

Internationally, there have been efforts to promote communication rights, including the report in 1974 to UNESCO on the Means of Enabling Active Participation in the Communication Process and the Analysis of the Report to Communicate. Subsequent resolutions, charters and declarations have been made ever since. In 2014, communication as a human right was articulated in the Universal Declaration of Communication Rights (Muclair, Pientranton & Williams 2018; International Communication Project 2014). The communication rights of all people as articulated in the UDHR 1948 was also reasserted and reframed in article 19 of the International Covenant on Civil and Political Rights and everyone, citizens or non-citizens (United Nations 1966a) must enjoy these. As Howie (2017:12) notes, the prevailing interpretation of the right to freedom of opinion and expression relates to civil and political rights because "free speech addresses the right to vote, free assembly and freedom of association which is essential to ensure press freedom". However, terrorism and anti- terrorism laws are now posing huge challenges to the freedom of the press (Anyanwu 2018, Howie 2017). The other ways in which the right to freedom of opinion and expression is under test is due to the changes in the ability to communicate through internet and social media (Kaye 2016).

In Africa, there have been efforts to articulate communication rights. In November 2019, the African Commission on Human and People's Rights adopted the

Declaration of Principles of Expression and Access to information in Africa to safeguard the rights to freedom of expression and access to information as guaranteed under article 9 of the African Charter. The Declaration expansively sets out and promotes principles of freedom of expression, access to information and internet rights in Africa. It adopted international standards under Article 19 of the UDHR and Article 19 of the International Covenant on Civil and Political Rights (ICCPR), which provides for the right to freedom of expression and access to information including the parameters of restrictions.

Social Media as Communication Tools

There are huge contestations over the meaning of the term social media (Effing, van Hillegersberg & Huibers 2011; Kaplan & Haenlein 2010; Xiang & Gretzel 2010). According to Carr and Hayes (2015), social media has been difficult to define both functionally and theoretically within communication studies. Early definitions of social media referred to digital technologies focusing on user generated content or interaction (Kaplan & Haenlein 2010; Terry 2009), channel characteristics (Kent 2010) and specific tools (Howard and Parks 2012). Extant definitions focused on the nature of the message (Russo et al 2008) or on ideological and technical foundations of web based 2.0, which allow exchange of user generated content (Agichetein et al 2008; Kaplan & Haenlein 2010). These definitions are simplistic and miss the unique technological and social affordances that distinguish social media (Carr & Hayes 2015). For example, Howard and Parks (2012:362) defined social media as:

> (a) the information infrastructure and tools used to produce and distribute content (b) the content that takes the digital form of personal messages, news, ideas, and cultural products; and (c) the people, organisations, and industries that produce and consume digital content.

This definition assumes that social media are denoted by looking at their specific applications of Facebook or YouTube. Social media is thus seen as a two way interaction and feedback with potential for real time interaction, reduced anonymity, a sense of propinquity, short response times and the ability to time shift or engage the social network whenever it suits a particular member (Kent 2010:645). Carr and Hayes (2015:50) proposed a definition of social media, which they claim, distinguishes social media, arguing that social media are:

> Internet- based channels that allow users to opportunistically interact and selectively self-present, either in real time or asynchronously with both broad and narrow audiences who derive value from user-generated content and the perception of interaction with others.

From the above definition, social media thus remains internet based and based on broader internet and not only web based but beyond. Social media is marked by channel distrainment where communication is facilitated by a particular channel in which the user participates when they can commit to participating as opposed to just face-to-face communication when both members of the communication dyad need to be committed at the same time. The other aspects of their definition include the perceived interactivity as opposed to predicted interactivity among users because it is critical that users perceive an interactive element to consider the medium social even if that interaction is not with others. Furthermore, the value of social media is also derived from contributions from or interactions with users rather than content generated by organisations or individuals hosting the medium. There is also an element of mass personal communication where there are instances where "mass communication channels are used for interpersonal communication, interpersonal channels are used for mass communication and when individuals simultaneously engage in mass and interpersonal communication (O'Sullivan 2005; Carr & Hayes 2015:52). Such tools include Facebook, YouTube and Twitter that allow individuals to broadcast messages to a large, yet often interpersonal mass audience of their own (Walther et al 2010). Social media is thus a tool for expressing and enjoyment of communication rights.

Social Media and Communication Rights in Africa

Social media has had a transformative role in democratic participation in Africa (Pindayi 2017; Boateng 2022). Nolle (2016) argues that the African situation in terms of access to free media means that social media plays an increasingly important role. The absence of access to free local media in Africa means that most citizens turn to social media for information, express their opinion and to organise protests (Nolle 2016). Furthermore, Africa is more reliant on social media as a political instrument and the exercise of democratic rights. Many African countries are still ruled by authoritarian regimes that suppress freedom of speech, using unconstitutional methods to stay in power. After the Arab Spring in 2011, more and more African rulers have ordered the outages of internet and telecommunications services to keep their population from politically rallying against the government and in most instances the suppression of these services in times of election hinders the process of democratisation (Nolle 2016).

Despite these setbacks, social media has the potential to facilitate political activities and expression in the form of demonstrations against high rates of unemployment, poverty, rampant government repression and corruption in Africa (Chatora 2012). Other critics like Nwafor (2013) argue that the coming of social media in Africa brought a new vista not only in the area of political communication but information sharing in general. Another important aspect of social media is that it has not created competition with mainstream media but has instead converged in complex ways in broadening the mediated public sphere in Southern Africa (Mare 2013). Social media has been instrumental in breaking news during protests and mainstream media has weighed in with verification, contextualisation and amplification with the convergence creating collaborative journalism practices and enabling the amplification of the voices of the previously silenced and legitimised activists (Mare 2013). The roles of social media as a new frontier in expanding the communicative possibilities in Africa are vast although they have to contend with other forces in the respective countries.

The Zimbabwean Communication Rights Scenario

The Zimbabwean Constitution (Amendment No.20) of 2013 in Section 61 recognises freedom of expression and freedom of the media which should be exercised with certain limits with regards to incitement of violence, hate speech, damage to reputations and privacy. The political environment in Zimbabwe pre- and post-Mugabe is punctuated by ingrained, enduring and deep-seated polarisation mainly along political lines. The ruling Zimbabwe African National Union Patriotic Front (ZANU PF) government has since the turn of the millennium played the role of victim of what they describe as regime change agenda by western countries led by Britain and the United States of America. This regime change agenda is attributed to the imposition of economic sanctions in the year 2000 over allegations of gross human rights abuses and disrespect of property rights after the government compulsorily acquired commercial farms owned by whites in a land redistribution exercise called the Fast-Track Land Reform Programme (FTLRP).

The formation of a formidable opposition political party, the Movement for Democratic Change (MDC) in 1999 which challenged the ZANU PF political hegemony threatening to push the ZANU PF government out of power had dire consequences on communication rights in Zimbabwe. This resulted in excessive curtailing of the right to communication mainly through restrictive media legislation for print and electronic media, closure of private newspapers, deportations of foreign correspondents, bombing of printing press and criminalisation of dissent and criticism. While over the years, there have been some concessions in terms of the operations of the press and licencing of other players in the broadcast sector – the full enjoyment of communication rights remains a challenge.

Communication Rights in Post Mugabe Zimbabwe

The history of media restrictions through media laws has been noted by various scholars (Mabweazara 2015; Moyo 2009; Tsarwe 2018, Tsarwe & Mare 2019). The new Zimbabwean leader President Mnangagwa in November 2017 promised widespread reforms including the restoration and expression of people's communication rights. Despite the promises, freedom of expression, legal and political landscape remains contested. According to Clement Nyaletsossi Voule, United Nations Special Rapporteur on Rights to Freedom of Peaceful Assembly and of Association, 843 people were detained and 1 055 charged and tried for protesting a 150% hike in fuel price by the Zimbabwean government in 2019. This act greatly curtails the ability of people to communicate their grievances and instils enduring fear.

Zimbabwe has also not fared well on freedom of expression rankings, and is ranked 126 out of 180 by Reporters without Borders Press Index (MISA 2021).

A myriad of laws still violate constitutional and international standards on freedom of expression, media freedom, access to information and privacy. Such laws include the Censorship and Entertainment Control Act, Official Secrets Act, sections of the Criminal Law (Codification and Reform) Act, Interceptions of Communications Act among others. The net effect of these laws is that they have a bearing on the citizen's rights to free expression and media freedom. Despite enacting the Freedom of Information Act, the Zimbabwean government has continued to infringe the privacy rights of citizens as in the case where in March 2020 then Zimbabwe National Army (ZNA) commander Lieutenant General Edzai Chimonyo was quoted saying the military would soon start snooping into private citizens to guard against subversion, as social media has become a threat to national security (MISA 2021). The fear of being arrested for posting critical information on social media also curtails alternative means of exercising and actualisation of communication rights.

Digital Media, Public Sphere and Communication Rights

Habermas' idea of the public sphere, defined as a metaphorical space where access to information affecting the public good is available, where discussion is ideally free from domination, and participation is on equal basis, is part of the critical role that the media play in a democratic society (Curran 2002). The media facilitate the formation of a public sphere by providing an arena for public debate and by reconstituting private citizens as a public body in the form of public opinion. However, while Habermas' idea of the public sphere illuminates debate on the significance of the media in democratic discourses, it has been broadened by the emergence of social media. The broadening of the public sphere through social media platforms can facilitate the realisation of communication rights in context where the media is muzzled by the state. Rasmussen (2013) argues that the internet has transformed the earlier public sphere theorized by Habermas (1989) and brought about a paradox in "democratization of media and an extended freedom of expression," which "imply less power for formal politics to fulfil what is envisioned precisely as democratization." While social media platforms assist to democratize communications rights in contexts such as Zimbabwe, these platforms are not largely accessed by the majority of citizens on account of economic challenges related to the cost of data, internet connectivity and lack of information communication technology gadgets that are expensive.

However, new technological changes have a bearing on how the roles of the media should be conceived in a democratic society as they are used to democratise power through access to information that citizens use to challenge concentrated power by governments. Polat (2005) argues that interactions stemming from the ease and relative cheapness of communicating via new media technology have improved some African countries' political structures and processes but the question is whether there is real inclusivity. Barber (2003:39) argues that digital media encourage "a politics of solitude" in which citizen's just sit "at home in front of electronic screens and view the world and its political choices as so many consumer alternatives."

Social Media as Communication Rights Platforms

Social media in Zimbabwe has largely been deployed in the communication rights which are political and as a way of engaging other citizens to raise concerns over the state of governance. This is mainly due to the history of silencing dissent and toxic political climate and debilitating economic meltdown since the year 2000. The most visible and pronounced early use of social media as a platform for demanding good governance was the 2013 *#ThisFlag* campaign led by Baptist Pastor Evan Mawarire which led to offline protests (Africa Country 2023). Mawarire used YouTube to express deep affection for his country and deeper frustration with the governance in Zimbabwe.

To show the power of social media and impact of *#ThisFlag* from a communication rights perspective, the video was posted on multiple applications, remixed, debated and reported across social media resulting in its popularity, including the arrest of Mawarire and a Statutory Instrument criminalising the draping of the Zimbabwean flag by individuals as that practice was regarded as a way of protest (Africa Country 2023). This move was in sharp contrast to earlier encouragement of draping the flag as a sign of patriotism, and in a veiled support for the ruling party Zimbabwe African National Union Patriotic Front (ZANU PF). *#ThisFlag* protests, which were supported by online audiences in and outside the country, were met by state organized, pro-government protests as ZANU PF recruited youths including bussing them from rural areas as a show of force that despite the online popularity, the party and regime had popular support (Africa Country 2023). Another interesting aspect of the opposition to social media protests was the claim by the government and attempts to downplay social media activism as an urban phenomenon and as of no consequence. What can be drawn from these attempts by the government is that social media was the new frontier for expressing communication rights after all the state suffocated other traditional media platforms.

As Kambarami noted, "social media channels like the almost ubiquitous *Facebook*, instant messaging *WhatsApp* provided an outlet of what one really thinks" including those in the rural areas. Kambarami is one of the optimistic critics who believe that in a country with 97% mobile perpetration and the anonymity of social media profiles and the protection of end-to-end encryption of instant messages allows for the first public glimpse of the real leanings of all Zimbabweans including those in the rural areas. Other social media activists who think that Zimbabweans are learning to utilize social media to speak about repressive rule and fight for a better future also share this optimistic view. The optimism that social media can reshape the communication landscape by activists is mainly in comparative terms due to the expansion of the internet and the liberalisation of ICT products importation from 2009 to 2013 during the period of the inclusive government in Zimbabwe. This liberalisation provided social media movements with a window of opportunity to establish pro-democracy and online reliant social media movements and spaces in Zimbabwe.

The other impetus for the use of social media in Zimbabwe is the lack of a properly fact checked and non-biased media where people analyse what is happening in government, talk about developments and give criticism. The closure of open spaces to communicate has given rise to alternatives such as social media as one human rights activist and lawyer Doug Coltart noted:

> I think social media has been very important in creating a space in which people are able to engage with one another and also with their elected representatives. It serves as a useful barometer in the country. It does not, however, represent the whole of society, since it's a disproportionately urban and young crowd that use it (Elm Magazine 2020).

In this sense, social media can be thought of as the new frontier for citizens to express themselves albeit with attendant limitations. Again, this optimism is derived from the several # movements headlined by the *#ThisFlag* which was translated into real action including the *#ZimShutdown* campaigns on Twitter and Facebook which were heeded by many Zimbabweans (Africa Country 2023). There are also a plethora of such platforms as the ones created by Magamba Network which are using creative ways to open up the democratic spaces. The most notable one was the *#ZimbabweLivesMatter* which was modelled along the George Floyd inspired *#BlackLivesMatter*. The *#ZimbabweLivesMatter* was hugely successful and led to the South African government abandoning its usual quiet diplomacy by sending a delegation to Zimbabwe to discuss the Zimbabwean situation during the period of COVID-19. These gains embolden digital rights activists on the prospects of social media as an expressive communicative tool. According to one digital media activist with Magamba Network, Munyaradzi Dodo:

> The government had been in denial that there was a crisis happening in the country. Then people started to share content under *#ZimbabweansLivesMatter* and it started trending in Zimbabwe and South Africa. Celebrities and politicians around Africa and US started reacting and sharing (Elm Magazine 2020).

This breakthrough has also been met with equal opposition as the government has sponsored social media activists openly encouraged by the President Mnangagwa to use social media platforms to harangue and denigrate government opponents. *Varakashi* ('Thrashers' or 'Destroyers'), are pro-government and ZANU PF trolls whose effect has been the polarization on digital platforms through misinformation, disinformation, deception, sexism and tribalism. Perhaps the government has realised that even if they shut down the platforms, they too will have no means to communicate with the same audience and have now resorted to fighting on the platforms. These contests, though characterised by undesirable acts, are a pointer that the fight for communication rights has now been taken online and audiences have moved to these platforms rendering the tight control of television and radio platforms irrelevant as people now follow content rather than media houses.

In addition, the government did not just respond through counter narratives but is in the process of enacting a cyber-security and data protection law which will largely criminalise communication in numerous ways. According to Ruhanya and Matsilele (2021) there is a thin line between being patriots and being enemies of the state and that, the admixture of social media and political dissidence has thrown many governments in a ceaseless panic reflected in a raft of legislation to control and constrain cyber activities. While local digital activists can be tracked down and arrested, those in the diaspora can continue to use the platforms to question any issue in the country and their views can reach those prevented from exercising their rights.

The shift of communication to online during the Covid-19 pandemic also appears to have enhanced the skills of people in terms of using social media platforms by citizens which might be used for communicative needs. Other sources of optimism for the potential of social media as alternative communication platforms stems from the its role in influencing policy decisions such as the Drax Gate Scandal which was exposed by NEZwire, an online newspaper which set social media platforms ablaze with citizens demanding corruption and demanding that then Minister of Health Obadiah Moyo resign due to incompetence and corruption within his ministry (Kubatana 2020).

The other examples of social media activism include the Big Saturday Read by the late Alex Magaisa which exposed the deep levels of systematic corruption in the Reserve Bank of Zimbabwe Farm Mechanization Scheme which led the former governor Gideon Gono to offer an explanation and clarifications. In addition, there is a firm belief that digital platforms can be an effective tool to reinvigorate advocacy and lobbying and activists must tap into social media tools in the same way the government is using these platforms to announce policy and engage followers (Kubatana 2020). Social media remains the main frontier where the battle for control of information dissemination will be fought. Mare's (2014) analysis of the *Occupy Grahamstown* (South Africa), the 20 July 2011 protests (Malawi), the 10 September 2010 food riots (Mozambique), the 1 April 2012 demonstrations in Swaziland, and the flash demonstrations by WOZA and Mthwakazi in Zimbabwe also give credence to the utility of social media as alternative communicative platforms in restrictive environments. Mare argues that social media was used differently in the respective phases of the protests from pre- demonstrations, ignition, escalation and post-demonstration of the protests. The notable takeaways are that despite Africa being the least connected in terms of internet, it is sprouting as pockets of resistance and more importantly even in what he calls the flawed democracies in Mozambique, Malawi and Zimbabwe where social media are the new protest drums creatively appropriated to convey not only warning signals but messages of indignation, discontent and that there is more interconnectedness between online and offline activism (Mare 2014). For Mare, in crisis times social media platforms present activists with an indispensable instrument for earl warning, bypassing state media blackouts, disarticulating the official state propaganda and passing on solidarity messages across space and time The utility of social media as a platform for demanding transparency from political leaders in order to improve their lives in Africa has also been noted Mustvairo (2021). However, Mustvairo argues that in Zimbabwe those who dare use such platforms demanding accountability from leaders such as Hopewell Chin'ono face arrests and detention for allegedly peddling falsehoods, a serious charge that could keep him in jail for two years if he is convicted.

Social Media: Challenges

Social media activists in Zimbabwe face a lot of challenges in using digital technologies in the fight for democratisation since the digital platforms are not guaranteed and can be shut down as the easiest way of silencing dissent. The arrests of social media activists entails that there are limitations of social media as instruments against digital authoritarianism in Zimbabwe (Mustvairo 2021). Another area which digital activism in Zimbabwe is found lacking is in terms of leadership, coordination and identity. The availability of social media especially Twitter has provided a new arena for public sphere of political communication which has some emancipatory connotations, claiming that social media allows people to openly participate in political deliberations online does not work in the African public sphere which is constrained (Mustvairo 2021; Fuchs 2014). While government critics see social media as an emancipatory tool, the government can block social media platforms and charge anti-government digital activists on treasonous charges (Mustvairo 2021). There are also other issues which limit the democratisation role of social media such as control and ownership, state policing and surveillance:

> Social media needs to be complemented with a strategy that is sustained, with more than one person at the head and with a level of awareness and appreciation by people who may not be involved in the struggle (Elm Magazine 2020).

Another issue that limits social media as a tool for enjoyment of communication rights is the high cost of data in an economy where many rural and urban people are living below the poverty datum line. Social media thus becomes exclusively and urban phenomenon, further limiting its utility as Dodo argues that:

> Social media users are mainly in urban areas, so conversations on Twitter might just represent an echo–chamber. The conversations are ...with people who have access to data and devices (Elm Magazine 2020).

Without access, the majority are left out and effectively excluded from these platforms and their communications rights continue to be violated. They thus remain outside the realm of communication activities as stipulated by various international statutes and the constitution and are not able to participate in activities that have a bearing on their everyday lives – a denial and violation of their rights. Social media, however, remains a tool for the enjoyment of communication rights despite all the attendant challenges.

Conclusion

While technological developments have aided human agency and participation in the enjoyment of communication rights, it is not obvious that these rights will be enjoyed without restrictions. Social media remains the new frontiers for the expression of communication rights even in competitive authoritarian regimes and restrictive environments. Social media platforms can be used to challenge concentrated state power by operating as conduits for democratic expression by broadening the

Habermasian public sphere. These platforms facilitate the realisation of communication rights through citizen participation and challenging government policies and practices as seen on online mobilisation of Zimbabweans to protect against the rise cost of living standards in post Mugabe Zimbabwe. The findings of this research validates arguments by African scholars like Ndlela and Mano (2020) who argue that the new digital tools have become "an important part of the political changes." They submit that the protests against Sudan's President Omar al-Bashir after 30 years in power, the forced resignation of Algeria's long serving President Abdelaziz Bouteflika in April 2019, the forcing of Congo President Kabila not to stand for re-election, visible protests against poor performance of the Paul Biya Government in Cameroon and protests in Uganda and Egypt to the power of social media. This study therefore submits that while there are challenges on accessibility by the broader masses, social media platforms are a critical site for the realisation of communication rights important for democratic accountability in developing contexts such as Zimbabwe.

References

AGICHTEIN, E, et al. (2008) *Finding High-Quality Content in Social Media.* [Online]. Available from: https://www.researchgate.net/publication/221520013_Finding_High-Quality_Content_in_Social_Media

AFRICA COUNTRY, (2023) *#ThisFlag, Social Media and Political Agency in Zimbabwe.* [Online]. Available from: https://africasacountry.com/2016/09/smartphone-activism-as-agency-in-zimbabwe

ANYANWU, C., (2018) Fear of Communicating Fear versus Fear of Terrorism: A Human Rights Violation or a Sign of Our Time? *International journal of speech-language pathology*, 20(1), 26-33.

BANDA, F., (2008) African Political Thought as an Epistemic Framework for Understanding African Media. *Ecquid Novi*, 29(1), 79-99.

BARBER, B. R., (2003) Which Technology and Which Democracy? In H. Jenkins. and D. Thorburn. (eds.). *Democracy and New Media.* London, Cambridge, pp. 3–47.

BOATENG, A. B., (2022) *Social Media Usage and Digital Rights Restrictions in the Republic of Chad.* [Online]. Available from https://www.researchgate.net/publication/36229 3646_DIGITAL_DISSIDENCE_AND_SOCIAL_MEDIA_CENSORSHIP_IN_AFRICA

CARR, C. T. and HAYES, R. A., (2015) Social Media: Defining, Developing, and Divining. *Atlantic Journal of Communication*, 23(1), 46-65.

CHABAL, E., (2014) Managing the Post Colony: Minority Politics in Montpellier, c. 1960–c. 2010. *Contemporary European History*, 23(2), 237-258.

CHATORA, A., (2012) Encouraging Political Participation in Africa the Potential of Social Media Platforms. [Online]. Available from: https://www.academia.edu/5451855/En couraging_political_participation_in_Africa_The_potential_of_social_media_platforms

CURRAN, J., (2002) *Media and Power.* London, Rutledge.

EFFING, R., Hillegersberg, J.V. and Huibers, T. (2011) *Social Media and Political Participation: Are Facebook, Twitter and YouTube Democratizing our Political Systems?* Berlin, Springer.

ELM MAGAZINE, (2020) *Social Media Creates New Space for Activism in Zimbabwe.* [Online]. Available from: https://elmmagazine.eu/adult-education-and-democracy/social-media-creates-new-space-for-activism-in-zimbabwe/Farcese, D. and Richer, S. (1973) *Social Research Methods.* New Jersey, Prentice Hall.

HOWARD, P. N. and PARKS, M. R., (2012) Social Media and Political Change: Capacity, Constraint, and Consequence. *Journal of Communication,* 62(2), 359-362.

HOWIE, E., (2018) Protecting the Human Right to Freedom of Expression in International Law. *International Journal of Speech-Language Pathology,* 20(1), 12-15.

INTERNATIONAL COMMUNICATION PROJECT, (2014). *Universal Declaration of Communication Rights.* [Online]. Available from: https://internationalcommunicationproject.com/get-involved/sign-the-pledge/

INTERNATIONAL LABOUR ORGANIZATION, (2013). *Constitution of Zimbabwe (Amendment number 20 Act) (2013).* [Online]. Available from: https://www.ilo.org/dyn/natlex/natlex4.detail?p_lang=en&p_isn=93498&p_country=ZWE&p_classification=01.01

JOHNSON, S., (1991) An Historical Overview of The Black Press in Studies on South African Media. Bellville, Anthropos Publishers.

KAPLAN, A.M. and HAENLEIN, M., (2010) Users of the World, Unite! The Challenges and Opportunities of Social Media. *Business Horizons,* 53(1), 59-68.

KAYE, D., (2016) *Report of the Special Rapporteur on the promotion and protection of the right to freedom of opinion and expression (A/ HRC/32/38).* Geneva, Switzerland: Human Rights Council.

KENT, M. L., (2010) Directions in Social Media for Professionals and Scholars. *Handbook of Public Relations,* 2, 643-656.

KUBATANA, (2020) *How Activists in Zimbabwe are Embracing Social Media to Influence Democracy.* [Online]. Available from: https://kubatana.net/2020/11/02/how-activists-in-zimbabwe-are-embracing-social-media-to-influence-democracy/

MABWEAZARA, H. M., (2015) Mainstreaming African Digital Cultures, Practices and Emerging Forms of Citizen Engagement, *African Journalism Studies,* 36(4), 1-11.

MARE, A., (2013) A Complicated But Symbiotic Affair: The Relationship Between Mainstream Media and Social Media in the Coverage of Social Protests in Southern Africa. *Ecquid Novi: African Journalism Studies,* 34(1), 83-98.

MARE, A., (2014) *Social Media: The New Protest Drums in Southern Africa?* Cham, Springer.

MATSILELE, T. and RUHANYA, P., (2021) Social Media Dissidence and Activist Resistance in Zimbabwe. *Media, Culture & Society,* 43(2), 381-394.

MCEWIN, A. and SANTOW, E., (2018) The Importance of The Human Right to Communication. *International Journal of Speech-Language Pathology,* 20(1), 1-2.

MCLEOD, S., (2018) Communication Rights: Fundamental Human Rights for All. *International Journal of Speech-Language Pathology,* 20(1), 3-11.

MEDIA INSTITUTE OF SOUTHERN AFRICA, (2021) *The State of Press Freedom in Southern Africa.* Harare, MISA.

MUTSVAIRO, B., (2020) *Why Social Media Activists Face an Uphill Struggle in Zimbabwe.* [Online]. Available from: https://democracyinafrica.org/social-media-activists-face-an-uphill-struggle-in-zimbabwe/

NDLELA, M. and MANO, W., (2020) *Social Media and Elections in Africa, Volume 1: Theoretical Perspectives and Election Campaigns* and *Social Media and Elections in Africa, Volume 2:*

Challenges and Opportunities. [Online]. Available from: https://www.academia.edu/ 42095501/Social_Media_and_Elections_in_Africa_Volume_1_Theoretical_Perspectives_an d_Election_Campaigns

MOYO, D., (2009) Citizen Journalism and the Parallel Market of Information in Zimbabwe's 2008 Election. *Journalism Studies* 10(4), 551–567.

MULCAIR, G., PIETRANTON, A. A. and WILLIAMS, C., (2018) The International Communication Project: Raising Global Awareness of Communication as a Human Right. *International Journal of Speech-Language Pathology*, 20(1), 34-38.

NOLLE, E., (2016) *Social Media and Its Influence on Democratization in Africa.* [Online]. Available from: https://www.ispsw.com/wp-content/uploads/2013/07/445_Nolle.pdf

NWAFOR, K. A, et al., (2013) Social Media and Political Participation an Africa: Issues, Challenges and Prospects. *Communication and the New Media in Nigeria: Social Engagement, Political Development and Public Discourse*, pp.64-84.

PINDAYI, B., (2017) Social Media Uses and Effects: The Case of WhatsApp in Africa. *Impacts of the Media on African Socio-Economic Development*, pp. 34-51.

POLAT, R. K., (2005) The Internet and political participation: Exploring the explanatory links. *European Journal of Communication*, 20(4), 435-459.

RASMUSSEN, T., (2013) Internet-Based Media, Europe and the Political Public Sphere. *Media Culture & Society*, 35(1), 97-104.

RUBEN, R. J., (2000) Redefining the survival of the fittest: communication disorders in the 21st century. *The Laryngoscope*, 110(2), 241-241.

RUSSO, A. et al., (2000) Participatory Communication with Social Media. *Curator: The Museum Journal*, 51(1), 21-31.

TERRY, M., (2009) Twittering Healthcare: Social Media and Medicine. *Telemedicine and e-Health*, 15(6), 507-510.

TSARWE, S., (2018) *Mobile Phones and a Million Chatter: Performed Inclusivity and Silenced Voices in Zimbabwean Talk Radio.* [Online]. Available from: https://www.researchgate.net/ publication/329326081_Mobile_phones_and_a_million_chatter_performed_inclusivity_and_si lenced_voices_in_Zimbabwean_talk_radio

TSARWE, S. and MARE, A., (2019) Journalistic Framing of Electoral Conflict in a Politically Fragile Society: A Comparative Study of the Zimbabwean Weekly Press. *African Journalism Studies*, 40(1), 18-35.

UNITED NATIONS, (1966) *International Covenant on Civil and Political Rights.* [Online] Available from: http://www.ohchr.org/EN/ProfessionalInterest/Pages/CCPR.aspx

UNITED NATIONS, (1989) *Convention on the Rights of the Child.* [Online]. Available from: https://www.unicef.org/crc/

UNITED NATIONS, (2006) *Convention on the Rights of Persons with Disabilities.* [Online] Available from: https://www.un.org/development/desa/disabilities/convention-on-the-rights-of-persons-withdisabilities.html

UNITED NATIONS, (2007) *Declaration on the Rights of Indigenous Peoples.* [Online] Available from: http://www.ohchr.org/EN/Issues/Peoples/Pages/Declaration.aspx

UNITED NATIONS, (1948) *Universal Declaration of Human Rights.* [Online] Available from http://www.un.org/en/universal-declarationhuman-rights/

VOA News, (2023) *Zimbabwe Activists Push Back on Social Media Restrictions.* [Online]. Available from: https://www.voanews.com/a/zimbabwe-activists-push-back-on-social-media-restrictions/4776684.html

WALTHER, J. B., CARR, C. T. and CHOI, S. S. W., (2010) Interaction of Interpersonal, Peer and Media Influence Sources Online: A Research Agenda for Technology Convergence. *A Networked Self*, 25-46.

World Health Organization and the World Bank. (2011) *World Report on Disability.* Geneva, World Health Organization.

XIANG, Z. and GRETZEL, U., (2010) Role of Social Media in Online Travel Information Search. *Tourism Management*, 31(2), 179-188.

The Role of Print and Online Newspapers in Protecting and Promoting Human Rights in Southern Africa: The Case of Zimbabwe

Isaac Mutelo and Steven Lishandi

Introduction

The notion of human rights refers to the norms, basic rights and freedoms that protect people from political, economic, legal, and social abuses or unjustified infringements. The Universal Declaration of Human Rights (UDHR) stipulates the fundamental human rights which ought to be universally protected. These rights are reflected in the Zimbabwean Constitution and other related legal documents. The promotion of human rights can be explored from various perspectives, including media. The media – especially print media, the news media, and broadcasting (radio and television) – can generally be regarded as an influential medium for the dissemination of political, social, economic and religious information. The media influences public opinion by changing the perception of listeners or readers regarding certain issues. For example, print and online newspapers make people aware of their fundamental rights, obligations and responsibilities, including the need to promote certain key democratic and constitutional values and principles in view of human rights. As Ray (2007:7) puts it, "the media can inform and educate the people of their rights and suggest ways and means by which they can solve their problems and thus empower them to protect their rights."

The media can be used as a channel to expose certain violations and infringements against human rights. It can also be used as a platform to publicise individuals, groups and organisations such as Media Alliance of Zimbabwe, Media Institute of Southern Africa and Zimbabwe Human Rights NGO Forum which engage in the promotion and securing of press freedom. As an essential platform, the media can play a major role in making the authorities aware of their duties and responsibilities towards citizens. As a means of transmitting information, the media play an important role in any democratic state that can help citizens advocate for and realize their human rights. It is important to explore the concept of human rights in general and specific to the Southern African context in order to outline the role and impact of media on the protection and promotion of human rights. This chapter advances the viewpoint that print and online newspapers are important in the promotion and protection of human rights due to its ability to inform and influence people, their thoughts and choices.

Print and Online Newspapers Media and Human Rights

The rational and civilised idea of human communication through designed channels dates back to thousands of years ago when several human civilisations painted on the walls of caves (Duignan 2023). Mass media generally refers to different forms of communication whereby opinion, information, literature, advocacy, publicity, advertising and other forms of entertainment, facts and expression are conveyed to masses. It includes radio, television, video, the internet, social platforms, recording and print through different forms such as newspapers and magazines. Janeau (2022) identifies six types of mass media, namely traditional media, print media, electronic/broadcasting media, outdoor media, transit media, digital advertising media:

> The first is traditional media, which is based on indigenous methods of information transfer, such as drama, paintings, and songs. The second type is print media, which is a form of information communication through print media. It includes magazines, newspapers, and brochures. The third type is electronic/broadcasting media, which involves communication through audio, visual, or audiovisual electronic systems. It includes televisions, radios, and motion pictures. The fourth type is outdoor media, which involves communication through outdoor channels. It includes billboards, posters, wallscape, and compark advertising. The fifth type is transit media, which consists of communicating information during movement. Examples include transit shelter advertising in train stations and bus advertising. Finally, the sixth type is digital media advertising, which provides communication through the internet. Digital media includes social media and SNS sites, emails, websites, and internet protocol television.

While the six types of mass media somewhat exist in most countries, there is a distinction between print and electronic media. Print media includes magazines, books and newspapers whilst TV, video recordings, smartphones and other forms of online content can be regarded as electronic media. The major forms of print and online newspapers in Zimbabwe include the two major state-owned daily newspapers, Herald and Chronicle, and various independent daily newspapers such as NewsDay and Daily News. The Herald and Chronicle are the two major daily government owned newspapers in Zimbabwe. They have been criticised for being one-sided by publishing news that supports the Zimbabwe African National Union-Patriotic Front (ZANU-PF) government and its manifesto (Musaka 2003:171). The NewsDay and Daily News are among Zimbabwe's most popular independent newspapers. For example, Daily News was founded in 1999 by a journalist and human rights activist Geoffrey Nyarota, based on the motto 'Telling it like it is'. The two independent newspapers have experienced several challenges in Zimbabwe. Geoffrey Nyarota was attacked, arrested and imprisoned several times which partly contributed to the International Press Freedom Award, Golden Pen of Freedom Award and UNESCO's Guillermo Cano World Press Freedom Prize. Several other journalists and editors of independent newspapers have been threatened, attacked and arrested. Apparently, for print and online newspapers to have an impact on society, accuracy, privacy, minimising harm, avoiding distortions, doing away with bribes and inducements and eliminating negative influences should anchor media practice across the board, while being trustworthy, transparent, accountable, honest and responsible in their conduct and behaviour. Thus, the media should place concern on actions of negligence and avoiding errors in areas of human sensitivity.

The promotion of human rights is a challenge for most African countries. The lack of proper education especially in rural areas, the poor economies, digital disparity and at times, the lack of good governance contribute to the ongoing violation and abuse of human rights. In most cases, print and online media including television have an important role in promoting and safeguarding human rights. As Singh and Pandey (2017:127) put it, "media has today become the voice of our society and it commands an enormous and significant influence on it." Print and online media such as newspapers are important to society and their impact is perceivable in most Southern African societies, including Zimbabwe. It is a reflection of society and it depicts what and how society functions. With advancements in technology, artificial intelligence and science, society continues to progress at the fastest rate. In such a context, different forms of media play an important role. Two features stand out in the contemporary conception of human rights, namely the idea of universality and the inclusion of economic and social rights under the rubric of general human rights. This universality assumption underpins the general definition of human rights. Linked to the concept of universality are the concepts of equality and inclusion. However, universality is logically meaningless if some humans are excluded or marginalised. Thus, human rights are authentically rights of all people, at all times and in all situations. Human rights are conceived as equal rights in the sense that each human being has the same human rights as every other human being (Donnelly 2013:10). In most cases, human rights are inalienable because one cannot dispose of his or her humanity in the same manner as he or she can dispose of material possessions. Hence, fundamental human rights are often respected, protected, fulfilled and promoted (Shapesea 2016:14, 18, 22).

Human rights are often prone to violations and abuse from individuals and groups of authority, including political and non-political institutions and organisations. Human rights advocates including individuals, associations and NGOs often face challenges and are sometimes targeted and labelled as opponents as they demand accountability, transparency, good governance and participation while exposing the social injustices and corruption. Examples of human rights abuses include unlawful arrests and detentions, death threats, assaults, torture, kidnappings and the suppression of the freedoms of speech, assembly, press and association. According to the 2022 Country Reports on Human Rights Practices in Zimbabwe, significant human rights violations include reports of:

> unlawful or arbitrary killings, including an extrajudicial killing; torture and cases of cruel, inhuman, or degrading treatment or punishment by the government; harsh and life-threatening prison conditions; arbitrary detention; political prisoners; arbitrary or unlawful interference with privacy; serious problems with the independence of the judiciary; serious government restrictions on free expression and media, including violence, threats of violence, and unjustified arrests or prosecutions against journalists, censorship, and arrests for libel; substantial

interference with the rights of peaceful assembly and freedom of association; restrictions on freedom of movement; serious and unreasonable restrictions on political participation; serious government corruption; serious government restrictions on or harassment of domestic and international human rights organizations… (Country Reports on Human Rights Practices 2022:1-2).

There are also cases whereby some people are being labelled as terrorists, some are disappearing suspiciously, physically assaulted and tortured, others are arrested, detained, and even presented before the courts on fictitious accusations, while some are killed and deaths are recorded.

State of Media Freedom in Zimbabwe

In Zimbabwe, the Constitution articulates the provisions for media freedom. Section 61(1-3) of the 2013 Constitution states that "(1) every person has the right to freedom of expression, which includes— (a) freedom to seek, receive and communicate ideas and other information… (2) Every person is entitled to freedom of the media, which includes protection of the confidentiality of journalists' sources of information. (3) Broadcasting and other electronic media of communication have freedom of establishment…" However, Section 61(5) states that freedom of expression and freedom of the media exclude "(a) incitement to violence; (b) advocacy of hatred or hate speech; (c) malicious injury to a person's reputation or dignity; or (d) malicious or unwarranted breach of a person's right to privacy." Moreover, other laws and regulations on media limit press freedom from the perspective of public security, professional confidentiality and the interest of defence. This indicates that in principle, all Zimbabwean citizens have the freedom to seek, receive and communicate information. This includes the promotion of media plurality that can be independently legitimated, and a sense of media liberalisation. In addition, the Zimbabwe Media Commission (ZMC) is mandated by the Constitution with "functions that include the duty to uphold, promote and develop media freedom, enforce good practices and ethics, as well as fair competition and diversity."

The quality of media freedom can be questioned for many reasons. Firstly, this is because cases of the violation of media freedom including the arbitrary arrests and torture of journalists continue to be reported. For example, in 2022 several journalists were harassed and arrested including Blessed Mhlanga, Chengeto Chidi and *ZimLive.com* Editor Mduduzi Mathuthu (Country Reports on Human Rights Practices 2022:13). Secondly, the President primarily appoints the chairperson and other officials of the ZMC although this is done in consultation with the Committee on Standing Rules and orders. Thirdly, various forms of media, especially state-owned media, operate under the influence and manipulation of some members of the executive branch of the government. The government has also continued to maintain censorship through strict registration and accreditation policies and regulations. The government has extensive powers to monitor and suppress the freedom of expression by barring the 'abuse of free expression.' For example, on August 3 2022, journalists Desmond Chingarande and Wisdom Mdzungairi were charged with transmitting 'false data messages'. The accusation followed their coverage of a legal dispute involving local authorities and their prosecution was carried out under a 2021 data protection law. Finally, certain laws are sometimes cited when silencing human rights defenders and advocates. For example, the Freedom of Information Act (FIA) was brought into effect in 2020 to replace the 2002 Access to Information and Protection of Privacy Act (AIPPA). While the new law was meant to replace the Access to Information and Protection of Privacy Act (AIPPA) which was regarded as repressive, the new legislation has brought very few changes due to the existence of the media authoritarianism in the post-Mugabe administration (Mututwa & Ndlovu 2021:89).

Media and the Promotion and Protection of Human Rights

The media plays a major role in protecting and promoting human rights in Southern Africa as it acts as the "watchdog" and frames the people's struggles. Independent newspapers such as NewsDay and Daily News have attempted to monitor and report on human rights violations in Zimbabwe by providing investigative reports and updates on elections, arbitrary detentions and media censorship thereby informing citizens, human rights organisations and the international community on the violations that require urgent actions. For example, on 17 November 2018 News Daily reported a rise in cases of arbitrary arrests and detention based on a report by Human Rights Watch (Daily News 2018). This example shows how print and online newspapers encourage and make key human rights known to ordinary citizens, help to safeguard the existing systems, and in some cases expose the violators and abusers of fundamental rights and freedoms. Newspapers in Zimbabwe have attempted to provide platforms and spaces for debate and dialogue on human rights issues by publishing opinion and editorial pieces on issues such as children's rights, gender equality, press freedom and political rights. For example, on 17 January 2023 NewsDay reported that Human Rights Watch (HRW) had accused the Zimbabwean Government of failing to prosecute security forces for human rights violations and the inability of the victims of human rights violations to access justice. It also reported that there had "been little progress on investigations into abductions, torture, arbitrary arrests, and other abuses against opposition politicians and activists" (NewsDay 2023). Similarly, on 28 July 2023 NewsDay reported that the Zimbabwe Human Rights Commission (ZHRC) had received 438 cases of human rights violations between January and June 2023 (NewsDay 2023). Media can make people aware of their rights and freedoms and enable society to focus on areas in need of the promotion and protection of human rights. For example, there have also been online newspapers such as *Zimlive* that have been actively engaged in critical journalism in Zimbabwe, including exposing cases of corruption and human rights abuses (Mututwa & Akpojivi 2020:82).

By reporting on cases of human rights abuse, the media makes people aware of the need to promote those ideals that are important to maintaining an open and democratic society. Moreover, the media has the power to influence people and greatly affects human life due to its ability to shape thoughts, opinions and perspectives. Media also helps in public education and makes people aware of the current circumstances, including human rights issues. During the Covid-19 pandemic for example, different forms of media in Zimbabwe played a vital role in various educational programmes, reports and raising awareness on health issues through ZBC, radio, and newspapers such as The Herald and Chronicle. Media can also initiate the provision of open-source information and the documentation of human right violations. What this means is that the media empowers citizens by keeping them constantly informed on human rights matters and issues. This indicates that "media has today become the voice of our society and it commands an enormous and significant influence on it. There are a variety of media platforms that have stimulated the thoughts of the young generation and other sections of our society, more eloquently" (Singh & Pandey 2017:127). By informing and educating people about their rights, more citizens became involved in the process of recommending ways and means to address their problems and the need to safeguard their rights. The different forms of media in modern democracies such as Zimbabwe can help to promote principles such as accountability, transparency and freedoms of speech. Media can also help to give publicity to individuals and organisations championing human rights across Africa. By reporting about people and organizations interested in the defence of human rights, others are inspired by the need to join the movement that promotes a society that has high regard for human rights. In Zimbabwe, online and print newspapers have also facilitated advocacy and human rights promotion by providing a platform to human rights organisations and activists to share information about human rights.

NewsDay and Daily News in Zimbabwe have featured the work of human rights activists such as Hopewell Chin`ono and local and international human rights organisations. This has not only helped human rights defenders to be heard but also encouraged public engagement and awareness. The media has traditionally called for public participation by conveying information to the public and unveiling certain violations and other scams. In some cases, this has led to active participation of people in the building of policies, hence promoting freedom of expression which encourages people to actively voice their opinions against unjust policies and regimes. This has promoted participation and exploration of new avenues in matters of human rights, since Zimbabwe is built on diverse cultural, political and social background. In this context, the media continues to help citizens reconcile and appreciate certain differences hence developing towards the common good.

Although print and online newspapers can contribute to the promotion and protection of human rights in many ways, governments have the primary responsibility of creating an atmosphere which promotes and respects the freedom of expression and freedom of the media. Unwarranted restrictions on individuals criticizing the government, harassment of journalists by security forces, officials, and supporters of the ruling party and censorship for members of the press and online media undermines the rule of law. At the same time, the media is faced with the fundamental need for the populace to be informed in a morally correct way. This implies the way information is sourced and verified, and affording individuals and organizations fairness. In other words, "the media, being a mass disseminator of information and an opinion leader, has to have strict values lest media organizations fan hatred, ethnic wars as was the case in Rwanda in 1994, genocide, despondency, stereotyping and other such ills" (Fungurani & Gunduza 2011:27). Hence, professional ethical codes should guide the way different platforms operate media so as to avoid infringing on the human common good. Due to the influence it has on society and citizen's perception, the media should be guided by law and moral values in its endeavours. Laws and morals are enacted for the common benefit of citizens and to improve the order of things and to happiness in general (Regan 2002:13).

For print and online newspapers to have an impact on society by promoting human rights, there is often a need for an independent press. This includes the need for journalists to be free from government or corporate interests. The role of print and online media is undermined in a context where the government strictly monitors and controls their reporting. While state-owned newspapers support the government, some independent newspapers focus on health, sports, and economy coverage while avoiding political issues. Because human rights are political issues, most newspapers in Zimbabwe rarely report on such matters, including independent newspapers. Where print and online newspapers are controlled either by the state or some private entity, the quality of the news is usually far from equality and is unbiased. The unwarranted restrictions on media freedom coupled with strict laws concerning licensing exert the dominance of the government over state-owned and independent media. The biased and one-sided way of delivering news by some print and online newspapers expose the level of censorship and political interference.

Conclusion

Different forms of print and online media such as newspapers have been attempting to play a pivotal role in protecting and promoting human rights in Zimbabwe. By acting as a 'watchdog,' several media platforms have been promoting transparency, accountability, educating, exposing certain human rights abuses and bridging the gap between the government and the populace. When there is press freedom, it influences society positively thereby bringing change, development and transformation, while helping eradicate conflicts and promoting peace. While online and print newspapers have the ability to safeguard human rights, government manipulation and restrictions have hampered this process. These include safety concerns, lack of access to information, the presence of laws that restrict media freedom and efforts to censor or restrict content by journalists and online media. Without adequate freedom, different forms of media are unlikely to promote democratic practices, good governance and the improvement of basic human living standards. Economic instability has made several online and print newspapers encounter financial constraints, which in turn affect their capacity to invest in the required equipment and quality journalism. The challenges deter the role the media should have in promoting and protecting human rights as stipulated by the Universal Declaration of Human Rights and the Zimbabwean Constitution. Regardless of the challenges, print and online newspapers, strengthened by professional journalism and good practices, can help to promote and protect human rights in any democratic society.

References

ALEXANDER, L., (1998) *Constitutionalism: Philosophical Foundations.* Cambridge, Cambridge University Press.

CHROUST, A. and OSBORN, D. L., (1942) *Aristotle's Conception of Justice.* [Online]. Available from: http://scholarship.law.nd.edu/ndlr/vol17/iss2/2

DAILY NEWS, (2018) *'Arbitrary arrests, detention rise'.* [Online]. Available from: https://dailynews.co.zw/arbitrary-arrests-detention-rise/

DUIGNAN, B., (2023) *Mass Media – Communications.* [Online]. Available from: https://www.britannica.com/topic/mass-media

DONNELLY, J., (2013) *Universal Human Rights: In Theory and Practice (Second Edition)* London, Cornell University Press.

FUNGURANI, G. and GUNDUZA, M. L., (2011) *Business Ethics and Corporate Governance in Zimbabwe.* Johannesburg, Eagle Press.

JANEAU, E., (2022) *Types of Mass Media and Their Impact in Society.* [Online]. Available from: https://study.com/academy/lesson/what-is-mass-media-definition-types-influence-examples.html

NAGEL, T. (2005) *The Problem of Global Justice.* New Jersey, Blackwell Publishing.

NEWSDAY, (2023) *ZHRC Records 438 Rights Violation Cases.* [Online]. Available from: https://www.newsday.co.zw/local-news/article/200014552/zhrc-records-438-rights-violation-cases

NEWSDAY, (2023) *Hold Security Forces Accountable For Human Rights Abuse.* [Online]. Available from: https://www.newsday.co.zw/local-news/article/200006242/hold-security-forcesaccountable-for-human-rights-abuse

MARKET BUSINESS NEWS, (2022) *What is Media? Definition and Meaning.* [Online]. Available from: www.marketbusinessnews.com.

MUSAKA, S. D., (2003) Press and Politics in Zimbabwe. *African Studies Quarterly*, 7(2&3), 171–183.

MUTUTWA, T., MUTUTWA, B. and NDLOVU, M., (2021) Policy Change or Tactical Retreat? MediaPolicy Reform in Zimbabwe's New Dispensation. *Communicare: Journal for Communication Studies in Africa*, 40(1), 89 – 106.

MUTUTWA, T. and AKPOJIVI U., (2020) Critical Journalism and Media Convergence during the COVID-19 Pandemic: Representation of Corruption in Zimbabwean Online News. In C. A. Draleg. and A. Napakol. (eds.). *Health Crises and Media Discourses in Sub Saharan Africa.* Chaim, Springer.

REGAN, R. J. (2002) *Aquinas: On Law, Morality and Politics.* Indianapolis, Hackett Publishing Company.

SHAPESEA, (2016) *The Fundamentals of Human Rights.* [Online]. Available from: http://shapesea.com/wpcontent/uploads/2016/02/HR-Textbook-Ch-1-Fundamentals-Ed-1.pdf.

SINGH, G. and PANDEY, N., (2017) *The Role and Impact of Media on Society: A Sociological Approach with Respect to Demonetisation. IMPACT: International Journal of Research in Humanities, Arts and Literature,* 5(10), 127-136.

UNITED NATIONS, (1948) *Universal Declaration of Human Rights.* [Online]. Available from: https://www.un.org/en/about-us/universal-declaration-of-human-rights

The Nexus between National ICT Policies and the Right to Information Access: An Analysis of ICT Policies in Selected Southern African Countries

Elisha Mupaikwa

Introduction

Freedom of information and the right to access information is globally recognised under international law as a basic human right that when enacted, promotes citizens' participation in governance and development initiatives that seek to improve their livelihoods (Salau 2017). According to Molomo and Molefe (2017), freedom of information is a critical facet of democratic governance and it is a prerequisite for an informed citizenry, capable of holding its government accountable. Across the globe, there are several examples where citizens have used their freedom of information to hold national leaders to account. For example, in Japan where lawyers forced the government to release information on government expenditure, in Canada where registry officers were forced to resign after the release of records of expenditure and in India's Rajasthan state where public administrators were forced to resign as a result of public demonstrations after the release of government expenditure information (Coliver 2006). This fundamental human right lies at the heart of democracy and respect for human rights and good governance.

Access to information fosters social benefits related to education, health, agriculture, children's rights, gender equality, environmental management and community development among several other sectors of human development. Governments that claim to be democracies, therefore, have to develop policies that support freedom of information, whether it is among citizens or between the government and its citizens. According to Molaba (2016), many rural communities in Africa, particularly in the Southern African region are excluded from participating in decision-making related to the development of their communities. For example, in Lepelle-Nkumpi Local Municipality of South Africa, community engagement in developmental activities was minimal and legislation did not provide for individual participation. Often development initiatives are not participatory, forced down from government bureaucracies, with minimum contribution from the potential beneficiaries. In the Lepelle-Nkumbi community of South Africa, developmental programmes were initiated by the local council and not by the community and community members lacked knowledge, information and expertise, which inhibited their participation in development (Molaba 2016). Additionally, governance information related to social and public services is rarely accessible among these communities (Mutula 2006).

Across the world, constitutional democracies have enshrined in their constitutions to facilitate access to information on governance and community development issues. Access to this information in recent decades has been facilitated by the technological developments of the internet and the world-wide-web. Freedom of information according to Svard (2018) creates governments that are more inclusive and promotes transparency and accountability. The United Nations and the African Union have both expressed their unflinching support for human rights and basic freedoms such as the right to access information through The United Nations' Universal Declaration on Human Rights (1948), (article 19) and the African Union (2007)'s African Charter on Democracy, Elections and Governance (Chapter 9, article 27). Chapter 9 (article 27) of the African Charter on Democracy, Elections and Governance emphasises the need for member states to embrace Information and Communication Technologies (ICTs) for political, economic and governance purposes while at the same time fostering partnerships related to developments between agencies such as civil society and the government. According to article 19 of the United Nations' Universal Declaration on Human Rights (1948), everyone has a right to freedom of opinion and without interference, the freedom to impart and receive information and ideas through any media regardless of frontiers. ICTs are key to the establishment of the right to information access and individual nations in Southern Africa. To this end, therefore, SADC countries have developed National ICT policies that seek to regulate and govern the establishment of ICT infrastructure and the use of these technologies.

However, for some governments, this freedom of information has been a challenge because it exposes governments to scrutiny, forcing these governments to limit their operations (MISA Zimbabwe 2020). On that basis, this chapter discusses the role of National Information and Communication Technology policies in promoting and protecting the citizens' right to developmental and governance information access in Southern Africa. A comparative analysis is carried out among selected countries in Southern Africa. The chapter also identifies limitations in national ICT policies that, when addressed, will make them effective in promoting and supporting the constitutional right to access information on governance and development.

ICT Policies and the Right to Information Access

Across all societies that claim to adhere to the principles of democracy and the rule of law, citizens' rights are at the core of governance systems and the state. From the end of the Second World War, principles of human rights have dominated all democratic governance systems, placing obligations on governments to comply with and to ratify international conventions and treaties such as the United Nations Declaration of Human Rights of 1948 and the African Charter on Democracy of 2007, Elections and Governance. Such emphasis on human rights is a recognition that these rights are inherent among all human beings and that humans are born with those rights, obliging societies to treat humans with dignity and respect. These rights define relationships between individuals and the state (The United Nations 2016). ICT developments of the 21st century have thrust upon humanity the information and knowledge society, transforming many aspects of how people manage their social and economic lives. The internet has become ubiquitous, enabling 24/7 global access and dissemination of information, enhancing citizens' right to freedom of information, and freedom of expression, and leading to a broader democratisation agenda.

The previously information-poor rural communities of southern Africa now have information on their tips but some governments have turned to surveillance technologies to monitor communication on the internet and social media and some countries reported to have done this are Botswana, Zambia and Zimbabwe (MISA & UNESCO 2022; USAID 2022). These governments have often argued that this has often been motivated by the need to counter cybercrime. Such actions have often been found to violate Principles 14 and 41 of the Declaration of Principles of Freedom of Expression and Access to Information in Africa which guaranteed individuals' rights to seek, receive and impart information and ideas in any media and that the state must take measures to protect media practitioners in their efforts to establish the free flow of information to the public (African Commission on Human Rights and People's Rights 2019). In the southern African region, the diversification of media sectors has been accompanied by legal and institutional frameworks that support media freedom as evidenced by new constitutions and constitutional amendments that have enshrined the right to freedom of expression although in some countries these constitutions have also retained sub-clauses that restrict media freedom citing national security concerns (Wasserman & Benequista 2017).

Despite the key role ICTs play, some countries' citizens have endured restricted access to information, yet nations have ICT policies purporting to support the utilisation of these technologies across various sectors of humanity (USAID, 2022). These nations have also enshrined in their constitutions, the citizens' right to freedom of accessing information, freedom of expression, freedom of opinion and freedom of the media. Some countries in Southern Africa, such as Malawi have gone further to develop national access to information policies which seek to promote people's freedoms and good governance and have sought to align this to both the National ICT policy and the national constitution (The Republic of Malawi, 2014). Freedom of expression and the right to disseminate and receive information is recognized as one of the major human principles of human rights. These principles are an integral part of basic human rights as defined in The United Nations' (1948) Universal Declaration of Human Rights whose article 19 reads:

> Everyone has the right to freedom of opinion and expression; this right includes freedom to hold opinions without interference and to seek, receive and impart information and ideas through any media and regardless of frontiers.

In its first session in 1946, before any other human rights declaration and treaties had been adopted, the United Nations General Assembly (UNGA) adopted a resolution stating that "freedom of information is a fundamental human right and....the touchstone of all freedoms to which the United Nations is consecrated" (Ndumbaro 2014:2). Access to information globally is believed to be a facilitator of human development and a catalyst for their participation in governance issues (IFLA

2017). Access to this information is often facilitated by the use of digital technologies, which have been proven key drivers of the information and knowledge society. Easy access to information is fundamental in enabling citizens to exercise their rights and monitor government activities as well as contribute to decisions that affect their lives (Marchant and Stremlau 2019). In principle, most countries in Africa proclaim that access to information is a basic right.

Asunka and Logan (2021) in an Afrobarometer survey, however, reported that most citizens in countries in Africa still believed that information access was restricted while some information was closed. Such views are then supported by various governments' actions who, despite acknowledging that access to information is a basic human right, have at some point shut down the internet and social media citing various reasons among these countries; Cameroon, Chad, Burundi, Ethiopia, Kenya, Morocco, South Sudan, Uganda, Egypt, Sri Lanka, India, Togo, Columbia, Democratic Republic of Congo and Zimbabwe. Molomo and Molefe (2017) point out that in Botswana, the Constitution provides free speech and a free press but laments the lack of legal protection for citizens in their efforts to freely access and disseminate information, citing Amnesty International as having flagged Botswana for harassment and intimidation of journalists. Such challenges have also been witnessed in the SADC region where some countries have taken steps that undermine internet access, penetration, and affordability, which weakens the potential of digital media to enhance free expression and civic participation in governance and development (MISA Zimbabwe 2022). MISA Zimbabwe (2022) also reported that countries in SADC had harmonised their domestic laws that govern the use of digital media to facilitate inter-state prosecution of offenders. These laws mainly focus on data protection, electronic transactions, computer crime and cybercrime.

Across Southern Africa, however, there have been significant barriers to information access and existing literature has recommended that besides repealing repressive media laws and policy regulations, investments in digital infrastructure must be a matter of priority among governments in the region. National ICT policies have further been developed to manage the use of ICTs and related infrastructure to support nations' development aspirations characterised by the information and knowledge society. Despite the importance of national ICT policies in guiding the development and communicational aspirations of societies there seems to be minimal research on the relationship between ICT policies and the right to information access. Nowadays, it is evident there exists a triad relationship between ICT policies, human rights and information access (Mlambo 2022). While there is so much literature about ICTs and their role in governance through e-government, there is little that has been done to match the influence of national ICT policies on the freedom of information and the right to access governance and developmental information.

ICT Governance and Information Access

ICTs have not only facilitated information exchange among individuals but have also done the same between government departments, between government and the private sector and between the government and its citizens and civic society.

Governments have also relied on ICTs to collect information about their citizens' sentiments about developmental programmes and governance systems to develop interventions for improving governance and initiating developmental programs to alleviate social and economic discomfort among citizens. ICTs have an important role in development and communication by facilitating an uninterrupted exchange of information, enabling services to function smoothly (Chari 2009).

With the attainment of independence of their states, many people in Southern Africa started to demand the democratisation of their governance and participation in government developmental programmes and decision-making (Adesida 2001). The colonial period had seen racially segregated developmental programmes that excluded the natives from critical decision-making about activities that affected their lives. The early years after independence for most countries seemed promising with the involvement of people in decision-making. However, as years went by, governments turned despots, and became autocratic, making unpopular unilateral decisions that would be forced down the throats of their citizens. High levels of corruption had crept into governance systems and people started to demand accountability from their governments. The turn of the century characterised by the digital revolution saw the emergence of the internet and the wider accessibility of these technologies to the public and this presented great challenges to the ruling elites who had enjoyed a monopoly over information. The public now had access to wider sources of information, which despotic governments could not censor.

Governance deals with how power is exercised. It describes how citizens, institutions, business and civic society express their interests and exercise their rights and obligations and how they relate with each other and their government (Adesida 2001). To contribute to governance, however, citizens require information and the information and knowledge society of the 21st century comprising a wide range of digital tools of communication provides a wide range of opportunities for information exchange to the extent of causing discomfort and insecurity among the ruling elites. Davids (2002) has demonstrated that personal freedoms and socio-economic aspirations were some of the key democratic attributes desired by the citizenry of southern Africa and that among these attributes dominant values desired were civil liberties and personal freedoms, the desire for socio-economic development and these were high in Botswana, Zimbabwe, Zambia, Malawi, Mozambique, Lesotho, Namibia and South Africa. However, Davids (2002) has also shown that across all countries studied in Southern Africa, less than 50% of the citizenry reported that their countries' governance systems were full democracies with Botswana scoring the highest score of 46%of the respondents supporting the proposition, while Zimbabwe had the least score of 9%. He further noted that citizens were relatively free to say what they thought with Mozambique scoring the least score of 49 % of the respondents agreeing to the proposition, followed by Zimbabwe(54 %), Lesotho (56%), Botswana (57%), Zambia (76 %), South Africa (77 %), Namibia (80%) and Malawi (89%) (Davids 2002). Democratic governance is key for establishing information and knowledge societies that would assist communities to realise their developmental aspirations and technological development of digital media technologies promise to be a key facilitator for realising this.

The information and knowledge society of the 21st century has become increasingly dependent on the internet to facilitate citizen participation and enhance the citizen's rights to freedom of information. The increased penetration of the internet in southern African countries promises to usher new promises to freedom of information. Despite such developments and opportunities, internet and social media shutdowns and slowdowns have posed challenges to the enjoyment of the right to information. Idea International (2021) reported that in Africa, there has been a trend for both partial and intentional internet shutdowns, internet slow down and the imposition of high internet access costs and surveillance to curb citizen mobilisation and information flow, particularly during election periods with some examples between 2020 and 2021 in Burundi, Guinea, Tanzania, Togo and Uganda (Idea International, 2021). Despite some writers having ranked Zimbabwe lowly in terms of human rights and good governance as evidenced by restrictive media laws (Mashingaidze & Buchanan-Clarke 2020), Rajah (2015) argues that Zimbabwe is one of the rare countries in Africa that commits to good governance and development of ICT initiatives for supporting good governance, development and information rights.

These global developments of the internet and the World Wide Web and the increased usage of social media have seen increased advocacy groups and the emergence of digital media that has unsettled state organs in not-so-democratic environments. Often this has resulted in media crackdowns and arrests of journalists. For nations in southern Africa, the fear of the replica of the Arab Spring that saw the usage of social media successfully mobilising demonstrations in Tunisia and Egypt is often attributed to such heavy-handedness in handling digital media and social media (source). In Zimbabwe, the power of social media and the internet in organising demonstrations was demonstrated during the Tajamuka riots and *#ThisFlag* demonstrations (Nyoka & Tembo 2021). Molomo and Molefe (2017) point out that in Botswana, the Constitution provides for free speech and a free press but laments the lack of legal protection for citizens in their efforts to freely access and disseminate information, reporting that Amnesty International had flagged Botswana for harassment and intimidation of journalists. According to the World Press Freedom Index 2021, a survey in Africa showed that press freedom in 23 of the 43 countries surveyed, press freedom violation was common and these violations included arbitrary censorship on the internet, arrests of journalists, citing cyber laws (Kimunwe et al 2022). Lack of tolerance towards dissenting views in Zimbabwe was also evident in a report by an online news publication, NewZimbabwe, where on 3 March 2023 a ZANU PF official Mr Tafadzwa Mugwadi was quoted threatening to disconnect satellite dishes at households of supposedly 'unpatriotic' Zimbabweans who watched foreign news stations. This was after Al Jazeera had announced its intention to broadcast a documentary on corruption in Zimbabwe. The ZANU PF official further declared that those who watched Al Jazeera, SABC, CNN, BBC, France 24, Sky News, Fox News, ABC News, Euro News, NBC News and Al Arabiya were not patriotic.

Contextualizing Digital Information Access in the SADC Region

Most rural communities in southern Africa are primarily agrarian and extensive users of the information on agriculture (May, Karugia & Ndokweni 2007; Kelil, Girma & Hiruy 2020). In addition, these communities also require information on education, health, community development and governance. However, most of these communities have faced several challenges related to government policies and the general lack of telecommunications infrastructure, which impedes the communication of governance and the development of information. A citizenry that has sufficient access to ICTs is capable of digitally participating in the governance of their nations. Digital participation enables individuals to engage in government decisions by providing input, participating in dialogical and discussion forums or even voting (Ingram & Dooley 2021). However, for citizens to participate in the governance of a nation, trust in the governance system is a prerequisite.

The turn of the century saw an increased penetration of mobile internet across the developing countries. Among countries that witnessed the increased penetration of mobile internet was Zimbabwe, where mobile internet access had increased to 60.6% in 2019 and this had been accompanied by the wider usage of social media platforms such as Whatsapp, Twitter and Facebook (Karekwaivanani & Msonza 2021). However, the impact of such developments can only be understood in the wider political contexts of the country (Karekwaivanani & Msonza 2021). Although there seems to be wide access and utilisation of digital technologies for communication among SADC countries, there is little evidence to support the view that the utilisation of these technologies has transformed the livelihood of communities in these communities. On the other hand, however, civic society and political parties have made noticeable progress in the dissemination of political content. Although SADC countries have pronounced policies aimed at establishing affordable and always-on internet availability, there has been low internet access penetration rates especially in rural communities (Mothobi, Chair & Rademan 2018). For example, Madagascar, the Democratic Republic of Congo and Malawi had the lowest penetration rates of 4.7%, 6.3% and 9.6% respectively (Mothobi, Chair & Rademan 2018). Across all SADC countries, the internet access gap has increased in rural areas, threatening efforts to ensure universal access to ICTs and their communication advantages. Besides such issues, according to a report by Minnar (2019) for MISA Zimbabwe, internet freedom in SADC countries has been declining since 2000 due to several factors. These include the weaponization the law to legitimise government actions, disruption of networks through internet shutdowns and jamming during and after protests, deployment of cyber-surveillance equipment, identification of all telecommunication users, increased mobile data prices, and the deployment of bots, cyber-attacks and disinformation such as the use of individual Facebook and Twitter account to propagate the ruling party propaganda.

According to Minnar (2019) governments in Africa have broadened measures to govern the internet, resulting in several laws being enacted to regulate and monitor the usage of the internet resulting in most African countries scoring lowly of the major indicators of freedom of expression, namely; transparency, civic space, protection, digital and media. In some countries such as Zimbabwe, a combination of factors has resulted in the decline of people using the internet. For example, a report by the Postal and Telecommunications Regulatory Authority of Zimbabwe (POTRAZ) at the end of December 2018 reported that 62.9% of Zimbabweans had access to the internet while another report at the end of June 2019 reported that this figure had declined to 57.2% (Karekwaivanani & Msonza 2019). In contrast to many Southern African countries however, South Africa has not sought to limit internet-based civic space by crafting repressive laws and has also not resorted to internet shutdown, jamming or arresting citizens or bloomers and journalists for expressing dissenting views online (Bosch & Roberts 2021).

While some studies have investigated the diffusion of ICTs in Africa, literature on the uptake of these technologies according to Cariolle (2020) is scant and several obstacles have been identified from the literature at both micro and local levels. Among these obstacles are demographic and individual characteristics, physical infrastructure proximity and competing policy (Cariolle 2020). One other challenge that has confronted many in accessing information, particularly in Africa is restrictions by governments. Bussiek (2022) notes that in addition to high internet costs, African governments have become renowned for restricting access to the internet to limit critics and opposition parties, through internet shutdowns or slowdowns (jamming), particularly ahead of elections or during elections. This has also been coupled with surveillance of personal communications without sufficient legal basis, for example in Zimbabwe, where interception is permitted without a warrant issued by a court. While the African Union (AU)'s declaration guarantees freedom of information by pledging to support individuals' rights to seek and receive information and to impart information and urges states not to interfere through removal, blocking or filtering of content, in many African countries, government's have continued to block and filter internet content purporting to protect national security (Bussiek 2022).

National ICT Policies, Cyber Laws and the Right to Information Access

Generally, governments in the SADC region have expressed their desire to integrate digital technologies into their developmental initiatives and developed national ICT policies to guide such developmental aspirations. On the other hand, ICTs have provided opportunities for governments to enhance good governance by strengthening citizens' rights to information and freedom of expression based on the wide opportunities offered by ICTs in generating and disseminating information in various forms such as audio, text, visual and multimedia. To balance the need for responsible use of ICTs for developmental purposes and the need to protect national security, various countries across the world have developed cyber laws. This suggests that there is a triad relationship among ICT policies, national constitutions and cyber legislations.

The diffusion of the internet to a previously digitally-disadvantaged world has created opportunities for unrestricted rights of information. However, this has brought with it challenges related to cybercrime, calling for governments to develop interventions to counter these crimes. This has created additional challenges with governments enacting repressive laws that have curtailed freedom of speech, freedom of expression and access to information among other information rights. Most countries in SADC have enacted laws that seek to regulate electronic communication. These laws include the Cybercrime and Computer-related Crimes Act of 2018 (Botswana), Cybercrimes Act of 2015 (Tanzania), Electronic Transaction Act (Mozambique), Electronic Transactions and Cyber Security Act of 2017 (Malawi), Cyber Security and Data Protection Act of 2021 (Zimbabwe), Cyber Security and Cybercrime Act of 2021 (Mauritius) and the Electronic Transactions Act 4 of 2019 (Namibia). Other laws include the Cyber Security and Cybercrimes Act of 2018 (Zambia), Computer Crime and Cybercrime Act of 2020 (Lesotho), Computer Crime and cybercrime act of 2022 (Eswatini) and the Cybercrimes Act 2020 (South Africa), Law of Electronic Communications and Information Society Services (Angola) and the Cybercrimes and Other Related Crimes Act 59 of 2021 (Seychelles).

According to MISA Zimbabwe (2022), some SADC countries that had cybercrime laws before the SADC model were Botswana, Zambia and Mauritius. However, these laws were less likely to infringe on individuals' rights to privacy when compared to the SADC model. The democratic cybercrime laws in Botswana, Zambia and Mauritius had been modelled along international cybercrime instruments and laws. In Mauritius, to counter the harmful use of the internet, the Cyber Security and Cybercrime Act of 2021 provides for lawful interception of contents data provided the investigating authority had reasonable grounds to believe that content data is relevant for investigation and prosecution and has made an application to the judge in Chambers. The Tanzanian Cybercrimes Act of 2015 among other limitations criminalises the transmission of unsolicited messages or intimating a relay of unsolicited messages.

While nations in Southern Africa have ICT policies, there seems to be little literature on how these policies have affected the right to information, freedom of expression, freedom of opinion and freedom of the media. These policies, however, seem to have focused on integrating ICTs in general developmental activities such as e-governance, e-health, e-agriculture and education among other applications. It is important to assess and evaluate the impact of these policies in addressing the challenges related to the freedom of information. The need for constant review of national ICT policies was reported as vital by the President of Zimbabwe, Emerson Mnangagwa while launching Zimbabwe's National ICT Policy in March 2018 (The Sunday Mail 2018). The president acknowledged the vitality of ICTs across all sectors of the economy but, however, pointed out that the ever-changing ICTs environment required constant reviews to make them relevant to the dynamic socio-economic environment and so that ICTs do not become antiquated fast. A review of national constitutions and National ICT policies to determine the level to which national ICT policies supported the citizens' right to information among SADC countries shows that all SADC countries have guaranteed freedom of information in their constitutions. Relevant ministries and government departments govern most national ICT policies. The right to information is expressed differently in its various forms from one country to the other. For example, while the phrase 'freedom of expression' is commonly used in Botswana, Eswatini, Lesotho, Malawi, Mauritius, Zimbabwe and Tanzania, in Malawi 'freedom of opinion' is more common.

Constitutionally, Botswana guarantees the protection of freedom of expression in Chapter II (Section 12) of the Constitution and the National ICT policy seeks to enhance this by providing access to relevant, localised and understandable information for all citizens (The Government of Botswana 2016). Additionally, the policy seeks to avail government services to citizens electronically (e-government). From these policy objectives, the ICT policy seems to ignore the ubiquitous and global reach of digital media. The Cybercrime and Computer-related Crimes Act passed in 2018 criminalises interception of non-public communication and the transmission of offensive content. The Cybercrime and Computer-related Crimes Act of 2018 section 9 criminalises the interception of non-public transmission without lawful justifications. The act also criminalises acts related to cyber extortion, cyber-harassment, cyber-stalking and offensive electronic communication (MISA Zimbabwe 2022).

The third chapter of the Constitution of Eswatini (section 24) guarantees the protection of freedom of expression (The Kingdom of Swaziland, 2005). To this end, the national ICT policy seeks to provide universal access to information to all citizens and to improve the quality of life through inclusive access to information on education, health, science and technology, culture and entertainment. For development purposes, the ICT policy also seeks to increase national consciousness of the role and potential of ICTs for sustainable development. Eswatini Computer Crime and Cybercrime Act of 2022 (Part II) criminalises the interception of non-public transmission without lawful justification. The act also criminalises sending of information that deceives, threatens or spreads hate speech using email, websites or social media. The act also bars service providers from disclosing information about criminal investigations under which communication is subject. It further criminalises the dissemination of information intending to coerce, intimidate, insult, harass or cause emotional distress to a person.

The second chapter of Constitution of Lesotho (article 14) guarantees freedom of expression under fundamental human rights and freedoms. Unlike other ICT policies, the Lesotho National ICT policy explicitly expressed the nation's commitment to the principles of freedom of the press and the right to the media. It also seems to fulfil aspirations of universal accessibility and inclusive access to ICT services and infrastructure among the citizens. The Computer Crime and Cyber Crime Act of 2020 seems to vary with other legislations in that it places no obligations on internet service providers to monitor data transmissions, therefore limiting the liability of internet service providers. This however enhances the citizens' rights to privacy as enshrined in the Constitution.

The Constitution of the Republic of Malawi breaks down information rights into various categories; namely, freedom of opinion, freedom of expression, freedom of the press, and access to information. Regarding national ICT policy, however, the key focus is on achieving universal access, promoting e-government services and promoting national security. This shows a gap between the Constitution and the national ICT policy. The national ICT policy does not fully address the information rights as enshrined in the Constitution. The Electronic Transactions and Cyber Security Act, however, protects freedom of information but places limitations on such acts as child pornography, incitement of racial hatred, xenophobia or violence. In addition to this, it seems to facilitate access to online communication but compliance with other laws of the republic. The Electronic Transactions and Cyber Security Act of 2016 under Section 87 (3) criminalises hacking but the act does not offer a statutory definition of the term "intercept". It defines the parameters of freedom of expression and its limits in political electronic communication. While it also promotes pluralism in the expression of thoughts and opinions, it prohibits the production and circulation of misleading adverts and the sending of unsolicited messages to consumers without consumers' prior consent. The Act punishes any person involved in recording, listening or monitoring content data in transit.

The second chapter of the Constitution of the Republic of Mauritius (section 12.1) pledges to support the protection of freedom of expression under the protection of fundamental rights and freedoms of individuals. The key issues the ICT policy seeks to achieve are accelerating e-government and providing a framework for guiding ICTs to enable the nation to attain its national development goals and to transform Mauritius into an information society where everyone has equitable and affordable access to ICTs. The Cyber Security and Cybercrime Act of 2021 section 8 criminalises the wilful interception of non-public data transmission. Section 21 of the act also criminalises downloading of movies and music for gain and places obligations on system administrators to moderate content that has been brought to their attention by the investigating authority. Section 26 also provides for the partial disclosure of traffic data where the investigating authority has reasonable grounds to believe that this requires criminal investigation.

The third chapter of The Republic of Namibia (article 21) guarantees fundamental freedoms. The national ICT policy seeks to support this by seeking to improve internet access, protect the rights of consumers and improve information security and privacy. It also strives to promote e-government. To fight cybercrime, Namibia promulgated the Electronic Transactions and Cybercrime Bill, which was criticised by the Legal Assistance Centre (LAC) and recommended that access to information should not be a province of cybercrime legislation (Links 2022). The third part of the Constitution of the United Republic of Tanzania (section 3) acknowledges the right of freedom of conscience and subsection 18 promotes freedom of expression (United Republic of Tanzania 2005). Like Mauritius, the ICT policy of Tanzania also seeks to provide a framework for enabling ICTs to contribute to the national development goals and to transform Tanzania into a knowledge-based society through the application of ICTs (The Republic of Tanzania 2016).

The third part of the Constitution of the Republic of Seychelles (section 22) on fundamental human rights and freedoms guarantees freedom of expression. The national ICT policy seeks to support this by ensuring the availability of accessible, universal, affordable, modern and high-quality ICT facilities. The Cybercrimes and Other Related Crimes Act 59 of 2021 criminalises the interception of non-public transmissions within a computer system and section 14 criminalises sending abusive, offensive, indecent, threatening, false, misleading or cause annoyance or inconvenience or is likely to cause stress or needless anxiety to any person. The third part of the Constitution of Zambia under (article 20) guarantees an individual's freedom of expression, freedom to receive ideas and information without interference, freedom to impart ideas without interference whether the communication is to the public generally or to any person or class of persons and freedom from interferences (The Republic of Zambia 2016). The Zambian ICT policy seeks to integrate ICTs in all sectors of the economy and seeks to achieve universal access to ICT infrastructure (The Republic of Zambia, 2006). The Cyber Security and cybercrimes act of 2018 was enacted to regulate the use of social media and to enhance cyber security. However, media houses have argued that this act infringes on internet freedoms by allowing the interception of internet communication and allowing the analysis of this information. The act also allows cyber inspectors powers to monitor and inspect any website or activity on the digital communication infrastructure but then prohibits the disclosure of the intercepted communication.

The second part of the Zimbabwean Constitution (section 61) guarantees freedom of expression and the media. Zimbabwe's national ICT policy seeks to support this by fostering the use of ICTs across all spheres of society and humankind and the government (The Republic of Zimbabwe 2013, 2016). The ICT policy also seeks to foster inclusive access and use of ICTs. The policy pronouncements however seem to exclude the media and freedom of expression. The cyber security and data protection act also borrows from the SADC model and enables the telecommunications regulatory authority POTRAZ to monitor the electronic communication of citizens and the Interception of Communications Act provides for surveillance of online communication. Some sections of the act have also been criticised for infringing on media freedom and freedom of expression. The act criminalises the transmission of information, which has the potential to incite acts of violence. The law makes it difficult for individuals to constructively criticise governments and promote transparency (MISA Zimbabwe 2022).

The preceding discussion shows that most Southern African countries have acknowledged the right to information as a fundamental human right. This is evident in their constitutional pronouncements on freedom of expression, freedom of opinion, freedom of speech and freedom of the media. These constitutional announcements have brought challenges related to the need to balance citizens' freedoms and national security. This has resulted in the development of legislation to strike a balance between national security and citizens' freedoms. As a regional block, the SADC countries have developed a model law to counter cybercrime across the region while individual states have used national ICT policies to guide the developmental aspirations. However, there still exists a gap between national ICT policies and national constitutions. National ICT policies have remained indifferent to freedom of information, freedom of opinion, freedom of expression and freedom of the media.

The extent to which National ICT policies address freedom of expression, freedom of opinion, freedom of information and freedom of the media is limited from an analysis of the national ICT policies of selected SADC countries. An analysis of the national ICT policies available showed that, although the SADC countries acknowledged the sanctity of these rights in their national constitutions, their ICT policies did not support these rights as shown by the gaps that exist between the national ICT policy and national constitutions. These gaps are further widened by the legislations that have been passed across various nations as a need to protect national security and to limit individual rights so that individuals' rights are limited concerning fellow citizens' enjoyment of their rights.

Conclusion

There is a gap between National ICT Policies, Cyberlaws and National Constitutions. The chapter, therefore, recommends multi-stakeholder engagements to reduce the gap that exists between these constructs of governance to ensure continued freedom related to information access, information dissemination and freedom of the media. This engagement must result in national ICT Policies clearly articulating how they contribute to media and information freedom. For several countries in the SADC region, research institutions play a vital role in policy formulation. Therefore, this multi-stakeholder engagement must include research institutions and parliamentary committees on ICTs and human rights. It is important to recognize the reality of cyber security threats that characterise the internet and social media. However, to balance the need to maintain the fundamental rights of information and the need to protect state security, where security threats are reasonably thought to exist and internet shutdown and surveillance are being considered, strong judicial processes must be followed. In some communities in the developing world, high costs of data and limited access to ICTs hinder effective access to information. To improve the accessibility of ICTs and improve access to information through these technologies, private and public sector collaboration and partnership must be enacted to facilitate infrastructural investments in ICTs. This must be coupled with subsidised data costs, particularly among rural communities with limited financial resources.

References

ADESIDA, O., (2001) Governance in Africa: The Role of Information and Communication Technologies. Abidjan, The Knowledge Network Centre.

African Commission on Human Rights and People's Rights. (2019) *Declaration of Principles on Freedom of Expression and Access.* [Online]. Available from: https://achpr.au.int/en/node/902#:~:text=The%20Declaration%20establishes%20or%20a ffirms,to%20express%20and%20disseminate%20information.

AFRICAN UNION, (2007) *African Charter on Democracy, Elections and Governance.* [Online]. Available from: https://au.int/en/treaties/african-charter-democracy-elections-and-governance

ASUNKA, J. and LOGAN, C., (2021) *Access Denied: Freedom of Information in Africa Falls Short of Public Expectations.* [Online]. Available from: https://www.afrobarometer.org/pu blication/ad452-access-denied-freedom-information-africa-falls-short-public-expectations/

BOSCH, T. and ROBERTS, T., (2021) *Digital Rights in Closing Civic Space: Lessons from Ten African Countries, South Africa Digital Rights Landscape Report.* [Online]. Available from: https://www.ids.ac.uk/publications/digital-rights-in-closing-civic-space-lessons-from-ten-african-countries/

BUSSIEK, H., (2022) *Digital Rights Are Human Rights: An Introduction to the State Of Affairs and Challenges in Africa.* [Online] Available from: https://library.fes.de/pdf-files/bueros/africa-media/19082-20220414.pdf

CARIOLLE, J., (2020) *International Connectivity and the Digital Divide in Sub-Saharan Africa.* [Online]. Available from: https://www.sciencedirect.com/science/article/abs/pii/S0167624520301451

CHARI, T., (2009) *Information and Communication Policy Formulation and the Divide in Zimbabwe.* [Online]. Available from: https://www.researchgate.net/publication/267269113_Information_and_Communication_Policy_Formulation_and_the_Information_Divide_in_Zimbabwe

COLIVER, S., (2006) *The Importance of the Right of Access to Information Held by Public Authorities, and the Need for the United Nations to take Steps to Further Elaborate, Codify, Protect and Promote this Right.* Warsaw, Open Society Justice Initiative.

DAVIDS, Y. D, et al., (2002) Measuring Democracy and Human Rights in Southern Africa. Uppsala, Nordiska Afrikainstitutet.

GOVERNMENT GAZETTE OF MAURITIUS, (2021) T*he Cyber Security and Cybercrime Act No. 16 of 2021.* [Online]. Available from: https://zimlii.org/akn/zw/act/2021/5/eng@2022-03-11#:~:text=An%20Act%20to%20provide%20for,driven%20business%20environment%20and%20encourage

GOVERNMENT GAZETTE OF MAURITIUS, (2021) *Cybersecurity and Cybercrime Act.* [Online]. Available from: https://ncb.govmu.org/ncb/legislations/THE%20CYBERSECURITY%20AND%20CYBERCRIME%20ACT%202021.pdf

GOVERNMENT OF BOTSWANA, (2016) Botswana's Constitution of 1966 with Amendments through 2016. [Online]. Available from: https://constitutions.unwomen.org/en/countries/africa/botswana

GOVERNMENT OF MADAGASCAR, (2010) *Madagascar's Constitution of 2010.* [Online]. Available from: https://faolex.fao.org/docs/pdf/mad128141.pdf

GOVERNMENT OF SEYCHELLES, (2017) *Seychelles's Constitution of 1993 with Amendments through 2017.* Online]. Available from: https://www.constituteproject.org/constitution/Seychelles_2017

GOVERNMENT OF ZIMBABWE, (2021) *Cyber and Data Protection Act [CHAPTER 12:07].* [Online]. Available from: https://www.veritaszim.net/node/5522

MOVEMENT OF ESWATINI, (2022) *The Computer Crime and Cybercrime Act.* [Online]. Available from: https://www.esccom.org.sz/legislation/COMPUTER%20CRIME%20&%20CYBERCRIME%20ACT.pdf

IDEA INTERNATIONAL, (2021) *The State of Democracy in South Africa and the Middle East 2021.* [Online]. Available from: https://www.idea.int/publications/catalogue/state-democracy-africa-and-middle-east-2021

INGRAM, G. and DOOLEY, M., (2021) *Digital Government: Foundation for Global Development and Democracy.* [Online]. Available from: https://www.brookings.edu/articles/digital-government-foundations-for-global-development-and-democracy/

KAREKWAIVANANI, C. and MSONZA, N., (2021) *Digital Rights in Closing Civic Space: Lessons From Ten African Countries.* [Online]. Available from: https://www.ids.ac.uk/publications/digital-rights-in-closing-civic-space-lessons-from-ten-african-countries/

KELIL, A., GIRMA,Y. and HIRUY, M., (2020) Access and Use of Agricultural Information in Africa: Conceptual Review. *Information and Knowledge Management,* 10(7).

KIMUNWE, P, et al., (2022) *The State of Media: Freedom and Safety of Journalists in Africa.* Kampala, CIPESA.

KINGDOM OF LESOTHO, (2018) *Lesotho's Constitution of 1993 with Amendments through 2018.* [Online]. Available from: https://www.constituteproject.org/constitution/ Lesotho_2018

KINGDOM OF SWAZILAND, (2005) *Eswatini's Constitution of 2005.* [Online]. Available from: https://www.constituteproject.org/constitution/Swaziland_2005

LINKS, F. (2022) *Familiar Flaws – Unpacking Namibia's Draft Cybercrime Bill.* IPPR.

MARCHANT, E. and STREMLAU, N., (2019) *Africa's Internet Shutdowns.* Oxford, University of Oxford.

MASHINGAIDZE, S and BUCHANAN-CLARKE, S., (2020) *Challenges and Opportunities: Media Independence and Press Freedom in Zimbabwe.* [Online]. Available from: https://digitalmallblobstorage.blob.core.windows.net/wp-content/2021/10/Zimbabwe-media-independence-and-press-freedom-Policy-Briefing.pdf

MAY, J., KARUGIA, J. and NDOKWENI, M., (2007) *Information And Communication Technologies And Agricultural Development In Sub-Saharan Africa: Transformation And Employment Generation.* African Economic Research Consortium (AERC).

MINNAR, I. (2019) *Information and Internet Rights in Zimbabwe.* Harare, MISA Zimbabwe.

MISA ZIMBABWE, (2022) *Cyber Security and Cybercrime Laws in the SADC Region. Implications on Human Rights.* Harare, MISA Zimbabwe.

MLAMBO, C., (2022) *The Nexus between Information Communication Technology and Human Rights in Southern Africa.* [Online]. Available from: https://www.mdpi.com/2078-2489/13/8/362

MOLABA, K. E., (2016) Community Participation in the Integrated Development Planning of the Lepelle-Nkumbi Local Municipality. Pretoria: University of South Africa.

MOLOMO, M. G. and MOLEFE, W., (2017) *Freedom of Information: Botswana Back Private Communication, Public Accountability.* [Online]. Available from: https://www.afro barometer.org/wp-content/uploads/migrated/files/publications/Dispatches/ab_r7_dispa tchno172_freedom_of_information_in_botswana.pdf

MOTHOBI, C., CHAIR, C and RADEMAN, C., (2018) *SADC Not Bridging the Digital Divide.* [Online]. Available from: https://researchictafrica.net/publication/sadc-not-bridging-digital-divide-2/

MUTULA, M. S., (2006) Freedom of Information in the SADC Region: Implications for Development and Human Rights. *Library Review,* 55(7), 440-449.

NDUMBARO, D. D., (2014) *The Cyber Law and Freedom of Expression: The Tanzanian Perspective.* [Online]. Available from: https://www.academia.edu/29661776 /THE_ CYBER_LAW_AND_FREEDOM_OF_EXPRESSION_THE_TANZANIAN_PERSPECT IVES

NEW ZIMBABWE, (2023) *Al-Jazeera Documentary Rattles ZANU As Part Official Threatens Satellite Dish Removal, Bar Zimbos From Watching Foreign TV Channels, Staff Reporter.* [Online]. Available from: https://www.newzimbabwe.com/al-jazeera-documentary-rattles -zanu-pf-as-party-official-threatens-satellite-dishes-removal-bar-zimbos-from-watching-foreign-tv-channels

NYOKA, P. and TEMBO, M., (2021) *Dimension of Democracy and Digital Media Political Activism on Hopewell Chin'ono and Jacob Ngarivhume Twitter Accounts Towards the July 31st Demonstrations in Zimbabwe.* [Online]. Available from: https://www.tandfonline.com/doi/full/10.1080/23311886.2021.2024350

RAJAH, H., (2015) E-government in Zimbabwe. An Overview of the Progress Made and Challenges Ahead. *Journal of Global Research in Computer Science,* 6(2), 11-16.

REPUBLIC OF MALAWI, (2014) *National Access to Information Policy.* [Online]. Available from: https://npc.mw/wp-content/uploads/2020/07/access_to_information.pdf

REPUBLIC OF MALAWI, (2017) *Malawi's Constitution of 1994 with Amendments through 2017.* [Online]. Available from: https://www.constituteproject.org/constitution/Malawi_2017

REPUBLIC OF MALAWI, (2017). *Electronic Transactions and Cyber Security Act.* [Online]. Available from: https://media.malawilii.org/files/legislation/akn-mw-act-2016-33-eng-2017-12-31.pdf

REPUBLIC OF NAMIBIA, (2010) *Namibia's Constitution of 1990 with Amendments through, 2010.* [Online]. Available from: https://www.constituteproject.org/constitution/Namibia_2010

REPUBLIC OF NAMIBIA, (2019) *Electronic Transactions Act 4 of 2019.* [Online]. Available from: https://www.lac.org.na/laws/annoSTAT/Electronic%20Transactions%20Act%204%20of%202019.pdf

REPUBLIC OF ZAMBIA, (2006) *National Information and Communication Technology Policy.* [Online]. Available from: https://thezambian.com/wp-content/uploads/2007/04/Zambia-Information-and-Communication-Technology-Policy.pdf

REPUBLIC OF ZAMBIA, (2016) *Zambia's Constitution of 1991 with Amendments through 2016.* [Online]. Available from: https://www.constituteproject.org/constitution/Zambia_2016

REPUBLIC OF ZAMBIA, (2021) *The Cyber Security and Cyber Crimes Act.* [Online]. Available from: https://cipesa.org/wp-content/files/briefs/Implications-of-Zambias-Cyber-Security-and-Cyber-Crimes-Act_on-Digital-Rights_2021.pdf

REPUBLIC OF ZIMBABWE, (2013) Zimbabwe's Constitution of 2013. [Online]. Available from: https://www.veritaszim.net/node/315

REPUBLIC OF ZIMBABWE, (2016) *Information and Communications Technology (ICT).* [Online]. Available from: http://www.zim.gov.zw/index.php/en/my-government/government-ministries/information-communication-technology

REPUBLIC OF SOUTH AFRICA, (2018) *Cybercrime and Computer-Related Crimes Act, (2018).* [Online]. Available from: https://www.bocra.org.bw/sites/default/files/documents/18%20Act%2029-06-2018%20Cybercrime%20and%20Computer%2 0Related%20Crimes.pdf

REPUBLIC OF BOTSWANA, (2018) *Cybercrime and Computer Related Crimes Act.* [Online]. Available from: https://www.bocra.org.bw/sites/default/files/documents/18%20Act%2029-06-2018%20Cybercrime%20and%20Computer%20Related%20Crimes.pdf

SALAU, A. O., (2017) The Right of Access to Information and National Security in the African Regional Human Rights. *African Human Right Law Journal,* 17, 367-389.

SVARD, P., (2018) *Access to Government Information: A Global Phenomenon but What are the Challenges?* [Online]. Available from: https://www.ajol.info/index.php/esarjo/article/view/179858

TANZANIA UNITED REPUBLIC, (2005) *Tanzania (United Republic of)'s Constitution of 1977 with Amendments.* [Online]. Available from: https://constitutions.unwomen.org/en/countries/africa/tanzania

UNITED NATIONS (1948) *Universal Declaration of Human Rights.* Geneva, United Nations

UNITED NATIONS (2016) *Human Rights: Handbook for Parliamentarians.* Geneva, United Nations.

UNITED REPUBLIC OF TANZANIA, (2016) *National Information and Communications Technologies Policy Ministry of Communications and Transport.* [Online]. Available from: http://www.tzonline.org/pdf/ictpolicy2003.pdf

UNITED REPUBLIC OF TANZANIA, (2015) *The Cybercrimes Act.* [Online]. Available from: https://www.parliament.go.tz/polis/uploads/bills/acts/1452061463-ActNo-14-2015-Book-11-20.pdf

WASSERMAN, H. and BENEQUISTA, N., (2017) *Pathways to Media Freedom in Sub-Saharan Africa: Reflection from Regional Consultation.* Washington, Centre for International Media Assistance (CIMA).

PART II:

CHILD RIGHTS, PRISONER'S RIGHTS

AND LABOUR RIGHTS

Birth Registration among Street Children of the Harare Central Business District, Zimbabwe: Challenges and Opportunities

Witness Chikoko

Introduction and Background

The chapter problematises the challenges associated with birth registration among the street children of the Harare Central Business District, Zimbabwe. Birth registration has been defined as a process involving the provision of birth records to a child soon after birth (Bluck et al 2022). Birth registration is a critical first step in ensuring the rights of a child and proof of identity and existence. A birth certificate is confirmation of a child's nationality, place of birth, parentage and age. In some countries, it is perceived as the key identity document, outweighing any other - a birth certificate is often needed to apply for a passport, driving licence or national identity card as the child becomes an adult (Plan International 2014).

Birth registration entitles a child to their rights and bestows the responsibility for that child throughout his or her life, depending on the state in which they are born (UNCRC 1989; ACRWC 1999). In several countries, proof of identity is essential for gaining access to basic services and for exercising fundamental human rights (Sanga et al 2020; Plan International 2014). Without a birth certificate, a child may not be able to sit for school examinations and receive immunisations, free healthcare, claim rights to inheritance, legal protection in courts of law or access social protection related services (Sanga et al 2020; Plan International 2014). Proof of age is critical in successfully prosecuting perpetrators of crimes against children such as child trafficking, sexual offences, early recruitment into armed forces, child marriage and child labour (Plan International 2014).

The process of acquiring a birth record is very important as it culminates in the acquisition of a birth certificate (Bluck et al 2022). As a result of a birth certificate, a child is officially recognised as a bona fide citizen of a given country. This is in line with the United Nations Conventions on the Rights of a Child (1989), the African Charter on the Rights and Welfare of Children (1999), the Children's Act 5.06 (Zimbabwe) and the Birth and Death Registration Act 5.02 (Zimbabwe). The United Nations International Children's Emergency Fund (2007:02) defines birth registration as "the official record of a child's birth by the administration of the state. It establishes a child's legal identity." The birth registration process should be done by a fully functional civil registration system (UNICEF 2007). A functional civil registration system is defined as universal, permanent, continuous and very confidential on personal data (UNICEF 2007). Birth registration is included in the Sustainable

Development Goals which ensure an improved vital registration system (Bhatia et al 2017). The improved birth registration is also crucial in terms of enhancing the monitoring of other child health goals, including under five mortality among others (Bhatia et al 2017).

Birth registration is one of the challenges affecting many parts of the world. Globally, an estimate of 230 million children do not have birth certificates (Bhatia et al 2017; UNICEF 2013). The low birth registration is widespread among African and Asian regions (Bhatia et al 2017). However, the lowest levels of birth registration are found in Sub-Saharan Africa at about 44 % (UNICEF 2013). In Eastern and Southern Africa, an estimate of 63 % of children do not have birth certificates (Chereni 2016 & 2017; Bluck et al 2022; Plan International 2014; UNICEF 2013). The low birth registration is more pronounced in orphans and other vulnerable children's categories such as those in street situations, child headed households, early and forced marriages, and child labour, among others (Bluck et al 2022). On the other hand, based on UNICEF's 2013 study, low birth registration is rampant among children living in rural areas, remote areas, with uneducated mothers, from poor households, and those from certain ethnic or religious groups, among others. In addition, children in armed conflicts are also severely affected with low levels of birth registration (UNICEF 2007).

There is severe paucity or dearth of academic studies that interrogate the challenges associated with birth registration among the street children of the Harare Central Business District, Zimbabwe. The chapter employs the child rights perspective to analyse and understand the realities of these children. Major challenges includes stigma and discrimination, inaccessibility and or lack of birth records, limited expertise by probation officers/social workers, inaccessibility of Registrar General's office, shortage of money, stringent Government of Zimbabwe legislations, policies and programmes, shortage of accessories from the Registrar's office. However, previous studies by Bourdillon (1991, 1994a, 1994b, 2000, 2009), Mella (2012), Mhizha (2010, 2014 & 2015), Mhizha and Muromo (2013), Chikoko (2014 & 2017), Ruparanganda (2008), Wakatama (2007), Chirwa and Wakatama (2000), Rurevo and Bourdillon (2003a and 2003b), Chirwa (2007), Dube (1997 & 1999), Manjengwa, Matema Tirivanhu and Tizora (2016), Chikoko et al (2020) were limited in articulating the challenges associated in acquisition of birth certificates among street children of the Harare Central Business District, Zimbabwe. On that basis, this chapter offers an updated contribution on the challenges affecting acquisition of birth certificates among these children.

Child Rights Perspective

The United Nations Convention on the Rights of a Child (UNCRC, 1989) divides child rights into four principles; namely, the best interest of the child, the right of a child to participation, non-discrimination and the right of a child to survival and development. Some of the key international and regional child rights legislations such as the UNCRC (1989) and the African Charter on the Rights and Welfare of Children (1999) have been ratified and domesticated by the Government of Zimbabwe.

Articles 7 and 8 of the UNCRC (1989) declare that governments should provide opportunities or platforms that enhance birth registration. The ratification and domestication by the Government of Zimbabwe is to ensure access fulfilment of the rights to a birth registration. The fulfilment of the right to a birth registration or certificate also includes children in the street situations.

In order to ensure access to birth registration among the citizenry, the Government of Zimbabwe developed a number of measures. Some of the strategies include the enactment of legislations such as the 2013 Constitution of the Republic of Zimbabwe, the Birth and Death Registration Act (5:02) and the Children's Act (5:06). In addition, the Government of Zimbabwe has also come up with child rights national programmes such as the National Action Plan for Orphans and Other Vulnerable Children (2004 to 2008, 2010 to 2015 & 2016 to 2020) and the Zimbabwe National Orphan Care Policy of 1999, among others. However, Boyden (2003) observes that notions of childhood derived from Western world thinking seem to be problematic when applied in different socio-cultural contexts. Bourdillon (2006) referred to child rights as 'romanticising childhood'.

Uvin (2007) observes that the human right discourse is mere rhetoric because of a number of reasons. He notes that the approach is project specific. Uvin recommends the need for the development community to be committed to the rights-based approach by not limiting the model to certain projects. He also notes that some of the development community should commit to a comprehensive application of rights-based approach to their own behaviours, thus promoting accountability. Uvin also suggests that the rights-based approach should address challenges associated with the global political economy that has triggered inequalities within societies. The development community occupy privileged positions in the global political economy and if they are serious on applying the approach it should start from there.

Stigma, Discrimination and Teenager Street mothers

Stigma and discrimination is one of the challenges that affects street children of Harare Central Business District to access birth registration. As a result of stigma and discrimination, the street children cannot have birth certificates. They are stigmatised and discriminated against as people of no fixed abode. They are referred as *magunduru (*a derogatory term referring to street children, derived from the notion of, *ideophone, "gunduru"* in Shona, literally, throw oneself about*) and *mastreet kids* among other terms. During in depth interviews one of the participants had this to say:

> *Hationekwe sevanhu nokuti tiri magunduru. Hapana ane basa nemagunduru munyika muno* (we are not seen as human beings because we are street children. No one is concerned with our situation in this country).

Street children are discriminated against and stigmatised to the extent that they cannot access birth registration in Zimbabwe. They are stigmatised and discriminated against as social misfits, deviants. The officers see no value in assisting such stigmatised and discriminated upon people. Moreover, low birth registration is associated with teenage street mothers on the streets of Harare Central Business

District, Zimbabwe. The majority of teenage street mothers are struggling to make ends meet. They do not also have birth certificates themselves. During the informal conversations, one of the teenager street mothers noted that:

Mudhara, hupenyu hwedu makwikwi mustreet. Vana vedu vatinoita mustreet havana mabirth certificates. Vanga mawana seiiko isu vana mai vacho tisinawo? Handina birth certificate ini. Handina mari yekundotora birth certificate racho. (Elder, our lives on the streets are tough. Our children do not have birth certificates. How can they be registered when the mother has not been? I do not have a birth certificate).

Apparently, the majority of teenage street mothers of Harare Central Business District did not have birth certificates. Some of them lose their birth certificates because of poor storage facilities. It is extremely difficult to keep such essential documents on the streets. Some of the teenage street mothers are of low levels of literacy who do not place much value on birth registration (Bluck et al 2022). Some of the street children of the Harare Central Business District do not have birth records as they were born on the streets. As a result of the lack of birth records it is extremely difficult for them to access birth certificates. Even in certain circumstances where the child was born in clinics and hospitals, the birth records are lost as they stay on the streets. During an informal conversation, one of the girls said:

Mudhara, mwana wangu uyu, hana birth certificate nokuti ndakamuzvarira mustreet. Handina kuenda kuchipatara. Kuzvipatara vanoda mari. Isu hatina mari. Varume vedu vemustreet havana mari yematernity (Elder, my child does not have a birth certificate because he was born on the streets. I did not have money for maternity fees demanded by council clinics and hospitals. My husband from the street is poor. He does not afford to pay for maternity fees).

Statutory Social Workers, the Registrar General Office and Financial Resources

Huge caseloads among statutory social workers are one of the challenges associated with low birth registration among street children of the Harare Central Business District. During informal conversations, one of the street boys indicated that the statutory social workers at Makombe Social Development office have huge caseloads. He noted that:

Mudhara ndakaenda kuMakombe Department of Social Development kakawandisa asi hapana chakabuda. Maofficers acho vanenge vane pressure yebasa. Nokuda kwekuoma kwehupenyu munyika, vanobatsira vanovapa mari. Manje ini ndiri musvuu ganda zvangu hazvibude. (Elder, I have visit Makombe Department of Social Development office several times, however to no avail. The Social Development Officer is always extremely busy. Because of the current socio-economic environment, they prefer clients that give them something. (Ironically) It is difficult for me because I am also very poor).

Social workers are sometimes overwhelmed by huge caseloads to an extent that sometimes they do not have enough time to do certain duties. For example, processing of birth certificates for abandoned, orphans and other children like those in street situations. The situation is also compounded by a number of factors such as massive brain drain that has hit the Department of Social Development, corruption, low staff morale among others (Mhizha and Muromo 2013; Chikoko 2014 & 2017). Furthermore, the inaccessibility of the Registrar General's office can be regarded as one of the reasons for low birth registration among the street children of the Harare Central Business District. The inaccessibility of the Registry's Office in the context of the attitudes, corruption, low staff morale among others. During in depth interviews, one of the street boys affirmed that:

> *Mudhara maofficers acho marukasi. Havana basa nevanhu vanoda mari. Vari corrupt. Plus, havasi kupihwa mari dzinotenga neGovernment. Saka vanopedzera shungu kwatiri isu. Saka kuwana birth certificate zvakadayi mahwani chaiwo.* (Elder the officers are rude. They do not care about people. They are corrupt. Plus, they are poorly remunerated by their employer. They displace their frustration on us. Therefore, to get a birth certificate in such circumstances it is not easy).

The Registrar General's office is very inaccessible as a result of a multiplicity of factors which includes negative or poor attitudes among officers, low staff morale, and corruption, among others (Bluck et al 2022; Gibberd et al 2016). Additionally, limited access to financial resources is one of the challenges affecting access to birth registration among the street children of the Harare Central Business District. Some of the street mothers do not have money which is required to pay at maternity hospitals to get birth records. As a result of their failure to raise the much-needed money for settling bills related to maternity services, they cannot get birth records. During in depth interviews one of the street mothers said:

> *Mudhara ini ndiri street mother. Pandakaenda kuHarare Hospital kwandakaponera mwana wangu uyu (achinongedzera mwana wacho aiyamwa mukaka). Ndakabva ndisina kubhadhara mari yematenet. Saka handina kubva zvakanaka. Ndakatiza ndichiuya muno mustreet. Handina kuwana birth record remwana wangu.* (Elder, I am a street mother. When I went to Harare hospital seeking for maternal health services, for my born baby (pointing at the lactating baby), I did not pay any single cent. Soon after the delivery of my child I ran away from the maternity ward to the streets of Harare Central Business District. Therefore, I did not get any birth record for my newly born child)

Clearly, some of the street children cannot access birth registration because of shortage of financial resources. Street mothers fail to clear maternity bills at some of the hospitals to the extent that they cannot access birth registration records. Finally, stringent measures associated with the Birth and Registration Act are some of the challenges that affect street children to get registered (Bluck et al 2022). The Birth and Death Registration legislation can be regarded as rigid. During informal conversations one of the street boys said:

> *Elder, mutemo wemabirth certificates hausi bhoo, wakaoma. Zvinodiwa kana uchidakutora birth mahwani. Vanoda zvakafanana nebirth record, vabereki vako, kana mawitnesses. Saka ini semunhu anogara mustreet handikwanise kuwana zvinhu izvozvo. Saka mahwani chaiwo. Ikarate paHarare.* (Elder, the Birth and Death Registration Act is not good. It is very rigid not flexible. Some of the

requirements for birth registration are difficult to fulfil. For example, bringing birth records, parents and or witnesses. As a person staying on the streets, it is very difficult for me to meet such stipulations).

The sentiments expressed above shows that some of the stipulations seem to be very rigid for children in street situations. This is because it is difficult to register birth certificates for the street children of the Harare Central Business District given the tough requirements from the Registrar General's office (Woden and Yedan 2019). As a result of the stringent measures, there has been low birth registration among the street children of the Harare Central Business District.

Recommendations

The following recommendations can help by ensuring increased accessibility of birth registration or certificates among street children of the Harare Central Business District, Zimbabwe:

- There is need to lobby and advocate the Ministry of Finance and Economic Planning to avail more resources towards Registrar General's Office.
- The corporate and non-governmental organisations should also fund some of the functions of the Registrar General's Office.
- There is need to reorient, retrain and capacity build Registrar General's Office staff members that they become more receptive and friendly to the vulnerable members of society such as elderly, orphans and street children.
- Civil society organisations should engage in lobbying and advocating initiatives for policies, programmes that fight stigma and discrimination against street children. This can be through policy briefs, Parliament portfolio on social services, breakfast meetings with key stakeholders among other strategies.
- The Department of Social Services should employ qualified and experienced social workers that have skills working with street children. This can go a long way in acquisition of birth certificates for street children.
- There is a need to repeal the current Birth and Death Registration Act (5.02) and Children's Act (5.06) so that street children can easily acquire birth certificates with little hustles or problems. The National Association of Social Workers in Zimbabwe can play a pivotal role in the process of lobbying and advocating for law reforms.
- There is a need to integrate birth registration into public services. For example, integration of birth registration with delivery of primary health care, immunisation, education services among others.
- There is a need for staff motivation for birth registration officials. If the birth registration officials are well remunerated, they are able to diligently do their work.
- There is a need to improve social cash transfer programmes as incentives to increase birth registration.
- There is a need to facilitate compilation of a database of all children without birth certificates by the District Child Protection Committees and Case management officers.

- There is need facilitate presentation of findings of the database of children without birth certificates by the District Child Protection Committee to the District Registrar General's office
- There is a need to facilitate mobile registration through working partnership with the Ministry of Home Affairs, Registrar General's office.
- There is a need to facilitate information giving to children, families and communities on the requirements on getting birth certificates.
- There is a need to facilitate awareness raising on the importance of birth registration to children, families, schools, communities.
- There is a need to facilitate lobby and advocacy at various levels.

Conclusion

As discussed above, there are numerous challenges that affect the acquisition of birth registration or certificates among the street children of the Harare Central Business District. The reasons are varied and multiple. Some of them include stigma and discrimination, shortage of money, lower levels of literacy among parents, lack of birth certificates among teenager street mothers, lack of birth records, stringent measures associated with Birth and Death Registration Act (5.02), lack of awareness on the importance of birth certificates, and inaccessibility of Registry's Office, among others. These challenges affect the enjoyment of the rights of street children as defined by international, regional and local child rights laws, policies and programmes. Rather, these challenges highlight huge child rights abuse and violations among the street children of the Harare Central Business District, Zimbabwe.

References

AFRICAN UNION, (1999) *African Charter on the Rights and Welfare of Children.* [Online]. Available from: https://au.int/sites/default/files/treaties/36804-treaty-african_charter _on_r ights_welfare_of_the_child.pdf

ARMSTRONG, L., (2014) Screening Clients in a Decriminalised Street-based sex industry: Insights into the Experiences of New Zealand Sex Workers. *Australian and New Zealand Journal of Criminology*, 47 (2), 207- 222.

BEAZLEY, H., (2003) Voices from the margins: Street children's subcultures in Indonesia *Children's Geographies,* 1(2), 181- 200.

BHATIA, A, et al., (2017) Who and Where are the Uncounted Children? Inequalities in Birth Certificate Coverage Among Children Under Five Years in 94 Countries Using Nationally Representative Household Surveys. *International Journal for Equity in Health,* 16(1), 148.

BHATTACHARYA, A. & NAIR, R., (2014) Girls on the Street: Their Lived Experiences and Vulnerability to Sexual Abuse. *Indian Journal of Social Work,* 75(1), 33-47.

BLUCK, P., MUZONDO, E. and ZVOMUYA, W., (2022) The Nexus between Children's Rights and Birth Registration in Zimbabwe: A Missing Link and Future Prospects. In Mabvurira, V., Murenje, M. & Mundau, L. (eds.). *Professional Social Work in Zimbabwe: Putting Children First*. Edenvale: Beyond the Vale Publishing.

BOURDILLON, M. F. C., (1991) *Poor, Harassed but Very Much Alive: An Account of Street People and their Organization.* Gweru, Mambo Press.

BOURDILLON, M. F. C., (1994a and 1994b) Street Children in Harare Africa. *Journal of the International African Institute,* 4(4), 516-533.

BOURDILLON, M. F. C., (2000) *Earning a life: Working Children in Zimbabwe.* Harare, Weaver Press.

BOURDILLON, M. F. C., (2009) Children's work in Southern Africa. *Werkwinkel,* 4(1), 103-122.

BOYDEN, J., (2003) Children under Fire: Challenging Assumptions about Children's Resilience. *Children, Youth and Environments,* 13(1), 1-29.

CHERENI, A., (2016) Underlying dynamics of child birth registration in Zimbabwe *International Journal of Children's Rights,* 24, 741-763.

CHERENI, A., (2017) Researching the Dynamics of Birth Registration and Social Exclusion for Child Rights Advocacy: The Unique Role of Qualitative. Research. *Qualitative Social Research,* 18(1), 1-28.

CHIKOKO, W., (2014) Commercial 'Sex Work' and Substance Abuse among Adolescent Street Children of Harare Central Business District. *Journal of Social Development in Africa,* 29(2).

CHIKOKO, W., (2017) *Substance Abuse among Street Children of Harare: A Case of Harare Central Business District.* Harare, University of Zimbabwe.

CHIKOKO, W., MHIZHA, S. and RUPARANGANDA, W., (2020) Adolescent Street Boys' Car Washing and Parking of Vehicles in the Harare Central Business District as Urban Resilience under Austerity Era. *Journal of Sociology and Social Anthropology,* 11(3-4), 206-214.

CHIRWA, Y., (2007) Children, Youth and Economic Reforms, An Expedition of the State of Street Children in Zimbabwe. In Maphosa, F., Kujinga, K. & Chingarande, S. D. (eds.). *Zimbabwe's Development Experiences since 1980, Challenges and Prospects for the Future.* Addis Ababa, OSSREA, pp. 76-93.

CHIRWA, Y. and WAKATAMA, M., (2000) Working Street Children in Harare. In Bourdillon, M. F. C (ed.). *Earning a life: Working Children in Zimbabwe.* Harare, Weaver Press, Harare, pp. 45-58.

DUBE, L., (1999) *Street Children: A Part of Organized Society.* Harare, University of Zimbabwe.

DUBE, L., (1997) AIDS-risk patterns and Knowledge of the Disease among Street Children in Harare, Zimbabwe. *Journal of Social Development in Africa,* 12(2), 61-73.

DUBE, L., KAMVURA, L. and BOURDILLON, M. F. C., (1996) Working with Street Boys in Harare. *Africa Insight,* 26(3), 260- 267.

EBIGBO, P. O., (2003) Street children: The Core of Child Abuse and Neglect in Nigeria. *Children Youth and Environment,* 13(1), 244-249.

GIBBERD, A., SIMPSON, J. M. and EADES, S., (2016) No Official Identity: A Data Linkage Study of Birth Registration of Aboriginal Children in Western Australia. *Australia and New Zealand Journal of Public Health,* 40(4), 388-394.

GOVERNMENT OF ZIMBABWE, (2001) *The Children's Act (5.06).* Harare, Government Printers.

GOVERNMENT OF ZIMBABWE, (2005) *The Birth and Death Registration Act (5.02).* Harare, Government Printers.

GOVERNMENT OF ZIMBABWE, (2013) *Constitution of the Republic of Zimbabwe.* Harare, Government Printers.

HASSON, D., (2003) 'Strolling' as a Gendered Experience: A Feminist Analysis of Young Females in Cape Town. *Children, Youth and Environments*, 13(1), 1-28.

KRUGER, J. M. and RICHTER, L. M., (2003) South African Street Children at Risk for AIDS? *Children, Youth and Environments*, 13(1).

MALINDI, M. J. and THERON, L. C., (2010) The Hidden Resilience of Street Youth. *South African Journal of Psychology,* 40(3), 318- 326.

MELLA, M., (2012) *An Investigation into the Nature and Extent of Economic Exploitation of Street Children in Zimbabwe: A case study of Harare Central Business District.* Harare, University of Zimbabwe.

MHIZHA, S., (2010) *The Self-Image of Adolescent Street Children in Harare.* Harare, University of Zimbabwe.

MHIZHA, S., (2014) Religious Self-Beliefs and Coping Vending Adolescent in Harare. *Journal of Religion and Health*, 53, 1487-1487.

MHIZHA, S., (2015) The Religious-Spiritual Self-Image and Behaviours among Adolescent Street Children in Harare, Zimbabwe. *Journal of Religion and Health,* 54, 187-201.

MHIZHA, S., et al., (2016) Ecological Self-Image and Behaviours for Children Living on the Streets of Harare. *Development Southern Africa* 33(1), 39-52.

RUREVO, R. and BOURDILLON. M. F. C., (2003a) Girls: The Less Visible Street Children of Zimbabwe, *Children, Youth and Environment,* 13(1):1-20

_____ (2003b) *Girls on the Street.* Harare, Weaver Press.

RUPARANGANDA, W., (2008) *The Sexual Behaviour Patterns of Street Youth of Harare, Zimbabwe, in the Era of the HIV and AIDS Pandemic.* Harare, University of Zimbabwe.

UNITED NATIONS, (1989) *The United Nations Convention on the Rights of a Child.* Geneva, United Nations.

SACKEY, E. T. and JOHANNESEN, B. O., (2015) Early identity and Respect through Work: A Study of Children Involved in Fishing and Farming Practices in Cape Coast Ghana. *Childhood,* 22(4), 447-459.

SANGA, C, et al., (2020) Decentralisation of Birth Registration to Local Government in Tanzania: The Association with Completeness of Birth Registration and Certification *Global Health Action,* 13(1).

TURNER, S. and SCHOENBERGER, L., (2012) Street Vendor Livelihoods and Everyday Politics in Hanoi, Vietnam: The Seeds of a Diverse Economy? *Urban Studies,* 49(5), 1027-1044.

OSTHUS, I. S. and SEWPAUL, V., (2014) Gender, Power and Sexuality among Youth on the Streets of Durban: Socio-Economic Realities. *International Social Work,* 57(4), 326- 337.

WAKATAMA, M., (2007) *The Situation of Street Children in Zimbabwe: A Violation of the United Nations Convention on the Rights of the Child (1989).* Leicester: University of Leicester.

WARRIA, A., Nel, H. and TRIEGAARD, T. (2015) Challenges in Identification of Child Victims of Transnational Trafficking. *Practice: Social Work in Action,* 27(5), 315- 333.

WODEN, Q. and YEDAN, A., (2019) Obstacles to Birth Registration in Niger: Estimates from a Recent Household Survey. *Journal of Health, Population and Nutrition,* 38(1), 26.

UVIN, P., (2007) From the Right to Development to the Rights-Based Approach: How 'Human Rights' Entered Development. *Development in Practice,* 17(4-5).

Substance Abuse and Sexual Behaviour among Street Children with Reference to the Child Agency Theory: The Case of Harare Central Business District, Zimbabwe

Witness Chikoko and Kudzai Mwapaura

Introduction

The abuse of substances and various sexual behaviours are the twin problems affecting street or homeless children (Embleton et al 2012; Chikoko 2017). The chapter problematizes the issue of sexual behaviours and substance abuse among the street children of the Harare Central Business District in Zimbabwe. Substance abuse can be defined as taking a drug too often or taking drugs or substances for wrong reasons (Makaruse 2010). A child is defined as any human being under the age of 16 years in terms of the Zimbabwe's Children's Act (5.06), whilst the United Nations Convention on the Rights of a Child (1989) as someone aged below 18 years. As part of the discussion, the chapter interrogates the various typologies of child agency, including thin agency, thick agency, self-destructive agency and ambiguity of agency within the context of sexual behaviours and substance abuse of street children.

The Child Agency Theory

Scholars such as Bell (2012:284) define agency as "a process whereby individuals are able to envisage different paths of action, decide among them and then take action along a chosen route." Chuta (2014:2) has also defined agency as "understood as an individual's own capabilities, competences and activities through which they navigate the contexts and positions of their life worlds fulfilling many economic, social and cultural expectations". The term agency is about choices or actions taken by individuals to survive or meet their daily needs. Bell (2012:284) also defines sexual agency among youth as "processes where young people become sexually active and the strategies, actions and negotiations involved in maintaining relationships and navigating broader social expectations." The various sexual behaviours of the street children of the Harare Central Business District, Zimbabwe could be part of sexual agency. Some of the sexual behaviours included; commercial sex work, masturbation, multiple sexual relationships, sodomy, unprotected sex, heterosexual relationships, oral sex, hook up among others (Ruparanganda 2008; Mhizha 2010; Chikoko 2014, 2017).

The childhood studies view children as social actors, not as passive citizens, and or vulnerable victims (Bordonaro & Payne 2012, Payne 2012, Allen 2009,

Gallacher & Gallagher 2008). As social actors, children are able to influence the super structures and institutions such as laws, policies among others through participation in consultative meetings among other critical meetings. The children's agency is demonstrated when they cope with various constraints. Some of the constraints might be because of certain socio-cultural, legal, economic, political, physical structures. The children as social actors are capable of demonstrating their power although in circumstances where they could be considered less powerful (Evers et al 2011). In the context of substance abuse among street children of the Harare Central Business District, street children as capable social actors, exercise their agency through excessive use of some of the substances, including traditional medicines. They also demonstrate their agency through sustaining their lives with commercial sex work (Chikoko 2014, 2017).

Children's agency demonstrates a number of key characteristics such as creativity, negotiation, resilience and inventiveness. The child agency theory disregards the child rights perspective, which view African children as victims, not as social actors (Evers et al 2011). In the context of street children, their social structure is restrictive, probably due to lack of enough resources for survival. The social structure is also enabling on the basis that street children are able to manipulate the existing social structures. For example, despite the limited resources and presence of police officers, street children continue to engage in substance abuse such as smoking marijuana and drinking alcohol even in undesignated areas and considering that they are under age. The street children of Lusaka, Zambia demonstrate their human agency by leaving their homes and surviving on the streets (Mtonga 2011). Mtonga also observed that human agency was illustrated by the street children's ability to manage their own lives by meeting daily needs while living on the streets of Lusaka, Zambia.

Furthermore, street children who abuse substances as social actors, also employ a number of coping mechanisms. Some of the mechanisms include the use of traditional herbs for treatment of sexually transmitted diseases and pregnancy management in an environment, which is restrictive and characterized by limited access to appropriate reproductive health services on the streets (Ruparanganda 2008). Street children of Harare Central Business District, as social actors also demonstrate their agency in using available traditional medicine, to cure ailments that confront them (Ruparanganda 2008; Chikoko 2017). Using traditional medicine, the street children of Harare Central Business District are able to influence the social structures.

The Ambiguity of Agency

The ambiguous nature of agency is one of the key concepts associated with child agency theory. Scholars such as Tisdall and Punch (2012:256) observes that "children and young people's agency should certainly be a contested and scrutinised concept rather than one which is taken for granted, unproblematized or assumed inherently to be positive and desired by all children and young people." Hartas (2008) notes that the children's agency can exert a lot of pressure on children and young people in a context of structural limits. There has been a growing debate on the ambiguity of the agency of the children, particularly when their social actions are clashing with culture and moral values. One can query the agency of street children, in the context of substance abuse and sexual behaviours, because such agency could be considered immoral. For example, the street children demonstrated their agency in sexual behaviours such as rape, sodomy, intergenerational sex and multiple sexual relationships, among others (Mhizha 2010, Tadele 2009, and Ruparanganda 2008).

Such sexual behaviours seem to clash with moral and cultural values of Zimbabwean society. In Zimbabwe children including those in the street situations, are not expected to engage in sexual behaviours (Chikoko, 2017). Such behaviours are strongly condemned in Zimbabwean society. Children, including those in street situations, are supposed or expected to have sex when they grow up and are married. The strong moral foundations of Zimbabwean society are such that when a daughter is married as a virgin she will be rewarded in the form of a cow (cattle). Everyone else from her family and friends would feel proud of that kind of a reward. The ambiguity of the agency is also explained when such behaviours also threaten the well-being of these children (Bordonaro & Payne 2012). Largely, the various sexual behaviours such as rape, sodomy, intergenerational sex and abuse of substances are not in the best interest of the children. These behaviours are not in the best interest of the street children of the Harare Central Business District because of the risks associated with the various sexual behaviours and abuse of substances. Some of the risks included death because of unsafe abortion and exposure to sexually transmitted diseases such as HIV, among others (Chikoko 2014, 2017).

The street children's human agency becomes ambiguous when it is explained to be at the expense of their own interests or interests of the community or society. For example, having street children to indulge in sexual behaviours or smoke marijuana is regarded as clashing with moral values of childhood (Bordonaro & Payne 2012). The behaviour of abusing substances is not in the 'best interest of a child' as defined in article three (3) of the United Nations Convention on the Rights of a Child (1989), the African Charter on the Rights and Welfare of Children (1999) and national child rights laws such as the Children's Act *(5:06)* and the Domestic Violence Act (5:16). Drawing from the Criminal Law (Codification and Reform) Act (9: 23), street children who abuse substances and engage in various sexual behaviours are referred as 'children in conflict with the law,' Such children are in conflict with the law because of the criminalisation of substance abuse and sexual behaviours among children in Zimbabwe, including those in the street situations.

In contrast, Bourdillon and Musvosvi (2014) affirm that, 'ambiguous agency,' as noted by Bordonaro and Payne (2012), falls away as children also have abilities of assessing the outcomes of their survival strategies for immediate needs and also for the development of entrepreneurial skills for their future lives. As much as academics talk about the agency of street children, there is a need to strike a balance between vulnerability and agency of these children. However, for children to resort to staying on the streets could be considered as a coping survival strategy and can be considered as agency but within structural limits.

The Self-Destructive Agency

Gigengack (2006, 2008, 2013) through his studies with street children and youth in Mexico City came up with the concept of self-destructive agency. The destructive agency is when street children make choices that have risks as they navigate through their childhood. Some of the choices would expose the street children to a number of risks. In his study, some of the risks included death because of substance abuse (Gigengack 2008). In relation to the street children of the Harare Central Business District, Chikoko (2017) applied the same concept of self-destructive agency and found that some of the street children's behaviour constitute self-destructive agency. He observed that excessive use of substances had intricate and or multidimensional relationships with a number of sexual behaviours of these street children (Chikoko 2017). The street children of Harare Central Business District abused a wide range of substances.

Some of the sexual behaviours included; multiple sexual relationships, unsafe abortion, unprotected sex, masturbation among others had huge risks among these street children thus self-destructive agency (Chikoko 2014, 2017; Chikoko et al 2019, Chikoko et al 2018). Some of the risks included death in the context of unsafe abortion. Some of the street children of Harare Central Business District succumbed to sexually transmitted diseases, including HIV and AIDS, because of various reasons. Some of the street children became vulnerable to sexually transmitted diseases because of the inaccessibility of reproductive health services. For example, Ruparanganda (2008) has cited a situation where street girls failed to access reproductive health services because of stigma and discrimination as a result of their homelessness situation when they approached public health hospitals. In other words, they impose social restrictions on themselves due to perceived stigmatisation.

Substance abuse has been cited as one of the reasons why the street children of Harare Central Business District succumb to sexually transmitted diseases (Chikoko 2017, 2019). As a result of excessive use of substances such as cannabis, some of the street children ended up contracting sexually transmitted diseases through unprotected sex with an infected person. On the other hand, Mahati (2015) has observed that some of the children are able to reduce risks that could confront them, thus in a way dismissing the self-destructive agency. However, the choices that are made by the majority of the street children of the Harare Central Business District in relation to substance abuse and sexual behaviours demonstrate the self-destructive agency of these children.

The Thin Agency

Klocker (2007:85) defines thin agency as "decisions and everyday actions that are carried out within highly restrictive contexts, characterised by few viable alternatives." Scholars such as Tisdall and Punch (2012) also define thin agency as characterised by limited survival options or opportunities for children. The concept seems to be applied to the situations of the street children of the Harare Central Business District. The streets of the Harare Central Business District are characterised by limited survival opportunities for street children. This is largely because of the multiple constraints that are characteristic of street life among children on the streets of Harare Central Business District. Therefore, when the street children of the Harare Central Business District engage in abuse of substances and various sexual behaviours that can be viewed within the thin agency (Chikoko 2017). This is because through such behaviours the street children of the Harare Central Business District were able to eke a living in an environment characterised by very limited survival options. Through trading or selling sex, the street girls of the Harare Central Business District were able to raise money for food, clothing among others, thus thin agency.

In addition, utilising the thin agency concept, the street children of the Harare Central Business District were able to navigate their daily experiences in a highly restrictive context through multiple sexual partnerships and abuse of substances (Chikoko et al 2019). The street children were also raising or getting financial resources through engaging in multiple sexual relationships (Chikoko et al 2019). In a way, the abuse of substances also facilitated the street children of the Harare Central Business District to sustain some of the multiple sexual relationships. On the other hand, the street children of Harare Central Business District also became addicted to some of the psychoactive substances as a result of traumatic related challenges associated with multiple sexual relationships (Chikoko et al 2019).

Weaknesses of the Child Agency Theory

Scholars such as Archer (1982), Turner (1991) have argued that the agency theory has a number of weaknesses. Craib (1992) observed that, the agency theory "is a series of definitions," and probably the line of arguments in these concepts is unclear. Scholars such as Tisdall and Punch (2012) and Vanderbeck (2008) argue that applying the child agency is associated with several debates from theoretical ideas in practice. The situation is compounded when there are social realities that are characterised by complex and contradictory contexts. To a certain extent, the child agency theory triggers a lot of theoretical debates to understand the sexual behaviours and abuse of substances of the Harare Central Business District, Zimbabwe. Ritzer (1992) criticises the agency theory as it seems not to have any end result, and is regarded as an endless cycle of agency and structure without any direction. Therefore, in such vagueness it then becomes problematic to apply or give a better explanation on the issues of sexual behaviours and substance abuse among the street children of the Harare Central Business District, Zimbabwe.

One of the weaknesses of agency theory is that it over emphasizes the capacity of individual actors in terms of influencing social structures (Ritzer 1992). For example, one wonders to what extent the street children that are abusing substances and engaging in various sexual behaviours could influence changes in the social structure of the streets of the Harare Central Business District, which is characterized by socio-economic and political issues. Kovats-Bernat (2006:7) observes that:

> the danger in emphasising the agency of street children lies in the erroneous
> assumption that they are not simultaneously victims of larger political and

economic machinations that severely impact their lives, complicate their survival and place them at higher risk of dying younger and more violently than other children.

In relation to the context of substance abuse among street children, these children end up engaged in abuse of substances so as to cope with the constraining environments. For example, as a result of using some of the traditional medicine in unsafe abortion, one of the street girls of Harare Central Business District ended up dead. Ursin (2013:35) argues that, "by emphasising agency on behalf of the surrounding context of extreme structural constraints, the researchers run a risk of unwittingly substituting vulnerability by responsibility." Despite the street children demonstrating their agency in various sexual behaviours and abusing substances, the researchers can argue that people should not forget that these children remain very vulnerable to abuse and exploitation, among other risks. As much as structure agency theorists argue that these children are demonstrating agency by abusing substances and engaging in sexual behaviours, some scholars from a child rights perspective view such behaviours as huge child rights violations.

Holt (2011:3) observes that the children's agency "is paradoxically integral to the marginalisation within contemporary societies of children and young people (and others such as disabled people) who cannot achieve this ideal of independence and autonomy." There are groups of people such as the disabled, who cannot independently work on their own (Chikoko 2017). Therefore, to consider agency among such a group of people would become problematic. For example, there are street children of the Harare Central Business District, Zimbabwe within such situations, who abuse substances and engage in various sexual behaviours. Such children are viewed as having multiple vulnerabilities.

Further, Ansell (2009) has noted that as much as the children's agency created a lot of interest among many stakeholders, including those in academia, the circumstances around the children's agency are perceived as negative, problematic or challenging. As much as the agency theory tries to explain human agency among street children, it has a number of flaws or limitations. In relation to street children of the Harare Central Business District, when street children engage in abuse of substance and sexual behaviours the social actions are perceived in a very negative way. In other words, the sexual behaviours and abuse of substances by the street children of the Harare Central Business District are seen as problematic to Zimbabwean society. They are viewed as problematic because of the negative perceptions of the Zimbabwean society on such sexuality related behaviours and abuse of substances among minors.

A further weakness of the agency theory is that it overshadows issues of culture, as noted by Ritzer (1992). The child agency theory does not consider socio-cultural issues. The socio-cultural issues are very important in any given society. For example, abusing substances like aphrodisiac and engaging in commercial sex work could illustrate human agency of these children (Chikoko 2014, 2017). Such kind of behaviour might be regarded as immoral within the context of African moral philosophies like *Ubuntu* and or *hunhu* (Mangena 2007 & 2012). The upholding of moral values is one of the cardinals of the Zimbabwean and other African societies countries. The *Ubuntu* or *hunhu* philosophy provides a moral compass for African society. It therefore becomes problematic and challenging for the street children of the Harare Central Business District to engage in sexual behaviours and abuse of substance. The social behaviours could be seen as an abomination in the Zimbabwe society.

However, when the street children of the Harare Central Business District engage in the various sexual behaviours and abuse of substances, who is to be blamed? It is the society that is blamed for producing such citizens with socially unacceptable behaviours (Chikoko & Ruparanganda 2020). It is every one's responsibility to ensure that the children including those in street situations are moulded in morally upright behaviours and citizens. Generally, the street children are not born on the streets of the Harare Central Business District (Ruparanganda 2008). To a certain extent, the street sub culture dictates that street children of the Harare Central Business District engage in various sexual behaviours and abuse of substances for them to survive. However, the street sub culture of the streets of the Harare Central Business District should be a mirror of the big picture of Zimbabwean society. Following the preceding discussion, the recommendations can be considered:

- There is need to align national, regional and international child rights legislations to reduce gaps that are exploited by potential perpetrators of child abuse and neglect.
- Key stakeholders such as the Government of Zimbabwe, civil society organisations and non-governmental organisations should urgently attend to the needs and rights of street children of the Harare Central Business District to reduce incidences of risks associated with sexual behaviours and abuse of substances.
- There is need to implement social protection programmes to arrests childhood poverty issues among the street children of the Harare Central Business District.
- Street children should be availed with more information on substance abuse and sexual behaviours such that they can make informed decisions or choices.

Conclusion

The attempt to understand the relevance of the child agency theory in terms of explaining sexual behaviours and substance abuse among the street children of the Harare Central Business District remain crucial. Several concepts within the child agency theory are useful in analysing the sexual behaviours and abuse of substances. These include self-destructive agency, thin agency and the ambiguity of agency, among others. In general, the child agency theory has a number of strengths when applied to understand substance abuse and sexual behaviours of the street children of the Harare Central Business District, Zimbabwe. However, the child agency theory has some weaknesses in terms of explanation of sexual behaviours and abuse of substance of street children of the Harare Central Business District, Zimbabwe. Some of them include the vagueness of agency, placing a lot of agency at the expense of structural issues, agency perceived as negative, problematic and challenging among others.

References

ANSEL, N., (2009) Childhood and the Politics of Scale: Descaling Children's Geographies? *Progress in Human Geography* 33(2), 190-209.

BORDONARO, L., (2011) From Home to the Street: Children's Street Ward Migration in Cape Verde. In S. J. Evers., C. Notermans. and E. Van Ommering. (eds.). *Not Just a Victim: The Child as Catalyst and Witness of Contemporary Africa.* Boston, Brill.

BORDONARO, L., (2012) Agency Does Not Mean Freedom: Cape Verdean Street Children and the Politics of Children's Agency. *Children's Geographies,* 10(4), 413-426.

BORDONARO, L. and PAYNE. R. (2012) Ambiguous Agency: Critical Perspectives on Social Intervention with Children and Youth in Africa. *Children's Geographies* 10(4), 365- 372.

CHANDAENGERWA, E. K., (2014) *Growing Up in the Era of AIDS: Childhood Experiences in Rural Zimbabwe.* Pretoria, University of Pretoria.

CHENEY, K. E., (2010) Expanding Vulnerability, Dwindling Resources: Implications for Orphaned Futures in Uganda. *Childhood in Africa,* 2(1), 8-15.

CHENEY, K. E., (2010) Deconstructing childhood vulnerability: An Introduction *Childhood in Africa* 2(1), 4-7.

CHENEY, K. E., (2012) Killing Them Softly? Using Children's Rights to Empower Africa's Orphans and Vulnerable Children. *International Social Work,* 56(1), 92-102.

CHENEY, K. E., (2014) *Conflicting Protectionist and Participation Models of Children's Rights.* In A. I. Twum-Danso. and N. Ansell. (eds.). *Children's Lives in An Era of Children's Rights: The Progress of the Convention on the Rights of the Child In Africa.* New York, Routledge.

CHIKOKO, W., (2014) Commercial 'Sex Work' and Substance Abuse among Adolescent Street Children of Harare Central Business District. *Journal of Social Development in Africa,* 29 (2).

CHIKOKO, W., (2017) *Substance abuse among the street children: A case of Harare Central Business District, Zimbabwe.* Harare, University of Zimbabwe.

CHIKOKO, W. et al., (2016) Nongovernmental Organisations' Response to Substance Abuse and Sexual Behaviours of Adolescent Street Children of the Harare Central Business District. *African Journal of Social Work,* 6(2).

CHIKOKO, W. et al., (2018) Forced Sex or Rape and Substance Abuse among Street Children of the Harare Central Business District. *International Open and Distance Learning Journal,* 3(2).

CHIKOKO, W. et al., (2019) Early Sexual Debut and Substance Abuse among Street Children of Harare Central Business District, Zimbabwe. *African Journal of Social Work,* 9(1), 79-87.

CHIKOKO, W. and RUPARANGANDA, W., (2020) *Ubuntu* or *Hunhu* perspective in understanding substance abuse and sexual behaviours of street children of Harare Central Business District in the *African Journal of Social Work/Special Issue,* (10)1.

CHUTA, N., (2014) *Children's Agency in Responding to Shocks and Adverse Events in Ethiopia.* [Online]. Available from: https://ora.ox.ac.uk/objects/uuid:ff5911b4-3562-45e6-898c-c6fb48dee65a

EMBLETON, L, et al., (2012) Knowledge, Attitudes, Substance Use Practices among Street Children in Western Kenya. *Substance Use and Misuse,* 47, 1234-124.

EVERS. S. T, et al., (2011) *Ethnographies of Children in Africa: Moving Beyond Stereotypical Representations and Paradigms* in Not Just a Victim: The Child as Catalyst and Witness of Contemporary Africa. Leiden, Brill.

GIGENGACK, R., (1994) Social Practices of Juvenile and Mortality: Child care Arrangements in Mexico City. *Community Development Journal,* 29(4), 380-393.

GIGENGACK, R., (1999) The Buca Boys from Metro Juarez, Leadership, Gender and Age in Mexico City's Youthful Street Culture. *Kids and Culture,* 12(2), 101-124.

GIGENGACK, R., (2000) La Banda De Gari-The Street Community as a Bundle of Contradictions and Paradoxes. *Focaal,* 36, 117-142.

GIGENGACK, R., (2006) *Young, Damned and Banda: The World of Young Street People in Mexican City 1990-1997.* Amsterdam, University of Amsterdam.

GIGENGACK, R., (2008) How Street Children Studies Can Address Self-Destructive Agency. *Focaal,* 36, 7-14.

GIGENGACK, R., (2013) *The Chemo and the Mona, Inhalants, devotion and street youth in Mexico City.* [Online]. Available from: https://www.sciencedirect.com/science/article/pii/S0955395913001254

GOVERNMENT OF ZIMBABWE, (2001) *The Children's Act (5:06).* Harare, *Government* Printers.

GOVERNMENT OF ZIMBABWE, (2006) *The Criminal Law (Codification and Reform) Act (9:23).* Harare, Government Printers.

HARTAS, D., (2008) *The Right to Childhoods: Critical Perspectives on Rights, Difference and Knowledge in a Transient World.* London: Continuum.

HOLT, L., (2004) The 'Voices' of Children: De-Centring Empowering Research Relations. *Children's Geographies,* 2(1), 13-27.

HOLT, L., (2011) Introduction: Geographies of Children, Youth and Families, Disentangling the Socio-Spatial Contexts of Young People Across the Globalising World. In L. Holt. (Ed.). *Geographies of Children, Youth and Families: An International Perspective.* London, Routledge, pp.1-8

KLOCKER, N., (2007) An Example Of Thin Agency: Child Domestic Workers in Tanzania. In R. Panelli., S. Punch. and E. Robson. (Eds.). *Global Perspectives on Rural Childhood and Youth: Young Rural Lives.* London, Routledge, pp.81-148.

MAHATI, S. T., (2015) *The Representations of Childhood and Vulnerability: Independent Child Migrants in Humanitarian Work.* Johannesburg, University of the Witwatersrand.

MANGENA. F., (2007) *Natural Law Ethics, Hunhuism and the Concept of Redistributive Justice among the Korekore-Nyombwe People of Northern Zimbabwe: An Ethical Investigation.* Harare, University of Zimbabwe.

MANGENA. F., (2012) *On Ubuntu and Redistributive Punishment in Korekore-Nyombwe Culture: Emerging Ethical Perspectives.* Harare, Best Practices Books.

MHIZHA, S., (2010) *The Self-Image of Adolescent Street Children in Harare.* Harare, University of Zimbabwe.

MTONGA, J., (2011) *On and Off the Streets: Children Moving Between Institutional Care and Survival on the Streets.* Trondheim, Norwegian University of Science and Technology.

MUGUMBATE, J. and CHERENI, A., (2019) Using African Ubuntu theory in Social Work with Children in Zimbabwe. *African Journal of Social Work,* 9(1), 27-34.

MUSHUNJE, M. T., (2006) Child Protection in Zimbabwe: Yesterday, Today and Tomorrow. *Journal of Social Development in Africa,* 21(1), 12-34.

NGULUBE, L., (2009) *A Study of the Sexual and Reproductive Health Challenges Faced by Adolescents Participating in the Streets Ahead Programs in Harare.* Harare, University of Zimbabwe.

NORMAN, A., (2014) *Children's Rights in the time of AIDS in KwaZulu-Natal, South Africa.* In A. I. Twum-Danso. and N. Ansell. (eds.). *Children's Lives in an Era of Children's Rights: The Progress of the Convention on the Rights of the Child in Africa.* New York, Routledge.

OKOLI, R. C., (2009) *Children's Work: Experiences of Street Vending Children and Young People in Enugu, Nigeria.* Edinburg, University of Edinburg.

PAYNE, R., (2012) Agents of Support: Intra-Generational Relationships and the Role of Agency in the Support Network if Child headed Households in Zambia. *Children's Geographies,* 10(3), 293-306.

RUREVO, R. and BOURDILLON, M. F. C., (2003a) Girls: The Less Visible Street Children of Zimbabwe. *Children, Youth and Environment,* 13(1), 1-20.

_____ (2003b) *Girls on the Street.* Harare, Weaver Press.

RUPARANGANDA, W., (2008) *The Sexual Behaviour Patterns of Street Youth of Harare, Zimbabwe, in the Era of the HIV and AIDS Pandemic.* Harare, University of Zimbabwe.

TISDALL, E. K. M and PUNCH, S., (2012) Not so 'new'? Looking Critically at Childhood Studies. *Children's Geographies* 10(3), 249-264.

URSIN, M. (2011) 'Wherever I Lay my Head is Home'- Young People's Experience of Home in the Brazilian Street Environment. *Children's Geographies* 9(2), 221-234.

URSIN, M. (2013) *'The Place Where I Buried My Bellybutton'- A Longitudinal Study of Transitions and belonging Among Young Men on the Street in Salvador, Brazil.* Nordland, University of Nordland.

UNITED NATIONS, (1989) *The United Nations Convention on the Rights of a Child.* Geneva, United Nations.

VANDERBECK, R., (2008) Reaching Critical Mass? Theory, Politics and the Culture of Debate in Children's Geographies. *Area* 40(3), 393-400.

WAKATAMA, M., (2007) *The Situation of Street Children in Zimbabwe: A Violation of the United Nations Convention on the Rights of the Child (1989).* Leicester, University of Leicester.

WATSON, D., CHENEY, K. and RAOU, E. H. (2015) Children and Young People in Times of Conflict and Change: Child Rights in the Middle East and North Africa. *Global Studies of Childhood,* 5(2), 115-121.

The Confluence of Child Rights, Duties and Parentage: The Case of Southern Africa

Isaac Mutelo and Oswald Mgaya

Introduction

An English jurist and politician, Sir William Blackstone (1723-1780), recognized maintenance, protection and education as the three primary parental duties to children. Over a century later in 1924, the League of Nations adopted the Geneva Declaration of the Rights of the Child which outlined the primary rights of a child, including the right to healthcare, shelter, protection against exploitation and the right to receive the requirements for normal human development. Since then, several other documents have unambiguously stipulated the rights of children, including the rights to healthcare, clean water, healthy food, education, family life, recreation and play, protection from abuse and freedom from any form of discrimination. While there is much discussion on the need to promote and protect the rights of children, there seems to be less attention on the implication this has on parenting and the duties and responsibilities of children themselves. Greater attention is paid to cases of the violation of children's rights than on parenting and helping children to effectively carry out their responsibilities.

Adult caregivers, especially parents, guardians, social workers, teachers and others have the responsibility of helping children to be responsible and accountable based on their level of human development and reasoning capabilities. Given that children's rights are intertwined with reciprocal duties and responsibilities (Liefaard & Jaap 2005:262), this chapter begins by discussing notions such as 'child' and 'children's rights' in the context of parenting. The chapter then discusses some of the core duties and responsibilities of children from the perspective of both parenting and rights. The chapter demonstrates that the discourse on children's rights cannot be divorced from the conversation on parenting and the rights and responsibilities of children to their parents, guardians and/or caregivers, their own growth and development and society in general.

Understanding the Child in the Context of Parenting

A child is a young person especially between infancy and puberty. The United Nations Convention on the Rights of the Child (UNCRC) defines a child as anyone under the age of eighteen. This is in line with Section 28 (3) of the South African Constitution which states that the word child refer to a person under the age of 18 years. In countries such as South Africa, Zimbabwe and Zambia, such an age period includes kindergarten (or nursery), primary and secondary schooling, a very sensitive and important period in human development, and crucial for installing authentic human values and knowledge in a growing human person. Based on Erik Erickson's (German-American psychoanalyst) psychological stages, between conception and one year the infant requires basic needs such as nourishment and affection, while between 1 and 3 years of early childhood the child develops a sense of independence. Through the help of parents, guardians, caregivers and others, between the age of 3 and 6 years, the child develops self-confidence when competent through daily tasks whereas between the adolescent ages of 12 to 18 develop a solid sense of identity and experiment through different roles, talks and daily interactions. These stages of development from infancy to adolescence are crucial since they indicate key aspects of personality development which are crucial and during each stage, the person experiences a psychosocial crisis that could positively or negatively affect personality development" (Mcleod 2023).

As the child grows and matures, the first human interactions and contacts which includes family members, caregivers, teachers and acquaintances have an important contribution to his or her overall growth and development. This includes self-understanding, socialization skills and the acquisition of knowledge and the relevant skills. As Forward puts it, "our parents plant mental and emotional seeds in us— seeds that grow as we do. In some families, these are seeds of love, respect, and independence" (Forward 1989:17). Integral human development especially at early stages becomes important as the child is influenced by various aspects including social media which shapes their overall social, intellectual and physical development. However, parents, guardians and other important early contacts of children sometimes contribute negatively to their growth and development directly or indirectly. The bad habits of parents, guardians and caregivers such as moral indecency, negative self-talk, managing stress incorrectly and smoking and drinking alcohol excessively affects the growth and development of children, especially mental and physical health. Forward notes that:

"No parent can be emotionally available all the time. It's perfectly normal for parents to yell at their children once in a while. All parents occasionally become too controlling. And most parents spank their children, even if rarely. Do these lapses make them cruel or unsuitable parents? Of course not. Parents are only human and have plenty of problems of their own. What better word than toxic to describe parents who inflict ongoing trauma, abuse, and denigration on their children, and in most cases continue to do so even after their children are grown?" (Forward 1989:18).

There are four main types of parenting styles, namely, authoritative, authoritarian, permissive and uninvolved (Sanvictores and Mendez 2022; Morin 2022). Because children require accompaniment and close monitoring, parents and caregivers ought to spend quality time with their children and learners. Uninvolved parents, guardians and caregivers tend to have little knowledge of what their children generally do. They set minimal irrelevant rules in the household. As a result, children may not receive much guidance, nurturing and parental attention. Uninvolved parents expect children to raise themselves. They do not often devote much time or energy into meeting children's basic needs. A parent with mental health issues or substance abuse problems, for example, may not be able to care for a child's physical or emotional needs on a consistent basis (Mower 1997:3). In some cases, uninvolved parents lack knowledge about child development or they may believe that their child will do better without their oversight. In other cases, they are simply overwhelmed with other problems, like work, paying bills, and managing a company. Children with uninvolved parents are likely to struggle with several issues including low self-esteem and poor academic performance. By contrast, authoritarian parentage which places an emphasis on strict and imposing dictates, rules and principles usually emanates from parents without consideration of the feelings and opinions of the child at stake (Xinwen et al 2018). Such parents are good at giving punishment and overlooking the role of the child in his or her own process of growth and development. They expect only compliance from their children. Children who grow up under strict authoritarian parents, guardians and caregivers tend to develop self-esteem problems, depression and other problems. They may also become hostile or aggressive in accord with parental expectations.

Permissive parents are lenient and often step in when there is a serious problem (Morin 2022). They are quite forgiving and adopt an attitude of 'kids will be kids.' When they apply consequences, they may not make those consequences minimal. They might give privileges back if a child begs or they may allow a child to get out of time-out early if they promise to be good. Permissive parents usually take on more of a friend role than a parent role. They often encourage their children to talk with them about their problems, but they usually don't put much effort into discouraging poor choices or bad behavior (Xinwen et al 2018). Children who grow up with permissive parents are more likely to develop holistically although they might struggle in some cases. For example, they may not appreciate authority and rules. Authoritarian parenting is often linked to authoritative parenting. Although this style of parenting might send rules and the related consequences, it also takes children's opinions into account. Authoritative parents often validate their children's feelings, while also making it clear that the adults are ultimately in charge. Authoritative parents invest time and energy into preventing behavior problems. They also use positive discipline strategies to reinforce positive behavior through praise or rewards. Children with authoritative parents are most likely to become responsible adults who feel comfortable self-advocating and expressing their opinions and feelings (Sanvictores and Mendez 2022). Children raised with authoritative discipline tend to be disciplined, mature and successful. They are also more likely to be good at making sound decisions and evaluating safety risks.

Apart from relying on their parents, guardians, caregivers and teachers, children today also rely on technology for learning, research, interacting with people in social situations, imagination, and innovation. Technology can also contribute negatively to the growth and development of children, especially from the perspective of explicit content, health, poor sleep quality, diminished attention span and poor social skills. The child is a particularly vulnerable member of society and, therefore, requires and deserves special protection and monitoring (Mower 1997:3). This is because of the many child abuse cases reported in Southern Africa render children vulnerable.

In May 2022, the Zambia Police "recorded 540 cases of child defilement from 6,915 cases of Gender Based Violence reported countrywide in the first quarter of 2022" (Lusaka Times 2022). In January 2023, two people were arrested in the Western Cape province of South Africa for allegedly abusing children. In the first case, a woman from George in the Western Cape was arrested for allegedly physically abusing a 2 year old child left under her care by a relative. The child was later taken to a local hospital for treatment due to sustained facial injuries and bruises. In a related case, a man was arrested for abusing and assaulting a one year old child with the "intent to commit grievous bodily harm" (McCain 2013). The arrest was made after a video of the incident was shared on various social media platforms.

The cited cases are mere examples of several reported cases of child abuse in countries such as South Africa and Zambia. The cases show the need for the safety and protection of children. Article 3 of the Convention on the Rights of the Child asserts that "In all actions concerning children, whether undertaken by public or private social welfare institutions, courts of law, administrative authorities or legislative bodies, the best interests of the child shall be a primary consideration" (Mower 1997:5). This indicates that the rights and dignity of the child should be considered as a priority by everyone. This requires that parents discern carefully the parenting styles that befit the current situation and context of children, and in some cases, going beyond authoritative, authoritarian, permissive and uninvolved parenting styles. Forward places a responsibility on parenting styles as he states:

> Many of the time-honored techniques of parenting that have been passed down from generation to generation are, quite simply, bad advice masquerading as wisdom (remember 'spare the rod and spoil the child'?). It is important to remember that all toxic parents, regardless of the nature of their abuse, basically leave the same scars (1989:22).

The development of science and technology has influenced the formation of parenting styles in Southern Africa and beyond. In a context where some children are more knowledgeable and informed about modern technology than their parents, the question becomes the extent to which such less knowledgeable parents can satisfy the needs and curiosity of their children. There is a need to equip parents with suitable and modern parenting styles to ensure better children in the modern world. This includes learning about what children do on their devices, the willingness to be taught by children about their digital lives, discerning what is important about technology and tailoring the media plan to the family. As parents, guardians and caregivers educate themselves about social media and how children use it, they will be able to educate their children about the associated common risks and how to ethically and responsibly navigate technologies (Gehan & Gawhara 2016:176). This stresses the importance of digital parenting whereby parents, guardians and caregivers support, supervise and regulate the online activities and digital environments of children.

Rights of Children

By the late nineteenth century, the standards of the safety and protection of children were not clearly outlined in most contexts, including industrialized countries. As a result, children worked alongside adults under unsafe and unhealthy conditions. Today, countries in Southern Africa are signatories to several international human rights instruments such as the United Nations Convention on the Rights of the Child (UNCRC) which recognize and protect the rights of children. National legal instruments such as South Africa's Children's Act of 2005, Zambia's Children's Code Act of 2022, Namibia's Child Care and Protection Act 3 of 2015 and Botswana's Children's Act of 2009 (No. 8 of 2009) provides a comprehensive legal framework for the promotion and protection of child rights. Moreover, most Constitutions today unambiguously recognize the rights of children. Section 28(1) of the South African Constitution states that children have the right:

> (a) to a name and a nationality from birth; (b) to family care or parental care, or to appropriate alternative care when removed from the family environment; (c) to basic nutrition, shelter, basic health care services and social services; (d) to be protected from maltreatment, neglect, abuse or degradation; (e) to be protected from exploitative labor practices; (f) not to be required or permitted to perform work or provide services that- (i) are inappropriate for a person of that child's age; or (ii) place at risk the child's well-being, education, physical or mental health or spiritual, moral or social development; (g)not to be detained except as a measure of last resort, in which case, in addition to the rights a child enjoys under sections 12 and 35, the child may be detained only for the, shortest appropriate period of time, and has the right to be - (i) kept separately from detained persons over the age of 18 years; and (ii) treated in a manner, and kept in conditions, that take account of the child's age; (h) to have a legal practitioner assigned to the child by the state, and at state expense, in civil proceedings affecting the child, if substantial injustice would otherwise result; and (i) not to be used directly in armed conflict, and to be protected in times of armed conflict.

Children have basic inalienable rights—to be fed, clothed, sheltered, and protected. But along with these physical rights, they have the right to be nurtured emotionally, to have their feelings respected, and to be treated in ways that allow them to develop a sense of self-worth. Children also have the right to be guided by appropriate parental limits on their behavior, to have their mistakes corrected, and to be disciplined without being abused. Naturally, as children grow older, parents, guardians and caregivers nourish their maturity by giving them certain responsibilities and duties, but never at the expense of their childhood (Forward 1989:46). In most cases, children listen to their parents, watch their parents, and imitate their parents' behavior. Because they have little frame of reference outside the family and the digital space, the things they learn at home and through media about themselves and others sometimes become universal truths engraved deeply in their minds. Parental role models are central to a child's developing sense of identity—particularly as he or she develops gender identity. Despite dramatic changes in parental roles over the last two decades, the same duties apply to parents. Parents, guardians and caregivers provide for children's physical needs, protect children from all forms of physical harm, provide for children's needs for love, attention, and affection and provide children's moral and ethical guidance.

Without a parental role models at this critical state of emotional development, a child's personal identity is set adrift in a hostile sea of confusion, thus, "death, neglect, and abuse of children must finally be placed alongside slavery, racism, and apartheid on the shelf reserved for those things no longer acceptable to humankind" (Mower 1997:6). When a parent, caregiver or teacher, acknowledges and encourages a child's interest, it fosters feelings of self-esteem and self-worth. It reinforces that significant adult's respect and value their interests, which serves as the foundation for furthering the student's desire to learn, discover and explore. Such encouragement provides the unique and individual child with the confidence to go forth and be the person that he or she is with fortitude and self-assurance (Lerner 2005:xii).

The key issue remains how to positively nurture a child's unique qualities and distinctive characteristics at the same time as the child is integrated into an educational, social environment and digital, so that childhood can be a magical time for growth, wonder and holistic development (Lerner 2005:6). Parents, guardians and caregivers usually consider it their responsibility to raise strong, independent children with a definite sense of self. When they become overprotective, then this might limit the holistic growth and development of their children. Given the centrality of trust in parenting, children require adequate room to develop unique values, principles and goals. This is paramount in the development of the solid parenting skills and strategies needed to raise a well-balanced child. Children react well to approval, which in some cases requires parents to listen to their children so that they may understand them, and journey with them better. In some cases, children become vulnerable to the environment which often affects their children's cognitive, emotional, social, physical, and language development. As such, healthy emotional bonds between children and parents become important in the child's development.

Because children are influenced by several internal and external factors, some parents, guardian and caregivers become frustrated and confused, leading to cases of child abuse. Tedd reminds parents, guardians and caregivers: "You must not be embarrassed to be authorities for your children. You exercise authority as God's agent. You may not direct your children for your own agenda or convenience. You must direct your children on God's behalf for their good" (Tripp 2005:13). For Tedd, the purpose of parental authority in the life of children is not to control, but to empower them to be mature and responsible people. Children desperately need to understand not only the external 'what' they did wrong, but also the internal 'why' they did it (Tripp 2005:15). A change in behavior that does not stem from a change in heart is not helpful. The goal is to form children who have better knowledge of the self, the world and the underlying duties.

Duties and Responsibilities of Children

Children themselves are also responsible for knowing and defending their rights whenever they find that they are in danger of becoming victims. They must know their best interest with the help of other human beings. This means that the best interests of the child shall be the guiding principle of those responsible for his or her education and guidance. Children have a grave duty to protect their rights especially when they reach an age of discernment and once they have attained a certain level of freedom of choice, the majority of children reach such a stage at the age of seven and above (Humanium 2023). They also have the duty to respond positively to the instruction and moral principles given to them by their parents, guardians and caregivers. If parents have the duty to direct their children towards their wellbeing, then children ought to participate actively in their own growth and development. They have the duty to learn as they grow by being teachable, open to correction, and gain certain soft and hard skills and to be responsible. However, in some contexts the duties and responsibilities of children are not emphasized since the focus is usually on rights – that is, children should know their rights and report when their rights have been abused (Western Cape Government 2022).

The emphasis on the duties and responsibilities of children highlight the importance of respect, hardworking, health awareness, spiritual growth and accountability on the part of children. It ensures holistic upbringing and the integrity of the human family rhymes with the claim that "Humanity must give children the best of itself"? (Liefaard and Jaap 2015:247). This requires that children be conscious of the sense of duty thereby creating a responsible human community:

> Whenever a child is born, he or she automatically becomes a part of the universal family of human beings. But that child also needs to become a member of a specific family to receive nurture and care and grow up healthy and strong. This child needs to be a member of a family not just a spectator from the sidelines. A member is involved and contributes to the affairs of a community. A member of a community is responsible and committed to the welfare of society (Warren 2002:136).

Due to the multicultural and pluralistic dimensions which are part of most societies in Southern Africa, shared values such as integrity, common good, social responsibility, justice and dignity of human life should be promoted by all human beings and institutions. Parents, guardians, caregivers and teachers have the responsibility to inculcate core human values in children so that they grow in knowledge and worth of human values. Education towards a sense of responsibility must also be cultivated in children. The formation of true conscience in the growing child will assist in the building of responsible citizens in the future. Children have the right to an education that develops their personality and abilities and encourages them to respect other people, cultures, and the environment and have the responsibility to make the most of their education and encourage others to develop their abilities. Children have mutual responsibilities to each other, including the need to nurture others (Humanium 2023). While children have the right to be treated fairly, they have the responsibility to treat others fairly. While they are to be respected, children have the duty to respect others. Parents and teachers have the duty to guide their children and students to recognize such duties and their corresponding rights even as they enjoy rest, play and learn.

Investment in education and parenting support programs is also important (World Bank 2012). Prioritizing such programmes can help ensure access to quality education which promotes holistic growth and development. Moreover, providing resources and raising awareness about child rights and the responsibilities of parents and caregivers through campaigns, workshops and educational materials can help prevent different forms of child abuse. Raising awareness on parentage and child rights requires the collaboration of international and regional organizations, governments and civil society. Encouraging the participation and involvement of children in decision-making processes, policy discussions and community initiatives also empower them to be responsible citizens (United Nations 2016). Moreover, combating violence and different forms of abuse against children by strengthening law enforcement mechanisms, establishing child protection units and providing specialized training which can help law enforcement agents to efficiently handle child-related cases should be prioritized (African Child Policy Forum 2021).

Conclusion

The confluence of parentage, child rights and duties in Southern Africa presents a complex and challenging landscape. Several international, regional and national legal frameworks provide a solid foundation for promoting and protecting child rights. Most Constitutions highlight the rights of children, including health food and clean water, a clean and safe environment, good healthcare, good education, non-discrimination, protection from harm, freedom of thought and access to relevant information. Children are increasingly becoming aware of their rights and the relevant channels to follow when their rights have been violated. Nevertheless, cases of child abuse from the perspective of sexual, physical, psychological abuse and child neglect continue to be reported. In some cases, they include different forms of maltreatment of a violent or threatening nature for the child. While cases of child abuse and the discourse on rights are important issues, aspects such as parenting and the rights and duties of children should be considered. While being aware of the rights of children, parents, guardians and caregivers should also understand the duties and responsibilities of children and help them to develop self-awareness and a sense of responsibility. Through modern parenting styles, parents, guardians and caregivers have the responsibility to nature, protect, educate and provide developmental, moral and ethical support to their children. Based on a good understanding of the rights of children, parenting styles can support healthy child growth and development. By prioritizing education, different forms of support, and legal protections for children, countries in Southern Africa can create an environment in which children are nurtured and empowered.

References

AFRICAN CHILD POLICY FORUM, (2021) *Child Marriage in Southern Africa: Trends, Challenges, and Opportunities.* [Online]. Available from: https://www.africanchildforum.org/clr/pdfs/sr-reports/Child%20Marriage%20in%20Southern%20Africa.pdf

FORWARD, S., (1989) *Toxic Parents. Overcoming Their Hurtful Legacy and Reclaiming Your Life.* New York, Bantam Books Publishers.

HUMANIUM, (2023) *Criticisms of Children's Rights.* [Online]. Available from: https://www.humanium.org/en/criticisms-of-childrens-rights/#:~:text=Lastly%2C%20children's%20rights%20are%20sometimes,live%20in%20the%20same%20conditions.

KANOY, K., (2013) *Emotional Intelligence in Children: How to Raise Children Who are Caring, Resilient, and Emotionally Strong.* Adams Media.

LERNER, S., (2005) *Kids Who Think Outside the Box: Helping Your Unique Child Thrive in a Cookie-Cutter World.* New York, AMACOM Books.

LIEFAARD, T. and JAAP D., (2015) *Litigating the Rights of the Child.* New York: Springer Books.

LUSAKA TIMES, (2022). *Lusaka Province Records the Highest Number of Child Defilement Cases.* [Online]. Available from: https://www.lusakatimes.com/2022/05/18/lusaka-province-records-the-highest-number-of-child-defilement-cases/

MORIN, A., (2022) *The 4 Types of Parenting Styles and How Kids are Affected: Learn if Your Style is Authoritative, Authoritarian, Permissive, Or Uninvolved.* [Online]. Available from: https://www.verywellfamily.com/types-of-parenting-styles-1095045

MOWER, G., (1997) *The Convention on the Rights of the Child. International Law Support for Children.* Connecticut, Greenwood Press.

MCCAIN, N., (2013) *Two People Arrested in Separate Child Abuse Cases in the Western Cape.* [Online]. Available from: https://www.news24.com/news24/southafrica/news/two-people-arrested-in-separate-child-abuse-cases-in-the-western-cape-20230103

TRIPP, T., (2005) *Shepherding a Child's Heart.* Wapwallopen, Shepherd Press.

SOUTH AFRICAN GOVERNMENT (1996) *The Constitution of the Republic of South Africa, No. 108 of 1996.* [Online]. Available from: https://www.gov.za/sites/default/files/images/a108-96.pdf

UNITED NATIONS, (2016) *Guideline on the Meaningful Engagement of Children in the Context of Southern Africa.* [Online]. Available from https://www.unicef.org/zimbabwe/media/1781/file/2016%20UNICEF%20SADC%20Guidelines%20Children%20Participation%20(2).pdf

WARREN, R., (2002) *The Purpose-Driven Life: What on Earth Am I here for?* Grand Rapids, Zondervan.

WESTERN CAPE GOVERNMENT, (2022) *Children, Know your Rights and Responsibilities.* [Online]. Available from: https://www.westerncape.gov.za/general-publication/children-know-your-rights-and-responsibilities

WORLD BANK, (2012) *Early Childhood Development in South Africa: Investing in the Future.* [Online]. Available from http://documents1.worldbank.org/curated/en/824201468330552539/pdf/751040WP0ECD00N0Box374374B00PUBLIC0.pdf

XINWEN, B, et al., (2018) *Parenting Styles and Parent–Adolescent Relationships: The Mediating Roles of Behavioral Autonomy and Parental Authority.* [Online]. Available from: https://www.frontiersin.org/articles/10.3389/fpsyg.2018.02187/full

ZIVS, S., (1980) *Human Rights: Continuing the Discussion.* Delhi, Progress Publishers.

An Analysis of the Tenets of a Social Contract in Relation to the Blanket Disenfranchisement of Pretrial Detainees and Prisoners in Zimbabwe

Dorcas Tatenda Chitiyo

Introduction

A full expression of the social contract envisages that the right to vote is a fundamental political right to participate in one's governance processes. It is included in the principles of good governance which bind the state and constitute a component of a good electoral system as indicated by the founding values of the Constitution of Zimbabwe (section 3, 155). Although the Constitution of Zimbabwe (section 67(3a) provides for the right to vote for every eligible adult citizen, no special measures have been made by the government to accommodate the enjoyment of the political right by citizens in prison or on remand. This chapter examines whether prisoners and pre-trial detainees have the right to vote in light of the provisions of the Zimbabwean Constitution. The absence of provisions in the Electoral Act as the primary legislation from the Zimbabwe Electoral Commission (ZEC) as the key institution that could enfranchise pre-trial detainees and prisoners are analysed to establish if the limitation of the right to vote which is expressly guaranteed to every adult citizen in Zimbabwe is justifiable in an open democratic society.

The chapter also discuss the current position of disenfranchisement because of incarceration as considered in the case of *Musarurwa, Madzokere and Maengahama v The Minister of Justice Legal and Parliamentary Affairs and 2 Others* (2022). The analysis of the judgement is canvassed to scrutinise whether any justification exists for the current disenfranchisement in so far as the judgement did not dwell on the substantive content of the right to vote. The current legal position in Zimbabwe in the context of the electoral laws and policies that enfranchise pre-trial detainees and prisoners in other jurisdictions such as South Africa is also considered. The analysis of the electoral laws and institutions responsible for managing elections in Zimbabwe will be considered in the context of the Constitution of Zimbabwe and the underlying principles of a social contract. The electoral framework as envisaged in the Constitution provides for the principles that must be observed in the Zimbabwean electoral system to impose a minimum threshold of standards that the critical state institutions' conduct must be juxtaposed against the obligations bestowed upon them by the Constitution. Thus, the chapter also analyse whether the current structure of the electoral legislation, which disenfranchises adult Zimbabwean citizens who are pre-trial detainees and prisoners, can withstand constitutionalism scrutiny and the underlying democratic principles such as the rule of law and the core tenets of social contract theory.

Musarurwa, Madzokere and Maengahama v The Minister of Justice Legal and Parliamentary Affairs and Ors (2022) HH 751

Arguments by the Applicants and Respondents

The matter before the High Court of Zimbabwe was that the applicants beseeched the court to declare that the Zimbabwean law allows prisoners to be registered as voters and to vote in elections when so registered. The applicants also sought to have the court compel the respondents to facilitate their and other prisoners' registration as voters and the enjoyment by prisoners of that right to vote (Veritas 2022). The applicants argued that they were approaching the court to vindicate their right to vote in elections and referendums as enshrined in the Constitution of Zimbabwe under section 67(3)(a). They also indicated that they were all registered voters who had participated in previous elections held before their incarceration and wished to participate in future elections regardless of their status as prisoners. They contended that while the legislation adequately protects people who are not imprisoned from exercising their political rights or participating in election processes, it does not adequately protect those who are detained. Regarding what should happen to individuals who want to vote while incarcerated, there is currently no legislation. They further argued that the state is obliged by the Constitution to take all appropriate measures, including legislative steps to ensure that all eligible citizens are registered as voters and are granted the opportunity to cast their votes (Veritas 2022). The basis of their case for eligibility was that they were all Zimbabwean citizens over the age of 18 and that none of them was prohibited from voting under the current law's disqualification standards.

The applicants also argued that much as they appreciated that the electoral law permitted the imposition of reasonable restrictions such as residence requirements for purposes of ensuring that persons are registered on the most appropriate voters' roll, any such restrictions had to remain *intra vires* the Constitution. Their status as prisoners was thus not a reasonable basis upon which their right to vote could be denied. By parity of reasoning, an omission by the law to make provision for mechanisms for the facilitation of enjoyment of the right to vote by prisoners is not sufficient justification for excluding them from participating in electoral processes. It is, therefore, incumbent upon the respondents to ensure that there is facilitation for the applicants to register as voters and that mechanisms are put in place to enable them to vote whilst in custody (Veritas 2022).

In essence, the first respondent's argument was that:

a. All prisoners in Zimbabwe are eligible to vote. The first respondent held this view on the backdrop of a comparison of the provisions of Zimbabwe's former Constitution and the current Constitution. In the former Constitution, prisoners serving sentences of imprisonment of six months and above were specifically barred from voting. Those serving lesser sentences could vote. That distinction was scrapped from the current Constitution. The only hindrance in the country's electoral framework is that prisoners do not meet the residence requirements prescribed by law. It is the residence criteria which make the prisoners' registration as voters impossible.

b. The criteria are permitted by paragraph 1(2) of the Fourth Schedule to the Constitution which allows the Electoral Act to prescribe such requirements.

c. As such the applicants cannot seek to compel the respondents to do that which is not permitted by law (Veritas 2022).

Thus the impugned law is not *ultra vires* the Constitution. The applicants' only recourse would be to lobby the legislative arm to change the law. The second and third respondents all filed a notice of opposition based on the following key arguments:

a. In terms of s 23(2) of the Act, a person ceases to be resident in a particular constituency if, for a continuous period of twelve months, he/she has ceased to reside in that constituency.

b. Section 51(1) of the Act obliges ZEC to establish polling stations in each constituency adequate to take a poll of the voters registered in that constituency. The polling stations must, by law, be physically situated in the constituency concerned. In addition, it is a requirement that every such polling station be located in a place which is readily accessible to the public including people with disabilities.

c. Although s. 51(2) of the Act allows the establishment of a polling station outside the physical boundaries of the constituency to which it relates it equally provides that such a polling station cannot be for more than one constituency (Veritas 2022).

High Court's Decision

The Court acknowledged that the parties both took the position that Zimbabwean laws allow prisoners to vote because the Constitution of Zimbabwe (section 67) accords to every Zimbabwean over the age of 18 years without distinction, the right to be registered as a voter and once registered, to vote in any election or referendum according to the law (Veritas 2022). The Court further observed that the Constitution expressly disenfranchised certain specified categories persons vis:

i. persons detained in terms of a statute as mentally handicapped or; ii those declared by a court that they cannot handle their own affairs for the duration of such declaration or; iii those convicted of an offence under the electoral law with a concomitant declaration by the High Court that such convicted person is disqualified from registration as a voter or from voting for the duration of such declaration (Veritas 2022).

Thus the Court concurred that the removal from the current Constitution of those groups of inmates puts beyond doubt the interpretation that the Constitution does not bar prisoners from voting. However, despite the above acknowledgement by the High Court the matter was ultimately not decided on merit for, the court upheld the objection raised *in limine* stipulating that the application was moot. The first point of mootness alleged was that the applicants had been released from prison which extinguished their personal interest in the application. At the time when the application was made, the applicants had been serving custodial sentences after being convicted of the crime of murder. However, at the time of rendering the judgement, the Court noted that the applicants had since been released from prison. Their convictions and sentence had been quashed on appeal by the Supreme Court of Zimbabwe (Zimbabwe legal Information Institute 2021). The Court thus highlighted that "there is no debate that they have lost their personal stake in the application before the court…there is nowhere in the application that they indicate that they are suing in the public interest or on behalf of a class or group of persons in terms of s 85(1)" (Veritas 2022).

The second point of mootness was that the Constitutional Court of Zimbabwe in the case of *Gabriel Shumba and 2 Others v Minister of Justice Legal and Parliamentary Affairs and 5 Others* in 2018 had decided on the issue of the residence requirements to determine whether or not the Constitution of Zimbabwe directly or indirectly, allows for the diaspora vote. Based on the two grounds, the High Court refused to exercise its discretion to determine the moot application on the merits and the application was dismissed. Thus, although the matter was not dealt with on the merits there is still an argument to be raised that a pretrial detainee or convicted prisoner in Zimbabwe not covered by the list of expressly disenfranchised categories contained in the fourth schedule of the Constitution of Zimbabwe Act 2013 must be allowed to exercise his or her right to vote and as such the state must create the necessary conditions for this right to be enjoyed. In Zimbabwe, there is currently a blanket disenfranchisement of detained and convicted people with a custodial sentence in the sense that there is no distinction or limitation of disenfranchisement based on the nature of the offence such that even non-electoral offences result in one being disenfranchised. The disenfranchisement of those who commit election-related crimes used to be contained in the old Constitution of Zimbabwe (Lancaster House Constitution), the fact that it is not contained in the current Constitution should be taken as a symbol of progressive democracy meant to enfranchise all citizens eligible to vote.

The term blanket disenfranchisement is used to describe the predicament of both pre-trial detainees and all prisoners serving custodial sentences. For pre-trial detainees, their disenfranchisement materialises from the moment one is arrested and remanded in custody, one loses access to voter registration and when already registered on the voting day there are currently no provisions and mechanisms accommodating for such people to vote (Levine 2010:194). This is despite there being a constitutional right to be presumed innocent until proven guilty as stipulated under section 70 (1)(a) of the Zimbabwean Constitution. In respect of convicted prisoners, the moment one is serving a custodial sentence there are no express means for them to register to vote and to cast their votes even if the offence they were convicted for is not an electoral offence as well as even if they do not fall within the category of the expressly disenfranchised people in terms of the Constitution. Resultantly, when there is blanket disenfranchisement, detained and arrested people are barred from exercising their right to vote and the opportunity to select a candidate to represent them through the ballot (Levine 2010:194). A blanket disenfranchisement as conceptualised herein, therefore, prevents detained and convicted people serving custodial sentences from voicing their opinion on the policies and legislation to which they will be subjected to and the core of social contract tenets.

Social Contract Tenets: Consent of the Governed

According to the Black's Law Dictionary, a social contract constitutes an express or implied agreement between citizens and their government whereby individuals agree to surrender certain freedoms in exchange for mutual protection (Garner 2014 1603-1604). This underlying hypothetical agreement among the members of an organised society or between a community and its ruler, therefore, forms a foundation for a political society that has defined rights and limits the consequences and duties of each. A social contract can also be understood as a human agreement to concentrate power in the hands of a single individual or group with a leadership mandate to govern (Dedi, Hidayat, Parjaman & Maruoko 2023:1; Dario 2015:6). Social contracts can be understood at the level of implementation as agreements made by and among individuals to renounce their rights and submit to authorities chosen via the democratic process (Dedi et al 2023:6).

The concept of the consent of the governed expressed through social contract has been expressed by scholars such as Jean-Jacques Rousseau who argued that societal laws are held up by the collective will of the citizens whom they represent (Miscevic 2013: 509; Dunn 2002:163, Rousseau 1913). The citizen "remains free" as a result of observing the law and sacrifice by abandoning unfettered freedom for the sake of the political community (Miscevic 2013:512; Dunn 2002:9). The establishment's will is the collective will when it comes to elections based on the consent by the people to rule over themselves. Hence if there is no corruption, the democratic government is wholly legitimate as the authority is legitimately recognised (Miscevic 2013: 514; Dunn 2002:10). Early criticism of the conceptualisation of social contract as an expression of tacit manifestation of the consent of the governed emerged from scholars such as David Hume. The ideal basis for a government, according to Hume, is the consent of the governed, but in practice, this has not generally been the case (Umezurike 2018:992). Hume's scepticism points to obedience as thus not optional but a means to maximise society's total utility a governmental system is thus a necessary evil (Umezurike 2018:991; Hume 1752).

Ideally, people agree to give up part of their liberties and submit to authority (the ruler or the will of the majority) in return for the preservation of their remaining rights or the maintenance of the social order, either expressly or tacitly (Dario 2015:4-12; Umezurike 2018:990). Thomas Hobbes, John Locke, and Jean Jacques Rousseau, among other social contract theorists, envisioned a social contract in which individuals consent to be governed by and subject to the rules of society in exchange for the protections and advantages that an organised political system provides (Weale 2013:12). In the conception of social contract theorists it is important to establish whether the Zimbabwean electoral system expressly condones disenfranchisement of detained and imprisoned people. From the perspective of the social contract theory, it is important to determine whether by virtue of departing from the law-abiding structure and design, due to incarceration and/or conviction with a custodial sentence an individual relinquishes his or her membership in society and their right to choose the leaders and policies in the future.

The Right to Vote

The right to vote is the foundation of a democratic society essential to demonstrate active participation and citizen engagement in the political process of a given society (Levine 2010:193). Most forms of democratic governments are founded upon the right to vote hence without this right democracy cannot exist. The marking of a ballot has thus been referred to as the mark of distinction of citizens of a democracy (Douglas 2013:81). This is because the right expresses the premise that every citizen's vote is a badge of dignity and personhood, as voting is the cornerstone of our whole democratic system. The right to vote is therefore a crucial working part of democracy and each vote invigorates any country's democracy. Zimbabwe as a democracy is anchored on the founding principles spelt in its Constitution. Among the key founding values of the Constitution (section 3) is good governance which is underlined by universal adult suffrage and free, fair and regular elections. The Constitution of Zimbabwe thus lays a premise on which the right to vote exists and thrives.

The right to vote is a fundamental component of the state-binding standards of good governance, a component of a good electoral system as outlined by the founding values of the Constitution of Zimbabwe. As highlighted in *Minister of Home Affairs v National Institute for Crime Prevention (*2004) ZACC 10, by its very essence, the right to vote imposes positive duties on the legislature and the administration, necessitating efficient procedures for its exercise. In this case, the South African Constitutional Court dealt with a challenge to the denial of voting rights for citizens incarcerated in South African prisons. The burden of providing the legal framework, infrastructure and resources necessary for the holding of free and fair elections rests on the legislative arm and the executive (Constitution of Zimbabwe Act 2013, section 157).

The right to vote implies participation in the formal expression of choice for a candidate for office or a suggested solution to a problem (Jason 2020; Douglas 2013:83). Defining the right to vote as a human right is significant because it gives this entitlement a weight that can be relied upon to guarantee that it is respected (Beckman 2009:1-2). As a human right, voting should be viewed as more than the instrumental choice of selecting a candidate, it must be perceived as a way in which a citizen asserts their place in the community (Fishkin 2012:1890). Thus exercising the right to vote in its entirety is the foundation of equal citizenship as voting is connected to dignity, thereby demonstrating that human rights are interdependent and interdependent (Fishkin 2012:1890). In the South African Constitutional Court case of *Minister of Home Affairs v National Institute for Crime Prevention* ZACC (2004, paragraph 24-25) the Court emphasised that the ability to vote provides people with a significant instrument to confirm and express their opinions of civic responsibility and pride in their citizenship in this nation. The right to vote in Zimbabwe is supplanted by firm bedrock that subscribes to the principles of good governance such as universal adult suffrage which make up the founding values of the Constitution of Zimbabwe Act 2013 (section 3(2)).

Suffrage is the right or privilege to cast a vote in a political election of a state (Garner 2014:1661). Adult suffrage is a democratic constrain on voting to put an age limit on who can vote thus adult suffrage is concerned with the right of a person who has reached adult age to vote in all public elections (Kijia 2020:222; Larsen, Levinsen & Kjaer 2016:435). In the Zimbabwean context, the concept of universal adult suffrage is laid out in the Constitution which provides that "every Zimbabwean citizen who is of or over eighteen years of age has the right to vote in all elections and referendums" (Constitution of Zimbabwe Act 2013, section 67(3)(a)). Beckman (2009:1) argues that the distribution of political rights should not discriminate unfairly between individuals based on irrelevant distinctions. This is because unjustified restriction of the right to vote severely undermines the wide acceptance of the legitimacy of the victor in an election (Beckman 2009:8). An inclusive franchise thus encourages all elements of society including marginalised fractions such as prisoners to perceive a stake in the existing political order that emerges from the elections (Pablo 2015:85).

Meeting the stipulated age for universal suffrage can be construed to mean that there ought to be no burdensome impediments against any citizen's registering to vote or casting a ballot (Kijia 2020:226-228). This is reinforced by Pablo (2015:119) who echoes that, the problem of imposing should always be construed in favour of a principled form of the franchise, which has as its central tenets the concept of the right to vote as a human right and the claim of universal suffrage as its logical conclusion. On that basis, every human being should have the right to vote, and the government's role should be confined to enabling and safeguarding this right. Wilson (2019:5) claims that political equality fundamentally requires electoral and law-making institutions that are consistent with the equal political status of citizens.

Furthermore, when a government ensures that each citizen's authority over everyday experience is respected, it creates egalitarian connections between people since equal status necessitates respect for each citizen's authority over common life as they live in the society (Wilson 2019:7). Thus, in the context of adult suffrage, voting equality means that all votes are ordered equally and that no vote has a greater weight than any other. The equality of votes ensures that no vote should count more than another. This principle also ensures that the right to vote is made available to everyone. Conti (2019:1-5) has observed that it has become commonplace to treat the concern about the presence of a diverse populace in the legislatures and other state institutions as intrinsic as a commitment to democracy itself. Central to this need is the democratic concept of adequate representation of the electorate through Parliament mirroring its society. This buttresses the concept of representative democracy which must thrive as a manifestation of the will of the consent of the governed to be ruled by those they elect.

Disenfranchisement

Disenfranchisement is the act of depriving an exercise of the right to vote in public elections from a citizen (Garner 2014:567). This act builds on the underlying logic of the right to vote, principles of democracy and good governance that are closely linked to social contract tenets such as consent to being governed by and submit to the laws of society in return for the protections and benefits that an organised governmental structure provides. It is important to consider the disenfranchisement of pretrial detainees and prisoners in Zimbabwe from the lens of interrogating whether or not it can be justified from the underlying tenets of the social contract applicable in a democratic society that accords adult suffrage to every citizen.

Disenfranchisement of Convicted Prisoners

According to Pablo (2015:23), criminal disenfranchisement generally refers to the taking away of a person's ability to vote and other political rights while they are a target of the state's punitive power. In this broad sense voting rights for prisoners are subject to restrictions and/or conditions, whereas in some cases people convicted of an offence are automatically disenfranchised for the period of their prison term, or even after they have served their time of parole (Penal Reform 2016:1). Thus, disenfranchisement includes not only prisoners but also other subjects criminally prosecuted who remain outside the prison system, pretrial detainees and even ex-convicts that have served their sentences in respect of countries such as in some states of the United States of America (Chowdhury 2017:1).

According to a survey carried out by the Penal Reform International (2016:3), international offenders serving non-custodial criminal sentences in most countries are entitled to vote. However, in some jurisdictions such as Belgium, Ethiopia and Tunisia, disenfranchisement can be handed down by the court as an additional sentence, which could result in the restriction of voting rights of those serving a non-custodial sentence. In other jurisdictions such as Brazil and Kuwait, the law does not distinguish between those deprived of liberty and those serving non-custodial sanctions and disenfranchisement following a final court decision can therefore also affect those serving a non-custodial sentence (Penal Reform International 2016:5).

Criminal disenfranchisement has a long history that dates back to Ancient Greece, when felons were forbidden from voting, serving in the military, giving speeches, and participating in gatherings (Travis, Western & Reburn 2014:208; Manza & Uggen 2006:38-39). During the Middle Ages, criminal disenfranchisement was typical throughout Europe, criminals received the punishment of "civil death," which involved losing all citizenship privileges (Behan 2015:3; Miller & Spillane 2012: 403; Pettus 2005:30). Resultantly, criminals lost society's protection and were often sentenced to death which can be taken as the withdrawal of social contract privileges of being governed, regulated and protected by the law of that society. In certain cases, the government could seize a criminal's property, and anyone, including those who are not part of the government, could kill a criminal without punishment (Behan 2015: 3-7; Pettus 2005:30). One could argue that remnant traces of the drastic measures of the Middle Ages are the application of blanket disenfranchisement of all convicted people.

Levine (2009:193) observes that arguing for disenfranchisement of prisoners from the social contract perspective rests on the flawed premise that by virtue of having broken the law, convicted people lose their right to vote and the ability to participate in selecting a politician to represent them and are muted from most forcefully voicing their opinion of the policies and laws to which they will be subjected. In addition, Levine (2009:196) criticises this reasoning on the basis that it constitutes a denial of the democratic entitlement to elect leaders who govern and represent them as well as their entitlement to participate publicly in state affairs that affect their welfare.

It has been argued by various scholars (Hoskins 2013: 33-38; Lippke 2001:82) that although convicted offenders retain some of their basic moral rights, thus while others are severely limited by legal punishment, they retain their core of being beings. This argument is rooted in the inalienable dignity of every human being which is a right from which no lawful limitation is permissible under the Constitution of Zimbabwe (section 86(3)(b)). Justification for disenfranchisement based on the social contract, therefore, negates the very essence of democracy itself. This is because a convict might have disregard for a certain law in the land but certainly has respect for its democratic institutions and systems and thus cannot be deprived of political franchise. (Pablo 2015; Barn 2014). In the case of *August and Another v Electoral Commission and Others* 1999, the court remarked that:

> Prisoners are entitled to all their personal rights and personal dignity not temporarily taken away by law, or necessarily inconsistent with the circumstances in which they have been given personal rights and their liberties are very considerable. They no longer have freedom of movement and have no choice regarding the place of their imprisonment. Their contact with the outside world is limited and regulated…Nevertheless, there is a substantial residue of basic rights which they may not be denied; and if they are denied, then they are entitled to legal redress. Of course, the inroads which incarceration necessarily makes upon prisoners.

The idea that being convicted of a crime is a violation of the social contract tenets is an over-simplistic interpretation of the concept because the people in prison are still very much part of the nation and as such should not be subjected to a blanket disenfranchisement (Hoskins 2013:40; Lippke 2001:85). Moreover, it is a fundamental leap to assert that those who break a few rules should lose the protection of them all. As observed by the South African Constitutional Court in *August and Another v Electoral Commission and Others (CCT8/99) [1999] ZACC 3,* if at all the convicts ought to have some of their rights curtailed, an account is then required to show which rights it is legitimate to curtail keeping into account proportionality. In the leading case of *Sauvé v Canada Chief Electoral Officer 2002,* the Canadian Supreme Court held that prisoners have a right to vote it held that:

> The social [contract] requires the citizen to obey the laws created by the democratic process. But it does not follow that failure to do so nullifies the

citizen's continued membership in the self-governing polity. Indeed, the remedy of imprisonment for a term rather than permanent exile implies our acceptance of continued membership in the social order...

The restrictive application of the social contract theory that serves as justification for the political disenfranchisement of prisoners is arguably incompatible with the values that underpin democracy, including the above-mentioned universal and equitable representation. In addition, this militates against the grain of any human right whose characteristics include being inherent to every human and thus not a privilege (Barn 2014). Disenfranchisement supported by a very narrow interpretation of the social contract is inconsistent with international law instruments such as the International Covenant on Civil and Political Rights (1966, article 25), the Banjul Charter (1981, article 13(1)), as well as of the Constitution of Zimbabwe Act 2013 (section 67(3)) which proclaims the right to vote, is fundamental for every citizen of Zimbabwe eligible to vote. The Universal Declaration of Human Rights (UDHR) (1948, article 21.3) grants everyone the "right to take part in the government of this country, directly or through freely chosen representatives." The UDHR is considered customary international law, and in Zimbabwe customary international is part of Zimbabwean law unless it is inconsistent with the Constitution or an Act of Parliament (Constitution of Zimbabwe Act 2013, section 326(1)).

Disenfranchisement under the Retribution Theory

The retributivist school of thought on disenfranchisement contends that breaking the law has grave repercussions since citizenship implies obligations in addition to rights and advantages (Barn 2014). The idea of forfeiture behind the disenfranchisement defence is that committing a crime results in a citizen's loss of some rights and advantages which dates from a time when obtaining a sentence meant losing citizenship, which included all property rights. Barn (2014) observes that the theory also has roots in social contract theorists such as John Locke who posit that, by putting ourselves in a state of war with another, we forfeit our natural rights not to be enslaved or to be denied our rights. Barn (2014) further argues that the implications for democracy based on the theory of the retributivist argument leading to disenfranchisement are that it is undermined.

Behan (2015:5) acknowledges that from the lens of social contract theory, the stripping of any citizen of political rights is problematic. However, for those who break the social contract, there must be a sanction. According to a contemporary theorist on disenfranchisement, Ramsay (2013:11), the rationale for disenfranchisement is that inmates have renounced their democratic citizenship rights by implicitly denying citizenship via their crime. Disenfranchisement is a proportional punishment since it lasts as long as a person is incarcerated, presumably for a serious enough offence to merit incarceration. Proponents of disenfranchisement following the logic above thus contend that only law-abiding individuals should have the right to vote on who should become lawmakers since they are the only ones who would appreciate that privilege of the law and order of their given society (Behan 2015:6).

When evaluated through the prism of contemporary democratic norms, such as universal adult suffrage, the arguments above justifying disenfranchisement as a commensurate punishment for reneging on the laws of society are flawed arguments. Pablo (2015:220) argues that criminal disenfranchisement cannot be justified as a democratic punishment, fails to overcome the democratic measure and therefore cannot constitute a legitimate exception to the principle of universal suffrage. The retributive theory asserts its conclusion on the premise that prisoners should not get the vote because they have broken the law, and are therefore now prisoners, who do not get the vote (Barn 2014). Further, a belief in the democratic process means that those who are not willing to accept the outcome of that process – the passing of laws – debar themselves from the right to participate in it (Behan 2015:7). This, however, does not explain why their voting rights should be revoked as a result of their offence. For Pablo (2015:246), relying on law abidance as the definitive rule of distributing the right to vote subverts the idea underlying the universal franchise, transforming the principle of "all those subjected to the law" into the principle of "only those law-abiding". In addition, this logic was criticised by the Canadian Supreme Court which held in the case of *Sauvé v Canada Chief Electoral Officer* SC (2002) that:

> Denying citizen law-breakers the right to vote sends the message that those who commit serious breaches are no longer valued as members of the community, but instead are temporary outcasts from our system of rights and democracy. More profoundly, it sends the unacceptable message that democratic values are less important than punitive measures ostensibly designed to promote order. If modern democratic history has one lesson to teach it is this: enforced conformity to the law should not come at the cost of our core democratic values.

Critics of the disenfranchisement of prisoners also contend that doing so is only practical if the penalty is appropriate to the offence (Chowdhury 2017:12; Ewald & Rottinghaus 2009:60). It is further argued, disenfranchising criminals may be a proper punishment to those found guilty of political crimes, but it may be an excessive response to offences unrelated to politics given that voting is a component of the political process (Ewald & Rottinghaus 2009:56). Furthermore, taking away voting rights can make them feel isolated from society, creating a future problem when it is time to renter society as it may make it harder for those who were previously denied the right to vote to reintegrate into society after serving their sentences (Miller & Spillane 2012:402).

Disenfranchisement as a Result of Theories on Rehabilitation

To justify disenfranchisement, it has also been advanced as justification that it can enhance an individual's sense of civic duty thus it has some retributive characteristics (Pablo 2015). According to Manfredi (2009: 277), "the rights of liberal citizenship entail a responsibility to avoid conduct harmful to other citizens." Additionally, it promotes the use of punishment to shape character by supporting the moral norm-setting of criminal law. Thus, denying the right to vote to untrustworthy individuals will foster respect for the law and may dissuade some from engaging in illegal conduct. Proponents of disenfranchisement think it sends the most potent message, both actual and symbolic, to law-abiding and non-law-abiding individuals about the significance of respecting the rules imposed by the people's representatives (Behan 2015).

To counter this argument it has been asserted that disenfranchisement could actually work against this edifying aim. Barn (2014) argues that as people who have broken the law, prisoners are among those most in need of civic education, and it seems that denying their participation in the civil process is not the best way to foster that participation. Social exclusion is seen as a major cause of crime and recidivism hence a ban on prisoner voting could serve to further exclude those already on the margins of society (Pablo 2015; Barn 2014; *Sauvé v Canada Chief Electoral Officer* 2002). The Supreme Court of Canada in *Sauvé v Canada Chief Electoral Officer* 2002 Supreme Court aptly described the importance of enfranchisement as a contributory factor to promoting democracy, rehabilitation and easier assimilation back into society once a prisoner has served his or her term. The court held that:

> Denying penitentiary inmates the right to vote is more likely to send a message that undermines respect for the law and democracy than messages that enhance those values. The legitimacy of the law and the obligation to obey the law flow directly from every citizen's right to vote. To deny the inmates the right to vote is to deny them an important means of teaching them democratic values and social responsibility…denying inmates the right to vote… removes a route to social development and undermines correctional law and policy directed towards rehabilitation…

Disenfranchisement for Non-custodial Penalties

Given the discussion above social contract tenets focusing on representative democracy where the members consent to live under the rules of a society it is worth asking if being accused of an offence is enough to merit disenfranchisement. If the argument was to be sustained that convicted persons have to be punished for undermining the spirit of social contract this logic and disenfranchisement conceptualisation as justified by the various theories above does not hold in respect of who are not yet convicted of any offence and are merely remanded in custody during the election period, there is need to create facilities for them. In terms of the Constitution of Zimbabwe Act 2013 (section 70 (1)(a)) every accused person has the right to be presumed innocent until proven guilty. This right, therefore, accords to pretrial detainees protection from any due limitation of their human rights for which it can be argued the current blanket disenfranchisement of all people who are in the custody of places of detention, remand and imprisonment are currently subjected to in Zimbabwe. Pablo (2015:24) posits that pretrial detainees are in a different situation from those that are still formally enfranchised but are deprived of a mechanism to exercise the vote from prison. The broad concept of anticipating the implications of a prospective criminal conviction provides a better explanation for this variable, taking into account the applicability of criminal disenfranchisement to non-sentenced inmates and non-incarcerated prosecuted people (Pablo 2015:48).

Enfranchisement

Enfranchisement entails granting of voting rights to a person (Garner 2014:645). Criminal disenfranchisement laws are intricately linked to the judicial branch of any given democracy in many ways. The courts have made a substantial contribution in recent years to the discussion of whether the law should support the reconfiguration of disenfranchisement laws (Ewan & Rottingaus 2009:34). Therefore, courts have significantly influenced disenfranchisement legislation and related discourse via their rulings in significant instances involving criminal disenfranchisement (Chowdhury 2017:14). The case of *Hirst v. The United Kingdom* 2004 European Court of Human Rights set a democratically sound precedent for enfranchisement. John Hirst, a prisoner convicted of murder, challenged the state's decision to revoke his voting rights in the United Kingdom in 2004. He argued that a blanket ban on voting violated Protocol No. 1 in Article 3 of the Representation of the People Act (1983), which requires court approval or established legislation before depriving prisoners of their right to vote. The European Court of Human Rights ruled that a blanket ban on voting as practised at the time in the United Kingdom was in violation of the protocol mentioned in Article 3 of the Representation of the People Act (Horne & White, 2015: 9).

In *August and another v Electoral Commission and Others* 1999, the case brought by the court was challenging the denial of eligible citizens incarcerated in South African Prisons to vote which the applicants claimed was unconstitutional. The questions raised in the application challenged the very essence of the meaning of democracy which is selectively practised (de Vos, 2004:1-5). In recognising the right to vote for prisoners in South Africa the court held that:

> The vote of every citizen is a badge of dignity and personhood. Quite literally, it says that everybody counts. In a country of great disparities between wealth and power, it declares that whomever we are whether rich or poor, exalted or disgraced we all belong to the same democratic South African nation; that our destinies are intertwined in a single interactive polity…Rights may not be limited without justification and legislation dealing with the franchise must be interpreted in favour of enfranchisement rather than disenfranchisement.

The decision of the South African Constitutional Court also endorsed the legal principle, *ubi jus ibi remedium*. The Latin legal maxim means *'where there is a right there is a remedy'*. The basic principle contemplated in the maxim is that, when a person's right is violated, the victim will have an equitable remedy under the law (Curie and De Waal 2013:144). The maxim also states that the person whose right is being infringed has a right to enforce the infringed right through any action before a court. This means that the existence of a legal rule implies the existence of an authority with the power to grant a remedy if that rule is infringed (Curie and De Waal 2013:144). Following that vein of thought, it is contended that the lawmakers could never have contemplated a right without a remedy. Therefore, the South African road to restoring the right to vote to prisoners was through a judicial intervention prompted by the need to address a constitutional right infringement.

As courts have weighed in on whether the law favours the sustainability of a prisoner's right to vote the trend of enfranchising felons those remanded in custody is slowly gaining momentum (Ewald & Rottinghaus, 2009:7). The automatic blanket restriction on inmates exercising their right to vote has been struck down by the supreme courts of Canada, South Africa, and Europe (Ewald & Rottinghaus, 2009:35). Allowing prisoners to exercise the franchise is, therefore, a great symbol of restoring a path of civic engagement otherwise thwarted by criminology theories which believe blanket disenfranchisement of the incarcerated men is part of a criminal sanction.

Chowdhury (2017:15) however also observes that although superior courts of various countries have played a significant role in advancing the enfranchisement of prisoners it is also important to note that the actions of the judiciary cannot be understood without taking into account the political environment and context in each of these countries. In countries where the judiciary is insulated from the other institutions of government, the decisions of that court may differ greatly from the more vulnerable court. Therefore, the wholesome welfare of any given democracy promoting good governance practices such as separation of powers tends to lead to a thriving society where there is recognition of the equality of votes and promotion of universal adult suffrage. As the situation stands in Zimbabwe, the court's ruling in the case of *Musarurwa, Madzokere and Maengahama v The Minister of Justice Legal and Parliamentary Affairs and 2 Others* (2022, High Court) perpetuates blanket disenfranchisement. Selective application of democracy and repression of adult suffrage as is currently the case in Zimbabwe where citizens who are eligible to vote are not included in the process of exercising that enfranchisement undermines the hallmarks of democracy.

Conclusion

The right to vote is a political legal right provided for in numerous regional, international and domestic legal instruments which guarantee it, specify how it is to be exercised and provides for regulation of the enjoyment of the right. The right to vote is anchored by international principles of democracy and it should be reinforced that the right to vote is a fundamental human right that is recognized by major human rights international instruments which have been ratified by most democracies in the world. It is a basic human right that empowers citizens to influence the governance of their nations and safeguard the protection of their other rights. Despite consensus on the importance of the right to vote, its inclusion in many international human rights treaties and its significance in protecting other important human derogations of voting rights remain widespread through practices such as blanket disenfranchisement. As a member of society, one is not severed from the protections expected from being a member of society that promote the tenets of a social contract. Enfranchisement for all is critical because the right to vote enables one to influence government policies by according to one the opportunity to participate in selecting those who occupy public office. Prisoners and pre-trial detainees have rights however some rights such as liberty may be limited during the period one is imprisoned or held in custody during the course of the trial this does not however justify the disproportionate stripping away of all rights bestowed on any human being who is a member of a given society. As discussed in the paper there are also various theories which justify the enfranchisement of prisoners and pre-trial detainees.

Given the importance of the right to vote highlighted throughout the paper, the current blanket disenfranchisement of pretrial detainees and prisoners amounts to detrimental harm especially if the exclusion is not justifiable in a democratic society as required by the Constitution. A derogation of the right of a citizen should only be accepted under circumstances where the law permits such derogation and also the limitation should be fair and reasonable. The idea that voting is not just a right but also a civic obligation to society that one should perform to also reassert their involvement as a member of that society is what underpins the shift in the dominant beliefs supporting disenfranchisement. It is also clear that the extent to which detained citizens can exercise their right to vote differs substantially from nation to nation. The incarcerated people and pre-trial detainees in Zimbabwe prisons who are eligible to vote ought to be considered as voters and mechanisms must be put in place for them to access and exercise their right to vote.

References

BARN, G., (2014) *Prisoner Disenfranchisement: The Supposed Justifications.* [Online]. Available from: http://blog.practicalethics.ox.ac.uk/2014/03/prisoner-disenfranchisement-the-supposed-justifications-3/

BECKMAN, L., (2009) *The frontiers of Democracy: The Right to Vote and Its Limits.* London, Palgrave Macmillan.

BEHAN, C., (2015) *Punishment, What is Justice? Prisoners and the Franchise.* Sheffield, University of Sheffield Howard League for Penal Reform.

CURRIE, I. and DE WAAL, J., (2013) *The Bill of Rights Handbook.* Cape Town, Juta.

CASTIGLIONE, D., (2015) The Logic of Social Cooperation for Mutual Advantage - The Democratic Contract. *Political Studies Review, 13,* 1-30.

CHOWDHURY, I. T., (2017) *Criminal Disenfranchisement Policies across Democracies: The Impact of Democracy, Punishment and Race.* Alabama, University of Alabama.

DEVOS, P., (2023) *South African Prisoner's Right to Vote. Civil Society Prison Reform Initiative.* [Online]. Available from: https://acjr.org.za/resourcecentre/South%20 African%20Prisoners%20Right%20to%20Vote.pdf

DUNN, S., (2002) A New Kind of Social Contract. In S, Dunn (ed.). *The Social Contract and the first and Second Discourses Jean-Jacques Rousseau.* New Haven, Yale University Press, pp. 9-33.

DEDI, A, et al., (2023) Social Contract Implementation in Elections in Indonesia. *Moderat: Jurnal Ilmiah Ilmu Pemerintahan, 9*(1), 1-12.

DOUGLAS, J. A., (2013) The Foundational Importance of Voting: A Response to Professor Flanders. *Oklahama Law Review,* 66(1), 81-100.

EUROPEAN COURT OF HUMAN RIGHTS, (2005). *John Hirst v United Kingdom.* [Online]. Available from: http://www.bailii.org/eu/cases/ECHR/2005/681.html

EWALD, A. C. and ROTTINGHAUS, B., (2009) *Criminal Disenfranchisement in an International Perspective.* Cambridge, Cambridge University Press.

FISHKIN, J., (2012) Weightless Votes. *The Yale Law Journal*, 121, 1888 -1910.

GARNER, B. A., (2014) *Black's Law Dictionary.* Minnesota West, St. Paul.

HOSKINS. Z., (2013) Ex-offender Restrictions. *Applied Philosophy*, 31(1), 33-48.

HORNE, A. and WHITE, I. (2015) *Prisoners Voting Rights (2005 to May 2015).* [Online]. Available from: https://commonslibrary.parliament.uk/research-briefings/sn01764/

HUME, D., (1752) *Of the Original Contract.* [Online]. Available from: https://cpb-us-w2.wpmucdn.com/blogs.cofc.edu/dist/8/406/files/2014/09/David-Hume-Of-the-Original-Contract-1kif9ud.pdf

INTERNATIONAL LABOUR ORGANIZATION, (2013). *Constitution of Zimbabwe (Amendment No. 20) Act 2013.* [Online]. Available from: https://www.ilo.org/dyn/natlex/natlex4.detail?p_lang=en&p_isn=93498&p_country=ZWE&p_classification=01.01

INTERNATIONAL LABOUR ORGANIZATION, (2004). *Electoral Act of Zimbabwe Chapter 2:13.* [Online]. Available from: https://www.ilo.org/dyn/natlex/natlex4.detail?p_lang=en&p_isn=85404&p_classification=01

JIKIA, M., (2020) Interrelation between the Universal Suffrage and its Restrictions. *Uluslararası Sosyal Bilimler ve Eğitim Dergisi*, 2(3), 220-235.

JASON, B., (2020) *The Ethics and Rationality of Voting.* [Online]. Available from https://plato.stanford.edu/entries/voting/

LARSEN, E. G., LEVINSEN, K. and KJAER, U., (2016) Democracy for the Youth? The Impact of Mockelections on Voting Age Attitudes. *Journal of Elections, Public Opinion and Parties*, 26(4), 435–451.

LEVINE, E. L., (2010) Does the Social Contract Justify Felony Disenfranchisement? *Washington University Jurisprudence Review*, 1(1), 193-224.

LIPPKE, R. (2001) Criminal Offenders and Right Forfeiture. *Journal of Social Philosophy*, 32: 78-89.

LOCKE, J. (1690) *Two Treatises of Government.* [Online]. Available from: https://www.yorku.ca/comninel/courses/3025pdf/Locke.pdf

MANZA, J. and UGGEN, C. (2006) *Locked Out: Felon Disenfranchisement and American Democracy.* New York, Oxford University Press.

MILLER, B. L. and SPILLANE, J. F. (2012) Civil death: An examination of ex-felon disenfranchisement and reintegration. *Punishment & Society*, 14(4), 402-428.

MISCEVIC, N., (2013) In Search of the Reason and the Right—Rousseau's Social Contract as a Thought Experiment. *Acta Analytica* 28(4), 509-526.

MICHAEL, O. (2015) *Prisoner Enfranchisement in Ireland.* [Online]. Available from: https://law.marquette.edu/facultyblog/2015/02/prisoner-enfranchisement-in-ireland/

OFFICE OF THE HIGH COMMISSIONER FOR HUMAN RIGHTS, (1966) *International Covenant on Civil and Political Rights.* Available from: http://www.ohchr.org/EN/ProfessionalInterest/Pages/CCPR.aspx

PABLO, M., (2015) *Criminal Disenfranchisement: A Debate on Punishment, Citizenship and Democracy.* Glasgow, University of Glasgow.

PETTUS, K. I., (2005) *Felony Disenfranchisement in America: Historical Origins, Institutional Racism, and Modern Consequences.* New York, LFB Scholarly Publishing.

PENAL REFORM INTERNATIONAL, (2016) *The Right of Prisoners to Vote: A Global Overview*. [Online]. Available from: https://www.penalreform.org/wp-content/uploads/2016/08/The-right-of-prisoners-to-vote_March-2016.pdf

RAMSAY, P., (2013) *Faking Democracy with Prisoners' Voting Rights*. London, London School of Economics.

REFWORLD, (1981) *African Charter on Human and Peoples' Rights*. [Online]. Available from: *https://*www.refworld.org/docid/3ae6b3630.html

ROUSSEAU, J. J., (1913) Social *Contract & Discourses: The Social Contract or Principles of Political Right*. [Online]. Available from: https://www.bartleby.com/lit-hub/social-contract-discourses/chapter-iii-elections/

SUPREME COURT OF CANADA, (2002). *Richard Sauvé v Canada (Chief Electoral Officer)*. [Online]. Available from: https://scc-csc.lexum.com/scc-csc/scc-csc/en/item/2010/index.do

TRAVIS, J., WESTERN, B. and REDBURN, F. S., (2014) *The Growth of Incarceration in the United States: Exploring Causes and Consequences*. Washington DC, National Academic Press.

UMEZURIKE, G., (2018). A Re-Examination of David Hume's Idea of Liberty and Republicanism: A Critique of Hume's Social Contract Theories of Thomas Hobbes and John Locke Evolutionary Account of Origin of Government. *World Applied Sciences Journal* 36 (8), 989-997.

VERITAS, (2022) *Musarurwa, Madzokere and Maengahama v The Minister of Justice Legal and Parliamentary Affairs and Ors (2022) HH 751*. [Online]. Available from: https://www.veritaszim.net/node/6013

WEALE, A., (2013) *Democratic Justice and the Social Contract*. Oxford, Oxford University Press.

WILSON, J. L. (2019) *Democratic Equality*. Princeton, Princeton University Press.

ZIMLII, (2018) *Gabriel Shumba and 2 Others v Minister of Justice Legal and Parliamentary Affairs and 5 Others*. [Online]. Available from: https://www.zimlii.org/zw/judgment/constitutional-court-zimbabwe/2018/4

ZIMLII, (2021) *Madzokere and 3 Others v The State 2021*. [Online]. Available from: https://media.zimlii.org/files/judgments/zwsc/2021/71/2021-zwsc-71.pdf (Accessed on 15 April 2023).

ZIMLII, (2022) *Musarurwa and 2 Others v The Minister of Justice, Legal and Parliamentary Affairs and 2 Others*. [Online]. Available from: https://zimlii.org/zw/judgment/harare-high-court/2022/751

ZIMBABWE LEGAL INFORMATION INSTITUTE, (2021) *S v Madzokere and 3 Others (71 of 2021) [2021] ZWSC 71 (4 June 2021)*. [Online]. Available from: https://zimlii.org/akn/zw/judgment/zwsc/2021/71/eng@2021-06-04

Competing Images of the Girl Child and Ending Child Marriages in Malawi

Peter Chikondi Matsimbe,
Reuben Chifundo Nazombe and Isaac Mutelo

Introduction

News reports and scholarly literature suggests that child marriages represent a looming disaster which developing countries like Malawi must adequately address in order to avert their daring consequences on the achievement of economic growth and development goals. In 2013, Malawi was ranked among 10 countries with the highest rates of child marriages: Niger 75%; Chad and Central African Republic 68%; Bangladesh 66%; Guinea 63%; Mozambique 56%; Mali 55%; Burkina Faso and Sudan 52% and Malawi 50% (World Health Organization 2013). For more than 140 million girls who marry before the age of 18, 50 million are under the age of 15 (World Health Organization 2013). Despite such alarming rates, "... little progress has been made toward ending the practice of child marriage.... In fact, the problem threatens to increase with the expanding youth population in the developing world" (World Health Organization 2013). Ending child marriages is important because girls married young are vulnerable to intimate partner violence and sexual abuse and pregnancy complications than those who marry late. Further, child marriages are the leading cause of death in young women aged 15-19 while girls who marry later have many chances to stay healthier, better education and build a better life for themselves and their families (World Health Organization 2013).

With such an alarming rate of child marriages and the catastrophic effects on young girls, any laws towards ending such marriages should be welcome. But what value does the law have in the efforts to curb child marriages? Such a question is necessary because the law itself does not address some subtle issues surrounding child marriages. The image of the girl child in particular, is very important in the fight against child marriages (Rwezaura 1998:265). Under the international human rights image of the child, a child is viewed as a rights holder. In the context of child marriages, such marriages are seen as a violation of the child's rights. In the Malawian context, as in many Sub-Saharan States, this image of the child is in competition with traditional images which in the end frustrate the conceptual basis of ending child marriages:

The basis for studying the conflicting perceptions of childhood in sub-Saharan Africa is that the traditional image of childhood is now widely contested and yet no concrete alternative perception of childhood has fully emerged. Moreover, given that over 47% of Africa's estimated total population of 758 million are children under the age of 16 years, we have to be concerned about the quality of childhood experienced by these youth because such experience will shape their future as well as the future direction of the region, if not the whole world (Rwezaura 1998:254-255).

Thus, the importance of having a resolved image of childhood in the efforts to improve the livelihood of children needs not to be overemphasised. Similarly, any efforts towards curbing child marriages will yield to nothing if this image of childhood is not resolved. This chapter argues that ending child marriages is more of a conceptual issue. It is when the issues around the conceptual image of the girl child are properly addressed that legislation can work efficiently in tackling child marriages. As Rwezaura (1998:254-261) puts it, "… when considering child protection in our region, the important question is not whether there are any laws, rather, whether these laws are effective in performing their protective task".

Competing Images of the Girl Child and Child Marriages

The image of childhood has been defined as "the manner in which a given society perceives its children at a particular historical juncture and how such children are expected to the adult world" (Rwezaura 1998:253). In Sub-Saharan Africa, this image is contentious and unsettled partly because "the traditional image of childhood is now widely contested and yet no concrete alternative perception has fully emerged" (Rwezaura 1998:254). The way a child is conceptualized has the effect of contributing positively or negatively to the struggle against child marriages. The image of a child that a particular society has is very important in understanding the rights that are allocated to the child. In Malawi, like in most countries in the Sub-Saharan region, the image of a child is a competitive issue since the "… traditional image of childhood has not lost force, it is still exerting its influence in many ways even in the face of determined challenge" (Rwezaura (1998:254). However, any effort towards ending child marriages without a proper conception of the image of the girl child will turn out to be meaningless.

In Malawi, the image of a girl child as an object of reproduction and male sexual gratification is prevalent largely in the rural areas. The girl child is mainly visualized as a material for child bearing and as a sexual tool for the males. The image is imbued in cultural beliefs and traditions associated with the development of the girl child:

> Under various customs within the region, a pubescent girl-child (usually about twelve years old) is eligible for the status of adulthood simply by reason of her biological capacity to bear children. Local cultures assume that because the primary role of a woman is to be a wife and mother, she attains adulthood as soon as she is biologically able to play that role…. That might explain the prevalence of child marriages in the region and the fact that very old men do not consider it embarrassing or shameful to marry women who are young as their grandchildren (Rwezaura 1998:260).

A key example can be seen in the initiation ceremonies or rites of passage. These are rites that children are made to undergo as they become adults (Malawi

Human Rights Commission 2006:35). In 2006, the Malawi Human Rights Commission (MHRC) established that most of the practices that pertain to rites of passage dwell much longer for the girl child for a married adult life whereas the same are less elaborate for boys. Thus training at the initiation camps is largely to do with how the girl child can satisfy the husband sexually and how she can be a good and subservient wife. One such rite of passage is *Msondo*, also called *Zoma* or *Chidoto* which involves girls from as young as six years old. Girls are taken to an isolated place, where they are kept in confinement for a period of two to four weeks, for purposes of concealment:

> During the evening of the day before the girls are taken to this isolated ... the *namkungwis*, accompanied by the *kholodzo* ... perform a dance through which a number of pieces of advice are given to the girls. This includes teaching the girl how to offer the best sex to their male counterparts. These women perform this dance while naked.... As they do this people from the community are free to watch and where they are amused, they ululate and give the particular woman money ... by placing money directly on the virginal area. During this time, the songs, usually obscene, are sung (Malawi Human Rights Commission 2006:37).

The close nexus between these rites of passage and child marriages becomes apparent when one considers rites of passage for young *Maasai* girls in Tanzania. In 2014, the Human Rights Watch found out that "cultural practices such as female genital mutilation (FGM) also contribute to child marriage in some communities". It was established that among the *Maasai* and *Gogo* ethnic groups, female genital mutilation is closely related to child marriage and is done "primarily as a rite of passage to prepare girls, aged 10–15, years for marriage" (Human Rights Watch 2014). Under female genital mutilation, it was established that Girls are cut between 10–15 years and get married 2–3 months after being cut. Under this image of the child, once a girl child reaches puberty, she is taken as ripe for marriage and thus at ages as low as 10-15, girls are married off without remorse as they are viewed to be ready for reproduction and capable to satisfy males sexually.

Unlike the boy child who enjoys a superior image, the girl child is treated as an inferior being and subject to control by parents. The case of *Chatema v Lupanda (1961-1963)* illustrates this point. In this case, the respondent brought an action against the appellant in Zomba African Urban Court to recover compensation in respect of sexual intercourse and subsequent birth of an 'illegitimate' child. The rationale of this case is that the girl child is in the nature of a chattel, to the extent that a father can claim for damages if she was impregnated since her value on the marriage market dwindles. The girl child is generally 'owned' particularly by the father. In *Chatema v Lupanda (1961-1963)*, Cram J said:

> The girl was unmarried, I consider, I can accept the well-recognized principle of African Customary law that the girl in the nature of her father's chattel could be obliged for him and that he suffered damage to his property. He suffered family disgrace and dishonor and the girl lost some of her value in the marriage market, he could suffer pecuniary loss which would amount to damage.

The appellant was found liable for gross and unwarranted sexual interference and was ordered to pay compensation of 25 Pounds. Since the girl child is being viewed as a chattel or a resource, "… girls may be viewed as an economic burden, as a commodity, or as a means for settling debts or disputes or securing social, economic or political alliances" (United Nations Population Fund 2012:12). By looking at the practice of *kupimbira* or *kupawira* as reported by the MHRC, the image of a girl child as in the nature of a chattel, a resource, a lesser human being becomes very apparent.

Based on its findings, the MHRC (2006:26) noted that the practice of *kupimbira* or *kupawira* demands that a young girl be given to a wealthy man as a form of debt payment for the debts of the parent or for other purposes. This practice takes a number of forms. In the most common form, which is practiced in the northern part of Chitipa District, a girl is given in marriage to a creditor as a form of debt payment in the case where the girl's parent gets into debt. The girl can be as young as 9 years old and the man 40 years old (MHRC 2006:25). In another variation, a young girl is given in marriage to a male tenant on an estate who is hardworking and has high prospects of financial success. It all starts when the parents of the girl ask the man to do work on their farm and then the parents fail to pay back the money; and in such cases, *lobola* (bride price) is not even paid. In a third form, parents send a girl child as young as 9 years old to stay with a rich man and by this time the parents and the rich man have already agreed and money and cattle have already been paid. In oblivion, the child finds herself graduating into a marriage with the rich man. The last form is that of *kutomela*. This is an arrangement between parents wanting to strengthen their family ties. A girl and a boy are brought into a marriage (Rwezaura 1998:260). As such, the girl child is likely to be forced into marriage by parents who view her as their property.

The image of the girl child as a rights holder has been championed by the international child rights law and the Constitution of the Republic of Malawi. The child holds rights and this in turn automatically creates duty bearers for these rights. In fact, the Constitution of the Republic of Malawi "protects people below 15 years from entering into a marriage or being involved in any treatment that is likely to be hazardous, interfere with their education or be harmful to their physical, mental, spiritual or social development" (MHRC 2006:78). This image is in a close competition with the other images since under it, child marriages are viewed as a violation of the rights of the girl child. The fact that the girl child has rights entails that there are correlative duties on the part of the society to respect, protect, promote and fulfil the rights of the girl child. The state, in particular, should protect the girl child from being forced into early marriages and any failure is viewed as a violation of the state's international obligations. This can be done through creation of legislative and policy frameworks that inhibit child marriages. The binding nature of international agreements entail that any "… departure from the obligations enshrined in these conventions is a violation of human rights. By becoming party to these Conventions, governments agree to hold themselves accountable for violations" (United Nations Population Fund 2012:10).

Child Marriages and Images of the Girl Child in Malawi

A child marriage happens when either one or both of the spouses are below the age of 18 (UNFPA 2012:10). This is in line with the usage under international law where anyone below the age of 18 is considered a child (Convention on the Rights of the Child 1990; Human Rights Watch 2014). They are also called forced or early marriages because in regard to the age of the child, they are not able to give free consent or an informed consent to their marriage partner or the timing of their marriage (UNFPA 2012:11). Apparently, the image of the girl child is at the centre of the struggle against child marriages. The image of the girl child as an object of male sexual gratification and reproduction and the image of the girl child as an inferior human being subject to control facilitate the forcing of young girls into early marriages. Such is the case because child marriages are viewed as culturally acceptable. Unfortunately, such images are the dominant ones in the areas where there is a high rate of child marriages, that is to say, rural areas. The United Nations Population Fund (2012:34) reports that girls living in rural areas of developing countries tend to enter into union twice the age of their counterparts in town, that is, 44% and 22% respectively. A competing image is that of the girl child as a rights holder which does not tolerate child marriages as they are viewed as interfering with the enjoyment of rights of the girl child as well not being in the best interest of the girl child.

In Southern Africa, the most important question is not whether there are any laws protecting children, but whether those laws are effective in the performance of their protective task (Rwezaura 1998:261). Further, the image that a particular community ascribes to childhood is very important in the understanding of the rights that are allocated to the child. Lack of clear image of the child is perhaps at the root of inconsistencies in ending child marriages as there is no certainty regarding the minimum age of marriage and such alone is enough to hamper the full protection of young girls from child marriages. There is a need to push this image of the girl child as a rights holder over other competing images if at all laws protecting the girl child from child marriages are to work. This calls for a clear paradigm shift in conceptualising the girl child and change of conception of this image should be the primary goal in any attempt to thwart child marriages in Malawi.

Ending Child Marriages and the Minimum Age for Marriage in Malawi

The Marriage, Divorce and Family Relations Act of 2015, has consolidated all regimes for marriage in Malawi, that is, statutory and customary laws on marriage and divorce. The Law Commission considered the marriage age and observed lack of consistency within various regimes of marriage. It noted that:

> only the statutory marriages set the age of 18 years as the minimum age for marriage... customary and religious marriages have no fixed age requirement and the attainment of puberty tends to be a critical determinant of capacity to marry... a marriage under the age of eighteen years is a health hazard; early marriage also

has negative development implications, and unless early marriages involving girls are discouraged, the attainment of the Millennium Development Goals; especially Goal 3 which emphasises the need for girl child education, or the goal on Human Capital Development under Poverty Reduction Strategy Paper may be elusive.

Thus, the Marriage, Divorce and Family Relations Act (2015) says that subject to Section 22 of the Constitution of the Republic of Malawi, two persons of the opposite sex who are both not below the age of eighteen years, of sound mind, may enter into marriage with each other. 'Subject to Section 22 of the Constitution' only means that marriage by persons aged 15 years are also permitted upon consent of their parents or guardians. Justice Fiona Mwale made the following comment on the status of Section 14 of the Marriage, Divorce and Family Relations Act in the light of the provisions in section 22 of the Constitution before the amendment:

> The Act provides that bearing in mind Section 22 of the Constitution, two people of the opposite sex who are not below the age of 18 years can enter into marriage. Since Section 22 of the Constitution allows children between 15 and 18 years to get married with consent of their parents or guardians, this suggests that though the proposed age of marriage is now 18, this is not a tight minimum age, since the lower age of marriage with consent under the constitution still applies (Mwale 2015).

The new Act had fuelled the confusion about marriage age. However, the amendments in sections 22 and 23 of the Constitution have consolidated the age of the child to 18, which is a path in the right direction. Although the recent amendment has put the marriage age at 18 in line with international human rights standards, the new law has in a way paved a way for continued perpetration of child marriages. One aspect of the new regime of marriage is that it has recognized marriages by repute or permanent cohabitation (Marriages, Divorce and Family Relations Act 2015). Marriage by repute and permanent cohabitation is provided for under section 13 of the Act, thereby providing a gateway to marriages of children under the age of 18.

According to section 13 of the Marriages, Divorce and Family Relations Act, marriage by repute and permanent cohabitation can only be recognized by a court of competent jurisdiction. In addition, the provision provides the following as factors for the court to consider before a finding as to whether there is marriage by repute and permanent cohabitation: the length of the relationship, which in event shall not be less than five years; the fact of cohabitation; the existence of conjugal relationship; the degree of financial dependence or interdependence and any agreement for financial support between parties; ownership, use and acquisition of property; the degree of mutual commitment to shared life; whether the parties mutually have care for, or support children; the reputation of the parties in the community as being married and the public display of aspects of their shared relation and any other factors that the court considers fit.

Apparently, the new law seeks to discourage child marriages by having a prescribed marriage age at law. However, marriage by repute and permanent cohabitation defeats this intention of parliament since it depends upon the finding of the Court. What this entails is that one can still stay with a girl under the age of 18 so long as the court does not find. Perhaps, this part of the law might have been drafted without foresight of the fact that children can find themselves in these marriages by repute or permanent cohabitation where no marriage formalities or requirements are complied with. It is trite that one moves the court where there are conflicts or disagreements. In this vein, if one cohabits peacefully with an underage girl, it seems the law condones such a malpractice. It is therefore evident; the new marriage has failed to correctly reflect the girl child as a rights holder.

Before the Constitution (Amendment) (No. 3) Act, 2017 there was no progress as far as the issue of ending child marriages is concerned as the law did not clearly address the competing images of childhood. This was visible in the huge inconsistencies between the Constitution and the consolidated law on marriage. Viewed as a whole, there were big loopholes under which this malpractice would be condoned. In the end, the violation of rights of children through child marriages was going to be perpetuated. However, the Constitution (Amendment) (No. 3) Act, 2017 is the new beacon of hope in as far as protection of children is concerned although it does not essentially settle down all the issues. The best achievement of the amendment is to bring the age of the child in Malawi to 18 in line with international standards. The other achievement is that it does not provide for marriages for persons below the age of 18. Nevertheless, the same law can be abused if someone chooses to cohabit with a child under a marriage by repute or permanent cohabitation.

Human Rights Violated through Child Marriages

Child marriage is a human rights and public health issue, which should be resolved. It is a violation of human rights enshrined under the Constitution of the Republic of Malawi. Child marriages also violate various international human rights instruments, such as the Convention on the Rights of the Child (CRC), the Convention on the Elimination of Discrimination against Women (CEDAW) and the African charter on Rights and Welfare of the Child (ACRWC). The Universal Declaration on Human Rights (UDHR), under article 16(2), states that marriage shall be entered into only with the free and full consent of the intending spouses. Article 16(1) (b) of the CEDAW states that States parties shall take all appropriate measures to eliminate discrimination against women in all matters relating to marriage and family relations and in particular shall ensure, on a basis of equality of men and women – the same right freely to choose a spouse and to enter into marriage only with their free and full consent. Article 16(2) of CEDAW states that the betrothal and the marriage of a child shall have no legal effect, and all necessary action, including legislation, shall be taken to specify a minimum age for marriage and to make the registration of marriages in an official registry compulsory. The CEDAW Fact Sheet No. 22 states that steps must be actively taken "… to ensure that women are able to exercise the same rights as men, including the right freely to enter into marriage and to choose a spouse. In keeping with the freedom of a woman to choose when and whom she should marry, a minimum age for marriage should be guaranteed by law" (UN Office of the High Commissioner for Human Rights 1995).

In the Program of Action adopted by the International Conference on Population and Development (ICPD), countries reached a consensus, agreeing on measures to eliminate child marriages as well as to strictly enforce laws to ensure that marriage is entered into only with free and full consent of the intending spouse (UNFPA 2012:10). The preamble to the Convention on Consent to Marriage, Minimum Age for Marriage and Registration of Marriages, adopted in 1962, reaffirms that all states:

> should take all appropriate measures with a view to abolishing such customs, ancient laws and practices by ensuring, inter alia, complete freedom in the choice of a spouse, eliminating completely child marriages and the betrothal of young girls before the age of puberty, establishing appropriate penalties where necessary and establishing a civil or other register in which all marriages will be recorded.

Article 1(1) of the Convention highlights the need for consent as it says that "… no marriage shall be legally entered into without the full and free consent of both parties, such consent to be expressed by them in person after due publicity and in the presence of the authority competent to solemnise the marriage and of witnesses, as prescribed by law". Keeping in line with the CEDAW and the CRC, this minimum age should be 18 as it is the internationally recognized age at which one ceases being a child. Considering the age of children, it is evident that they are not able to give free and full consent as such marriages are not in the best interests of a myriad number of children particularly girls who find themselves in such marriages. It follows that lack of a consistent minimum age for marriage, and having a marriage law that allows children below the age of 18 to get married is a complete violation of the children's right to be free from child marriages. In 2016, the Human Rights Watch noted that:

> Under article 22 of the Constitution, a person who is 18 years of age may enter into marriage without parental consent, while persons between 15 and 18 must obtain parental consent before entering into marriage. The Constitution does not prohibit marriage of children below 15, but provides that the state is obliged merely to "discourage" marriages where either party is under age 15. The 1903 Marriage Act, which sets 21 as the minimum age of marriage, also allows for marriage of children below 18 years with parental consent. The Child Care, Protection and Justice Act does not provide for a minimum age of marriage nor prohibit child marriages, but provides criminal penalties for those who force a child to marry.

The perpetuation of child marriages by the inconsistencies in the law meant that the rights of children to freely, fully and competently consent to married life. The child is not capable of making an informed decision when consenting and may end up making wrong decisions.

Secondly, the right to health "… is a fundamental human right indispensable for the exercise of other human rights…" and as such each and every human being "… is entitled to the enjoyment of the highest attainable standard of health conducive to living a life in dignity" (Committee on Economic Social and Cultural Rights 2000). According to Article 24(1) of the CRC and article 12 of the ICESCR, the state should recognize the right of the child to the enjoyment of the highest attainable standard of health. This is a closely connected right and highly dependent upon:

> the realization of other human rights, as contained in the International Bill of Rights, including the rights to food, housing, work, education, human dignity, life, non-discrimination, equality, the prohibition against torture, privacy, access to information, and the freedoms of association, assembly and movement. These and other rights and freedoms address integral components of the right to health (Committee on Economic Social and Cultural Rights 2000).

The right to healthy is also an all-embracing right, meaning it embraces a "… wide range of socio-economic factors that promote conditions in which people can lead a healthy life, and extends to the underlying determinants of health, such as food and nutrition, housing, access to safe and potable water and adequate sanitation, safe and healthy working conditions, and a healthy environment" (Committee on Economic Social and Cultural Rights 2000). The state is enjoined to take all effective and appropriate measures with a view to abolishing traditional practices prejudicial to the health of children. Child marriages violate the rights of the girl child to the highest attainable standard of health. Child marriages lead to early pregnancies at a time when the bodies of the young girls are not fully matured to contain the pregnancy. Consequently, this leads to maternal deaths and many other serious health complications such as, obstetric fistula, a disability associated with early childbirth which leaves the girls in constant pain, vulnerable to infection, incontinent and often shunned by their husbands, families and communities (UNFPA 2012:11). A pregnancy too early in life before a girl's body is fully matured is a major risk to both the mother and the child and that complications of pregnancy and childbirth are the main causes of death among adolescent girls of ages between 15-19 years old in the developing world. Child marriages are thus identified as a contributing factor to poor health outcomes, including the high maternal mortality rate (Human Rights Watch 2014). They have a harmful effect on the health and physical development of the girl child since most of them end up pregnant as soon as they get married (MHRC 2006:79). The right of the girl to the highest achievable form of health is therefore violated and this is a very bad signal to any country's development.

Thirdly, the right to education for everyone is enshrined in a number of international instruments including article 26 of the UDHR, articles 13 and 14 of the ICESCR, article 10 of the CEDAW, article 28 of the CRC, article 17 of the ACHPR, article 11 of the ACRWC, as well under Section (24) of the Constitution of the Republic of Malawian (1994). The importance of education cannot be overemphasised as the committee on the CESCR (1999) notes that the right to education has been classified as "a civil right and a political right, since it is central to the full and effective realisation of those rights as well. In this respect, the right to education epitomises the indivisibility and interdependence of all human rights". Child marriage leads to the violation of the right to education. When girls are married at a tender age, it mostly means the end of education of the girl child. In its study on cultural practices, the MHRC (2000:78-79) found that:

> Once children entered into marriage, they did not continue with education. They were expected to take care of their husbands, do household chores and attend to

farm work among the many tasks demanded of them. In a family where the young girl was not the first wife, she was treated like a slave by the older wives who assigned her various tasks. This bordered on servitude. For many young girls, the problem also arose when they started bearing children. The chances that they would give birth and return to school were almost non-existent. Thus, the girl's right to education was greatly compromised if not completely denied.

Early marriages therefore interrupt the girl's education or deny them access completely (Human Rights Watch 2014). The lack of education by young mothers means that they will be condemned to being housewives for the rest of their lives. Essentially, they will entirely depend on their husbands, and they will be subjected to various forms of abuse. Often, they cannot voice out or move out of the marriage since they have no financial independence due to lack of education. Furthermore, these young mothers are the seed for a generation of children that will not attend school hence being empowered unlike their counterparts that attend school.

The Image of a Girl Child as a Rights Holder and Ending Child Marriages

A new image of the girl child is inevitable if the legislative initiatives on ending child marriages are to be anything but effective because "… such efforts are unlikely to bear fruit without a determined endeavour at the local and regional levels to translate the existing good will into a concrete and sustained aspiration for a new conception of childhood" (Rwezaura 1998:267). Such an image needs a proper institutional machinery to ensure support for the new image. Social mobilisation and education are an important starting point in creating greater rights awareness. Lack of community awareness chokes any effort in raising the status of children. It further affects victims from reporting abuses for instance. Thus, a great awareness of the fact that children have rights will go a long way in tackling child marriages.

Moreover, Bart observes that the fact that many families in the Sub-Saharan Africa region face economic hardships account for the many problems that children face in the region (Rwezaura 1998:267). Gender inequalities also account for the problems as mostly women do not have voices in their families on decisions affecting their children. Empowerment of the family should involve raising the status of women in the family and participation of women in the family decision making process is seen as a step towards greater protection of children. Perhaps, mothers who were forced into child marriage would not want their children to go through the same ordeal they went through. Moreover, it is important to establish institutions that can act as a watchdog and as an advocate of the new image of childhood. This institution has the power to be flexible in playing the steering and coordinating work (Rwezaura 1998:267). Such an institution would explore inconsistencies in the law which led to confusion in the successful prohibition of child marriages. Thus, there is a need to move to a single consistent image of the child, in particular the girl child towards a successful ending of child marriages in Malawi.

Conceptualising the girl child as a rights holder entails a child rights-based approach to ending child marriages. There are four goals that the child rights-based approach seeks to achieve. These include survival, development, participation and protection (Convention on the Rights of the Child 1990). Survival is critical from the moment of conception. There is a need for that life to be protected. Then development follows, since the child that has survived should turn into a matured adult person. The child has to participate in matters that affect them and this has to be done according to their evolving capacities. Children also have to be protected from anything that interferes with the enjoyment of their rights. On that basis, forcing a girl child into early marriages frustrates the realisation of the two goals, development and protection.

Development entails that the child develops properly physically, psychologically and academically before they embrace the world. Child marriages stop such development since "girls who enter into marriage early also have a high chance of having many children early in their lives" (MHRC 2000:79). Such girls are robbed of their childhood early and are therefore deprived of the opportunity to develop physically, emotionally and psychologically. These young mothers are further prone to early deaths due to over use of their not fully developed uteruses. She is forced into the stressful demands of marriage. The goal of protection is also frustrated because the girl child is exposed to sexual exploitation. Child marriages in a way frustrate the realisation of child rights goals. The underlying principle of child rights is the best interest of the child and should be a primary consideration when making decisions about the child (Convention on the Rights of the Child 1990; African Charter on the Rights and Welfare of the Child 1990; Constitution of the Republic of Malawi, Section 23). There is a difference between the best interest of the child as is enshrined in international treaties like the CRC and the ACRWC and the welfare of the child as has been added in the Malawian Constitution, since best interest of the child connotes a higher standard in coming up with the decision concerning the child unlike welfare of the child. Early marriages frustrate both the realization of child rights goals and the enjoyment of other rights by the child. Marriages of girl children go against the underlying principle of child rights law. Thus, "… for myriads of girls, marriage is anything but safe, and also inconsistent with their interest" (UNFPA 2012:11).

Nature of the Obligation to Protect Girls from Child Marriages

As opposed to the duty to respect, the duty to protect is horizontal because it concern the relations between individuals as opposed to relations between the individual and the state. It requires that the state protects the individual from activities of another individual. In the case of the girl child, it means the state has a duty of protecting her from child marriages. Article 2 of the ICSECR states that:

> Each State Party to the present Covenant undertakes to take steps, individually and through international assistance and cooperation, especially economic and technical, to the maximum of its available resources, with a view to achieving progressively the full realization of the rights recognized in the present Covenant

by all appropriate means, including particularly the adoption of legislative measures.

In general, conduct can be passive and active, active where the state takes the step and passive where the state does not interfere with the right. The step has to be deliberate, concrete and targeted towards the realization of the right. The initial step includes a plan of action, in this case, ending child marriage action plan. The state is not expected to go backwards after initiating a step and such retrogression action is regarded as a violation. Legislative measures include the need to amend, repeal or adopt legislation. In this case, it would mean passing legislation that forces all customary marriages to be registered at the District Commissioner's office, as well as putting appropriate criminal sanctions on those that fail to comply with such requirements.

Whatever legislative measure is enjoined to possess the following characteristics; it should have targets and goals, institutional responsibility, national mechanism for monitoring, remedies intended in collaboration with civil society, international organizations and private sectors. The plans of action must be based on a human rights-based approach and must cover all aspects of rights and corresponding responsibility, clear objectives and targets within a time frame. Moreover, progressive realisation contemplates that the right will not be achieved immediately. In *Soobramoney v. Minister of Health (Kwazulu-Natal)*, Madala described the rationale behind this as follows: "In its language, the Constitution accepts that it cannot solve all of our society's woes overnight, but must go on trying to resolve these problems. One of the limiting factors to the attainment of the Constitution's guarantees is that of limited or scarce resources". This requires that the state should use resources that are available to it to the maximum in the realisation of the rights. As noted in *Government of the Republic of South Africa and Others v Grootboom and Others (CCT11/00) [2000]*, the meaning of this is that "… both the content of the obligation in relation to the rate at which it is achieved as well as the reasonableness of the measures employed to achieve the result are governed by the availability of resources". Indicators include structural, process and outcome. Process includes policy and budgetary commitments. For example, how much money has been specifically allocated to ending child marriages in the national budget? In *Government of the Republic of South Africa and Others v Grootboom and Others (CCT11/00) [2000]*, it stressed that there is a balance between goal and means, and that "measures must be calculated to attain the goal expeditiously and effectively but the availability of resources is an important factor in determining what is reasonable". Though the international community has a duty to assist, it is necessary to have a coordinated effort in order to use resources at their disposal effectively.

At the very centre, there is a girl child who is the rights holder. Then there are immediate care givers, family and the community. These are very close to the girl children and therefore very crucial in the fight against child marriages. If these duty bearers have a conception of the girl child as a rights holder, that will go a long way in addressing this problem. From the community one finds the band of institutions, and subnational structures. From the national level, one finds the international community as a duty bearer. If this country has about 50% of girls getting married before 18 years, it is because there is a haemorrhage in the carrying out of duties. It is pointless to bark in the media, if there is a collapse in the obligations pattern at different levels, more girls are still going to get married young. There is a need for a concerted effort from the government, to include a critical appraisal of this pattern among the measures to end child marriages in the country.

Child Based Approach and the Struggle against Child Marriages

Most children are forced into marriages due to poverty and early pregnancies. The efforts of ending child marriages cannot have any effect if they end up on the television, for instance, which cannot be accessed by most of the people in rural areas. The girl child is particularly vulnerable due to the predominant image in the country which encourages child marriages. The need to empower children and promote their rights ensure that the girl child is protected from early marriages. For this to happen, it is required that the duty bearers at all levels carry out these duties. It is pointless to embark on outlining measures for the realisation of rights of children without improving the capacity of claim holders to claim their rights and duty bearers. Section 23 of the Child Care, Protection and Justice Act defines conditions under which a child can be regarded as one in need of care and protection. It stipulates that a child is in need of care and protection if the child has been or there is substantial risk that the child will be physically, psychologically or emotionally injured or sexually abused. Child marriages put young girls under the risk of physical, psychological, and emotional abuse, hence they qualify as children in need of care and protection (MHRC 2006:79).

Section 23(1) (b) says a child is in need of care and protection if the child has been or there is substantial risk that the child will be physically injured or emotionally injured or sexually abused and the parent or guardian or any other person, knowing of such injury, risk or abuse, has not protected or is unlikely to protect the child from such injury, risk or abuse; by the parent or guardian or a member of the family or any other person. In practices like 'Kupimbira' or 'Kupawira', parents and guardians often support child marriages. This is despite the fact these marriages are not in the best interest of the children as they expose them to physical, emotional or sexual injury.

Section 23(1) (g) further describes as a child in need of care and protection if the child behaves in a manner that is, or is likely to be, harmful to the child or to any other person and the parents or guardians are unable or unwilling to take necessary measures to remedy the situation or the remedial measures taken by the parents or guardians have failed and as a result the child cannot be controlled by his parents or guardians. The girl child's behaviour sometimes can lead to early pregnancies. Early pregnancies are a leading cause to child marriages as such they also qualify as children in need of care and protection. Similarly, Section 23(1) (j) says a child is in need of care and protection if the child frequents the company of immoral, vicious, or otherwise undesirable persons or is living in circumstances calculated to cause or induce the seduction, corruption or prostitution of the child. Section 23(1) (i) describes a child in need of care and protection as one that cannot be controlled by his or her parent or guardian or the person in custody of the child.

Section 24 says that a police officer, social welfare officer, a chief or any member of the community, if satisfied on reasonable grounds that a child is in need of care and protection, may take the child and place him or her into his or her temporary custody or a place of safety. In line with the image of a girl child as a rights holder, these people become duty bearers to protect the children from getting into child marriages and they should discharge their duties properly. This child who is taken into a place of safety under section 24 shall be brought before a child justice court within forty-eight hours (Child Care, Protection and Justice Act 2010). If it is not possible to bring a child before a child justice court within the time specified above, the child shall be brought before any magistrate who may direct that the child be placed in (a) a place of safety; or (b) the care of a fit and proper person, until such time as the child can be brought before a child justice court (Child Care, Protection and Justice Act 2010).

Where a child in need of care and protection is brought before a child justice court, the court shall, if the age of the child is not known, refer him or her to a probation officer for age estimation (Child Care, Protection and Justice Act 2010). If a child is in a place of safety or in the care of a fit and proper person: (a) the person in charge of the place of safety or such fit and proper person shall have like control over, and responsibility for the maintenance of, the child as the parent or guardian of the child would have had; (b) the child shall continue to be in the care of the person referred to in (a) above notwithstanding that the child is claimed by the parent or guardian or any other person (Child Care, Protection and Justice Act 2010).

Section 25(5) says that a social welfare officer, police officer, chief or any member of the community who takes a child to a place of safety under this section shall, immediately upon such taking, cause the parent or guardian of the child to be notified of such taking if the parents are known and if it is practicable to do so. A police officer, chief or any member of the community who takes a child into temporary custody under this section shall, immediately upon such taking, notify the social welfare officer of such taking. The Child Care Protection and Justice Act creates a duty on family members in Section 35(4) to immediately inform a social welfare officer or a police officer if they believe that the child in the family is in need of care and protection. Failure to do so attracts a criminal liability and one shall be released on a binding agreement on conditions to be determined by the court (Child Care, Protection and Justice Act 2010). The image of a girl child as a rights holder will move a family member to report when one child of the family is forced into an early marriage. The same duty is also on the child care providers as well as members of the community and failure to report attracts a criminal offence and one is liable to a fine as well as three months imprisonment (Child Care, Protection and Justice Act 2010). Even though the law is clearly spelt out, it takes the image of the girl child as a rights holder to convince a member of the community to view a girl in a child marriage as one in need of care and protection and subsequently to report to the social welfare officer.

The child justice court may do the following when it is satisfied that any child brought before it under is a child in need of care and protection: (a) order the parents or guardians to enter into a binding agreement to exercise proper care and guardianship for a period specified by a child justice court; (b) make an order placing the child in the custody of a fit and proper person for a period specified by the child justice court; (c) without any other order or in addition to an order made under paragraph (a) or (b), make an order placing the child under the supervision of (i) a social welfare officer; or (ii) some other person appointed for the purpose by the child justice court, for a period specified by the child justice court. If this image of a child as a rights holder is promoted, a girl in a child marriage will be viewed as a child in need of care and protection and the duty bearers within the communities will perform their roles efficiently.

Section 81 of the Child Care Protection and Justice Act says that no person shall; (a) force a child into marriage; or (b) force a child to be betrothed. Any person who contravenes this section commits an offence and shall be liable to imprisonment to ten (10) years. Section 136 of the Penal Code criminalises sex with girls below 16 as defilement with up to 14 years imprisonment. Consent of the victim in this case is irrelevant as the girl below the age of 16 is deemed not capable to give consent to sexual intercourse. Section 132 of the Penal Code defines rape as follows:

> Anyone who has unlawful carnal knowledge of a woman or girl without her consent, or with her consent if the consent is obtained by force or means of threats or intimidation of any kind, or by fear of bodily harm, or by means of false representations as to the nature of the act, or in the case of a married woman, by personating her husband, shall be guilty of the felony termed rape.

Does the girl child below the age of 16 in a child marriage have the capacity to consent to sex? Is this not rape then? There is confusion as to how these penal provisions relate to child marriages as the Human Rights Watch (2016) has observed:

> A precise legal definition of a child that is consistent with international human rights law is essential to ensure a coherent application of laws protecting children. Malawi's Penal Code in article 138(2) criminalises sex with a girl below 16 as defilement, and those convicted under this provision can be sentenced to 14 years in prison. Article 132 defines rape as having "unlawful carnal knowledge of a woman or girl without her consent, or with her consent if the consent is obtained by force or means of threats or intimidation of any kind, or by fear of bodily harm." How the current definitions of rape and defilement apply to sexual intercourse in the context of child marriage is unclear.

Given that according to the CEDAW, to which Malawi is a party, child marriages are void and have no legal effect, cases of sexual encounter with girls below the age of 16 in such unions should be treated as defilement cases in line with Section 136 of the Penal Code and the purported husbands should be under criminal responsibility. Those who force girls below 18 years should be criminally liable under Section 81. However, for such penal sanctions to work, the image of a girl child as a rights holder is vital, as it will prompt people to report such instances and pursue the cases with relevant authorities.

Conclusion

The challenges of child marriages on the girl child castrate their education and put their health at risk. Among the causes of child marriages, the image that is assigned to the girl child in a particular locality is crucial in the effective tackling of child marriages. In Malawi, there is an interplay of images of the child, that is to say, a number of images of the girl child are in competition. There is an image of a girl child as a resource, as an inferior being subject to control. The other image is that of a girl child as a tool for male sexual gratification and reproduction. These images justify child marriages since young girls are married off as soon as they reach puberty. These images are faulty, for instance, even if the child can reproduce at puberty, they are not physically and or psychologically prepared to take up the mammoth task of child bearing. Being forced into early marriages also entails curtailment of their enjoyment of the right to education. This is so because it implies dropping out of school as a consequence. The other competing image is that of a girl child as a rights holder. This image of the child is dominant in both international and domestic child rights discourse. This image entails that there are correlative duty bearers in relation to that right. The duties include respect, protect, promote and fulfil the rights of the child. The duties are held at different levels from community level, national level and international level. The image of a child as a rights holder is the one that is very critical in ending child marriages and unless such an image is popularised, efforts to thwart child marriages through legislative initiatives will remain illusory for a long time.

References

AFRICAN UNION, (1981) *African Charter on Human and Peoples' Rights.* [Online]. Available from: https://au.int/sites/default/files/treaties/36390-treaty-0011_-_african_charter_on_human_and_peoples_rights_e.pdf

AFRICAN UNION, (1990) *African Charter on the Rights and Welfare of the Child.* [Online]. Available from: https://au.int/sites/default/files/treaties/36804-treaty-african_charter_on_rights_welfare_of_the_child.pdf

HUMAN RIGHTS WATCH, (2014) *'I've Never Experienced Happiness': Child Marriage in Malawi* [Online]. Available from: https://www.hrw.org/report/2014/03/06/ive-never-experienced-happiness/child-marriage-malawi

HUMAN RIGHTS WATCH, (2014) *No Way Out: Child Marriage and Human Rights Abuses in Tanzania.* [Online]. Available from: https://www.hrw.org/report/2014/10/29/no-way-out/child-marriage-and-human-rights-abuses-tanzania

HUMAN RIGHTS WATCH, (2016) *Submission to the Human Rights Committee Consideration of Malawi's Periodic Report.* [Online]. Available from: https://tbinternet.ohchr.org/Treaties/CCPR/Shared%20Documents/MWI/INT_CCPR_CSS_MWI_17468_E.pdf

MALAWI HUMAN RIGHTS COMMISSION, (2006) *Cultural Practices and Their Impact on the Enjoyment of Human Rights, Particularly the Rights of Women and Children.* Lilongwe, Malawi Human Rights Commission.

MWALE, A., (2015) *Marriage, Divorce and Family Relation Act & DEWIPA.* Workshop for Magistrates on Jurisdiction, Victoria Hotel, 22 May, 2015.

NATION ON SUNDAY, (2014) *Why Ending Child Marriage Can No Longer Wait*. [Online]. Available from: https://wcaro.unfpa.org/en/node/4897

OFFICE OF THE HIGH COMMISSIONER FOR HUMAN RIGHTS, (1979) *Convention on the Elimination of all Forms of Discrimination against Women (CEDAW) 1979*. [Online]. Available from: https://www.ohchr.org/en/instruments-mechanisms/instruments/convention-elimination-all-forms-discrimination-against-women

OFFICE OF THE HIGH COMMISSIONER FOR HUMAN RIGHTS, (1966) *International Covenant on Economic, Social and Cultural Rights 1966*. [Online]. Available from: https://www.ohchr.org/en/instruments-mechanisms/instruments/international-covenant-economic-social-and-cultural-rights

OFFICE OF THE HIGH COMMISSIONER FOR HUMAN RIGHTS, (1995) *Factsheet No. 22, Discrimination against Women: The Convention and the Committee*. [Online]. Available from https://www.refworld.org/docid/47947740d.html

RWEZAURA, B., (1998) Competing 'Images' of Childhood in the Social and Legal Systems of Contemporary Sub-Saharan Africa. *International Journal of Law, Policy and Family,* 12(3), 253-278.

SOUTH AFRICAN LEGAL INFORMATION INSTITUTE, (2000) *Government of the Republic of South Africa and Others v Grootboom and Others (CCT11/00) [2000]*. [Online]. Available from: http://www.saflii.org/za/cases/ZACC/2000/19.html

SOUTH AFRICAN LEGAL INFORMATION INSTITUTE, (1997) *Soobramoney v Minister of Health, KwaZulu Natal (1997) 12 BCLR 1696 (CC)*. [Online]. Available from: http://www.saflii.org/za/cases/ZACC/1997/17.html

INFORMEA, (1996) *The Social and Economic Rights Action Center, et al. v. Nigeria*. [Online]. Available from: https://www.informea.org/en/court-decision/social-and-economic-rights-action-center-et-al-v-nigeria

UNITED NATIONS COMMITTEE ON ECONOMIC, SOCIAL AND CULTURAL RIGHTS, (2000) *General Comment No. 14: The Right to the Highest Attainable Standard of Health (Art. 12 of the Covenant)* E/C.12/2000/4. [Online]. Available from: https://www.refworld.org/docid/4538838d0.html

UNITED NATIONS CONVENTION ON THE RIGHTS OF THE CHILD, (1990) *Convention on the Rights of a Child 1990*. [Online]. Available from: https://www.unicef.org/media/56661/file#:~:text=The%20Convention%20on%20the%20Rights,be%20taken%20away%20from%20children.&text=This%20text%20is%20supported%20by,the%20Rights%20of%20the%20Child.

UNITED NATIONS WOMEN (2010) *Child Care, Protection and Justice Act 2010, No. 10 of 2010*. [Online]. Available from: https://evaw-global-database.unwomen.org/en/countries/africa/malawi/2010/the-child-care-justice-and-protection-act-2010#:~:text=Brief%20Description,and%20harmful%20practices%20against%20children.

UNITED NATIONS POPULATION FUND, (2012) *Marrying Too Young: End Child Marriage*. New York, UNFPA.

UNITED NATIONS, (1945) *Universal Declaration on Human Rights* (UDHR) 1945. [Online]. Available from: https://www.un.org/en/about-us/universal-declaration-of-human-rights

WORLD HEALTH ORGANISATION (WHO), (2013) *Child Marriages – 39 000 Every Day: More than 140 million Girls will Marry between 2011 and 2020*. [Online]. Available from: https://www.who.int/news/item/07-03-2013-child-marriages-39-000-every-day-more-than-140-million-girls-will-marry-between-2011-and-2020

ZOMBA AFRICAN URBAN COURT, (1961-1963) *Chatema v Lupanda 1961-63 ALR Mal. 162*. Zomba, Zomba African Urban Court.

Labour Rights as Human Rights:
A South African Perspective

Thandekile Phulu

Introduction

Common law, legislation and international labour law have had an impact on South African labour law. South Africa has a dark history of racial oppression which was based on the apartheid system. Apartheid caused racial and gender imbalances in the South African labour market. The interim Constitution which was enacted in 1993, after the end of the apartheid regime was intended to prepare the path for the new political regime by enshrining ideals and principles, embracing equality, human rights and restoring human dignity. Its preamble emphasized the need to establish a new legal system in which South Africans would be entitled to a common citizenship in a sovereign and democratic state. These values were later included into the Constitution of the Republic of South Africa (the Constitution), which was ratified in 1997.

The ethos of the Constitution, like that of the interim constitution, is based on ideals of justice, non-discrimination and equality within South African society. Additionally, labour regulations such as those in the Labour Relations Act of 1995 (LRA) and the Employment Equity Act of 1998 (EEA) have been enacted to curb employment discrimination. These labour laws were enacted to fulfil the constitutional obligation of ensuring equality and justice at workplaces. Against this background, the concerns that will be analysed in this chapter include employee rights as protected by different pieces of legislation.

Labour Rights as Human Rights

Labour rights are entitlements that are explicitly related to the function of an employee. Some of these rights are exercised individually, while others are exercised collectively (Smit van Eck 2010:50). These include the right to work in a job of one's choice, the right to fair working conditions, which can include issues as diverse as a fair wage or the protection of one's privacy, the right to be protected from arbitrary and unfair dismissal, the right to belong to and be represented by a trade union, the right to strike, and many others. These rights may be founded on many principles, such as liberty and dignity (Mantouvalou 2012:160). Relevant International Labour Organisation's (ILO) treaties provide a human rights foundation for a variety of rights. Governments that ratify these treaties pledge to preserve certain human rights. The ILO was founded as part of the Versailles Peace Treaty after the conclusion of World War I. The ILO constitution states that it aspires to help nations achieve fair competition through the adoption of standard-setting protective principles and to build social harmony through equitable working conditions (ILO Constitution 1919).

South Africa, the Netherlands and the United Kingdom were among the founding members of ILO in 1919. The United States joined in 1934, left in 1977, and re-joined in 1980. South Africa withdrew from the International Labour Conference in 1964 as its apartheid practices became a topic of contention. South Africa re-joined the ILO on May 26, 1994, after its first democratic elections (Grawitzky 2011:50; Webster and Forrest 2021:330) The ILO, in support of workers' rights and labour standards issued a Declaration in 1998, titled the Declaration on Fundamental Principles and Rights at Work and Their Implementation (ILO Declaration), calling on its Member States to respect and promote the ILO Declaration's underlying principles which form the basis of the ILO's core conventions.

Moreover, the United Nations' Universal Declaration of Human Rights (UDHR) of 1948 includes labour rights as a component of human rights. Article 23 of the UDHR states that individuals should have the right to work, equal compensation for equal effort and the right to establish and join trade unions. Article 24 states that working hours should be fair. Although it is recognised that the UDHR is not a legally enforceable treaty, it may be regarded as a profoundly significant and cornerstone human and labour rights treaty. South African history shaped the current labour relations from the Native Labour Regulations Act 1911 to the current LRA.

Labour rights are rights founded on several foundations, such as liberty, dignity or capacity. These fundamental foundations should be considered when interpreting labour rights. The legal protection afforded to labour rights by the international community demonstrates their significance as human rights. In recent years, the ILO has certified a number of work rights as human rights. In 1998 the ILO approved the Declaration of Fundamental Principles and Rights at Work. The Declaration binds all ILO Member States, regardless of whether they have ratified the relevant conventions, and contains four human rights: freedom of association and collective bargaining, the abolition of forced or compulsory labour, the abolition of child labour, and the abolition of employment discrimination.

On the other hand, another recently drafted human rights document, the European Union Charter of Fundamental Rights (EUCFR), which became legally binding with the Lisbon Treaty of 2009, contains a list of labour rights as human rights. These include the right to information and consultation, protection from unfair dismissal and the prohibition of forced labour. Mantouvalou contends that the nature of labour rights as human rights is supported if either state and international institutions, such as courts, or civil society groups, such as trade unions and non-governmental organisations, are effective in advocating them as such (Mantouvalou 2012:156). Against this background, it can be noted that through the enforcement of labour rights under the Constitution, LRA and other pieces of legislation, labour rights can be regarded as human rights in South Africa.

History and Development of Labour Rights in South Africa

A precursor of the historic development of South African labour law is needed in order to understand the current labour legislative frameworks and labour rights protections. In the 1970s, employment relationships were founded on the notion that every employment contract was entered into freely, and that any party was free to terminate it at any moment if they provided proper notice and there was no contractual provision to the contrary (Lichtenstein 2013:30). Discrimination against employees on the basis of race and gender was not only permissible, but also legally enforced under apartheid. Moreover, the legislation gave employers the ability to discriminate on the basis of religion, disability, or political viewpoint. As a result of such harsh working circumstances, it was difficult for workers to grow and become productive, since they were oppressed at work and in other aspects of SA society (Lichtenstein 2013:30).

For instance, the 1973 Durban strikes were a series of labour conflicts and worker-led rallies that took place in Durban in 1973. African employees in many areas withheld their labour intentionally in an effort to demand greater salaries and improved working conditions. Mass strikes broke out and persisted for three months till the end of March. According to Buhlungu (2009), the strikes engaged over 60 000 African employees and affected over 100 businesses. The greatest number of strikes occurred at textile, metal and chemical factories on the outskirts of Durban. While the number of strikes reduced after March, it was believed that 100,000 African and Indian employees had engaged in some sort of industrial action by the end of 1973 (Buhlungu 2009).

A spate of victimisation cases characterised the era of union expansion that began in the mid-1970s, as documented in legal records. All of these judgements were based on criminal restrictions in South African labour law barring employers from dismissing employees for their participation in works committees or trade unions. *Kubheka v Imextra (Pty) Ltd 1975 (4) SA 484* was the first documented case in the series of victimisation cases. A group of employees claimed that they were dismissed on notice by their employer because they actively engaged in efforts to form a works committee at their company. Section 24 of the Bantu Labour Relations Regulation Act 1973 stated that employers who dismissed employees under such circumstances would be guilty of a criminal offence, and that if convicted, the criminal court could reinstate affected employees and/or compel compensation for any damage incurred. The employees sought an order in a civil court declaring their dismissal. They were denied. The court determined that the remedies given by the statute were innovative and only applicable in the context of a criminal prosecution, not in civil proceedings.

In another case, *P E Bosman Transport Works Committee v Piet Bosman Transport (Pty) Ltd* (1980) *ILJ* 66 (*Bosman*), a works committee, an unregistered trade union and a group of employees sought an interdict to prevent an employer from dismissing employee in violation of section 24 of the Bantu Labour Relations Regulation Act. Two of the employees had been dismissed. The court ruled that neither the works committee, the union, nor the dismissed employees had standing to seek such remedy. It was claimed that the works committee was a statutory organisation with restricted duties that had no authority to 'take up the cudgels on behalf of the employees.' Similarly, the unregistered union was found to have little more than a financial or commercial interest in the result of the case, which was insufficient to satisfy the common-law standing requirements. The court further held that employees could therefore bring a case and hope that if the employer is convicted, the court convicting them would order reinstatement in the exercise of its discretion.

In 1977, the Wiehahn Commission was established as a matter of urgency to study South African labour policy. The development of black unionism and increased worker militancy and the Durban strikes prompted its establishment (Kooy et al 1979:5). The Wiehahn commission's mandate was extraordinarily broad, including analysing all laws under the supervision of the Department of Manpower. The most crucial aspect of the Wiehahn Commission's recommendations was their suggestion that the discriminatory premise underpinning South African labour policy be repealed and black and white employees be subjected to the same labour laws (Kooy et al, 1979:5).

In the years following 1979, the government carried out this recommendation in a variety of ways, most notably by repealing the Black Labour Relations Regulation Act 48 of 1953 through the enactment of the Labour Relations Regulation Act 57 of 1981 and amending the definition of 'employee' in the Labour Relations Act (formerly the Industrial Conciliation Act 28 of 1956) to remove the exclusion of black employees from the Act's ambit. Nonetheless, many of the legal reforms mirrored developments that had already occurred on the factory floor (O'Regan 1997:20). During this period, trade unions represented just a small proportion of the overall number of black employees. White union recognition gave some assistance for collective bargaining, but no protection from dismissal for striking for such employees. Every employment was essentially governed by the employment contract (Van Eck, Boraine & Steyn 2004:910). Employers could therefore dismiss any employee on notice, for good or bad reasons.

The labour market was almost fully restricted based on race. Salaries set through collective bargaining and extended to black employees were often explicitly discriminatory (Maylam 1990:60). Similarly, job reservations existed in mines and numerous state-owned industries and businesses. Job reservation meant that certain skilled grades of employment were reserved for white people. According to apartheid regulations, black employees who had no right to dwell in urban areas had to register for employment at state labour bureaux in rural regions as it regulated access to jobs (Crush 1992:389). Such employees were only granted permission to live and work in cities for a period of 12 months, and dependants and family members were not authorised to join them (Coleman 1991: 179)

The post-democratic era saw a significant transition in the development of labour law. The statute prohibiting employment discrimination is no longer in force. Particularly among black employees, unionism has gradually grown. Currently, 25% of the South African labour force is unionised, a change which occurred during the previous two decades (Buhlungu 2003:199). The post-independence safeguards protect all employees, whether unionised or not, as well as those in traditionally unregulated areas such as agriculture and domestic labour (Fioramonti & Olivier 2007:410). Some of these improvements are unquestionably the product of the democratic transition of 1994. Nonetheless, considerable changes in labour relations and labour law occurred as a consequence of rapidly shifting attitudes and practises on the shop floor, particularly in response to the demands of the emerging trade unions (Webster & Omar 2003:196). Chapter 2 of the South African Constitution contains several provisions relevant to employment and labour law, including: "the right to equality; the right to dignity; the right to be free from servitude, forced labour, and discrimination; the right to work; and protection for children against exploitative labour practises and hazardous work".

Every labour legislation must be interpreted in light of the Constitution. Section 23 of the Constitution addresses labour relations directly, stating that everyone has the right to fair labour practices, including the right to create and join a trade union, engage in the activities and programmes of a trade union and the right to strike. Section 23(1) of the Constitution is an uncommon provision since it is so wide and overarching as it specifically safeguards the right to fair labour practises (Ramolotja & Mpedi 2000:422). Fair labour practices are challenging to define precisely because they are a dynamic subject of law anchored on socioeconomic rights. Section 23(1) refers to "everyone," which covers more than just employees, it also includes applicants, employers and legal entities.

Every employer has the right to create and join an employers' organisation, and engage in the activities and programmes of an employers' organisation. Every trade union and employers' organisation has the freedom to select its own administration, programmes and activities. The trade union also has the right to organise and join a federation; and lastly, every trade union, employers' organisation, and employer has the right to negotiate collectively (section 23 of the Constitution). The LRA, the Basic Conditions of Employment Act 77 of 1996 (BCE), the EEA and the Skills Development Act 97 of 1998 (SDA) all brought in new labour law trends in labour relations. These Acts implement international treaty provisions into national law. They also represent a departure from the previous attitude, which was based primarily on beliefs that contradicted international standards. These Acts protect basic rights enshrined in the Bill of Rights.

The LRA was enacted as the 'national legislation' referenced in subsections 23(5) and 23(6), which state that "national legislation may be enacted to regulate collective bargaining" and "national legislation may recognise union security arrangements contained in collective agreements." Moreover, item 2(3) of the Code of Good Practice: Dismissal (Code) contains a clause prohibiting unfair discrimination against employees. The Code forms part of the LRA schedule 8. This Code addresses some of the most important components of terminations for misconduct and capacity-related reasons. The LRA gave substance to the constitutional right to equality through eliminating job discrimination. This was SA's first effort to implement anti-discrimination laws within the framework of an employment relationship. It was made very clearly in item 2(1)(a) of schedule 7 of the LRA's residual unfair labour practices. Furthermore, EEA supplements both Acts by replicating the Constitutional equality provision in its entirety, adding that discrimination based on human immunodeficiency virus (HIV) status is prohibited (EEA). Dispute resolution mechanisms lie with the bargaining councils, the Commission for Conciliation, Mediation and Arbitration (CCMA) and Labour Courts. However, the Constitutional Court may examine labour court decisions on disputed subjects such as the dismissal of striking employees if the petitioners have exhausted the processes provided to them under labour law. In *National Union of Metal Workers of South Africa and Others v Bader Bop (Pty) Ltd and Another (CCT14/02) [2002]*, the Constitutional Court reversed a Labour Appeal Court judgement that narrowly construed the LRA. The court recognised the importance of collective bargaining and bargaining councils, which aid in the formation of trade unions for majority unions. The court held that minority unions may not strike in support of claims for organisational powers reserved under the EEA.

Labour Rights Protection in South Africa

Apart from being a constitutional right, the right to equality is protected by the EEA, a statute that promotes workplace equity, ensuring that all employees have equal opportunity and that employers treat employees equally. The Act protects an employee from unfair treatment and discrimination in any form. The legislation stipulates that an employer may not directly or indirectly discriminate against an employee through an employment policy or practice on the basis of race, gender, pregnancy, marital status, family responsibilities, ethnic or socioeconomic origin, colour, sexual orientation, age, disability, religion, HIV status, conscience, belief, political stance, culture, language, and birth are all factors to consider (section 6 of EEA). The Act's objective is to achieve workplace fairness through eliminating unjust discrimination in the workplace to promote equal opportunity and fair treatment. HIV testing is forbidden unless the Labour Court rules that it is reasonable (section 7 of EEA). Psychological testing and comparable examinations are also forbidden unless the test is scientifically accurate and trustworthy, applicable to all employees equitably, and not prejudiced against any person or group (section 8 of EEA).

Moreover, the right to fair labour practices is guaranteed under Section 23 of the Constitution. Section 23(1), like other constitutional enactments, was intended to move the law from a limited positivist approach to a rights-based perspective (Tshoose 2014:280). Section 23(1) of the Constitution also establishes the legitimacy of an employer's disciplinary authority for dismissals. It establishes essential employees' rights in the context of fair labour practices. The South African Constitution was drafted with the appropriate Industrial Court decisions on fair labour practices in mind (Bhorat & Cheadle 2009). As a consequence, the right to fair labour practises was included in the South African Constitution's Bill of Rights. Fair labour practices, including the right to a fair dismissal, are built on equitable principles of fairness.

Section 186(2) of the LRA states that unfair labour practice refers to (a) unfair conduct by the employer relating to the promotion, demotion, probation (excluding disputes about dismissals for a reason relating to probation) or training of an employee or relating to the provision of benefits to an employee; (b) the unfair suspension of an employee or any other unfair disciplinary action short of dismissal in respect of an employee; (c) a failure or refusal by an employer to reinstate or re-employ a former employee in terms of any agreement; and (d) an occupational detriment, other than dismissal, in violation of the Protected Disclosures Act 26 of 2000), because the employee made a protected disclosure as defined in that Act.

Since the establishment of section 23 (1) was based on equity, it is contended that the LRA, although attempting to convey a section 23(1) requirement, cannot be understood without constitutional purposes guiding equity. In *National Education, Health, and Allied Workers Union v University of Cape Town* (2003) 24 *ILJ* 95 (CC), the Constitutional Court found that the idea of a fair labour practice is devoid of exact description and that defining the term is neither required nor desirable. The court went on to say that the notion should derive its meaning from the judgements of the specialised tribunals on an individual basis. The employment axis should be used to analyse the concept of unfair labour practices. A practice that does not stem from this connection is not a labour practise (Cheadle & Davis 2005:140).

Article 2 of ILO's Termination of Employment Convention of 1982 (C158) protects employees from unfair dismissal. According to article 2(5), member states may exclude various types of employees from some requirements of C158 based on the size and nature of the employer's company. Pre-dismissal conditions are addressed in Articles 4 to 8 of C158. According to Article 4 of C 158, the employment of an employee should not be terminated unless there is a justifiable reason for such termination related to the employee's capacity, misconduct or based on the operational needs of the enterprise, establishment, or service. This makes it evident that the ILO only recognises three kinds of admissible reasons for terminating an employee's services: conduct, capacity or the employer's operational reasons. It is also evident that dismissal must be based on a reasonable cause that falls into one of these categories. This right is also entrenched in section 185 of the LRA which states that every employee has the right not to be unfairly dismissed; and subjected to unfair labour practice. Section 186(1) of the LRA defines dismissal by outlining six types of circumstances that may be considered a dismissal:

> When an employer terminates an employment contract without notice. Failure to renew a fixed term contract. However, this is not a dismissal unless the employee had a reasonable expectation that the employer would renew the fixed-term contract or retain him/her indefinitely and can substantiate that expectation, for example, by demonstrating that the employer had previously renewed similar contracts or represented to the employee that the contract would be renewed, and so on. When an employer renews a fixed-term contract or keeps an employee indefinitely, but on much less favourable terms and circumstances, this may also constitute a kind of dismissal. An employer refused to allow an employee to return to work after she took maternity leave in accordance with any law, collective agreement, or her employment contract; When an employer dismisses a group of employees for the same or comparable cause, such as collective misconduct, then subsequently offers to re-employ some but not all of them, the employees who are not included in the offer are deemed to have been dismissed as of the day they were not re-employed. A constructive dismissal occurs when an employee resigns because the employer made ongoing employment intolerable for the employee.

Whether a firm is transferred as a going concern or in bankruptcy, the new employer succeeds the former employer, and the employees' employment continues. Nevertheless, if the "transferred" employees are given working conditions or circumstances that are much less favourable than those offered by the previous employer, an employee may resign, resulting in a unique sort of constructive dismissal.

Moreover, section 187 state that dismissing an employee for any of the following reasons is automatically unfair:

Being pregnant, intending to get pregnant, or any other pregnancy-related cause; Membership to a trade union or participating in its operations; Participating in or supporting a protected strike, or expressing a desire to do so; Refusing or showing an intention to refuse to perform the job of another employee who is participating in a protected strike or is lawfully locked out, unless the activity is required to avoid an actual threat to life, personal safety, or health; Refusal to accept an employer's demand on a topic of mutual interest, such as refusing to accept a lower salary demand from an employer during a strike and being fired as a result; Any arbitrary basis, including (but not limited to) race, gender, sex, ethnic or social origin, colour, sexual orientation, age, disability, religion, conscience, faith, political opinion, culture, language, marital status, or family responsibilities; The employee made a disclosure protected by the Protected Disclosures Act of 2000 Act.

The LRA lays down the procedures to be followed before an employee is dismissed.it also provides that every dismissal must be substantive and procedural fair (section 188). The Code explains the guidelines that should be followed in order to determine the fairness of a dismissal for conduct and capacity. It is every employer's duty to pay an employee reasonable compensation for services rendered. Minimum wages have been introduced in many developed and developing economies. In 2018, South Africa joined these countries by enacting the National Minimum Wage Act 9 of 2018 (NMWA). It is illegal and unfair labour practices for an employer to unilaterally change working hours or other employment circumstances in order to implement the NMW. The NMW is the amount payable for normal working hours and excludes allowances (such as transportation, tools, food, or housing), compensation in kind (boarding or lodging), tips, bonuses, and gifts. The NMWA mandates the NMW Commission to examine the rates on a yearly basis and offer recommendations to the Minister on any changes to the national minimum wage, while also taking into account alternative viewpoints, including those of the public.

An employer cannot breach an employee's privacy unless the employee has a right to such privacy. In general, the right to privacy has been founded on a reasonable expectation of such right by the person seeking its protection (Pagnattaro 2003:625). It would be inaccurate to claim that an employer may never monitor an employee's online activity. Consequently, an employer that has reason to fear an employee using the Internet to expose trade secrets, for example, would take proper efforts to either confirm or ease such concern, and monitoring would be an effective manner of doing so (Carbone 2015). In today's world, Internet use has grown so pervasive that employees often use it for personal or semi-personal purposes with no intent or intention to hurt their employers. It can be argued therefore that an employer has no right to infringe upon an employee's private conduct or behaviour especially if the conduct has nothing to do with the employer or the employer's business. Employees should enjoy their right to privacy without worrying about the employer's prying eyes. The employees' rights are protected by various pieces of legislation. The 1992 Interception and Monitoring Prohibition Act prohibits telephone and postal communications monitoring and interception. The IMPA prevents eavesdropping on important data. The Electronic Communications and Transactions Act of 2002 (ECTA), section 1(a), defines personal information as:

> Information relating to the individual's race, gender, sex, pregnancy, marital status, national, ethnic or social origin, colour, sexual orientation, age, physical or mental health, well-being, disability, religion, conscience, belief, culture, language, and birth.

The Promotion of Access to Information Act (PAIA) enforces the Constitution's information right by permitting access to public records, including personal information. The PAIA applies to employer data collection. Employers seek employee data from data controllers as third parties under the PAIA. The growing diversity and innovations in communication technologies, the globalisation of the telecommunications business, and the convergence of the telecoms, broadcasting and IT industries led to the 2002 Regulation of Interception of Communications and Provision of Communication Related Information Act (RICA). This Act bans intercepting direct or indirect communication without permission. RICA intercepts and monitors most workplace and private telecommunications. Section 2 of RICA reads, "No person may wilfully intercept or attempt to intercept, or authorise or procure any other person to intercept, any communication in the course of its occurrence or transmission at any site in the Republic".

At the municipal, regional and international levels, the right to safe and healthy working conditions has acquired significance. Most governments have recognised the significance of the human right to safe and healthy working conditions by enshrining it in domestic laws and regulations (Tshoose 2014:281). As a result, from a human rights standpoint, the right to occupational health and safety allows individuals to claim a vital component of their life. The United Nations General Assembly has recognised that the right to health encompasses a broad variety of socioeconomic variables that support circumstances in which individuals may live a healthy life. This includes the underlying factors of health, safety, and a good working environment.

The ILO's tripartite structure of employer, employee and government is ideally adapted to initiating and facilitating large-scale programmes to realise the ILO's Global Strategy on Occupational Safety and Health. Its tripartite system implies that governments, employers, and employees are all represented, and their representatives may vote at the International Labour Conference.

At the national level, South African legislation requires all employers to provide a healthy and safe working environment for their employees. This commitment is based on constitutional values. Section 29 of the Constitution, in particular, guarantees everyone the right to an environment that is not damaging to their health or well-being. Additionally, section 8 of the Occupational Health and Safety Act 85 of 1993 puts a general obligation on every employer to establish and maintain a safe and risk-free working environment for employees. Moreover, many pieces of legislation govern occupational injury and sickness in South Africa. For example, the Compensation for Occupational Injuries and Diseases Act 130 of 1993 (COIDA) deals with the aftermath of an employee's occupational injury or sickness while on the job. This regulation also covers compensation for workplace illnesses and injuries.

The Occupational Diseases in Mines and Works Act 78 of 1973 requires the reporting and payment of specific benefits to mine employees who acquire defined occupational lung illnesses, as well as the provision of benefits to dependents of workers who die from such diseases. In terms of the Mine Health and Safety Act 29 of 1996 (MHSA), an inspector who has reasonable grounds to believe that any occurrence, practise, or condition at a mine endangers or may endanger the health or safety of any person at the mine may issue an instruction necessary to protect the health or safety of any person at the mine. This includes a directive to suspend activities at the mine or a portion of the mine in order to protect employees.

Moreover, dignity is a tenet of the country's Constitution, which was drafted in reaction to the country's apartheid history. According to Section 10 of the Constitution, everyone has inherent dignity and the right to have that dignity acknowledged and preserved. According to the Constitution, all people's dignity and value as members of society must be recognised. Characteristics of this right include those rights inherent in the status of the human being and linked to any individual by the fact of being a person. These rights are prerogatives, and some writers see them as primal, while others regard them as essential human rights. These rights apply to any other person as privileges derived from birth. In the case of *Kylie v CCMA* (2010) 31 *ILJ* 1600 (LAC), the court held that employees have a right to be treated with dignity by their employers, and that section 23 of the Constitution, at its heart, protects the dignity of people in employment relationships.

According to the Philadelphia Declaration article 2, all human beings, regardless of race, creed, or gender, have the "right to seek both their material well-being and spiritual growth under conditions of freedom and dignity, economic stability, and equal opportunity." This statement is similar to one contained in the ILO Constitution. It is therefore vital to protect an employee's interest in job security to the degree that it is consistent with the right to dignity and the promotion of autonomy. The belief that each employee has dignity that must be respected and serves as the basis for the right not to be dismissed unfairly.

Freedom of association is compatible with democracy. As a consequence, the ILO's freedom of association principles played an important role in bringing South Africa closer to genuine democracy (Tajgman 1994:50). The LRA in section 4 describes the right to freedom of association, as guaranteed by ILO Freedom of Association and Protection of the Right to Organise Convention, of 1948 and Sections 18 and 23 of the Constitution. The core of employees' freedom of association is their ability to associate or organise together, as well as create or join trade unions.

Employers have the same freedom to combine with other employers and create an employers' association (section 23(3) of the Constitution; section 6 of the LRA). According to Section 4(1) of the LRA, everyone has the right to participate in the formation of a trade union or federation of trade unions, as well as to join a union pursuant to its constitution. The LRA also specifies important features of freedom of association, such as the right of every member of a trade union, subject to the trade union's constitution, to engage in its legitimate activities and to vote for its office-bearers, officials, or union representatives.

Section 5(1) of the LRA enshrines these rights by declaring that no one may discriminate against an employee who exercises any of the rights granted by it. Moreover, the LRA provides protection not just to employees but also, according to Section 5(2), to job seekers. As a result, any Act, law, or agreement that may have the effect of limiting or depriving an employee, job seeker, or employer of the right to freedom of association will be in conflict with the LRA and the Constitution, and thus invalid and unconstitutional, unless such limitation complies with the constitutional limitation clause (section 36 of the Constitution). This is supported by Section 2 of the Constitution, which states that the Constitution is the supreme law of South Africa: any legislation passed by Parliament or administrative decision made by the executive that is inconsistent with the entrenched rights (including employment rights) in the Bill of Rights is void to the extent of the inconsistency with the provisions of the Constitution.

South African National Defence Union v Minister of Defence (CCT27/98) [1999] demonstrates the importance of freedom of association. The Constitutional Court ruled that section 126b(1) of the Defence Act 44 of 1957 was unlawful and unconstitutional because it violated section 23(2) of the Constitution. Sections 126B(1), (3) and (4) of the Defence Act forbade permanent force personnel from joining a trade union or engaging in strikes, acts of public protest, or similar actions. The Constitutional Court found justification for this momentous ruling in ILO Convention No. 87. Accordingly, article 9(1) of the Convention which states that "the degree to which the guarantees provided for in this Convention shall apply to armed forces and the police shall be established by national laws or regulation". Also, "any Member's ratification of this Convention must not be interpreted to undermine any existing legislation, custom, or agreement under which members of the armed forces or police enjoy any right granted by this Convention" (article 9(2)). In general, Chapter II of the LRA, which contains numerous technical rules governing the right to freedom of association, provides full effect to the Constitution's guarantee of freedom of association.

The employees' right to strike is a necessary component of their right to freedom of association, and the right to strike is one of the tools used by trade unions when collective bargaining fails. Strike action is the most visible form of collective action during labour disputes, and it is often seen as workers' organisations' final choice in pursuing their goals. Employees cannot freely use their right to freedom of association unless they are protected by the right to strike. According to Olivier, if the right to collective bargaining and strike are not sufficiently recognised, the right to freedom of association will be rendered useless (Olivier 2006:67). Sachs (1995:697) observes that the ability to establish and join a trade union, to bargain collectively, and to strike are the essential components of the right to freedom of association. Employees' most important and basic rights are those that allow them to fight for and protect their rights (Sachs 1995:697). Without the ability to strike, trade unions devolve into pitiful, weak organisations, and management's dominance becomes absolute. For employees, the right to strike is essential to good industrial relations and the collective bargaining system.' Without the right to strike, the right to negotiate collectively is jeopardised. Consequently, there can be no meaningful collective bargaining without the right to strike, and collective negotiation will be nothing more than collective begging (Manamela & Budeli 2013:310). Strikes are typically protected under international human rights legislation, which is reflected in agreements, laws, and principles intended at safeguarding and advancing universal human rights. It is also protected by international labour law.

Finally, the LRA offers dispute resolution options in situations of unfair dismissals and unfair labour disputes. Such disputes may be referred to Bargaining Councils or the CCMA for resolution. Depending on the nature of the disagreement, the dispute is arbitrated by the council or CCMA or adjudicated by the Labour Court if conciliation fails. The Basic Conditions of Employment Act [No. 75 of 1997] establishes channels for the collection of overdue payments, whilst the Employment Equality Act allows for the adjudication of discrimination cases.

Conclusion

International human and labour rights legislation is founded on international treaties ratified by the United Nations (UN). With ratification, members of the United Nations are bound by international instruments on the international plane. Because of this, it is important for all countries to safeguard employees' labour rights and promote a conducive work environment. Labour rights are human rights, and the capacity to exercise these rights at work is required for employees to enjoy a wide variety of other rights, whether economic, social, cultural, political, or otherwise. All applicable international and regional human rights treaties should be ratified by states. South Africa should ensure that everyone has access to labour rights, regardless of occupation, industry, or immigrant status. Employee rights guarantee that employees are treated fairly at work. All applicable international and regional human rights treaties should be ratified by states. States should ensure that everyone has access to labour rights, regardless of occupation, industry, or immigrant status. Employee rights guarantee that employees are treated fairly at work. Employers may abuse their employees, pay them unjustly, and terminate them without reason if they do not have employee rights. Employee rights shield employees from such abuses and guarantee that they are treated with dignity. Labour rights, employers might abuse their employees, pay them unjustly, and terminate them without reason. Employee rights shield employees from such abuses and guarantee that they are treated with dignity.

References

BHORAT, H. and CHEADLE, H., (2009) *Labour Reform in South Africa: Measuring Regulation and a Synthesis of Policy Suggestions.* [Online]. Available from: https://papers. ssrn.com/sol3/papers.cfm?abstract_id=2176756

BUHLUNGU, S., (2009) The Rise and Decline of the Democratic Organizational Culture in the South African Labor Movement, 1973 to 2000. *Labor Studies Journal,* 34(1), 91-111.

BUHLUNGU, S., (2003) The State of Trade Unionism in Post-Apartheid South Africa. *State of the nation: South Africa,* 43, 184-203.

CARBONE, C. E., (2015) To be or Not to be Forgotten: Balancing the Right to Know with The Right to Privacy in the Digital Age. *Va. J. Soc. Pol'y & L,* 22.

CHEADLE, H. and DAVIS, D., (1997) The Application of the 1996 Constitution in the Private Sphere. *South African Journal on Human Rights,* 13(1), 44-66.

COLEMAN, K. M., (1990) South Africa: The Unfair Labor Practice and the Industrial Court. *Comp. Lab. LJ,* 178.

CRUSH, J., (1992) The Compound in Post-Apartheid South Africa. *Geographical Review,* 82(4), 388-400.

FIORAMONTI, L. and OLIVIER, G., (2007) Altruism or self-interest? An exploratory study of the EU's external image in South Africa. *European Foreign Affairs Review,* 12(3), 401–419.

GRAWITZKY, R., (2011) *Collective Bargaining in Times of Crisis: A Case Study of South Africa.* [Online]. Available from: https://ideas.repec.org/p/ilo/ilowps/994676283 402676.html

HEINONLINE, (1975) *In the case of Kubheka v Imextra (Pty) Ltd 1975 (4) SA 484.* [Online]. Available from: https://heinonline.org/HOL/Page?handle=hein.journals/iljuta2&div =17&g_sent=1&casa_token=

KOOY, A, et al., (1979) *The Wiehahn Commission: A Summary.* Cape Town, University of Cape Town.

INTERNATIONAL LABOUR ORGANIZATION, (1973) *Bantu Labour Relations Regulation Act 1973.* [Online]. Available from: https://www.ilo.org/dyn/natlex/natlex4.detail?p_lang =en&p_isn=15792

INTERNATIONAL LABOUR ORGANIZATION, (1998) *ILO Declaration on Fundamental Principles and Rights at Work.* [Online]. Available from: https://www.ilo.org/declaration/lang-- en/index.htm#:~:text=The%20ILO%20Declaration%20on%20Fundamental,our%20social% 20and%20economic%20lives.

INTERNATIONAL LABOUR ORGANIZATION, (1948) *Freedom of Association and Protection of the Right to Organise Convention, 1948 (No. 87).* [Online]. Available from: https://www.ilo. org/static/english/inwork/cb-policy-guide/freedomofassocandrighttoorganiseno87.pdf

INTERNATIONAL LABOUR ORGANIZATION, (1982) *C158 - Termination of Employment Convention, 1982 (No. 158).* [Online]. Available from: https://www.ilo.org/dyn/normlex/en/f?p= NORMLEXPUB:12100:0::NO::P12100_ILO_CODE:C158#:~:text=The%20employment% 20of%20a%20worker,the%20undertaking%2C%20establishment%20or%20service.

LICHTENSTEIN, A., (2013) *From Durban to Wiehahn: Black workers, employers, and the state in South Africa during the 1970s.* Johannesburg, University of the Witwatersrand.

MANAMELA, E. and BUDELI, M., (2013). Employees' Right to Strike and Violence in South Africa. *Comparative and International Law Journal of Southern Africa,* 46(3), 308-336.

MANTOUVALOU, V., (2012) Are Labour Rights Human Rights? *European Labour Law Journal*, 3(2), 151-172.

MAYLAM, P., (1990) The Rise and Decline of Urban Apartheid in South Africa. *African Affairs*, 89(354), 57-84.

MITRUS, L., (2019) Potential Implications of the Matzak Judgment (Quality of Rest Time, Right to Disconnect). *European Labour Law Journal*, 10(4), 386-397.

NATIONAL ARCHIVES AND RECORDS SERVICE OF SOUTH AFRICA, (1956) *Labour Relations Act No. 28 of 1956.* [Online]. Available from: http://www.nationalarchives.gov.za/ sites/default/files/ITEM_COD-0079-0026-_-003.pdf

O'REGAN, C., (1997) 1979-1997: Reflecting on 18 Years of Labour Law in South Africa. *Indus. LJ*, 18.

PAGNATTARO, M. A., (2003) What Do You Do When You are Not at Work: Limiting the Use of Off-Duty Conduct as the Basis for Adverse Employment decisions. *U. Pa. J. Lab. & Emp. L.*, 6.

PANSU, L., (2018) Evaluation of 'Right to Disconnect' Legislation and Its Impact on Employee's Productivity. *International Journal of Management and Applied Research*, 5(3), 99-119.

RAMOLOTJA, M. A. and MPEDI, L. G., (2000) Labour Law in Southern Africa: A Look at South Africa and Swaziland. *S. Afr. Mercantile LJ*, *12*, p.420.

SACHS, A., (1995) Constitutional Developments in South Africa. *NYUJ Int'l L. & Pol.*, 28.

SAFLII, (2010) *Kylie v Commission for Conciliation Mediation and Arbitration and Others (CA10/08) [2010].* [Online]. Available from: http://www.saflii.org/za/cases/ ZALAC/2010/8.html

SAFLII, (2002) *National Education Health & Allied Workers Union (NEHAWU) v University of Cape Town and Others (CCT2/02) [2002].* [Online]. Available from: http://www.saflii.org/za/cases/ZACC/2002/27.html

SAFLII, (2002) *National Union of Metal Workers of South Africa and Others v Bader Bop (Pty) Ltd and Another (CCT14/02) [2002].* [Online]. Available from: http://www.saflii.org/za/cases/ZACC/2002/30.html

SAFLII, (1980) *P E Bosman Transport Works Committee v Piet Bosman Transport (Pty) Ltd (1980) ILJ 66.* [Online]. Available from: https://www.saflii.org/za/cases/ ZAGPJHC/2014/238.rtf

SAFLII, (1999) *South African National Defence Union v Minister of Defence (CCT27/98) [1999].* [Online]. Available from: http://www.saflii.org/za/cases/ZACC/1999/7.html

SMIT, P. P. and VAN ECK, B. B., (2010) International Perspectives on South Africa's Unfair Dismissal Law. *Comparative and International Law Journal of Southern Africa*, 43(1), 46-67.

SOUTH AFRICAN GOVERNMENT, (1977) *Basic Conditions of Employment Act 75 of 1997.* [Online]. Available from: https://www.gov.za/documents/basic-conditions-employment-act

SOUTH AFRICAN GOVERNMENT, (1993) Compensation for Occupational Injuries and Diseases Act 130 of 1993. [Online]. Available from: https://www.gov.za/documents/compensation-occupational-injuries-and-diseases-act#:~:text=The%20Compensation%20for%20Occupa tional%20Injuries,such%20injuries%20or%20diseases%3B%20and

SOUTH AFRICAN GOVERNMENT, (1975) *Defence Amendment Act.* [Online]. Available from: https://www.gov.za/sites/default/files/gcis_document/201504/act-1-1976.pdf

SOUTH AFRICAN GOVERNMENT, (2000) *Protected Disclosures Act 26 of 2000.* [Online]. Available from: https://www.gov.za/documents/protected-disclosures-act

SOUTH AFRICAN GOVERNMENT, (1998) *Employment Equity Act 55 of 1998.* [Online]. Available from: https://www.gov.za/documents/employment-equity-act

SOUTH AFRICAN GOVERNMENT, (1996) *Mine Health and Safety Act 29 of 1996.* [Online]. Available from: https://www.gov.za/sites/default/files/gcis_document/201409/act29of1996s.pdf

SOUTH AFRICAN GOVERNMENT, (2018) *National Minimum Wage Act No. 9 of 2018.* [Online]. Available from: https://www.gov.za/sites/default/files/gcis_document/202112/45649gon 1616.pdf

SOUTH AFRICAN GOVERNMENT, (1973) *Occupational Diseases in Mines and Works Act 78 of 1973.* [Online]. Available from: https://www.gov.za/documents/occupational-diseases-mines-and-works-act-21-apr-2015-1257#:~:text=The%20Occupational%20Diseases%20in%20 Mines,matters%20Incidental%20thereto.

SOUTH AFRICAN GOVERNMENT, (1993) *Occupational Health and Safety Act 85 of 1993.* [Online]. Available from: https://www.gov.za/sites/default/files/gcis_document/201409/ act85of1993.pdf

SOUTH AFRICAN GOVERNMENT, (1998) *Skills Development Act 97 of 1998.* [Online]. Available from: https://www.gov.za/documents/skills-development-act

SOUTH AFRICAN GOVERNMENT, (1996) *The Constitution of the Republic of South Africa.* [Online]. Available from: https://www.gov.za/documents/constitution/constitution-republic-south-africa-1996-1#:~:text=The%20Constitution%20of%20the%20Republic%20of%20South% 20Africa%2C%201996%2C%20was,the%20provisions%20of%20the%20Constitution.

TAJGMAN, D., (1994) *International Labour Standards in Southern Africa.* Cape Town, University of Cape Town.

TSHOOSE, C., (2014) Placing the Right to Occupational Health and Safety within a Human Rights Framework: Trends and Challenges for South Africa. *Comparative and International Law Journal of Southern Africa,* 47(2), 276-296.

UNITED NATIONS, (1948) *United Nations' Universal Declaration of Human Rights (UDHR) of 1948.* [Online]. Available from: https://www.un.org/en/udhrbook/pdf/udhr_ booklet_en_web.pdf

VAN ECK, S., BORAINE, A. and STEYN, L., (2004) Fair Labour Practices in South African Insolvency Law. *South African Law Journal,* 121(4), 902-925.

WEBSTER, E. and FORREST, K., (2021) The Role of the ILO during and after Apartheid. *Labor Studies Journal,* 46(4), 325-344.

WEBSTER, E. and OMAR, R., (2003) Work Restructuring in Post-Apartheid South Africa. *Work and Occupations,* 30(2), 194-213.

PART III:

HUMAN RIGHTS, DEMOCRACY

AND THE ENVIRONMENT

Has Democracy Lost its Aura?
Elections, Military Coups, and Human Rights: Selected Cases from Southern Africa

Daglous Makumbe

Introduction

The African Charter on Democracy, Elections, and Governance and the Protocol on Amendments to the Protocol on the Statute of the African Court of Justice and Human Rights stipulates that member states shall adopt all necessary measures to reject unconstitutional changes of power such as military coups by prosecuting the perpetrators of such egregious crimes. The two African establishments also state categorically and emphatically that they shall suspend the perpetrators from all activities of the African Union. The offenders of such crimes will also be thwarted from participating in the ensuing elections or occupying any positions of responsibility in the political institutions of their state. Apart from imposing sanctions on such perpetrators, the latter are also liable for prosecution before the African Criminal Court. The Southern African Development Community (SADC) also strongly condemns coups and has a zero-tolerance to unconstitutional government changes. Unconstitutional changes of power manifest themselves in different forms. A head of state may prolong his/her reign by tinkering with the constitution to prolong their stay in power. Such constitutional coups are typically instituted through referendums to legitimise the unconstitutional tenures. An incumbent leader may also prolong their tenure by failing to hold elections at the stipulated times. The leader may give excuses for not conducting the elections, such as the absence of finances to fund the elections, the need to update the voters' roll or the absence of a clear roadmap to the elections. The incumbent regime may also be removed from power through a military coup. Whichever way it happens, the three forms outlined above constitute unconstitutional changes of power and are outlawed by SADC and other continental bodies.

SADC has been found wanting in its approach to dealing with unconstitutional government changes in the region. Its stance on military, constitutional coups, and other term prolongations has been inconsistent, incompetent, and dismal. The Madagascan coup was the first instance that SADC was confronted with an illegitimate change of government in the region. The organisation failed to abide by institutional principles, which strongly outlaw illegitimate power changes. In the Madagascar and Zimbabwe situations, the world has witnessed SADC's successful legitimisation of coup governments, contrary to its institutional rules. In the Namibian and Democratic of Congo (DRC) situations, Africa has witnessed how constitutions can be manipulated to prolong an incumbent's tenure (Namibia) and how a head of state can utilise flimsy excuses and quiet diplomacy to prolong his tenure (DRC). Sam Nujoma of Namibia set the pace for constitutional prolongation, which became contagious to other African leaders. As a pioneer in third-termism, he set a bad precedent for many African leaders, who later emulated his constitutional stratagems to prolong their terms in office. The Madagascar situation became SADC's acid test to evaluate its institutional mechanisms to eliminate unconstitutional government changes. It was an excellent maiden testing ground to evaluate its efficacy in upholding and enforcing its protocols on democracy and good governance (Zounmenou 2009). SADC's poor handling of the Madagascan crisis can justifiably be asserted as setting a bad precedent for successive coups such as the Zimbabwean 2017 one. Its failure to thwart Sam Nujoma from extending his term can also be justifiably asserted as setting an alarming pace for other power-hungry African leaders who intended to prolong their tenures of office.

The Zimbabwean coup was elusive, clumsy, and camouflaged. The coupists tried to cover it up so that it did not appear to be a coup, but the events brazenly displayed a coup's characteristics. Some called it a 'soft coup,' while others called it a coup in 'slow motion' (Souare 2006). The military responsible for the coup preferred lightly calling it military constitutionalism or a bloodless correction. Rather than calling it a coup, the military tried to reduce it to an operation codenamed 'Restore Legacy.' SADC's approach to conflict resolutions, such as military and other unconstitutional changes and prolongations of power, has been inconsistent and shrouded in controversy. In Zimbabwe, for example, it first condemned the military takeover as a coup, then later affirmed it as not a coup. The Nordic Africa Institute (2018) notes:

> In practice, the principles that guide SADC's crisis responses are constantly renegotiated by the members of the Summit, whose composition is heterogeneous. The dominance of liberation-party governments, the lack of democratic commitment from some members, and SADC's limited capacity to enforce its principles in non-compliant regimes mean that stability and sovereignty tend to take precedence over democracy.

Military coups and all other forms of constitutional manipulations to prolong an incumbent's tenure of office deprive citizens of their right to vote for their preferred candidate, and hence to choice. Such rights are enshrined in national constitutions and regional and continental statutes. A breach of such fundamental rights manifests a dearth of democracy, which may breed dissent and insurrection.

The Notion of Democracy

Democracy is derived from two Greek words *demos*, which means people, and *kratos*, which means rule. It, therefore, means rule by the people or popular sovereignty (Becker & Prime 2008). Democracy can manifest itself in direct, representative or participatory forms of rule by the people, depending on the polity (Day 2022; Becker & Raveloson 2008). Democracy encompasses the rule of law (legality), judicial independence, separation of powers, majority rule, and the respect of minority rights. It also includes freedom of expression, association, and upholding human rights (Bassiouni et al 1998; Becker & Raveloson 2008). Human rights are a fundamental bedrock of democracy, and some of them include political and civil rights. They also incorporate social and economic rights, third generation rights such as the right to development and to the environment (Becker & Raveloson 2008). Genuine democracy entails that each individual be free to participate in the governance and all political activities of one's country. Democracy takes its stand on two significant cornerstones of constitutionalism and liberalism (Bassiouni 1998; Day 2022). Since elections are a defining characteristic of democracy, they should be fair, free, regular, and credible. A democratic election should be equitable, secret, and transparent. The results should also be announced timeously. Practices such as the usurpation of power through a military or constitutional coup are detrimental to democracy and undermine the essence of constitutionalism and majority rule.

Constitutional Coups

Namibia's Sam Nujoma: The Namibian Pioneer Multi-Term President

The prolongation of presidential tenures and manipulation of constitutional loopholes in Africa was pioneered by the former Namibian President Sam Nujoma. The behaviour had spill-over effects on other leaders, such as former Burundian President Pierre Nkrunzinza, who emulated Nujoma's tactics. The first president of the Republic of Namibia, Sam Nujoma, was elected before independence by the members of the Constituent Assembly and sworn in on Independence Day on 21 March 1990 (Melber 2015). Among the new constitutional provisions incorporated in the Namibian constitution was the fundamental provision that stipulated that any president was mandatorily allowed to serve for two five-year terms. It meant that President Nujoma, who assumed the Namibian highest office in 1990 and was re-elected to a second term in 1995, was supposed to end his second and final term in 2000, after which the constitution would forbid him to run for another term (Dulani 2011). There has been one significant constitutional amendment to the Namibian Constitution, that of Article 29(3). In 1999 it was amended to allow President Sam Nujoma to run for a third term of office (LeBeau 2018). South West African Peoples' Organisation's (SWAPO) first constitutional change was in 1998 when its two-thirds majority in parliament modified the two-term clause for presidents. Sam Nujoma was not directly elected by the people the first time by being appointed by the Constituent Assembly, so he was allowed to stand for re-election by popular vote for another third term (LeBeau 2018). Namibia's 1990 constitution, which contained term limits, was changed in 1999 to allow President Nujoma, who had been in power since 1990, to run for a third term. However, the two-term limit was not scrapped but amended for Nujoma only.

To quell domestic and international detractors who were suspicious and concerned about a possibility of a president-for-life syndrome, Nujoma's loyalists manipulated a constitutional loophole on technical grounds. They argued that since a Constituent Assembly had first elected the president in 1989, his first term of office fell outside the ambit of the constitutional definition of elections as being through direct universal and equal suffrage (Article 28 (2) of the Namibian Constitution 1990).

This narrow reading of the constitution reflected not only the manipulation of institutional rules to advance a personalistic agenda but also placed Namibia among a long list of countries that departed from adhering to the spirit of the constitution by focusing on the minutiae of the wording of the law itself. The third-term debate ultimately led to the tabling of a parliamentary motion in the Namibian legislature in 1998 seeking to amend the constitution to allow Nujoma to run for a third term. Although the lethargic Namibian civil society and opposition made frantic efforts to thwart this constitutional amendment, they were overpowered by SWAPO's parliamentary majority, which pushed the amendment bill without difficulty. Nujoma hastily signed the bill into law, paving the way for him to run for a third term in the 1999 elections, which he convincingly won with 77 per cent of the vote (Africa Elections Database 1999). All subsequent presidents have since been limited to two terms. Nujoma stepped down in 2004 because his party did not want to change the constitution again (Tull & Simons 2017). The Namibian constitutional manipulation set a bad precedent for successive African governments in Burundi, Uganda, Rwanda, and the Democratic Republic of Congo (DRC). It has led to the emergence of multi-term presidents in the continent, giving rise to military coups as the only remedy for removing such presidents.

SADC failed to thwart Sam Nujoma from extending his term of office, setting a bad precedent for other African heads of state across the continent. The Southern African organisation was supposed to prevent Nujoma when the malady was nascent. By failing to thwart Nujoma, it became difficult to do so when the third-term pandemic had become a norm in many African states. It became difficult to stop leaders such as Robert Mugabe and Joseph Kabila from abiding by their countries' constitutions and refrain from meddling with them to prolong their tenures. Sam Nujoma, as the third-term pioneer president, started on a comprehensive rational model in which other African heads of state incremented. The failure of SADC to stop him from the onset paved the way for the organisation's failure to do so in other countries bedevilled by such political pathologies. Term prolongations through toying with constitutions is thus one political tool that some Southern African leaders are utilising to stay in power for a long time. It is the region's undoing as it is counterproductive to democracy and is a brazen violation of citizens' rights to choose their preferred leaders.

Democratic Republic of the Congo

Presidential term prolongation in a quest to tamper with the constitution to run for a third term is a political spirit that gripped the Democratic Republic of Congo (DRC) under former President Joseph Kabila. From 2015 tensions in the country grew. In the majority opinion, former president Joseph Kabila was manoeuvring to secure a prolongation of his tenure in the face of term limits (Africa Elections Database 1999). Six months before the end of his constitutional mandate, Kabila gave few signals on crucial questions which had been gripping the country for months. Without presidential declarations, Kabila's lieutenants and members of the presidential majority spoke on the one hand about a peaceful change of power at the end of the mandate.

In contrast, others talked of the inevitable delay of the elections. Others mentioned an ardent desire to see Joseph Kabila pursue (for as long as possible) his mission as the head of the country (Libebe 2016; Wolters 2018). Kabila vowed to remain silent over whether he would step down at the end of his term. The courts, the National Independent Electoral Commission, and the National Assembly were manipulated because a single man wanted to stay in power. It was against the will of most Congolese, who wanted to see the constitution implemented to guarantee the end of the second term and democratic change (Libebe 2016). The silence came to be because all the institutions that should be independent and impartial were subservient to Kabila's regime (Libebe 2016).

The Democratic Republic of Congo, just like other upcoming African democracies, established term limits in their constitutions in perpetuity to safeguard against the long-term personal rule. The rejection of personal rule and the support for term limits is perceptible at the level of public opinion. In a survey across 34 African states, Dulani (2015) found that 73 percent of citizens favour term limits, perhaps partly because elections offer only slim chances to oust incumbents, making term limits all the more relevant (Dulani 2015). In January 2014, demonstrations occurred in the DRC after former President Joseph Kabila attempted to modify the constitution and electoral laws to stay in power for more than two terms. It resulted in the death of 27 demonstrators. It also culminated in the Congolese parliament amending Article 220 from the updated constitution. The amendment would have allowed Joseph Kabila to remain in power after December 2016, when his second term ended (Camara 2016). The quest to meddle with the constitution and prolong Kabila's presidential term was Kabila's undoing. It delayed the country's presidential and legislative elections by two years (Wolters 2019).

A dilemma over power maintenance or peaceful transition remained prevalent as Kabila maintained his silence over whether he would step down or contest the 2016 presidential race. He was elected in 2006 and re-elected in 2011 amidst allegations of a fraudulent electoral process (Mbiatem 2018). Kabila made several attempts to cling to power and prolong his term. The first attempt was in June 2015, when he suggested that the presidential and parliamentary elections should be contingent upon completing a new electoral roll. The proposal sparked violent demonstrations, leading to over 40 people dying in violent clashes with the police (Mbiatem 2018). Protesters were angry with the decision to carry out a national census ahead of the poll, which many considered could delay the polls for years, thus allowing the President to postpone standing down. Kabila also sought to extend his presidential term by postponing elections from December 2016 to April 2018, a move that the Catholic Church and the main opposition coalition parties vehemently opposed (Maclean & Burke 2016). Kabila's second attempt to cling to power was when he struggled to organise a national dialogue with the opposition, which some opposition parties and civil society members boycotted. It intended to maintain him at the helm of an eventual national unity government (Maclean & Burke 2016). The third attempt was to increase the number of provinces from 11 to 26 as of 30 June 2015, which many observers viewed as a ploy to gain political momentum from loyalists he appointed to rule the new provinces, hence weakening political opponents (Engel 2010).

SADC failed to respond promptly to the DRC crisis when former President Joseph Kabila failed to conduct elections before his constitutional term expired. Kabila's quiet diplomacy plunged the country into a political catastrophe as people became anxious and restless. The ensuing demonstrations that rocked the country as people demanded elections had tragic consequences. SADC has therefore been found wanting to thwart the emerging and sophisticated political stratagems that modern African leaders are adopting to stay in power. It became challenging to prevent the third-term presidential stampede when it had consolidated in the region. The failure to stamp its authority to curb the problem in the Namibian situation meant that it grew in scope and magnitude, making it challenging to eradicate.

Military Coups

Madagascar Military Coup

SADC's incompetence, inconsistency, and ambiguity can also be realised in the Madagascar situation. Unlike the Sam Nujoma and Joseph Kabila constitutional prolongation, the Madagascan political transition was a debilitating military coup, the first such case in Southern Africa. In March 2009, the Madagascar military staged a coup against the then President Marc Ravalomanana. The official behind the coup was the then Antananarivo mayor Andry Rajoelina, who in 2008 had indoctrinated opposition members that Ravalomanana was consolidating his presidential powers and constricting freedoms. It was exacerbated by other anti-government protesters remonstrating allegations of government corruption and the deteriorating economic conditions (Plock & Cook 2012). Massive anti-government demonstrations of monumental proportions claimed 70 lives (Lanz & Gasser 2013). The army's mutiny was a critical factor that made Ravalomanana resign, compelling him to relinquish power to the military officers on 17 March 2009 (World Peace Foundation 2017). The army's intervention in the country's political transition tainted the military-led regime with illegality. It was thus unconstitutional and a brazen usurpation of power. When Ravalomanana went into exile in South Africa, he claimed his legitimacy since he had been ousted unconstitutionally. It gave rise to his supporters to carry out massive demonstrations in which they clashed with Rajoelina supporters. The clashes led to deaths on the streets (Lunn 2012). Plock (2010) notes that in the subsequent weeks, over 135 people were killed in demonstrations and riots. According to the country's constitution, when the president resigns, power should be ceded to the parliament speaker, and elections be held within two months following that resignation.

Although SADC invested some efforts in the Madagascan crisis, it failed to abide by institutional rules, legitimising an illegitimate regime. The organisation's efforts were an antithesis to organisational rules that explicitly delegitimize unconstitutional power changes. It suspended Madagascar from the regional family of nations in March 2009 in response to the military coup (Africa et al. 2009). The former stressed its stance of suspending Madagascar from all SADC structures through its Double Troika Summit Communique issued at Maputo in June 2010. The ban would be lifted if the Rajoelina-led coup regime restored constitutional order in the country (Chigara 2018). With its lead negotiator, former Mozambican President Joaquim Chissano, SADC led the negotiations and mediation process (Lanz & Gasser 2013). The negotiation efforts led to a power-sharing deal in Maputo (The Maputo Accords) on 9 August 2009 (Bearack 2009). The Maputo Accords stipulated a 15-month transition period followed by elections. The latter would culminate in an inclusive government headed by a president, prime minister, and two parliamentary bodies (Lanz & Gasser 2013). The agreement was, however, ephemeral as neither side could agree on who should assume the role of president in the transition period. SADC was restricted by protocol rules and regulations that outlawed coup leaders and did not require them to remain in office (Nathan 2013). SADC proposed the use of military means to reinstate Ravalomanana. However, a United Nations mediation entourage member found it unfavourable to mediation. Such a stance, it was proposed, would leave Rajoelina convinced that SADC preferred the ousted Ravalomanana at his expense (Nathan 2013).

The realisation of SADC's strong anti-coup stance motivated Ravalomanana to shun any SADC negotiations with an illegitimate power usurper. At the same time, it also convinced Rajoelina that the negotiations would not offer him anything. Consequently, Ravalomanana and Rajoelina's perceptions of SADC became pessimistic. Both parties became convinced they were better off without SADC-initiated negotiations (Nathan 2013). The staunch French High Transitional Authority (HAT) and military support for Rajoelina dissuaded Ravalomanana from participating in the negotiations. SADC's robust institutional stance against military coups demotivated Rajoelina from cooperating in the negotiations. It led to the combined SADC, African Union (AU), the International Organisation of the Francophonie (OIF), and United Nations (UN) team failing to mediate between the two belligerent parties effectively (Nathan 2013). The Addis Ababa Additional Act of November 2009 exposed SADC's lack of policy consistency and abidance to institutional rules. It is because the belligerent parties signed a treaty that made Rajoelina a transitional president and flanked by two co-presidents from the other two parties. The two co-presidents will be executing subordinate roles. This act indeed legitimised the Rajoelina coup, making it de jure. It deviated from SADC's stance on zero-tolerance to unconstitutional changes of power. Such an act may also motivate other potential coupists from other African countries to do the same, hoping their illegitimate acts will ultimately be legitimised, as in the Rajoelina situation.

Rajoelina had promised to conduct elections in 2010 but instead held a unilateral constitutional referendum that lowered the presidential age from 40 to 30 years. It necessitated him to stand for the presidency. The SADC Troika also concurred that the minimum age threshold that one can stand for the presidency could be reduced from 40 to 35, as proposed by the Rajoelina-propelled constitution, which enabled him to contest. The act of affirmation by the SADC Troika seemed to legitimise Rajoelina's illegality and his perpetuation to stay in power (Lunn 2012). It also stipulated that an inclusive transitional government would be formed and legislative and presidential elections held within twelve months from the day of the agreement. It also stated that the interim president, Andre Rajoelina, would remain president (Lunn 2012). SADC's decision could be interpreted as justifying and consolidating illegitimacy, thereby deviating from its institutional rules. By continuing to vest presidential powers to Rajoelina in a transitional government, it showed its inconsistency, ambiguity, and lack of policy consistency. The softening of the organisation's stance towards unconstitutional changes of power compromised organisational standards, ethics, and values, making a mockery of the organisation.

In September 2011, the belligerent Madagascan political parties signed an agreement to hold elections within the next 12 months. In the amnesty that followed the transitional government, SADC encouraged Rajoelina to allow Ravalomanana to return to the country, with the option for him to be incarcerated and prosecuted upon arrival. It was a poor decision by SADC because the ousted legitimate president was becoming a perpetrator under the SADC mediation process. The illegitimate president had been bestowed with powers to prosecute as if he was legitimate. SADC was also supposed to be wary of politicised prosecutions initiated to keep Ravalomanana out of the political landscape. In December 2012, SADC convinced Rajoelina to contest in the forthcoming elections. The belligerent leaders were urged to accept the 'ni-ni' option (Ploch 2010). Although Ravalomanana accepted and nominated his wife to stand for the elections, Rajoelina also backed out and entered the presidential race (Fabricius 2013). Rajoelina also missed the deadline for submitting his nomination papers and was still accepted. His participation in the ensuing elections had adverse effects on SADC and Madagascar. It tainted the organisation's image as a trusted force in restoring legitimacy. It also deprived the people of Madagascar of freedom of choice and expression under a coup regime. It is also economically detrimental to lifting economic and political embargoes under illegitimate circumstances (Dewar et al. 2013).

SADC's approach to crises such as military and constitutional coups has proven to be impotent, ambiguous, contradictory, and inconsistent. They allowed Rajoelina to be in power for two years as an interim president despite usurping power through a coup. The decision also contradicts its zero tolerance to unconstitutional changes of government. It also contradicts the African Charter on Democracy, Elections, and Governance and the Protocol on Amendments on the Statute of the African Court of Justice and Human Rights, of which SADC is part. The two statutes stipulate that they shall adopt all necessary measures to reject unconstitutional power changes, such as military coups, by prosecuting the perpetrators of such egregious crimes. The two continental establishments also state categorically and emphatically that they shall suspend the perpetrators from all activities of the African Union, a sanction that SADC failed to institute. The offenders of such crimes will also be thwarted from participating in the ensuing elections or occupying any positions of responsibility in the political institutions of their state, a sanction that SADC failed to implement on Rajoelina. Apart from imposing sanctions on such perpetrators, the perpetrator will also be liable for prosecution before the African Criminal Court, a sanction SADC failed to implement, even prosecuting Rajoelina at its Tribunal.

The SADC response to the Madagascan crisis may be construed as promoting and rewarding military coupists in Madagascar, particularly in Southern Africa. South Africa, a leading SADC member, also made a controversial move in January 2012 when it invited Rajoelina to the African National Congress' 100th Anniversary

(Centenary Celebrations). The gesture affirmed and consolidated Rajoelina's position as the legitimate president of Madagascar. The move may also send waves of suspicion to the international community that South Africa was behind the Rajoelina coup and backing it. Many argue that representing Madagascar and masquerading as the country's legitimate president violated the decisions and statutes of the African Union, which had imposed a travel ban on Andre Rajoelina (Businessday 2012).

Zimbabwe Military Coup

SADC failed the Zimbabwean situation as a trusted peace and legitimacy restoration force. It failed to restore legitimacy when the army usurped power through a military coup in November 2017. Although some scholars may argue that the coup was elusive and soft, that view may be construed as lazy and incompetent scholarship because it is not the president (Robert Mugabe) who deployed the armed forces, one of the core duties that a Commander-in-Chief does. All the characteristics of a military coup were present when the military took over power in Zimbabwe. The army took control of the parliament, the State House, and the Zimbabwe Broadcasting Corporation. It also subjected then-President Robert Mugabe and his family to house arrest. Senior army officers who took charge of the broadcasting services replaced the national radio and television presenters. The then army General Constantin Chiwenga and Major General Sibusiso Moyo made announcements on national radio and television services. The army also took control of the parliament and Mugabe's home in Borrowdale, where he was held hostage. Mugabe's close allies, such as the former police Commissioner-General Augustine Chihuri, and cabinet ministers, such as Saviour Kasukuwere and Jonathan Moyo, were all subjected to house arrest.

Although the army repackaged the coup by furnishing it with names such as 'military constitutionalism,' 'bloodless correction,' and 'Operation Restore Legacy,' the actions and developments could not harbour its brazen illegality. It also camouflaged the coup by mobilising the masses to march to the state house and the former president's private home. It was deliberately intended to legitimise the coup and make the outside world believe that the people of Zimbabwe were removing their president (Makumbe 2017). The military also referred to Mugabe throughout the coup as the Commander-In-Chief of the defence forces and the President of Zimbabwe, even if they had subjected him to house arrest. They also allowed him to make international calls to other SADC regional leaders. He was also allowed to perform his ceremonial role to cap graduates at the Zimbabwe Open University as the Chancellor. Mugabe was also allowed to give a televised address to the nation, followed by senior army officers who saluted him after the broadcast session. The Zimbabwe Defence Forces (ZDF) further tried to camouflage the coup by engaging with the media that Operation Restore Legacy was not a coup and therefore did not violate any democratic structures in SADC and AU constitutional statutes (Roessler 2017). The military said the coup aimed to eliminate criminals around Mugabe and restore the situation to normalcy (The Guardian 2017).

The Zimbabwean military coup received widespread support from the masses, who perceived it as an emancipatory move to thwart Mugabe from establishing a family dynasty in the country, imposition of arbitrary rule, and the neglect of the ethos of the liberation struggle (Roessler 2017). Zimbabweans from all walks of life and political affiliations unanimously welcomed the military coup with great enthusiasm, pomp, pageantry, fanfare, and ceremony to mark the political demise of a dictator. They endorsed the military coup by flooding the streets across the country. They utilised placards and social media platforms, exhorting SADC and the AU to stay away from meddling in Zimbabwean politics and the then state of affairs (Chigara 2018). There were tweets and retweets on social media to keep SADC away, such as the hashtag *#SADC Back off Zimbabwe* and other posts declaring SADC, the AU, and former South African President Jacob Zuma to stay away from Zimbabwean politics or they would face severe consequences (Institute for Security Studies Today 2017). Mackintosh (2017:11) says:

> It immediately attracted spontaneous, voluntary, universal support of all Zimbabweans who then fanned its power fervently and unrelentingly from literally every part of the country. This sui generis operando compelled Western media to introduce a new vocabulary, namely, 'a coup d'état that is not a coup'.

All these seemingly-legitimate events and developments camouflaged the coup and gave Operation Restore Legacy some veneer of legality, making it appear like anything but a coup. The dexterous manoeuvre by the army to usurp power in this way appeared to disable and confuse SADC's hand of intervention to maintain its zero-tolerance on unconstitutional government changes.

Although Robert Mugabe had fallen out of favour with the international community and many African leaders, SADC failed him by failing to intervene and restore legitimacy effectively. Former Zambian President Edgar Lungu denounced such an unconstitutional usurpation of power. Lungu (2017:19) declares, "The military's illegal takeover of power in Zimbabwe is not in tune with modern politics. SADC will negotiate the way forward with Mugabe as Head of State. The army goes back to the barracks." Zambian media houses further noted that President Edgar Lungu was prepared to send his troops to Zimbabwe to uphold and support Mugabe's regime and restore legitimacy (Mukori 2017). As the coup was unfolding, SADC was caught in the unenviable position of either condemning and intervening in the coup and appearing to be supporting a dictatorial and oppressive regime of Mugabe or supporting the coup and risking neglecting its principles of zero tolerance to unconstitutional changes of power. SADC preferred the latter option because the coup was popular, and many regional and international partners no longer preferred Mugabe. Roessler (2017:8) avers:

> In stark contrast to the Peace and Security Council's immediate and forceful rejection of nearly every other coup since the African Union was founded in 2002, the African Union tacitly supported the forcible removal of Mugabe from power, a position that the Southern African Development Community (SADC), which the African Union was happy to defer to in managing the crisis, also held. To justify its inaction, the African Union ultimately declared the Zimbabwe Defence Forces intervention did not constitute a coup d'état, after initially suggesting the opposite.

The failure of SADC to restore legitimacy in Zimbabwe can be revealed by Mugabe's interview in 2018. He unequivocally stated that his regional counterparts in SADC neglected him, especially South Africa, which had the most remarkable military strength in the region. He stated that the South African Defence and Security ministers dispatched to Zimbabwe by the then South African President Jacob Zuma misrepresented the situation as tranquil and pleasing. They also misrepresented Mugabe by reporting to the South African government that they had talked to Mugabe and the soldiers, respectively, and all agreed that there was no need to intervene (News24 2018). SADC failed Mugabe, democracy, and its fundamental principles on unconstitutional power changes. It was supposed to condemn the coup, whether de facto or de jure, suspend Zimbabwe from SADC and the AU, impose sanctions on the military junta, and intervene militarily to restore legitimacy. Such a response was to strengthen SADC's stance on anti-coup norms.

On the contrary, by failing to intervene, SADC endorsed a factional coup by the Zimbabwe military and its former Vice President Emmerson Mnangagwa. SADC now sees the coup perpetrators in key positions in the post-Mugabe government in direct contravention of the organisational ethos and regulations. Philip Roessler laments that SADC got it wrong by failing to intervene to thwart Operation Restore Legacy. Roessler (2017:38) says:

> The African Union, in alignment with SADC, got it wrong and missed a valuable opportunity to strengthen and expand its non-coup regime to include de jure and de facto coups. In narrowly focusing on the removal of the sitting head of state as the defining feature of a coup rather than the unconstitutional use of force to coerce elected leaders to relinquish power, it sets a dangerous precedent that threatens to undermine the strong gains the region has made to move beyond politics by the gun.,

From the Zimbabwean 2017 coup experience, it became apparent that for SADC, the prohibition of unconstitutional changes of government was based on a peace and security craft that considered factors such as stability and popular support of the coup, which necessitated them to compromise their stance towards the illegitimate usurpation of power. For SADC, when the coups are bloodless and popular, they are tolerated, affirmed, and legitimised. The Nordic Africa Institute (2018) corroborates:

> By accepting the de facto coup, SADC not only displayed its impotence vis-à-vis the Zimbabwean 'securocrats' and its unwillingness to pay the high cost of enforcing democratic principles but also set a dangerous precedent, signalling that the Community would tolerate unconstitutional changes of government and military meddling, just so long as they were thinly dressed up in constitutional clothing.

The usurpation of power through military coups deprives Zimbabweans of their right to choose a leader of their own. A coup also comes with restrictions on human rights, such as the right to free movement, assembly, and expression. When the Zimbabwean military junta was in charge of the country, the subsequent 2018 elections were not free and fair as the military government shot and killed fifteen demonstrators who were protesting against the procrastination of election results on 1 August 2018. The suppression of human rights is one real detriment of military coups, counterproductive to democracy.

Has Democracy Lost Its Aura?

Evidently, democracy is losing its aura in the 21st century. Constitutions are rigged as incumbent leaders are tinkering with constitutions to prolong their terms. Elections are rigged and widely contested, often ending up in the constitutional courts in such countries as Zimbabwe and Kenya. While there is a proliferation of elections in the world more than ever before, the average quality of democracy worldwide has deteriorated for the last decade. The primary reason is that authoritarian regimes are now conversant with how to manipulate and rig elections (Cheeseman & Klaas 2018). Military and constitutional coups have become rampant, compromising the efficacy and efficiency of democracy. Military coups have ravished countries like Zimbabwe, Madagascar, Egypt, Mali, Sudan, Cambodia, Thailand, Myanmar Gambia, and Burkina Faso, amongst other states. Constitutional coups are also a new form of rigging which is currently experienced in countries such as Rwanda, Uganda, Zimbabwe, the Republic of Congo, Democratic Republic of Congo, Madagascar, Burundi, Equatorial Guinea, Togo, Belarus, Turkey, North Korea, and Russia. As Bratton, Mattes and Gyimah-Boadi (2005:36) assert, "…their genesis lies in the previous military and one-party arrangements, now adapted for survival in a more open environment. Leaders have learned how to manipulate the rules of the democratic game and to stage-manage low-quality elections to their advantage."

Democracy is also losing its sensation as election results are being deliberately procrastinated to massage the results in favour of the incumbent. In Thailand, elections take up to 45 days to be announced, while in Zimbabwe, they may take up to 60 days, for example, in the run-off of the 2008 elections. Bizarre and awkward formulas to calculate the election figures have also been adopted to outsmart the opposition. In contrast, some crude tactics have been utilised, such as hitting the opposition leader(s) with multiple legal cases to bar them from contesting. In Zimbabwe, opposition legislator Job Sikhala failed to contest due to continual incarceration and multiple state allegations that barred him from contesting. Former opposition leader Morgan Tsvangirai was continually dragged to court over high treason charges, while in Uganda, opposition leaders Kiza Besigye and Robert Kyagulanyi Ssentamu (Bobi Wine) were continually persecuted through the courts. The incumbent leaders are also gerrymandering constituencies in areas where they have more significant support, such as rural areas. Former Nigerian President Shehu Shagari and Robert Mugabe of Zimbabwe gerrymandered constituencies to give them a legislative numerical advantage. Ballot stuffing and applying tipp-ex correction fluid to alter voters' choices have also been Africa's undoing, and it has caused democracy to lose its aura. Ballot stuffing flawed the Kenyan 2007 elections, leaving more than 1000 people dead, while the 2019 Malawian elections were nullified when supporters of former President Peter Mutharika altered ballot papers by applying tippex correction fluid in their favour.

Vote-buying has also caused democracy to lose its impression because it constitutes electoral corruption. The distribution of goodies such as food, clothing, and money has compromised elections. During the time of Robert Mugabe and the incumbent Mnangagwa regime, Zimbabwe has been known for vote-buying and was one of the major complaints of the opposition in the 2018 constitutional court challenge. Cheeseman and Klaas (2018:4) say "Between 2012 and 2016, more than two-thirds of elections in Africa and almost half of all elections in Asia and post-Soviet Europe featured significant vote-buying. Worse still, more than a third of these regions' elections saw state violence targeting opposition parties and their supporters." Democracy has also been undermined by incumbent regimes which menace and persecute the opposition, resurrect the dead in the voters' roll so that they get to vote for the ruling parties, and the launching of disinformation campaigns to indoctrinate people with false information, cast fear or intimidate them. In Zimbabwe, for example, the rural folk have been made to believe that voting for the opposition party is tantamount to returning the country to Rhodesia's former white colonial regime. In some states such as Ukraine, the ruling party matches the opposition leader's name with a similar name on the ballot paper to confuse voters and disenfranchise the opposition; for example, Yulia Tymoshenko found her name next to Yulia V. Tymoshenko (Cheeseman & Klaas 2018).

Some barbaric tactics that cause democracy to lose its impression have also been utilised to disenfranchise and annihilate the opposition parties, such as matching political parties on the ballot paper and with similar emblems and slogans. In the Zimbabwean 2008 harmonised elections, for example, there were four Movement for Democratic Change parties lining up in sequence on the same ballot paper and with similar emblems and slogans. There was MDC-Tsvangirai (MDC-T), MDC-Ncube (MDC-N), MDC-Mutambara (MDC-M), and MDC-99. In Zimbabwe, again, fearful of the opposition leader Nelson Chamisa, the ruling party pundits were on a drive to amend the legislation to raise the presidential age for aspiring candidates from 40 to 65. Excluding the opposition leader from contesting in the 2023 harmonised elections was advocated. In some states, such as Benin, setting financial rules for a prospective candidate in 2018 disqualified all opposition candidates, leaving the election a one-person race and an obvious winner. In some states, people vote without choosing, hence short-circuiting democracy. In Mobutu Sese Seko's Zaire (now the Democratic Republic of Congo), the former regularly conducted elections in which he was the sole candidate. North Koreans, for example, elect their puppet legislature using ballot papers containing a single name, without even a box to tick. Sometimes ballot boxes and all other polling materials are delivered to opposition strongholds in the late hours of the last day of voting to disenfranchise the opposition, such as in the Ugandan 2016 elections and the Zimbabwean 2023 harmonised elections. In other states, such as Côte d'Ivoire, crude tactics have been utilised by the ruling party against the opposition, such as excluding opposition candidates from the ballot paper.

Anti-democratic manoeuvres have also been utilised to outsmart the opposition, such as assassinating the opposition leader. In Pakistan, for example, opposition leader Benazir Bhutto was assassinated in 2007, while in Kazakhstan, Zamanbek Nurkadilov was also assassinated, excluding him from the 2005 elections. Opposition politicians have also been murdered, even in local government elections. Cheeseman and Klaas (2018) notes: "in Brazil, 22 people were murdered in the run-up to the local government elections in 2002, leading 410 towns to request additional security from the police." International support for democracy and free and fair elections is also on the decline as the United States of America and its Western counterparts are now prioritising other issues such as climate change, Lesbians, Gay, Bisexual, Transgender, and Queer (LGBT) issues, war on terror, global warming and the Russo Ukraine-NATO war and the current Middle East Hamas-Israeli war. Authoritarian regimes like Russia and China are gaining momentum in international politics and countering the West, attracting other states such as the African continent, India, Iran, Saudi Arabia, North Korea, Argentina, and Brazil. The election of Donald Trump in 2016 in the United States has also led democracy to take a nosedive. From repudiating the election defeat to the 6 January 2021 ransacking of the Capitol, Trump has been accused of diminishing democracy. He has also been accused of doing the same by hobnobbing with authoritarian regimes of North Korea, Russia, the Philippines, Egypt, and Turkey. It has sent optimistic waves to other authoritarian regimes that the United States no longer sanctions them but can ally with them. American foreign policy has thus made states maraud democracy rather than uphold it.

Do African States Still Need Democracy?

Africa has reached a point where it is questioning whether it needs democracy. The answer is affirmative because the moment Africa perceives democracy as alien will be tantamount to stooping so low from a de-colonial perspective. When Africa ostracises democracy, it admits it is accustomed to tyranny and dictatorship, and democracy does not belong to it. Africa only has to question whether it needs Western liberal democracy as a template, as a universalisation of democracy, as Francis Fukuyama would say. One is justified to differ in proposing that Western liberal democracy appeals to the African developmental trajectory. It is because democracy is facing an incipient decline. Since Donald Trump took over the presidency in 2016, democracy has been in free flow. Democracy has been going down the precipice. Authoritarianism as an alternative form of government is on the increase, is on the rise. Authoritarianism in some quarters has since proved that one does not necessarily need democracy to be developed or to be competitive globally. Some examples are China and its charming effect and its rise. Russia is another example of an authoritarian state at war but progressing.

In Africa, Paul Kagame's Rwanda is an authoritarian regime that is doing well. If one scrutinises Kagame's government, it is sad news. However, regarding economic developmental trajectory issues, Rwanda has since proved that a country can still develop without necessarily democratising. Thus, democracy is now cosmetology, face powder, to conceal the dictatorship and autocracy inherent in many African states. Democracy is thus now a façade. We are witnessing a scenario where almost all African states are characterised as competitive authoritarian regimes with every democratic posture and structure in place. However, the truth is that no structure would torpedo the status quo, resulting in the ruling party or incumbent losing power, ceding power, and paving for the opposition.

Democratic and Undemocratic Countries

Southern African states with a dearth of democracy may need to emulate what other democratic states are doing in their jurisdictions to attain democracy in order to strike a balance. To harmonise democracy between them, those states deemed to lack democracy may need to emulate the institutions, ways, and values of the democratic states. For SADC states that have been deemed to lack democratic values, they need to adopt the Mauritius example. Mauritius' mature and stable democracy is a good advertisement for the country. It is the only country in the SADC region classified as fully democratic in Sub-Saharan Africa in 2021 by the Democratic Index, a survey premised on five democratic categories. They include electoral processes, the functioning of a state's government, pluralism, civil liberties, political participation, and culture (Statista 2023). Mauritius scored a democratic milestone of 8.08 points, which earned it the enviable status of the most democratic state in the entire African continent (Statista 2023). It is traditionally a country with a democratic and peaceful transition through free, fair, credible, and regular elections. There are no instances of coups, both constitutional and military. All fundamental human rights are observed, respected, and practised. Unlike other SADC member states' constitutions, the Mauritius one is unique because it incorporates inclusivity. It allows the country's electoral commission to allocate up to eight additional seats to unsuccessful candidates from minority communities that are underrepresented. It is done through a process called the Best Loser System (US Department of State 2022). Therefore, unlike other SADC states, there are no winners or losers in elections but partners in Mauritius. SADC states with a dearth of democracy may need to copy the Mauritian example to revamp democracy in their jurisdictions.

SADC member states that lack democracy may also need to emulate the Botswana and South African democratic principles, institutions, and conducts. Although the two countries are classified under a flawed democracy, they ranked well in the democratic index. Botswana ranked second from Mauritius, and South Africa ranked fourth from Cape Verde (Statista 2023). Although Botswana's democracy and human rights record is in general decline under President Mokgweetsi Masisi (US Department of State 2022), the country's democratic history shows that there has never been a constitutional or military coup. There is also a clear separation of power since attaining independence in 1966. The South African example can also be emulated due to its democratic posture. Since the attainment of independence in 1994, the country has managed to maintain democratic and constitutional transitions. South Africa has never experienced unconstitutional government changes through a military or constitutional coup. Its elections have been peaceful, free, fair, regular, and democratic. It is one country where election results have never been contested and acts as a shining star and torch-bearer of democracy in Africa. Although the country's unscathed democratic record has deteriorated under Presidents Jacob Zuma and Cyril Ramaphosa (through undemocratic tendencies such as corruption (state capture), xenophobia, riots, and lootings) (US Department of State 2022), South Africa remains a credible democratic model that other SADC states with a dearth of democracy can emulate.

Conclusion

SADC still needs to contain unconstitutional changes of government in the region. Such illegitimate means range from presidential term prolongations to coup d'états. The Madagascar crisis was an acid test for SADC to assess its efficacy in dealing with military coups. The poor handling of the Madagascan crisis may have motivated the Zimbabwean coupists to manipulate SADC's impotence and stage a coup in 2017. Sam Nujoma became Namibia's third-term pioneer president. He embarked on an unconstitutional third term unfettered and set a bad precedent for future regional leaders. In both the Madagascar and Zimbabwe situations, SADC has been seen to vacillate and alter organisational rules to support the perpetrator. SADC failed to capitalise by thwarting Nujoma from extending his presidential term from the onset. It became difficult to do so when other African presidents followed the same trend. Although the African Charter explicitly states zero tolerance to unconstitutional government changes, SADC has failed to take stern measures to change the status quo. It has often affirmed the illegality, mocking its institutional rules and regulations. Democracy has lost its aura in this period as authoritarianism and dictatorship have gained momentum. The rise of Russia and China, perceived as autocracies, has countered that of the United States, making autocratic tendencies counter democracy. Democracy has also lost its splendour as autocracies are devising discreet and sophisticated methods that cannot be detected by election monitors, making it difficult to condemn or nullify an election. The Trump administration in the United States allegedly changed the democratic pendulum by transmogrifying it. Authoritarian regimes have been fraternised, hardening them and making them more repressive and aggressive. Although democracy is in a general decline, Africa still needs it, for to ignore or ostracise it will be tantamount to sliding back to the barbarous ages. The threat to democracy has drastically threatened human rights such as the right to choice, freedom of association, expression, and assembly.

References

AFRICAN UNION, (2012) *African Charter on Democracy, Elections and Governance*. [Online]. Available from: http://www.ipu.org/idd-E/afr_charter.pdf

AFRICAN UNION, (2009) *Africa Union Peace and Security Communique CLXXS1*. [Online]. Available from: https://www.sites.tufts.edu/wpf/files/2017/07/Madagascar-brief.pdf

BASSIOUNI, C, et al., (1998). *Democracy: Its Principles and Achievement*. Geneva, Inter-Parliamentary Union.

BASSIOUNI, C, (1998) Toward a Universal Declaration on the Basic Principles of Democracy: From Principles to Realisation. In Bassiouni et al. (ed.). *Democracy: Its Principles and Achievement*. Geneva, Inter-Parliamentary Union.

BEARACK, B. (2009) *Madagascar Political Rivals Agree to Power-Sharing Deal*. [Online].
Available from: https://www.nytimes.com/2009/08/10/world/africa/10madagascar.html

BECKER, P. and RAVELOSON, J. A. (2008) *What is Democracy?* [Online]. Available from:
https://library.fes.de/pdf-files/bueros/madagaskar/05860.pdf

BRATTON, M., MATTES, R. and GYIMAH-BOADI, E., (2005) *Public Opinion, Democracy and
Market Reform in Africa*. Cambridge, Cambridge University Press.

CAMARA, K., (2016) *Here is how African Leaders Stage "Constitutional Coups." They Tweak the
Constitution to Stay in Power.'* [Online]. Available from: https://www.washingtonpost.com/
news/monkey-cage/wp/2016/09/16/heres-how-african-leaders-stage-constitutional-coups-
they-tweak-the-constitution-to-stay-in-power/

CHEESEMAN, N. and KLAAS, B., (2018) *How to Rig an Election*. New Haven, Yale University
Press.

CHIGARA, B. A., (2018) Operation Restore Legacy (2017). Renders Southern African
Development Community (SADC) Constitutionalism Suspect in the Coup D'état that was
not a Coup. *Oregon Review of International Law*, 20(1), 1–43.

DAY, J., (2022) *Principles of Democracy: Democracy and Justice*. [Online]. Available from:
https://www.liberties.eu/en/stories/principles-of-democracy/44151

DEWAR, B., MASSEY, S. and BAKER, B., (2013) *Madagascar: Time to make a Fresh Start*.
[Online]. Available from: https://www.chathamhouse.org/sites/default/files/
public/Research/Africa/0113pp_madagascar.pdf

DULANI, B. M., (2011) *Personal Rule and Presidential Term Limits in Africa*. Michigan,
Department of Political Science.

DULANI, B. M., (2015) *African Publics Strongly Support Term Limits, Resist Leaders' Efforts to
Extend their Tenure*. [Online]. Available from: https://www.afrobarometer.org/wp-
content/uploads/migrated/files/publications/Dispatches/ab_r6_dispatchno30.pdf

ENGEL, U., (2010) *Unconstitutional Changes of Government: New African Union Policies in
Defence of Democracy*. Stellenbosch, South African Association of Political Studies.

FABRICIUS, P., (2013) *Time for SADC to Admit Defeat in Madagascar as it has, Effectively, in
Zimbabwe*. [Online]. Available from: https://issafrica.org/iss-today/time-for-sadc-to-admit-
defeat-in-madagascar-as-it-has-effectively-in-zimbabwe

LANZ, D. and GASSER, R., (2013) A Crowded Field: Competition and Coordination in
International Peace Mediation. *Mediation Argument Working Paper Series*, 12.

LEBEAU, D., (2018) Multiparty Democracy and Elections in Namibia. *Journal of African
Elections,* 4(1), 1–26.

LIBEBE, M., (2016) *Congolese Concern: Will Kabila Stand*? [Online]. Available from:
https://www.peaceinsight.org/en/articles/congolese-concern-will-kabila-stand/?location=
dr-congo&theme=conflict-prevention-early-warning

LUNGU, E., (2017) *Zambian Army to Invade Zimbabwe to Help Mugabe*. [Online]. Available
from: https://www.lusakantimes.com/2017/11/16/illeal-takeover-power-zimbabwe-not-
tune-modern-politics-president-lungu/

LUNN, J., (2012) *Madagascar's Political Crisis.* [Online]. Available from:
https://www.researchbriefings.files.parliament.uk/documents/SN05962.pdf

MACKINTOSH, E., (2017) *Zimbabwe's Military Takeover was the World's Strangest Coup*.
[Online]. Available from: https://edition.cnn.com/2017/11/20/africa/zimbabwe-military-
takeover-strangest-coup/index.html#:~:text=What%20is%20a%20coup%20d'%C3%

A9tat%3F&text=From%20the%20moment%20it%20began,out%20like%20any%20ordi nary%20coup.

MACLEAN, R. and BURKE, J., (2016) *The Democratic Republic of the Congo "Faces Civil War" if President Fails to Quit.* [Online]. Available from: https://www.theguardian.com/world/ 2016/nov/10/democratic-republic-of-the-congo-faces-civil-war-if-president-fails-to-quit

MAKUMBE, D., (2018). Military Dynamics in the Democratisation of Zimbabwe: Demystifying the Conundrum. *International Journal of Humanities and Social Science Invention (IJHSSI)*, 7(6), 57–72.

MBIATEM, A., (2018) Presidential Term Limit Divide in the Democratic Republic of Congo: Another Security Threat in the Great Lakes Region? *The Journal of Political Science*, 2(1), 1–3.

MELBER, H., (2015) From Nujoma to Geingob: 25 Years of Presidential Democracy. *Journal of Namibian Studies,* 18, 49–65.

MUKORI, W., (2017) *Zambian Army to Invade Zimbabwe to Help Mugabe: Lungu, Keep your nose out of Zimbabwe Affairs.* [Online]. Available from: https://bulawayo24.com/index-id-opinion-sc-columnist-byo-122178.html

NATHAN, L., (2013) Mediating in Madagascar: By-passing the African Union Ban on Coup Legitimisation. *Kujenga Amani*, December 5.

PLOCH, L., (2010) *Madagascar's Political Crisis.* [Online]. Available from: https://www.https://www.everycrsreport.com/files/20110711_R40448_c4242d98b2c6b9 016d7234927fc3588d7aeb61d3.pdf

PLOCH, L. and COOK, N., (2012) *Madagascar's Political Crisis.* [Online]. Available from: https://www.sgp.fas.org/crs/row/R40448.pdf

SCHNEIDER, J., (2015) Lessons from Burundi's Unrest. *New African*, June 2015, 36-38.

ROESSLER, P., (2017) *How the African Union Got It Wrong on Zimbabwe.* [Online]. Available from: https://www.aljazeera.com/opinions/2017/12/5/how-the-african-union-got-it-wrong-on-zimbabwe

STATISTA, (2023) *Democracy Index in Sub-Saharan Africa in 2021, by Country.* [Online]. Available from: https://www.statista.com/statistics/1204750/democracy-index-in-sub-saharan-africa-by-country/

SOUARE, I. K., (2006) *Civil Wars and Coups D'état in West Africa: An Attempt to Understand the Roots and Prescribe Possible Solutions.* Michigan, University Press of America.

NEWS24, (2018) *South Africa Could Have Done 'Much More' to Save Me: Mugabe.* [Online]. Available from: https://www.news24.com/news24/Africa/Zimbabwe/sa-could-have-done-much-more-to-save-me-mugabe-20180323

THE NORDIC AFRICA INSTITUTE, (2018) *Peace and Security Challenges in Southern Africa: Governance Deficits and Lackluster Regional Conflict Management, Policy Note No. 4: 2018.* [Online]. Available from: https://www.https://reliefweb.int/report/democratic-republic-congo/peace-and-security-challenges-southern-africa-governance-deficits

THE GUARDIAN, (2017) *The Situation has moved to another level: Zimbabwe Army Statement in Full.* [Online]. Available from: https://www.theguardian.com/world/2017/nov/15/the-situation-has-moved-to-another-level-zimbabwe-army-statement-in-full

TULL, D. M. and SIMONS, C., (2017) The Institutionalisation of Power Revisited: Presidential Term Limits in Africa. *Africa Spectrum*, 2, 79–102.

UNITED STATES DEPARTMENT OF STATE, (2022) Country Reports on Human Rights Practices: Botswana. [Online]. Available from: https://www.state.gov/reports/2022-country-reports-on-human-rights-practices/botswana/

UNITED STATES DEPARTMENT OF STATE, (2022) *Mauritius 2022 Human Rights Report.* [Online]. Available from: https://www.state.gov/reports/2022-country-reports-on-human-rights-practices/mauritius#:~:text=Significant%20human%20rights%20issues%20included,lack%20of%20investigation%20of%20and

UNITED STATES DEPARTMENT OF STATE, (2022) *Country Reports on Human Rights Practices: South Africa.* [Online]. Available from: https://www.state.gov/reports/2022-country-reports-on-human-rights-practices/southafrica/#:~:text=Although%20the%20constitution%20and%20law,well%20as%20reports%20of%20assault.

VAUDRAN-LOUW, L., (2017) *The African Union's Chequered History with Military Coups.* [Online]. Available from: https://issafrica.org/iss-today/the-african-unions-chequered-history-with-military-coups

WOLTERS, S., (2018) *Will Kabila Stand Again?* [Online]. Available from: https://issafrica.org/iss-today/will-kabila-stand-again

WOLTERS, S., (2019) *Opportunities and Challenges in the DRC.* [Online]. Available from: https://issafrica.org/research/central-africa-report/opportunities-and-challenges-in-the-drc

WORLD PEACE FOUNDATION, (2017) *Madagascar Short Brief.* [Online]. Available from: https://www.sites.tufts.edu/wpf/files/2017/07/Madagascar-brief.pdf

ZOUNMENOU, D., (2009) Madagascar's Political Crisis: What Options for the Mediation Process? *African Security Review*, 18 (4), 71-75.

Leadership Crisis, Democracy and Human Rights

Mundende James

Introduction

Leadership constitutes a greater segment of the superstructure of world affairs, national or any given grouping of people. Leaders are a product of the social set-up of any given geography (Meredith 2007:50-54; Hobbes 1954:13-24). People in societies sometimes have leadership they deserve; this is to say, either poor or good leadership reflects their (masses) aspirations and prospects with the motive that the leaders are fairly selected. On that basis, leadership crisis in some contexts reflects inadequacy on the part of followership. This chapter argues that human rights have become an area of protestations in Africa due to some incompatible conditions that undergird Western democracy. The world is somehow democratising along Western cardinalities and Africa is not an exception as many countries, Zimbabwe included, have recently gravitated towards such leadership style following the demise of colonial rule; such metamorphosis has led to hybrid authoritarian (Pisirayi 2020:215; Hadebe 2020; Muzondidya 2009:188-195).

Western democracy is underpinned by a plethora of complexities in which the African body-politic struggles to entrench them for they are contravening some endogenous and inherent issues stemming from African heritage, culture, religion and organic political discourses. To some extent, democracy can be regarded as an imposed concept of leadership with some incongruities that are contrary to the organic and pristine endogenous issues (Rodney 1972:50-67). Some African governments are struggling to democratise accordingly due to culture, religion and organic political ethics. This chapter holds the view that overtime and across the world, there are numerous democracies, which vary spatially and from time to time. In Africa, there was organic democracy in Africa before Whites came since such leadership was enhanced by value consensus among members of the society (Mlambo 2014:30-45); Palmer 2002). The problem that had put locals in the dull light had set in when local leadership attempted to undergo through some adjustments to fit into the imported values according to the protagonists of the Pan-Africanist movement who had the privilege of leading their countries notably (Rodney 1972; Nkrumah 1973). This chapter avers that, in Zimbabwe, there are divergent complexities in the democratic leadership and its relationship to human rights. The chapter also proffers some scathing and open critiques to the democratic processes and fundamentals, which in many contemporary respects, can be regarded as incompatibles or inconsistencies.

Leadership Crisis and Human Rights in Zimbabwe

Democratic leadership has its indices and fundamentals undergirded by plurality in political parties, periodic elections, recognition of all forms of human rights, rule of law hinged on national constitutions, among others. Nhemachena (2023b), Mhango (2018:30-43) and Lumumba (2016) postulate that democracy's emphasis on pluralism has brought cutthroat competition in the internal politics in authoritarian regimes. Lumumba (2016:1-16) reasons that when the electorate does not know what it wants even in a democratic situation, it create a confederacy of bad leaders. Since democratic leadership has been adopted though in quasi, its processes must be put under critical scrutiny. The struggle to have full democracy is that which is deemed as a leadership crisis, and this has historically and gradually been melted away into the domains of illegitimacy (Ndlovu-Gatsheni 2020:77). Scholars such as Ruhanya (2020:183), Mlambo (2009:100) and Muzondidya (2009:176) argue that human rights are being infringed in Zimbabwe due to politics of hatred, poverty, diseases and ignorance on the part of the masses. Such problems reflect political leadership crises in a country, and they constitute the context to which democratic deterioration has found a fertile ground. AS such, authoritarian intrigues and manipulations require social context to thrive such as socio-economic impoverishment and ignorance. The ignorant part of the masses is largely enhanced by covert indoctrination which is subtle courtesy of the deliberate use of state-controlled and non-state institutions, mass media, education, family and churches in particular. On the other hand, systematic impositions and intimidation can also compromise and shrink democratic space and it is a part coercion which is the next-best alternative method of power distribution (Graham (2022). Such is associated with the elitist type of governance that shrinks proper citizen participation into the mainstream issues of governance. Therefore, it is regarded by Way et al (2010) as leadership for its own sake and not for human rights preservation and security.

At independence in 1980, the Zimbabwean government promised to hold democratic leadership, with President Mugabe pledging to stick to the policy of reconciliation and toleration (Meredith 2007:30; Mhanda 2011:22). However, reconciliation was never beyond rhetoric aimed to hoodwink the conflicting parties internally; namely, the Zimbabwe People's Revolutionary Army (ZIPRA) cadres and the Rhodesians and the international community. The international community had already casted some doubts on Zimbabwe. Mugabe seemed to have preferred socialism like that of Tanzania's Julius Kambarage Nyerere, Ghana's Kwame Nkrumah and Mozambique's Samora Machel, among others. Some of these leaders experimented socialism, with one-party state being their preferred antidote to the seemingly endemic challenges (Lumumba 2017), but the one-party system failed largely based on ingenuity and pragmaticism.

The failure of Tanzania's *Ujamaa* ('fraternity' in Swahili) social policy by President Nyerere should have spoken loudly about the infeasibility of socialism based on structural and ethnographic incapacitation of the local environment. Regarding reconciliation, a policy praised by many African leaders and some pro-conservationists (Meredith 2007:65-80), turned to be its opposite, retaliation. Reconciliation without irreducible reconciliatory mechanisms turned into a resumption of the Shona-Ndebele stalemate of the late 19th century (Ndlovu-Gatsheni 2006:58-81). Poor leadership on the part of the government, made the *Gukurahundi* genocide possible where close to 20 000 people were killed in some parts of Midlands and largely in Matabeleland (Nkomo 2001:80; Hadebe 2020:173). Gukurahundi was a serious human rights crisis that had set a foundational justification for the politics of violence since such skirmishes were left to die unresolved and unattended despite the hyped reconciliation processes which are said to have been taken by the government itself intermittently since 1987 (Ruhanya 2020:188).

The idea that Mugabe's government chose to pursue Marxist political economy upon attainment of independence worsened the prospects of democracy in so many ways. Hadebe (2009:177) and Raftoplous (2009: 201-210) contend that the Zimbabwean government gravitated to Marxist model of the political economy which midwifed the morphosis of privatisation to nationalisation of the business entities; such has laid some foundation of infringements.

Regarding the economic situation of Zimbabwe, Mtisi, Barnes and Nyakudya (2009:133-148) point to the 'Welfarist' policies adopted to improve social lives but with no due consideration of the economics of such pro-people programs: "pro-people policy which missed its target". The government failed to weigh its options properly and the detrimental consequences were borne by the masses. The country set itself in a precarious position, which made it susceptible to international pressures, notably, Economic Structural Adjustment Programs (ESAP). ESAP was adopted as a mechanism to increase the country's credit-worthy through cutting-down huge government expenditure on consumer goods. Such "liberalisation of the indigenous economy" led to a further decline of social lives of the people and again had an insidious impact on the possibility of upholding the fundamental rights of the people (Muzondidya (2009:188). Gradually, the leadership crisis had become visible as the economy disintegrated giving rise to opposition politics, which changed the political landscape thereby putting the masses into a limited democratic space (Muzondidya 2009:172-178). For example, the formation of MDC in 1999 was a major headway towards democratisation, as political choice seemed to have been created. Such a change on the political landscape in Zimbabwe increased people's political choices only in theory for their choices expressed through periodic elections were not sanctified, respected and preserved. Despite the so-called widening of democratic space with the turn of the new millennium, the space for democracy to thrive remained shrunk.

Complexities of Democracy in Zimbabwe

Democratic processes have not been fully entrenched in Zimbabwe and indeed in many African nations since the 1960s and the reasons are embedded in the complexities of western democracy. Democratic processes include recognition of fundamental human rights seem to be impractical and non-beneficial ever since time of colonial rule as the successive governments from the British South Africa Company (BSAC) regime (1890-1923), Settler regime (1924-1952), Federation, (1953-1963), Unilateral Declaration of Independence (UDI) regime (1965-1979),

Mugabe regime (1980-2017) and the new dispensation. None of these, pre and post-colonial regimes, passed a democratic litmus test of democracy, as brutality has remained a key characteristic (Campbell et al 2005:67). Pan-Africanist perspective admits that democracy has some peculiarities which made it incongruous to Zimbabwe, as there are some cultural and heritage beliefs which do not synchronise well with some democratic tenets. Ruhanya (2020:205-2017) outlines that in many occasions, the government and the people had a remarkable opportunity to entrench democracy but it did not happen as anticipated due to many reasons and such golden opportunity was squandered due what he avers as "militarization of ruling party and the militarization of state institutions".

In contrary to such perspective, it is important to note that armed movements morphed into political parties and thus the main reason for continuous presence of militarised leadership in Zimbabwe (Pisirayi 2020:211). With the leadership composed of actors once subjected to brutality of colonialism, the hope has been to strengthen democracy (Meredith 2007:80) although reality has proved contrary to that expectation. Such expectation in which people had at independence synchronises neatly with the Hegelian philosophy, which argues that every historical change brings anything opposite to that which such change is said to have occurred. On that basis, Ian Smith's rule was undemocratic, racial and unconciliatory, which ought to be replaced with an exterior opposite; opposite rule in terms of race, culture and structural forms. But such remains imagined because the brutality and victimisation in every election cycle are on an upward spiral since 2000 in Zimbabwe (Levytisky & Way 2010). As such, the independence of Zimbabwe was attained out of evolutionary morphism and not the purported revolutionary one for the former denoted structural continuity of the colonial dogmas; while the latter, in theory, called for a disjuncture from the body-politic in which the blacks were fighting for that long from 1896 throughout the 20th century. In the words of Chikerema and Chakunda (2014), "electoral fraud and brutal campaigns have correctly defined Zimbabwe's political landscape since 1980". Further, Levytsky and Way (2010) talks of hybrid state which is authoritarian, described as a government whose preoccupation is on holding power and shrinking democratic spaces, and Zimbabwe suits such description since the Mugabe to Mnangagwa transition is still a matter of open scrutiny with some calling it "militarised and uncivilised transition" (Moyo 2021:90). The same is conceptualised by some as a coup. The 'Politico-military nexus' has always been the source of ZANU-PF led government in its *modus operandi* (Moyo 2021:90).

Political interaction between Government and Citizens

The interaction between the government its citizens is in theory positive in many Southern African countries, Zimbabwe included, though in practice such is characterised by some hidden countervailing, unreconciliatory and suspicion. Mlambo (2014:204) and Lumumba (2016:8) argue that the government-people relations presuppose that the government and its citizens have contractual relations. For Rousseau, leadership must be executed on contractual basis; where the two major participants, government and citizens, have to willingly and wittingly enter into that contractual agreement (Carr 1958:19). A contract entails that both parties involved must have a say in the decision-making. However, masses are often hoodwinked into the entrapment of an illusion that they are part of the governance processes though they may not. Such illusion is psychogenic but with no practicality and in fact it cannot be possible for citizens in their complex totality to actively decide their affairs; this is why there is democracy by representation which has some inadequacies found because human interests vary spatially.

A hind analysis demonstrates that prior to colonial establishment people in Zimbabwe were united structurally and conflicts emerged intermittently and were solved (Mlambo 2014:11-29), and the neutral position is that, the colonialist politics further widened the ethnic fissures which were not that pronounced back then. Unification through reconciliation by the former President Robert Mugabe was progressive but did not take shape. Mugabe's government failed largely on reconciliation, demobilisation and reintegration (Mlambo 2014:199-201). Reintegration of the former freedom fighters failed to kick-off legitimately as it was principally supposed, hence the dis branches became certain.

In addition, free and fair elections and multi-party politics periodically, which are critical to democracy, have remained very much contested rendering them into impracticalities (Lumumba 2016:9). Representative democracy is not reflecting the nature of the people's aspirations given the situation that interests vary from person to person and from time to time, therefore representation is just but a creation of illusion among the masses so that they feel good with the government that they are perceiving to have created. Regarding media freedom, the information in Zimbabwe is censored and there is limited freedom of association. While the state-controlled media has remained partial and suggestive, private media has always been preoccupied by opposition politics, critical to the ruling party (Muzondidya 2009:178-198; Hadebe 2020:155-177).

There is often no innovation and objectivity in the media, which leads to disinformation and misinformation. Inadequacy in knowledge and information is an abuse of human rights since the masses are bound to make wrong electoral decisions when it comes to selecting preferred candidates to occupy public office since the media houses show no impartiality. As such, Zimbabwe portray certain elements of a totalitarian state. The country can be described as exhibiting 'totalitarianism which is not total' due to public manipulations and intimidation of citizens. Further, the presence of critical indices of democracy such as periodic elections and plural party politics become a cover-up due to the presence of a constitution without constitutionalism. Among other reasons, it appears that Western democracy is not practical to African politics given the complexities of the local societies, which are full of divisions along ethnic lines and religion among others. Some government out of fear of labels from the Western powers chose to pursue democratic path, but in fact, there is no democracy, despite some modicum of it in some instances. Apparently, Western democracy is yet to be fully instituted in Zimbabwe and other African countries despite some purported claims by various heads of state suggesting that Africa is democratising.

Way Forward

For the purposes of good and servant leadership, Southern African nations must work towards achieving institutional independence. Institutions of power such as the judiciary, legislative, executive, army, media and electoral management mechanisms should work independently. Such independence will ensure that democracy and human rights thrive (Ndlovu-Gatsheni & Ruhanya 2020 4-19; Mlambo 2009:33). Moreover, political ignorance on the part of the masses needs urgent attention because such inadequacy increases the masses' susceptibility to machinations. Therefore, there is a need for an investment into the knowledge dissemination through mass media and education to avoid chances of the masses to be continuously and systematically derided and subjugated by the leadership they themselves elect into offices of influence.

The general masses are active and relevant only for supporting its leadership during the election cycle but manipulated in the favour of those in the power distribution matrix. They often do not make necessary and genuine demands courtesy of inherent factors, contextually, laitism. As Levystky (2010:24) argues, there is no democracy in a country whose leadership believes in totalitarianism that underpins centralization of key authorities and systems; namely, judiciary, legislature and the executive. Zimbabwe is struggling to entrench Western democracy partly because the leadership is still part of the former freedom movements, commonly known as War Veterans, that had emerged from the 'bush' to wage liberation war and subsequently morphed into political parties without striking down structures and ideologies. Moreover, there is need for Zimbabwe to consider the indigenous systems of governance, which are premised on the organic principles or heritage-based structures. Lumumba (2017: 11-19) notes that African countries must find their own ways of governance with "genuineness in transparency and accountability," not to rely on the systems which have proved to be disastrous.

Conclusion

The Zimbabwean case represents that of a "hybrid political landscape or system" (Levystky & Way 2010), suggesting that there is a form of centralization and shrinkage democratic space. Zimbabwe, a country that became independent in 1980, has remained subjected to continue to undergo a leadership crisis, coupled with lack of respect for human rights and the principles of democracy. Key aspects such as periodic elections and the media have continue to be manipulated. Mlambo (2014:60) describes the media as ZANU-PF's tool of ideological indoctrination to cement its hegemony, since it is vulnerable to censorship. For example, state media was silent on salient issues such as *Gukurahundi* and the 2008 horrors in which it misconstrues the details for a reason.

As such, democracy has not been fully actualized in Zimbabwe despite the adoption of cyclical elections, the constitution, multiparty politics, the purported media freedom and plurality, among others. The deterioration of human rights from 2000 onwards was partly due to vibrant opposition formations which gave the ZANU-

PF led government intense competition for electorate (Raftoplous 2009:201-231; Ndlovu-Gatsheni 2006:55), thus increasing the susceptibility of the masses to ideological manipulations and violence. Despite of the challenges, there are some institutions that could have been used in enhancing democracy and servant leadership though they are accused of serving their own interests and not the masses hence there is no symbiosis between the leaders and the led. Further, the incongruity of the democratic leadership is sufficiently explained on the basis of cultural and heritage underpinnings of the indigenous populations who belong to different ethnic political parties. For democracy to thrive there is need for genuine institutional independence, free flow of information and enhancement of public awareness. Attempting organic leadership style that is heritage-based can be in line with the African rigid and diverse culture and ethnographic fragilities.

References

CAMPBELL, R, H & TAUBAMAN, J., (2005) *Towards A Theory of Democratic Compliance: Security Council Legitimacy and Effectiveness After Iraq*. New York, Book Series.

Carr, E. H., (1958) *The Bolshevik Revolution*. New York, University of New York Press.

GATSHENI, S, J. and RUHANYA, P., (2020) *The History and Political Transition of Zimbabwe From Mugabe to Mnangagwa*. London, Palgrave Macmillan.

GRAHAM, T., (2023) *The Precarious Future of Russian Democracy*. [Online]. Available from: https://www.cfr.org/article/precarious-future-russian-democracy

GRAMSCI, A., (1971) *Selections from the Prison Notebooks of Antonio Gramsci [Translated by O. Hoare and G. N. Smith]*. New York, International Publishers.

HOBBES, T., (1954) *Leviathan: Or Matter, Form and Power of a Commonwealth Ecclesiastical and Civil*. London, Collier-Macmillan.

HADEBE, S., (2020) *The Ethnicization of Political Mobilization in Zimbabwe: The Case of Pro-Mthwakazi Movements*. In P. Ruhanya. and S. Ndlovu-Gatscheni. *The History and Political Transition of Zimbabwe from Mugabe to Mnangagwa*, pp. 155-178.

LEVITSKY, S. and Way, L. (2010). *Competitive Authoritarianism: Hybrid Regimes After the Cold War*. Cambridge, Cambridge University Press.

LUMUMBA, P, L. O., (2017) *Thoughts on the Role of African Professionalism the Quest for Development*. [Online]. Available from: https://www.coursehero.com/file/12728 3791/Patrick-Lumumba-Role-of-African-Professionals-in-the-Quest-for-Developmentpdf/

LUMUMBA, P, L. O., (2016) *Fighting Corruption in Africa: The Case for an African Association of Anti-Corruption Authorities*. [Online]. Available from: https://www.igg.go.ug/static/files/publications/Presentation_by_PLO_Lumumba_Confer ence_-_CASE_FOR_AN_AFRICAN_ASSOCIATION

MAMDANI, M., (1996) *Citizen and Subject: Contemporary Africa and the Legacy of Late Colonialism*. Princeton, Princeton University Press.

MARX. K., (1977) *Capital: A Critique of Political Economy [Translated by B. Fowkes]*. New York, Vintage Books.

MEREDITH, M., (2007) *Mugabe: Power, Plunder and the Struggle for Mugabe's Future*. New York, Perseus.

MHANDA, W. A., (2011) *The Role of War Veterans in Zimbabwe's Political and Economic Processes*. Harare, SAPES Trust Policy Dialogue Forum.

MHANDA, W. A., (2011) *Dzino: Memories of a Freedom Fighter*. Harare, Weaver Press.

MHANGO. N. N., (2018) *How Africa Developed Europe, Deconstructing the His-story of Africa, Excavating Untold Truth and What Ought to Be Done and Known*. Langaa Research and Publishing Common Initiative Group.

MLAMBO, A, S., (2014) *A History of Zimbabwe*. Cambridge, Cambridge University Press.

MLAMBO, A, S. and RAFTOPLOUS, B. (2009). *Becoming Zimbabwe*. Harare, Weaver Press.

MOYO, D., (2010) *Dead Aid: Why Aid Is Not Working and How There Is A Better Way for Africa*. New York, Farrar, Straus and Giroux.

MTISI, J., NYAKUDYA, M. and BARNES, (2009) *Social and Economic Developments during the UDI Period*. In A. S. Mlambo. and B. Raftoplous. (eds.). *Becoming Zimbabwe*. Harare, Weaver Press, pp.115- 140.

MUZONDIDYA, J., (2009) From Buoyancy to Crisis, 1980–1997. In A. S. Mlambo. and B. Raftoplous. (eds.). *Becoming Zimbabwe*. Harare, Weaver Press, pp.167-200.

NDLOVU-GATSHENI, S., (2006) Nationalist-Military Alliance and the Fate for Democracy in Zimbabwe. *African Journal on Conflict Resolution*, 6(1), (49–80).

NDLOVU-GATSHENI, S., (2020) *The Zimbabwean National Question: Key Components and Unfinished Business*. In A. S. Mlambo. and P. Ruhanya. (eds.). *The History and Political Transition of Zimbabwe From Mugabe to Mnangagwa*. London, Palgrave Press, pp.51-84.

NHEMACHENA, A., (2013a) Chisi Chako Masimba Mashoma/Kunzi Pakata Sandi Kunzi Ridza: Anthropological Musings on the Coloniality of Dispossession in Africa. *Journal of Black Studies*, 1-24.

NHEMACHENA, A., (2023b) *Kukumirwa Semombe Dzamavhu: When Voices Begin to Erupt from Bottoms, African Anthropology Becomes Colonial*. [Online]. Available from: https://link.springer.com/article/10.1007/s12111-022-09601-6

NKRUMAH, K., (1973) *The Rhodesian File*. London, Panaf Books.

PISIRAYI, P., (2020) *Social Media and Politics in the Context of the "Third Chimurenga" in Zimbabwe*. In P. Ruhanya. and S. Ndlovu-Gatscheni. (eds.). *The History and Political Transition of Zimbabwe From Mugabe to Mnangagwa*. London, Palgrave Press, pp.202-220.

RAFTOPLOUS, B., (2009) *The Crisis in Zimbabwe, 1998–2008*. In A. S. Mlambo. and B. Raftoplous, (eds.). *Becoming Zimbabwe*. Harare, Weaver Press, pp.201-231.

RODNEY, W., (1982) *How Europe Underdeveloped Africa*. Washington, Howard University Press.

RODNEY, W., (1972) *How Europe Underdeveloped Africa*. Washington DC: Howard University Press.

The impact of the shrinking of Democratic Space in Zimbabwe on National Development: A Case of the Second Republic of Zimbabwe

Mazuruse Irony

Introduction

Shrinking of democratic space is continuing to be the major problem among many African countries even though they claim to have attained their independence and Zimbabwe is not an exceptional case. In the 21st Century, democracy has turned out to be the most cherished political tool for development and social change, which has attained near global acclaim and admiration by many world leaders. Democracy is crucial and it plays a very important role in promoting good governance as well as national development. Although democracy is necessary for the development of a country, some countries today are still struggling to achieve or introduce it in their development policies. It is against this background that this chapter demonstrates the effects of shrinking of democracy space on national development with reference to the Second Republic of Zimbabwe. The chapter draw the linkages between compliance to human rights, democracy, and national development. The chapter maintains that democracy has undermined issues of economic justice like basic needs while recognising the impact of non-compliance to human rights and democracy on national development.

Understanding Democracy and Human Rights

A functional democracy that accommodates diversity, promotes equality, and protects individual freedoms is increasingly becoming the best bet against the concentration of power in the hands of a few and the abuse of human rights that inevitably results from it. In turn, the greatest protection of human rights emanates from a sustainable democratic framework grounded in the rule of law. The general characterises of a democratic system includes regular elections whereby the people elect their representatives in free and fair elections, active participation of citizens in public life, protection of human rights for all citizens and the rule of law, that is, the law applies equally to all the citizens (Diamond 2004). Democracy is an old concept that existed in ancient Athens around the 5th Century BC, with the purpose of restricting tyranny.

The recent decades have witnessed a renewed attention and interest towards the concept, especially with the spread of the so-called 'third wave' of democracy (Huntington 1991), the fall of the soviet regime and the start of democracy building efforts in the newly independent states. For Keane (2010:188), democracy implies 'self–government of equals' and serves to restrict and impose control and checks over unlimited power. Democracy gives room for participation of citizens, civil society organisations as well as recognition of human rights. Therefore, human rights and democracy are inseparable. Human rights constitute basic rights and freedoms to which all humans are entitled regardless of race, colour, nationality, sex and religion (Robinson et al 2006). The international human rights discourse has become broad to include categorization of human rights. There has been categorization of civil rights, political rights, liberties among other terms that have been developed in the human rights lexicon. One is exposed to the first generation, second generation and third generation of human rights.

Historical Background of Human Rights and Democracy in Zimbabwe

Before independence, the white-minority government abrogated the civil, social, political and economic rights of the black majority. The white minority government employed repressive laws and relied on state security apparatus to violate the rights of the black majority. One of the many grievances that led to the liberation war was the totally racially discriminatory and unfair distribution of resources. Upon the attainment of independence in 1980, the issue of social justice led to the fair re-allocation land and other resources. The policies implemented since independence can be distinctly categorised into three decades where the first decade was more preoccupied with the reconciliation and distribution policies. Feltoe and Sithole (2010) notes that the first decade after independence in 1980 saw huge expansion in social and economic rights in areas such as health, education, and rural development. The second decade is the period of the late 1990s, which coincided with the Structural Adjustment Programmes (SAPs) which failed to usher the country's macro-economy to prosperity, and casted it further into a recession that then continued to rampage Zimbabwe, and which saw a reversal of the human rights that had been guaranteed in the first decade.

After the adoption of SAPs, the third decade of policy implementation in the 2000s witnessed economic meltdowns in the country (Zhou and Zvoushe 2012:220). This period was characterised with violence, economic decline (hyperinflation), political instability, regressive legislation for political control and survival of citizens by the influential society (Zhou and Zvoushe 2012:220). It is in this last decade that we begin to see the controversial land reform programme which attracted a lot of condemnation from the international community. The democratic space and human rights deteriorated as shall be demonstrated in this section. In 1981, a reconciliation policy that was pursued was slanted towards the necessity to reshape essential peaceful co-existence, sustainable peace and equality between ethnic groups and races in the country. This policy epitomised a well-timed recap that the racial discrimination of yesteryears was to come to a sudden conclusion and that there was going to be harmony in the country. Davies, Smith and Simpson C (1981:206) note that after the first democratic elections the then Prime Minister Robert Gabriel

Mugabe took upon himself the necessity of creating an environment with "space for everyone…a sense of security for both the winners and the losers- forgiveness and forgetting." The policy was initially forged by the interactions between former white rulers and blacks as well as between the two major political parties then, Zimbabwe African National Union-Patriotic Front (ZANU-PF) and Zimbabwe African People's Union Patriotic-Front (PF-ZAPU).

In the years between 1982 and 1987, the country experienced tension between the two political parties - ZANU-PF and PF-ZAPU - and the government resorted to a 'dissident cleansing' which resulted in violence and bloodshed through the 'Gukurahundi' genocide where the Fifth Brigade army tortured and killed civilians. There was massive violation of human rights and demonstrated that the government was prepared to use violence as a tool to contain dissent. According to Zhou (2012:213), the Gukurahundi came to a halt in 1987 where there was a signing of the Unity Accord between ZANU and ZAPU and this showed a negative start and chapter of Zimbabwe post-independence with regards to the human rights discourse. Whilst, pro poor policies were in place like the Growth with Equity policy, Health and Education for All, the Gukurahundi occurrence was a dent on the government particularly when it came to human rights issues. Nevertheless, a welfarist approach adopted by the First Republic in the first decade was critical for the sustenance of human rights.

The second decade was characterised by the government abandoning the massive pro poor social outreach programme because of the Economic Structural Adjustment Programme (ESAP). This marked a reversal of the human rights gained that were realised under the first decade. ESAPs at the behest of the World Bank and International Monetary Fund (IMF) are "neo-liberal market-driven policy measures" that are authoritarian clarifications that were implemented so as to look into the economic catastrophes of the 1980s. Structural Adjustment Programmes (SAPs) provided "conditional lending" (Thomson 2010). Conditional, in that governments receiving debt relief were obliged to adjust their economic policy. These policy measures were underlined by the imperative need to reduce government expenditure by at least 25 per cent in all aspects of the government when it came to commercialization (Thomson 2010). The Economic Structural Adjustment Policy Document (1990:6) in Zimbabwe sought to "de-emphasize its expenditure on social services and emphasise investment in the material production sectors such as agriculture, mining and manufacturing". To 'de-emphasize its expenditure on social services' meant that the government had to abandon its pro poor stance which had an effect of a reversal of the social gains that had been realised in education and health. SAPs were a failure in Zimbabwe because "by the 1994/95 fiscal year, it had increased to 13 percent of the Gross Domestic Product (GDP) while inflation levels also worsened in the years, going beyond set targets" (Hardlife & Zhou 2012:214) The standard of life deteriorated hence many poor citizens could not afford or access basic commodities.

By the late 1990s, the country faced economic challenges, emanating from serious mismanagement of the economy and rampant corruption. The economy received a huge number of body blows, the most significant of which was the 1997 political award of massive unbudgeted increases in the stipends for a discontent war veteran around the same time the army was deployed to the Democratic Republic of the Congo financially which was also costly (Feltoe & Sithole 2010). Towards the end of the 1990s, the Government's popularity started to wane because of the economic hardships. The government encountered serious food riots and demonstrations, and then with the first major challenge to its strong grip on power the birth of the Movement for Democratic Change (MDC). The MDC that was formed in 1999 received massive support from the main labour confederation, the Zimbabwe Congress of Trade Unions.

The Fast Track Land Reform programme had immediate implications on international relations because it led to the West and international community condemning the country for its radical approach to the land reform. The international community felt that Zimbabwe had reneged on its commitments as prescribed in the agreements that had taken place regarding agrarian issues. However, one cannot thoroughly comprehend this argument without appreciating the background of the fast-track land reform program. Beginning in 2000, led by the war veterans of the Chimurenga war, landless blacks began to invade farms and seize white owned land. While this process fundamentally changed the inherited agrarian structure, it created new problems, especially among farm labourers (Chiweshe & Chabata 2019) and other vulnerable groups such as widowed women. The new agrarian structure, while more democratic in terms of land ownership across farm and class categories, 'has created a platform for new agrarian class formation processes and struggles' (Moyo 2011). Because of its radical nature, the FTLRP triggered an imperial backlash, with the European Union (led by Britain) and the United States imposing so-called targeted sanctions on Zimbabwe. According to Masiiwa (2003), this led to its isolation from international financial markets and lack of foreign direct investments, which forced the country to adopt a 'Look East' policy and a heterodox macro-economic policy in order to address the after-effects of spiralling inflation and economic stagnation. Thus, from this perspective, the FTLRP triggered the look east policy and invited wrath from the West nations. Zimbabwe was declared a pariah state and received the strongest backlash which can also explain the economic challenges Zimbabwe is facing. The chaotic Land reform was also characterised by brute force and massive violation of human rights. The government also resorted to arm-twisting the judiciary to settle its issues about land hence violation of constitutionalism.

In fact, the Mugabe administration professed that these invasions were spontaneous, and were reflective of land hunger and the need to re dress land imbalances (Sithole 2012). In fact, there is evidence to suggest that Mugabe regime choreographed these invasions with a clear political motive, to extinguish the support for the MDC on white commercial farms and to use land redistribution as paraphernalia to win back electoral support from rural Zimbabweans. The disastrous economic decline persisted apace after the widespread violence surrounding the 2000 elections and subsequent elections. The land reform programme impacted negatively on the economy as it only benefited the elite and women were strongly undermined by the programme. Agricultural production decreased which in turn necessitated an economic decline and meltdown. The imposition of sanctions harms more citizens as the government is crippled to cater for its citizens (Mararike 2018). From a human rights perspective, human rights were violated because of the land reform programme and its subsequent impact on the economy.

The second decade since attainment of independence proved to be a litmus test for the government regarding its commitment to democratic values and the protection of human rights. There had been widespread human rights abuses in Zimbabwe appearing soon after 1980. ZANU (PF) has always firmly believed that because it fought and won the liberation war and freed the country from colonialism, it alone has the right to govern the country in perpetuity (Feltoe & Sithole 2010). In line with this view, throughout the 1980s the Government signalled its desire to pass legislation to make Zimbabwe a de jure one-party State. Although it abandoned this plan in 1990, it continued to take measures to ensure that the country remains a de facto one-party State. As previously indicated, in the 1980s the Mugabe government launched a brutal military campaign against the entire civilian population in areas of Matabeleland and Midlands where ZAPU had strong support (Feltoe & Sithole 2010). In 2000 it became apparent that ZANU-PF was in danger of being booted out of power through elections; it responded by unleashing extreme violence on the MDC. In the run-up to the General Election in June 2000, it embarked upon a violent campaign to control political opposition, using the land issue to mask its true objective, the retention of power.

Between 2000 and 2008, ZANU-PF employed violence as a political tool, conducting a widespread and systematic campaign of violent persecution directed against the MDC in defiance of democratic principles leading to violation of human rights. It was not a coincidence that the violence against the opposition heightened at the time of Parliamentary and Presidential elections. A series of amnesties have been granted to the perpetrators of this violence. The government resorted to law-fare where it used legislation to thwart democratic space in Zimbabwe. This resulted in the enactment of repressive legislation that was passed that were used to clamp down on protest and dissent. These are the Public Order and Security Act (Chapter 11:17) (Act No. 1 of 2002) (POSA) and the Access to Information and Protection of Privacy Act. (Chapter 10:27) (Act No. 5 of 2002) (AIPPA). According to J Mapuva (2007), the provisions of these pieces of laws were regularly misunderstood or deliberately misapplied by the police. The organisers of a gathering are required to 'notify' the police; the section does not state that the police must 'give permission.' Police deliberately cancelled meetings of perceived threats in contrary to the provisions of the constitution and democracy. On the other hand, pro-Mugabe gatherings were freely allowed, often with the police providing escorts for the demonstrators.

According to Mapuva and Muyengwa (2012) POSA and AIPPA complement each other to further entrench ZANU PF and curtail voices of dissent. Dissent would be any form of opposition such as independent media. AIPPA aims to control the free flow of information as the government has been empowered to determine what type of information eventually reaches citizens. According to Mapuva and Muyengwa (2012), media freedom and independent newspapers have been under threat as many of their staff have been arraigned before the courts of law for publishing what the state views as prejudicial to state security, which under sections 23-30 of AIPPA is a criminal offence. The selective application of sections of AIPPA to intimidate the independent media has resulted in the development of a huge rift between the state and the independent media, with The Daily News being bombed and eventually closed in 2003. The closure on 12 September 2003 of Associated Newspapers of Zimbabwe (ANZ), publishers of The Daily News and The Daily News on Sunday is a classic example of how the legislative framework was used to thwart democratic space in the country.

In a democratic country the police force, the prison service, the prosecution service, the army and the intelligence services will be politically neutral professional agencies that will serve the national interest. Everyone is entitled to equal protection from the law and the law will be applied equally to all without discrimination. This was not the case in Zimbabwe as these services were employed by the ruling party in its bid to retain power. The net result of this process of political transformation of these agencies is that the law was now being applied selectively. It was used as a weapon against opponents of ZANU (PF). There are several reported cases of the police arresting the victims of political violence instead of the perpetrators when the victims have gone to police stations to report the crimes committed against them.

The law enforcement agencies became a major perpetrator of human rights abuses in Zimbabwe. They were employed to aid ZANU-PF, to suppress opposition and retain power. When these agencies operate in combination with the army, there are often increased levels of brutality. For opponents of Mugabe, the law enforcement agencies became an instrument of violence against them rather than an institution that offered them protection. They lived in fear of the very agencies that were supposed to protect them. Independent judges were purged out of the judiciary and were replaced by ZANU-PF loyalists (Gubbay 2010). A democratic institution requires an independent judiciary for the safeguarding of fundamental freedoms.

The government implemented Operation Murambatsvina (OM) in 2005, which was also very controversial. It aimed at cleaning up the urban areas by destroying the unregistered structures (Nzewi & Nyathi 2013). With the implementation of OM in 2005, for an economy that is already in crisis, this had repercussions on the economy of the country. The impact of OM was great; it created many problems for the country namely, transport woes, homelessness, cold weather, starvation, loss of assets, increased an immediate demand for accommodation and exposure to disease (ibid). The main opposition party, the MDC, believed that the real motive behind the campaign was to punish the urban poor for voting in substantial numbers for the opposition party in the March election.

The brutal suppression of opposition and dissent convinced the United States of America and European countries on the need to impose sanctions upon members of the Mugabe administration. Bilateral financial assistance to the Mugabe government was also terminated and the United States ensured that credit lines through the Bretton Woods institutions were no longer extended through the Zimbabwe Democracy and Economic Recovery Act (ZIDERA). On the other hand, considerable sums of money were channelled to human rights and humanitarian organisations operating within Zimbabwe. The political turmoil in the country also led to dis investment or lack of new investment which further weakened the economy. Industries reliant on goodwill such as tourism completely dwindled.

In the March 2008 elections the main opposition party, the MDC, won a majority of the parliamentary seats and Morgan Tsvangirai acquired more votes than Robert Mugabe in the first round of the Presidential election. However, in the re-run of the Presidential election ZANU PF unleashed a widespread campaign of violence that led to the deaths of some 200 MDC supporters and injuries to many other MDC members (Feltoe & Sithole 2010). This campaign of violence compelled Tsvangirai to withdraw from the re-run of the Presidential election to spare his supporters from further violence. This shows how democracy and human rights were not a priority for a power-hungry ruling party. The South African led political mediation process eventually led to the inclusive government deal entered in February 2009. This entailed a power sharing arrangement in which power was to be shared between the two factions of the MDC and ZANU-PF. The inclusive government led to the adoption of multi -currency and the drafting of the 2013 Constitution which was passed into law by citizens during a referendum. This stride was commended as democratic as it embraced democratic tenets. The inclusive government had a lifespan of 4 years and again ZANU PF won elections amid massive rigging of elections. Mugabe continued to be in power until he resigned in 2017. The study is also an attempt to examine whether the second republic deviated from the old republic ways of handling human rights and democratic issues.

The demise of former President of Zimbabwe Robert Mugabe signified a new era of democracy taking into cognizant his system, which had used repressive and retrogressive measures shrinking the democratic space in Zimbabwe (Marongwe 2018). It goes without saying that people embraced the new dispensation with open arms. Their hope which had so far eluded them for the past three decades was awakened. Whilst the opposition enjoyed the right to campaign freely in contrast to the Mugabe era, much still needs to be done in respect of the human rights situation and democracy in Zimbabwe. Human rights and democracy in Zimbabwe reached a low point when the military shot civilians after the July 30, 2018, elections (Magaisa 2018). The August 1, 2018 are a dent on the credibility of the new dispensation in regard to human rights situation and democracy. This appears to be a perpetuation of the 'gun leads politics' in which the military plays an integral role in the political landscape of Zimbabwe. This is perceived by many as a perpetuation of the Mugabe era politics in which the strategy was to use military force to neutralise demonstrators. What is evident is that the deaths of six people after the July 30 elections is part of collateral damages in democratic spaces.

Upon the realisation that the shootings by the army was catastrophic for international re- engagement the president Emmerson Mnangagwa played a Donald Trump card of opening an enquiry of commission into the findings of what exactly transpired. It should be noted that it is the commission of enquiry which concluded that the army was complicit in the august killings and further to that the commission recommended that the responsible people be brought to justice. This key recommendation up to date has not been realised. The reluctance of the administration in bringing perpetrators clearly epitomises the undemocratic nature of the government. The January 2019 killings because of massive protests fuelled by a fuel increase clearly indicates how the second republic continues to violate human rights. During the January shutdown in 2019, human rights violations have been attributed to the security apparatus. The harassment and unlawful detention of the Zimbabwe Congress of Trade Unions members by the state apparatus which is the Zimbabwe Republic Police bears testimony to this claim. Further to that, the curtailment of the freedom of expression is seen by the apprehension of protesting teachers who demanded their salaries be paid in United States dollars. A 270 km trek from Manicaland provincial capital of Mutare by nine members of the Amalgamated Rural Teachers Union of Zimbabwe (ARTUZ) - who were subsequently locked behind bars after being ordered by the police to stop their demonstration, appears to signify high handedness.

On the infringement of the freedom of expression, the example of using the courts to deem the doctors' strike illegal justifies the rejoinder and narrative of human rights and democratic issues in the country. The doctors' complaints included, among others, unhealthy working conditions that they perceive to be, in part, putting their lives at risk of contracting deadly diseases. The Labour Courts appear to view unfolding industrial action as thorns in the flesh of the new dispensation. Furthermore, as if not enough, the doctors were suspended following a curious court ruling. The government appears to justify suspensions through repressive measures. The appointment of Acting President, Constantine Chiwenga, who himself has a military background – as a negotiator does not bode well in terms of industrial democracy. This violation to the freedom of expression was also experienced in 2018 when 16 000 protesting nurses were initially dismissed from work before they were later reinstated. It is against such a background that the second republic resembles the first but clearly provides a fertile ground for research regarding democracy, human rights, and national development.

Human Rights Violation and Democracy by The Second Republic of Zimbabwe

From 1980 up to November 2017, Zimbabwe was under the leadership of Mugabe which is regarded as the first Republic, and the ascendance of Munangagwa through the assistance of the army took over Zimbabwe and the era is affectionately known as the Second Republic. Democracy needs the development of generally accepted core values that ensure fair electoral practice, predicated on representation, accountability, inclusiveness, transparency, gender equality, tolerance and respect for diversity. The Second Republic of Zimbabwe was ushered by a controversial yet disputed electoral process where the incumbent President Munangagwa became the leader of the 'new dispensation' on the back of a military coup in November 2017 (Noyes 2020). President Mnangagwa popularised just after the coup the terms "Second Republic" and "New Dispensation" to show that his regime differed from Mugabe's in terms of governance style (Rwodzi 2019). The most dominant debate after the ouster of Robert Mugabe in November 2017 has been on the forms and content of 'democracy' in Zimbabwe under the new government led by President Emmerson Mnangagwa.

The relationship between democracy and human rights is intricate, symbiotic, and mutually constitutive. A rights-based approach to democracy grounded in the rule of law is considered increasingly the most consistent safeguard against human rights abuses. There is an intrinsic relationship between human rights and democracy, which is necessary for development. Democratic government is based on the will of the people, expressed regularly through free and fair elections. Democracy has as its foundation respect for the human person and the rule of law. Democracy is the best safeguard of freedom of expression, tolerance of all groups of society, and equality of opportunity for each person. The birth of the second Republic in Zimbabwe is controversial as it was from the 'sanitised *coup d'etat'*. The ouster of Mugabe has never been democratic and the architectures of the ouster of Mugabe were the very people who constituted the government of the Second Republic. One can easily predict the reign of the leader of the second republic to rule with an iron fist to preserve his leadership hence violation of human rights and democracy.

ZANU-PF and President Mnangagwa won the disputed 2018 elections with a narrow margin of 50.8 per cent, avoiding the need for a Presidential run-off. The election results were contested, and the opposition MDC-Alliance filed a court case, which it lost. International election observers were critical of certain flaws but condoned the elections, and therefore the international community considers the ZANU-PF government legitimate. Despite incremental improvements from past elections, domestic and international observers noted serious concerns and called for further reforms to meet regional and international standards for democratic elections. Numerous factors contributed to a flawed election process in 2018, including: the Zimbabwe Election Commission's lack of independence; heavily biased state media favouring the ruling party; voter intimidation; the unconstitutional influence of tribal leaders; failure to provide an electronic preliminary voters' roll; politicisation of food aid; security services' excessive use of force; and lack of transparency concerning election results (Zimbabwe Human Rights Report 2022).

Successful democratic governance must inevitably focus on promotion and protection of human rights and fundamental freedoms. For without this protection there can be no democracy in any meaningful sense. The ouster of Mugabe gave the impression to the general population of Zimbabwe and other countries at large that Zimbabwe was going to have undisputed elections for the first time in history, but it was not like that. Numerous factors contributed to a flawed overall election process, including: the Zimbabwe Election Commission's (ZEC) lack of independence; heavily biased state media favouring the ruling party; voter intimidation; unconstitutional influence of tribal leaders; disenfranchisement of alien and diaspora voters; failure to provide a preliminary voters roll in electronic format; politicisation of food aid; security services' excessive use of force; and lack of precision and transparency around the release of election results (Zimbabwe 2019 Human Rights Report). Members of the opposition were given free way to penetrate the rural areas which was a positive mark, however they were not given access to state media coverage. In this scenario there was no difference with the 1st republic which caused a lot of people to totally subscribe to the notion that the opposition was given 'cosmetic' freedom. The election resulted in the formation of a government led by the ruling Zimbabwe African National Union-Patriotic Front (ZANU-PF) party with a supermajority in the National Assembly but not in the Senate.

The government of the Second Republic since its inception until today is mainly characterised by violation of human rights and democracy of which it tends to raise the assumption by the general populace that it is worse than the Mugabe regime. Significant human rights issues included: unlawful or arbitrary killings of civilians by security forces; torture and arbitrary detention by security forces; harsh and life threatening prison conditions; political prisoners; arbitrary or unlawful interference with privacy; serious problems with the independence of the judiciary; the worst forms of government restrictions on free expression, press, and the internet, including violence, threats of violence, or unjustified arrests or prosecutions against journalists, censorship, site blocking, and the existence of criminal libel laws; substantial interference with the rights of peaceful assembly and freedom of association; restrictions on freedom of movement; restrictions on political participation; widespread acts of corruption; crimes involving violence or threats of violence targeting women and girls; and the existence of laws criminalizing consensual same-sex sexual conduct between adults, although not enforced.

Human rights groups reported government agents continued to perpetrate physical and psychological torture. According to Zimbabwe 2019 Human Rights Report, human rights abuses and violations included 16 rapes, one sexual assault, 26 abductions, and a minimum of 586 assault and torture cases involving security forces from January 14 to February 5, 2019. In January, February, August, and November, uniformed and plainclothes soldiers and police officers systematically assaulted civilians in the Harare central business district and suburbs. Soldiers accused many of the victims of participating in the January 14-16 and August 16-21 demonstrations. In November 2019, police officers assaulted civilians who gathered at an opposition party's headquarters to hear a speech. Other abuses included 11 abductions and assaults, 34 assaults, 77 arrests, one tear gas victim, and one undetermined. Of the 47 cases requiring medical attention, the NGO classified the cases as 13 severe, 26 moderate, and eight mild (Zimbabwe Human Rights Report 2019).

There were protests in 2019 that were triggered by a 150% increase in the price of fuel in the middle of a quickly deteriorating economic environment. Countrywide protests in January 2018 over economic hardships, sparked by a sudden rise in fuel prices, were met with a brutal backlash by the army and police. According to the Zimbabwe Human Rights NGO Forum, 17 people lost their lives. Various civil society organisations such as the #ThisFlag of Pastor Mawarire and the Zimbabwe Congress of Trade Unions were at the centre of the protests (Mutlokwa 2020). This turmoil resulted in the government imposing an internet shutdown during the period of the protests apart from a violent military crackdown that left a trail of over 1,803 human rights violations (Zimbabwe Human Rights NGO Forum 2019). The order to shut down the internet was issued by the then Minister of State Security, Owen Ncube, through the Central Intelligence Organisation Director General, Isaac Moyo, using the Interception of Communications Act of 2007 (Veritas 2019). Social media was used to not only mobilise protests, but also record human rights violations. Thus, the internet shutdown was designed to not only undermine the efforts of labour unions and civil society leaders and other organisers to direct protests. It was also meant to close the spreading of images of state violence against demonstrators to the external world (Amnesty International 2019:19). One important underlying condition of a properly functioning democracy is access to information (Harrison & Sayogo 2014).

During the protests over the price hike of food, the government unilaterally switched off the internet for the whole country to ensure that citizens would not be updated of what was taking place in the country. Accordingly, the internet closure of 2019 and related government responses, like those of July 2016, violated a number of human rights, especially those related to the internet to access information, share ideas and express oneself. They were counterproductive to peacebuilding and development because they not only closed opportunities for the state to engage with citizens through social media platforms. They also worsened instead of addressing urban populations' grievances further posing a high risk for sustainable peace and development. However, internet access was restored on 21 January 2019 after the high court ruled that the blackout was unlawful (Kuwaza 2019). The shutting down of the internet was a clear indication of violation of human rights whereby citizens were denied access to information in a proclaimed democratic state. Civil society acknowledged that the protests were solely designed to register disgruntlement with the declining economic circumstances where, among other worries, citizens were not able to meet the expense of buying bread, sugar and bus fare to and from work while the government appeared uninterested to address the challenges. The government's proclivity to use dictatorial methods exacerbates citizens' objections, with extensive implications for peace and development. The protests came at the height of Mnangagwa and his government's 'Zimbabwe is open for business' mantra, in an effort to attract much-needed foreign direct investment. Potential investors frowned at the level of human rights abuses by the administration and thus the people of Zimbabwe continued to suffer at the hands of misrule and human rights abuses by the government.

The constitution and law prohibit arbitrary arrest and detention, although other sections of the law effectively weaken these prohibitions. The government's enforcement of security laws often conflicted with the constitution. Security forces arbitrarily arrested and detained persons, particularly political and civil society activists, labour leaders, street vendors, and journalists perceived as opposing the government. Several people are victims of arbitrary arrest in Zimbabwe. The Mnangagwa administration, akin to the Mugabe regime before, continues to equate any opposition with foreign-sponsored meddling resulting in it seeking to effectively outlaw dissent to 'pre-empt regime change'. A good example can be drawn for a popular journalist Hopewell Chin'ono who was accused of inciting violence as well as opposition members of parliament Job Sikhala and Godfrey Sithole for public order offences Citizen Coalition for Change (CCC). Job Sikhala who is by the time of this publication is still languishing in prison on remand for almost a year. According to

Zimbabwe Human rights report (2022), On May 7, police arrested journalists Blessed Mhlanga and Chengeto Chidi after they photographed police attempting to arrest the opposition member of parliament Job Sikhala in Chitungwiza, a suburb south of Harare. Police responded by attempting to break the journalists' phones to destroy the footage.

In a democratic system, the principles of constitutionalism are strictly adhered to, leaders come and go, free and fair elections are promoted, there is respect of human rights, freedom of expression and accountability are upheld and the respect of the rule of law is observed to. Currently the main opposition party the CCC is claiming that since the start of 2022, almost 100 of their supporters have been arrested and spent periods in detention without trials. Its rallies were banned and president Mnangagwa's administration of clamping down on its dissent and rights of assembly. Political parties in Zimbabwe must seek police clearance at least two weeks before an event. The opposition is claiming that the security agencies have refused permission for any opposition gatherings, saying there is no work force to guard the events. Corruption and nepotism are also the biggest huddle for the government of the Second Republic in Zimbabwe. The issue of smuggling gold from Zimbabwe, which was recently exposed by the Al Jazeera journalists, is a further indication that the government of the Second republic is after looting the precious minerals of the country hence violating human rights and democracy.

Importance of Human Rights and Democracy on National Development

In the contemporary world, democracy is regarded as the best system of governance given that it is people centred and development oriented. Democracy, over the years and across the globe, has been presented and perceived as a condition for national development (Egena 2013). Indeed, the positive relationship between democracy and development is globally acclaimed because its practice has the potential to enhance development. Virtually, all African nations, largely for this reason, have adopted democratic system of government. Yet the majority of these countries have remained mired in poverty and underdevelopment. The Second Republic of Zimbabwe, being the focus is for instance, apparently characterised by underdevelopment in its various dimensions. Mugabe left in 2017 through a coup and president Munangagwa is a product of the army. The 2018 elections were just a cosmetic activity to endorse the coup. The army created a regime that they controlled after the coup hence you can never build democracy based on coup the foundation is flawed. Therefore, one can easily assume that the method by which the government was formed will continue to use the same features to govern the country as there is no way one can expect a leopard to change her spots.

The state of underdevelopment in general in Zimbabwe has been reinforced by authoritarianism, political instability, ethnic and religious conflicts, and civil wars. Since attaining independence in 1980, Zimbabwe has been plagued by some form of political conflict. This has included the civil war between the Ndebele and the Shona (Gukurahundi) and disputed elections to mention but a few. Zimbabwe in the Second

Republic is still plagued by unlawful and arbitrary killings, while citizens' rights, peaceful assembly and freedom of association are constantly violated. The core of the argument that democracy helps promote development (more than the other way around) rests on some of the key institutional features of democratic systems-namely, its accountability mechanisms and checks and balances provisions. These features play an essential role in limiting the abuse of executive and state power more broadly, and through elections and other processes, they also provide a predictable (in terms of rules, not outcome), transparent, periodic and reliable system of rewards and punishments. According to Sen (1999a), for example, these institutional characteristics of a democracy explain why famines have never occurred in democratic systems.

Democracy plays a very important and crucial role in promoting good governance and national development. The relationship between democracy and national development is widely appreciated. This is because democracy plays a very important and crucial role in promoting good governance and fostering national development. The common feature of democratic governance is its emphasis on improving the socio-economic welfare of the people and this is synonymous with the idea of national development. Thus, the individual and his quality of life must be the centre of conception of national development (Amucheazi 1980). Democracy is perhaps the most cherished form of government. This is because of the rising degree of countries in the world today claiming to be democratic and the number of the populace who yearn for it. Good governance can also not be separated from democracy. Good governance denotes the best way to govern and manage the affairs of the state or institutions, at all levels, within a complementary view of political, social, economic and administrative sectors. Good governance envisages a just leadership based on rationality, recourse to law, respect for public liberties, consolidation of democracy, participation, equality, serving public interests and social development. Good Governance contributes to the realisation and reinforcement of human well-being and the expansion of human capabilities and their economic, social, and political choices, opportunities and freedoms, especially for the poorest and most marginalised. Good governance allows for public debate on the impact of public policies - and helps in the reduction of the divergent and improper policies through public accountability of politicians and civil servants. Citizen participation is recognized as an important attribute and one of the main pillars underpinning the institution of democracy. In a democracy, citizens acquire not only rights and freedoms, as it is commonly known, but also responsibilities and duties – participation in the political and civic lives through voting during elections, creating and joining associations, taking part in decision-making and policy formation, demanding transparency, and holding the governments accountable (Sargsyan 2016).

Foreign Direct Investment affected

Non -compliance to human rights, democracy has a negative impact on development as it scares away foreign direct investment (FDI). According to Carothers (2000), authoritarian regimes have inconsistent economic reforms that have resulted in many shunning investments, in the political setup. Though there is a multiparty system in Zimbabwe, the country is still far in terms of being democratic as the ruling party dominates everything. This has undermined democracy as investors have expressed little confidence in a government accused of vote rigging hence trampling upon democratic principles. To that effect, investors feel insecure about investing in the nation. It is a fact to argue that the country due to its undemocratic nature has been scaring away investment as evidenced by many companies closing. Marongwe and Mawere (2018) argued that nondemocratic nations have a tendency of not respecting property rights which has an effect of investors declaring those areas a no-go zone. Foreign Direct Investment brings much needed revenue which is critical for development but due to democracy being eroded the country continues to experience low levels of development hence the democracy development nexus is clear. Consequently, countries perceived to be human rights violators are shunned by investors and receive very little Foreign Direct Investment and goodwill-dependent industries like tourism suffer. The arguments here miss the point that not only is FDI affected as domestic direct investment (DDI) is also impacted negatively by the absence of human rights protection and respect for democratic ethos.

Global Isolation, Sanctions and Brain Drain

Zimbabwe is facing myriad of challenges that can explain the retarded development such as corruption, nepotism, maladministration, poor governance but certainly undermining democracy and violation of human rights has led to the country being isolated from the international community. The world is becoming a global village and Zimbabwe needs the international community. Zimbabwe Democracy and Economic Recovery Act (ZIDERA) imposes that assistance will be provided on the conditions that democracy and rule of law is respected (Chingono 2010). ZIDERA was amended during the reign of the Second dispensation and imposed further sanctions on the second republic of Zimbabwe (Mararike 2019). The country by failing to access much needed foreign intervention has failed to develop hence it is clear that there is need for the country to democratise and respect human rights if they are to be assisted hence perpetuating development in some way. This also tallies well with the country's plans to be re admitted in the Commonwealth which is also demanding that the country pursues several raft policies that promote human rights and democracy. The Trump administration amended the ZIDERA due to the growing belief that the second dispensation continues to violate human rights to this end, the study establishes the link between human rights, democracy and development and therefore advocates for the government to consider compliance to the two.

Brain Drain refers to the emigration of highly trained or qualified people from a particular country. A large section of the productive and innovative population is likely to remain incapable of contributing to development simply because their rights are inadequately protected by reason of their political allegiance. The ideas and industry of the millions of young men and women are now invested in other countries simply because there is inadequate protection of human rights in most African countries (Magaisa 2018). No amount of foreign currency can fill the gap left by these people. The education and the health sectors are heavily affected with brain drain. The covid-19 pandemic left many European countries in need of care workers. Many professionals left the country to Europe, mainly America and Britain to pursue manual jobs as they do not have confidence with the Second Republic to stabilise the economy. It may be politically expedient to castigate those in the diaspora, but a more principled approach requires self-critical analyses to understand why such a huge labour force has migrated and how it can be persuaded to return. It should be noted that barriers to their participation in development processes, is lack of freedoms. To this effect, it can be noted how human rights violations have led to massive brain drain which in turn compromised development.

Conclusion

Foreign direct investment has been affected leading to global isolation and sanctions, brain drain, and the negative impact on tourism and corruption has impeded on development of the Zimbabwean nation. The 'open for business' mantra by the Second Republic has been largely ignored by serious Western foreign investors. This is because of the nation's record in human rights violations. The August 2019 killings indeed played a part in scaring potential foreign investment. Potential investors frowned at the level of human rights abuses by the administration and thus the people of Zimbabwe continued to suffer at the hands of misrule and human rights abuses by the government. Findings of this chapter reflect that non -compliance to human rights and democracy by the second republic of Zimbabwe can explain low levels of economic development. It reflects that, due to the reasons discussed above. Foreign direct investment has decreased, sanctions have been renewed, the nation continues to face global isolation and the country continues to suffer from brain drain as intellectuals are running away from the despair and gloomy non-productive atmosphere. Despite the efforts by human rights activists and many other key players, there remain hindrances towards the promotion and respect of human rights and democracy in the second republic of Zimbabwe.

References

AMNESTY INTERNATIONAL, (2019) *'Open for Business', Closed for Dissent: Crackdown in Zimbabwe during the National Stay away 14–16 January 2019.* [Online]. Available from: https://www.amnesty.org/download/Documents/AFR4698242019ENGLISH.pdf

AMUCHEAZI, E. C., (1980) *Readings in Social Sciences: Issues in National Development.* Enugu, Fourth Dimension Publishing Company Ltd.

AYALEW, Y. E., (2019) The Internet Shutdown Muzzle(s) Freedom of Expression in Ethiopia: Comparing Narratives. *Information & Communications Technology Law*, 28(2), 208–224.

DIAMOND, L., (1999) *Developing Democracy: Toward Consolidation.* Baltimore, Johns Hopkins University Press.

DIAMOND, L., (2004) *What is Democracy?* [Online]. Available from: http://web.stanford.edu/~ldiamond/iraq/WhaIsDemocracy012004.htm

EGENA, I. O., (2013) *Democracy and Good Governance as a Tool for Growth and National Development.* Kumasi, Applied Research Conference in Africa.

FELTOE, G., LININGTON, G. and MAHERE, F., (2016) *Worlds Apart: Conflicting Narratives on the Right to Protest: Case Notes on 1.* [Online]. Available from: https://zimlii.org/zw/journal/2016-zelj-01/%5Bnode%3Afield_jpubdate%3Acustom%3AY/worlds-apart-conflicting-narratives-right.

HARRISON, T. and SAYOGO, D., (2014) Transparency, Participation and Accountability Practices in Open Government: A Comparative Study. *Government Information Quarterly*, 31, 513–525.

HELLUM, A, et al., (2013) *Rights Claiming and Rights Making in Zimbabwe.* Human Rights, Power and Civic Action: Comparative Analyses of Struggles for Rights in Developing Societies, 22.

HUNTINGTON, S. P., (1991) *The Third Wave: Democratization in the Late Twentieth Century.* Oklahoma, University of Oklahoma Press.

KEANE, J., (2010) *The Life and Death of Democracy.* [Online]. Available from: http://fora.tv/2010/08/07/John_Keane_The_Life_and_Death_of_Democracy

KILLANDER, M. and NYATHI, M., (2015) Accountability for the Gukurahundi Atrocities in Zimbabwe Thirty Years On: Prospects and Challenges. *Comp. & Int'l LJS Afr*, 48, 463.

CHIWESHE, M. K. and CHABATA, T., (2019) The Complexity of Farmworkers' Livelihoods in Zimbabwe after the Fast Track Land Reform: Experiences from a Farm in Chinhoyi, Zimbabwe. *Review of African Political Economy*, 46(159), 55-70.

LYSIAS D, G., (2015) *Democracy and National Development in Nigeria: Challenges and Prospects.* [Online]. Available from: https://iiste.org/Journals/index.php/JAAS/article/view/25617

MAODZA, T., (2018) *President Hits Back at Critics.* [Online]. Available from: https://www.herald.co.zw/president-hits-back-at-critics/.

MURISA, T. and CHIKWECHE, T., (2015) *Beyond the Crises: Zimbabwe's Prospects for Transformation.* Harare, Weaver Press.

MASIIWA, M., (2005) The Fast Track Resettlement Programme in Zimbabwe: Disparity Between Policy Design and Implementation. *The Round Table*, 94(379), 217-224.

MOYO, S., (2011). Changing Agrarian Relations after Redistributive Land Reform in Zimbabwe. *Journal of Peasant Studies*, 38(5), 939-966.

NOYES A, H., (2020) *A New Zimbabwe? Assessing Continuity and Change after Mugabe.* California, RAND Corporation.

NDIMANDE, J. and MOYO, K. G., (2018) 'Zimbabwe is Open for Business': Zimbabwe's Foreign Policy Trajectory under Emmerson Mnangagwa. *Afro Asian Journal of Social Sciences Volume,* 12(2).

RWODZI, A., (2019) *Democracy, Governance and Legitimacy in Zimbabwe since the November 2017 Military Coup.* Lisbon, Centro de Estudos Internacionais.

SEN, A. (1990) Development as Capacity Expansion. In K. Griffin. and J. Knight. (eds.). *Human Development and the International Development Strategy for the 1990s.* New York, Macmillan.

SARGSYAN, G., (2016) *Democracy and Development in the Making: Civic Participation in Armenia; Challenges, Opportunities.* Trento, University of Trento.

UNITED STATES DEPARTMENT OF STATE, (2018) *Zimbabwe 2018 Human Rights Report.* [Online]. Available from: https://www.state.gov/wp-content/uploads/2019/03/Zimbabwe-2018.pdf

UNITED STATES DEPARTMENT OF STATE, (2022) *Zimbabwe 2022 Human Rights Report*. [Online]. Available from: https://www.state.gov/wp-content/uploads/2023/02/415610_ZIMBABWE-2022-HUMAN-RIGHTS-REPORT.pdf

Zimbabwe Human Rights NGO Forum, (2019) *The New Deception: What Has Changed? A Baseline Study on the Record of Zimbabwe's 'New Dispensation' in Upholding Human Rights*. Harare, The Zimbabwe Human Rights NGO Forum.

Zimbabwe Human Rights Commission, (2019) *Monitoring Report in the Aftermath of 14 January to 16 January 2019 "Stay Away" and Subsequent Disturbances*. [Online]. Available from: http://www.zhrc.org.zw/monitoring-report-in-the-aftermath-of-the-14-january-to-16-january-2019-stay-away-and-subsequentdisturbances/.

ZHOU, G. and ZVOUSHE, H., (2012) *Public Policy Making in Zimbabwe: A Three-Decade Perspective*. [Online]. Available from: https://www.ijhssnet.com/journals/Vol_2_No_8_Special_Issue_April_2012/26.pdf

Intersecting Human Rights and Environmental Rights in South Africa

Thandekile Phulu

Introduction

Human dignity and environmental quality have evolved simultaneously, but independently in contemporary legal instruments. The right to a healthy environment is recognised in most constitutions, as is the right to human dignity. Moreover, many constitutions share features such as defining causes of action, *locus standi*, the scope of judicial review, and remedies regarding these rights (May & Daly 2016:240). The health of the environment is directly related to the pleasure of humans in life. A healthy environment is necessary for human material and spiritual prosperity. International concern for human rights, health, and environmental preservation has developed significantly during the previous several decades. To address environmental awareness, the international community has developed a wide range of international legal instruments, specialised organisations, and agencies at the global and regional levels (Shelton & Pippitt, 2007:340). The links between human rights, health, and environmental preservation have been apparent since the Stockholm Declaration of the United Nations Conference on the Human Environment in 1972, the first international conference on the human environment. The connection was reflected in the preamble of the concluding declaration at the Stockholm session, in which the participants declared, "man is both a creature and a shaper of his environment, which provides him with physical sustenance and allows him to grow intellectually, morally, socially, and spiritually" (Stockholm Declaration 1972).

The Environment and Sustainable Development

In South Africa, the National Environmental Management Act (NEMA) mainly regulates environmental management. According to NEMA, an environment refers to the natural surroundings in which people live:

> the earth's land, water, and atmosphere, microorganisms, plant, and animal life; any component or combination of the first two things on this list, as well as their interrelationships; and the physical, chemical, aesthetic, and cultural features and circumstances of the aforementioned that impact human health and well-being.

Moreover, the 1989 Environment Conservation Act defines the environment as "the collection of things, events, and causes that affect the life and habits of man or any other creature or group of creatures." The influence of human beings as the shaper of the environment is highlighted in the above definitions. Environmental rights are always associated with sustainable use and sustainable development. In order to shape and reshape the environment in a way that is beneficial to future generations, human beings should utilise the environment in a sustainable manner. According to the 1983 World Commission on Environment and Development, sustainable development is "development that meets the needs of the present without compromising future generations' ability to meet their own needs" (Imperatives 1987:23). The first crucial principle in this aspiration is the concept of needs, namely the vital needs of the world's poor, which must take primacy. The second is the concept of technological and societal restrictions put on the environment's capacity to fulfil existing and future requirements. Sustainable development attempts to disprove the concept that as civilization moves away from traditional energy sources, it must forego growth, innovation, and progress. This implies that if used properly, technology and innovation can aid sustainability. Furthermore, NEMA states that sustainable development requires the state to protect, promote and fulfil the social, economic and environmental rights of everyone and strive to meet the basic needs of previously disadvantaged communities (NEMA Preamble).

Intersecting Human Rights and Environmental Rights to Achieve Sustainability

Environmental rights are human rights that demonstrate holistically and legally the integrated relationship between people and the environment, as well as an individual's entitlement to a certain level of environmental quality (Boyd 2011:9). In general, the scope of these rights extends beyond people's natural environment to include cultural legacy, human habitat, and health. With a few exceptions, environmental rights include both action and receipt rights. Rights of recipients emphasise what right holders have the right to expect or receive, while rights of action emphasise what right holders have the right to do. The role of public involvement in environmental rights realisation, environmental rights as autonomous substantive rights of beneficiaries needing public participation in their execution are given specific study (Cullet 1995:30).

Recognizing the pervasive influence of local and global environmental situations on the attainment of human rights needs the inclusion of an environmental component to the human rights debate. Legally, the new links will boost protection in both domains, since environmental protection will benefit from current technology while human rights protection will be strengthened by the incorporation of hitherto disregarded interpretative factors (Moysiadis et al 2021:346). There are numerous ways to include environmental concerns into the fulfilment of human rights (Buhmann, Jonsson & Fisker 2019:389). One of them is through enforcing judicial remedies in remedying environmental rights violations. Additionally, businesses have a duty to protect human rights, avoid damage, and perform due care in their operations.

Environmental protection is intricately related to a variety of other human rights, and it arises as both a precondition and a result of the exercise of several rights (Lee et al 2020:643). This is because international human rights institutions have addressed environmental dimensions of a variety of human rights, including the rights to life, religion, and property, health, water, food, and culture. They have addressed the right to a healthy environment explicitly on occasion, but have mostly concentrated on the environmental implications of more recognised rights. An environmental right encompasses two distinct concepts: the right to a clean and healthy environment, as well as the right to protect natural resources for human life (Lyster 1992:528). Environmental rights are "moral" rights that might be seen as birth rights - rights that are granted just by virtue of being human. As a result, just like the right to life, the primary duty of the state and its institutions is to safeguard the continuous flow of environmental quality (Iyalomhe 1999:518).

Attempts to promote environmental sustainability will be ineffective unless they occur within the context of enabling legal frameworks that ensure human rights such as the rights to knowledge, participation, and access to justice. Addressing transboundary environmental issues like climate change, biodiversity loss, pollution, and ecosystem management necessitates an international coordinated response based on shared human rights and environmental principles like solidarity, accountability, transparency, equity, and justice. The International Covenant on Civil and Political Rights, the International Covenant on Economic, Social, and Cultural Rights, the Convention on the Elimination of All Forms of Discrimination against Women, and the Convention on the Rights of the Child all contain significant provisions concerning human rights and the environment. Moreover, regional human rights agencies, such as the Inter-American Commission and Court of Human Rights, the African Commission on Human and Peoples' Rights, and the European Court of Human Rights, have highlighted these connections in their decisions.

Global entities such as the Human Rights Council, the International Court of Justice, and the World Bank Inspection Panel have addressed the links between human rights and the environment. According to the most recent Human Rights Council (HRC) resolution on climate change, "human rights obligations, standards, and principles have the potential to inform and strengthen international, regional, and national policy making in the area of climate change, promoting policy coherence, legitimacy, and long-term outcomes" (OHCHR 2023). The most recent HRC resolution on human rights and the environment contains crucial human rights and environmental measures (OHCHR 2023). Regional human rights bodies' decisions, such as the Inter-American Commission and Court of Human Rights, the African Commission on Human and Peoples' Rights, and the European Court of Human Rights, encourage states to consider further, among other aspects, respect for and promotion of human rights within the framework of the United Nations Framework Convention on Climate Change (UNFCCC) calls on them to respect, protect, and fulfil human rights, including in all actions undertaken to address environmental rights(OHCHR 2023).

The 2030 Agenda for Sustainable Development expressly acknowledges the connections between human rights, development, and the environment, particularly biological variety and climate change. The relationship between environmental sustainability is based on reducing environmental damage while also preserving the role of natural resources and ecosystem services in promoting human wellbeing, economic opportunities, and social and ecological resilience (United Nations 2023).

Ecosystem health, biodiversity, pollution in all kinds, and climate change are rapidly being regarded as major challenges to human health, dignity, and well-being. The 2015 Paris Agreement, for example, defines climate change as a shared concern to all people and expressly calls on states to uphold, promote, and consider human rights while pursuing climate action. The paragraphs below are a discussion on the regulation of environmental rights in South Africa.

Environmental Rights in South Africa

The 1970s heralded a worldwide environmental watershed. Numerous new laws were adopted in South Africa, as well as some novel concepts. Several key Acts were also updated, such as the Environment Conservation Act 73 of 1989. After apartheid, South Africa's environmental justice movement made a number of significant gains, most notably the development of an environmental right and legislation that implicitly and officially recognises environmental justice. Early iterations of the African National Congress's Reconstruction and Development Plan reflected the party's position on environmental issues at the time (Trevor and Patrick 2020:70). Post-apartheid environmental laws and policies were created through a participatory process that included South Africans from all across the country. The notion of community engagement was incorporated into NEMA as a result of this participatory approach. This piece of legislation represented a significant departure from traditional environmental management by providing those affected by environmental degradation with a means of redress through mechanisms for conflict resolution, fair decision-making, the protection of those reporting on environmental transgressions, as well as recognition of people's right to refuse to work in hazardous environments (Murcott 2015:23). South African environmental rights also arose in reaction to distinct and serious socio economic challenges (De Villiers & Van Staden 2006:780).

Within the context of specific treaties, United Nations organs concerned with human rights have addressed the links between human rights, health, and environmental preservation. The former United Nations Human Rights Commission appointed a Special Rapporteur on human rights duties related to the enjoyment of a safe, clean, healthy, and sustainable environment. The goal of the human rights and environment mandate is to investigate the human rights obligations related to the enjoyment of a safe, clean, healthy, and sustainable environment and encourage best practices for applying human rights to environmental policy. It also intends to overcome impediments to universal recognition and implementation of the right to a safe, clean, healthy, and sustainable environment, as well as to conduct country visits and respond to human rights violations (OHCHR 2023).

The International Covenant on Economic, Social, and Cultural Rights (IESCR) 6 of 1966, for example, safeguards the right to safe and healthy working conditions (article 7b), as well as the right of children and young people to be free from hazardous labour (article 10-3). Article 12 of the Convention on the Rights of the Child (CRC) also mandates states parties to "improve all aspects of environmental and industrial hygiene, as well as the prevention, treatment, and control of epidemic, endemic, occupational, and other diseases." The CRC discusses environmental protection in regard to children's right to health. States parties are obligated to combat disease and hunger "by providing enough nutritious meals and safe drinking water, while taking into consideration the dangers and risks of environmental pollution" (article 24(2)(c) of the CRC) and the transmission of hygiene and environmental sanitation knowledge and teaching to all segments of society (Article 24(2)(e) (e) of the CRC). The intersection of environmental rights with other rights and the enforcement of these rights will lead to sustainability.

In Africa, the right to the environment is also included in Article 16 of the African Charter on Human and Peoples' Rights of 1991. This article indicates that every person has the right to the best physical and mental health possible, while article 24 states that all people have the right to a generally adequate environment conducive to their development. The case law emanating from the African Charter on Human and Peoples' Rights takes a far more progressive position towards the notion of environmental rights as 'collective' rather than merely individual entitlements (Francioni 2010:43). The African Charter on Human and Peoples' Rights guarantees the right to health rather than the right to the environment. Both the right to health and the right to the environment have recently been asserted before the African Commission on Human Rights.

Almost all international and regional human rights organisations, particularly those concerned with the right to health, have investigated the link between environmental degradation and legally recognised human rights, such as the right to life. The complaints made in almost every instance are not based on a specific right to a safe and healthy environment, but rather on rights to life, property, health, information, family, and home life (Shelton 1991:334). Pollution, deforestation, water contamination, and other types of environmental devastation are at the root of the concerns. These examples demonstrate several benefits of using one or more rights-based approaches to environmental and health challenges (Huntjens 2021:205).

The right to social security, which encompasses environmental rights, is contained in the South African Bill of Rights and is being enhanced by legislative and constitutional revisions, as well as the creation of case law in the courts (Choma 2008:12). There is a clear need to broaden the discipline's knowledge through systematic research and training at several levels. The majority of African countries' constitutions provide the right to a healthy environment. In contrast to the international and regional systems, the bulk of environmental rights-related concerns are absent from South Africa's domestic system. South Africa is fortunate to have, at least on paper, regulations that facilitate access to courts with the goal of safeguarding or conserving the environment (Kidd, 2010:28). In conformity with how international agreements define environmental rights, Section 24 of the South African Constitution was framed as an individual right rather than a collective one. Because environmental degradation often affects groups of people, one may argue that the right should protect groups rather than individuals. Section 24 states that everyone has the right –

(a) to an environment that is not harmful to their health or well-being; and (b) to have the environment protected, for the benefit of present and future generations, through reasonable legislative and other measures that I prevent pollution and ecological degradation; (ii) promote conservation; and (iii) secure ecologically sustainable development and use of natural resources while promoting conservation.

The South African Constitution explicitly states that constitutional rights must be protected and enforced. It is an important feature of the South African Constitution that courts have extensive discretion to devise new remedies for the protection of constitutional rights and the performance of constitutional obligation (Kotzé 2007:348). The inclusion of the environmental right implies that people may seek this right at the 'highest' constitutional level conceivable. This considerably expands the number, type, and breadth of judicial remedies available to enforce it, particularly since one may use all constitutional remedies to vindicate this right (Kotzé 2007:301:350). Judicial interpretation and elaboration of the state's duties inherent in this right are critical in guiding the legislative and executive actions in connection to environmental governance (De Wet & Du Plessis 2010:158).

The NEMA is South Africa's major environmental management framework law, and it covers a number of environmental principles. Section 2(4)(f) states that all interested and affected parties must be encouraged to participate in environmental governance. All people must have the opportunity to develop the understanding, skills, and capacity required for equitable and effective participation, as well as ensuring the participation of vulnerable and disadvantaged people in environmental governance. Section 2(4)(g) strengthens the latter clause by requiring decisions to take into account the interests, needs, and values of all interested and affected parties. The National Environmental Management: Waste Management Act of 2008, provides explicit, albeit fragmented, opportunities for public involvement in environmental issues. The Act states, for example, that when a mining company submits a licence application to the Department of Environmental Affairs and Tourism (DEAT), the agency must take steps to bring the application to the attention of interested parties and the public. The details of any industry's waste management strategy, for example, should be made available for debate. Any comments received about a waste management, authorization and application must be examined, and a copy of all comments must be delivered to the authorities together with the application documentation. As a consequence, and commendably, the Waste Management Act mandates that the outcomes of public engagement processes, as well as the content of existing waste management plans, be included in licence application procedures. Applicants must also inform people who objected to their waste management permission application of the decision and the reasoning behind it.

Recognition in the National Water Act 36 of 1998 (NWA) provides that there must be equitable access to water. The Act also gives the state the responsibility to ensure that water is protected, used, developed, conserved, managed, and controlled in a sustainable and equitable manner, for the benefit of all persons and in accordance with its constitutional mandate. The National Environmental Management: Air Quality Act 39 of 2004 (NEMAQA) recognises that "the burden of health impacts associated with polluted ambient air falls disproportionately on the poor," necessitating legislation to ensure the improvement of ambient air quality for the benefit of all people. Additionally, the Marine Living Resources Act 18 of 1998 seeks to reform the fishing industry in order to correct historical imbalances and provide justice across all fishing industry sectors.

The Municipalities Systems Act of 2000 establishes the fundamental concepts, structure, and processes that municipalities must follow in order to develop their communities socially and economically while also ensuring affordable universal access to essential services. The Act relates to the provision of fundamental municipal services that are required to guarantee an acceptable and reasonable quality of life, public health, safety, and the environment. The municipality exercises legislative or executive authority by providing services, either directly or through service providers; monitoring or regulating those services; imposing and recovering rates and taxes, among other things; monitoring the impact and effectiveness of services, policies, programmes, or plans; and promoting a safe and healthy environment.

Judicial Consideration and Locus Standi in Environmental Rights

The evolution of constitutional environmental law is essentially dependent on the courts' ability and willingness to concretise the meaning of any rights that may have an influence on the environment. Given this, it is critical to establish a court system that is both independent and impartial in order to interpret, administer, and enforce substantive environmental rights. The courts thereafter create a body of environmental rights jurisprudence that could guide the efforts of all authorities and others to respect, protect, promote, and fulfil a right that aims to ensure the protection and enjoyment of the environment as well as the health, well-being, and quality of life for this generation and future generations (Kotzé & Du Plessis 2010:348). The main question regards who has the capacity to approach the court for redress when an environmental right is infringed upon. The current approach as the Constitution states is that anyone listed in section 38 has the right to petition a competent court, alleging that a right guaranteed by the Bill of Rights has been violated or threatened, and the court may grant appropriate relief, including a declaration of rights:

> Anyone acting in their own interest; anyone acting on behalf of another person who cannot act in their own name; anyone acting as a member of, or in the interest of, a group or class of persons; anyone acting in the public interest; and an association acting in the interest of its members may approach a court (Constitution of South Africa Section 38).

Furthermore, NEMA later altered the common law situation by providing the same range of people and organisations (including those working in the public interest) standing to seek the courts for appropriate redress in the event of a violation or threatened infringement of environmental legislation. Section 32 of NEMA states that any person or group of persons acting in their own interest may seek appropriate relief for any breach or threatened breach of any provision of NEMA, a specific environmental management Act, or any other statutory provision concerned with environmental protection or natural resource use.

Ministry of Health and Welfare v Woodcarb (Pty) Ltd 1996 (3) SA 155 (N) was the first time a court in South Africa examined an environmental right. In this case, the Minister's request was an interdict to prohibit the defendant from engaging in a 'planned procedure' in violation of the Air Pollution Control Act. The court rejected the respondent's allegation that the Minister lacked the essential *locus standi* to seek an interdict. The judgement was based on the notion that the Act obliged the Minister to control the installation and use of scheduled processes throughout the country, and that the interdict was one of the essential tools at her disposal to carry out her duties under the Act. Furthermore, the court determined that the respondent's acts violated section 9 of the Air Pollution Act. Nonetheless, the court emphasised that the respondent's actions were not only illegal under the Air Pollution Prevention Act, but also infringed on the rights of the respondent's neighbours to an environment that is not injurious to their health or well-being, as guaranteed by section 29 of the Constitution. On this basis, the Minister would have had the constitutional authority to seek a restraining order against conduct that violates the environmental rights of the respondent's neighbours.

In *BP Southern Africa (Pty) Ltd v. MEC for Agriculture, Conservation and Land Affairs 2004 (5) SA 124 (WLD),* an application for authorization to establish a new petrol/gas filling station was applied for. The environmental authority refused the application after considering the statutorily obligatory environmental impact assessment technique. It reached its determination based on a number of decision-making criteria, some of which were socio economic in nature rather than just environmental. The authority's mandate, according to the petitioner, was limited to looking into environmental issues. The authority claimed that its jurisdiction included both socioeconomic and environmental problems, citing the constitutional right to the environment and NEMA. In this case, the court held that environmental authorities had a constitutional commitment to carry out section 24, which included enacting necessary legislative and other measures, as well as developing and executing decision-making criteria. The court explained that these remedies, in addition to being reasonable, must contribute to the eventual realisation of the applicable right. Consequently, the court concurred with the environmental authority's decision to refuse the sought environmental licence.

According to the court, pure economic criteria will no longer decide whether a development is acceptable. Economic and financial sound development will be balanced by its environmental impact in the future, taking into account the principle of intergenerational equity and the sustainable use of resources in order to achieve integrated environmental management, sustainable development, and socioeconomic concerns. As noted in In *BP Southern Africa (Pty) Ltd v. MEC for Agriculture, Conservation and Land Affairs 2004 (5) SA 124 (WLD)*, South Africa firmly started out on a route that will lead to the aim of attaining a protected environment through an "integrated plan that takes into consideration, among other things, socioeconomic concerns and values."

The contribution of In *BP Southern Africa (Pty) Ltd v. MEC for Agriculture, Conservation and Land Affairs 2004 (5) SA 124 (WLD)* case to an understanding of section 24 can be found in the following: a) confirmation of the socioeconomic factors in the relationship between people and the environment; b) view that the entire environmental right must be interpreted in the context of intergenerational environmental protection and within the context of sustainable development; and c) emphasis on the fact that the positive duties that the state incurs in terms of environmental cohesion are not limited to the state itself.

In *Petrol Retailers Association of South Africa (Pty) Ltd v. Director General Environmental Management Mpumalanga and Others CCT 67/06 (2007) ZACC 13* (PRASA case), the Constitutional Court addressed the environmental right for the first time. Like the BP case, this case addressed the nature and scope of the environmental authority's role to analyse the social, economic, and environmental effects of a proposed gasoline filling station, as well as whether the environmental authority met that requirement. The Constitutional Court found that environmental preservation and social and economic development, as well as their effect on environmental decisions and environmental agencies' duties in this regard, are essential constitutional issues. In addition, the Court emphasised, citing Section 24 of the Constitution, that socioeconomic advancement must be balanced against environmental protection. In order to create a balance between social, environmental, and economic issues, the Court stated, among other things, that: development promotion implies environmental conservation. The environment, however, cannot be protected if development overlooks the repercussions of environmental degradation. As a result, the environment and development are closely linked (PRASA case).

Judicial Remedies for Violations of Environmental Rights in South Africa

When environmental degradation causes human harm that violates accepted human rights norms, a human rights committee, commission, or court may provide a remedy that can effectively contribute to the reversal of both the underlying environmental degradation and the human rights violation (Pasternack and Malone, 2002). In order for the court to grant relief, the petitioner must have satisfied the standing criteria, and his rights must have been violated and/or jeopardised (*De Kock v. Ministry of Water Affairs and Forestry* (CCT 30/05) [2005]). Environmental rights are not unique, and no special remedies are necessary. Nonetheless, the litigation around these rights often reveals characteristics that need the development of new and more effective remedies. The following are typical features: The activity is being taken to help communities or groups of people rather than single individuals; the lawsuit is being pursued to benefit communities or groups of people rather than a few individuals; the affected people are often impoverished and politically and socially vulnerable. They are those who depend on the state for fundamental socio economic services but lack the political and social authority to get them without the involvement of the courts. Therefore, individuals have a stake in the state's affirmative obligation to provide socioeconomic services.

Sections 172 (1)(b) and 167 (7) of the South African Constitution empower courts to make any just and equitable decision when considering any matter touching the interpretation, protection, or enforcement of the Constitution. When using their remedial discretion, they are guided by justice and fairness (Choma 2008:12). The subject is brought up many times in the Bill of Rights. According to section 38, when a fundamental right is infringed or endangered, only what is fair, reasonable, and suitable is taken into account. Environmental human rights claims are generally rejected unless three conditions are met: (1) environmental degradation; (2) a nation-state action or omission that causes or contributes to environmental degradation; and (3) a deprivation of human rights as a result of environmental degradation (Malone & Pasternack 2002:368).

The creation of a substantive right is still contested in certain circles since it introduces a number of new and problematic components to the idea of human rights. Second, it must guarantee that the living circumstances offered to persons are suitable for a reasonable standard of life. Local ecosystems and livelihoods, as well as global ecosphere balance, are required by these two requirements. It is critical to remember at this point that environmental rights holders cannot claim a specific state of the environment, a perfect environment (which has never existed since humans first appeared on Earth), or a local environment similar to those in other parts of the world, because unequal resource distribution precludes the existence of identical environmental conditions everywhere. As previously said, the theory must be global, but its execution must be decentralised and sensitive to local challenges, since most people are afraid or upset only when a problem directly threatens them (Cullet 1995:33).

The Role of NGOS

A number of new generation environmental justice non-governmental groups (NGOs) exist, including the Federation for a Sustainable Environment and Biowatch South Africa (FSE). The FSE, which was created in 2008, advocates for public involvement and environmental justice (the FSE's current water dispute is detailed in section V). Biowatch is a research and advocacy group founded in 1997 to promote biodiversity and sustainable living in rural areas, particularly among the poor (Dugard & Alcaro, 2013:20). The South Durban Community Environmental Alliance (SDCEA) is also relevant when considering environmental rights. SDCEA was founded in 1995 as a collaboration of civic and resident groups from various fields advocating for stricter environmental regulatory requirements for South Durban's industry. SDCEA has been able to battle for environmental justice on the local, national, and international levels, with a focus on justice for the poor, gaining notoriety in the field over the years for its ability to organise across the region's historic racial divisions (SDCEA 2023).

SDCEA has lately expanded its environmental outreach into some of Africa's most impoverished communities, such as Umlazi, which are often resistive to conventional environmental outreach. Although not a popular movement in and of itself, SDCEA views itself as an important component of South Africa's greater battle for environmental justice, as well as a key factor in the fight against the worldwide danger of climate change. SDCEA utilises a variety of strategies, but its primary emphasis is advocacy, and it has undertaken long-term efforts to pressure corporations to comply with environmental standards. SDCEA's successful approaches have included the development of precise scientific competency in pollution, including the ability to monitor pollution levels via sample collection and analysis. This information is disseminated across the community in order to empower local residents and boost SDCEA's legitimacy in the eyes of the state. For example, SDCEA's fight against air pollution caused by the Engen oil refinery led to Engen implementing a technology that lowered its sulphur dioxide emissions by a fourth in 2000. SDCEA has also been effective in ensuring that local concerns are addressed by the media and that industry and government are continually urged to achieve environmental justice.

Rising Concerns: Environmental Rights and Other Competing Rights

Constitutional human rights are of such a character that they cannot operate in isolation and may sometimes give birth to incompatible principles. The court should offer direction on how to handle conflicting rights and grasp the position of the right to a healthy environment in relation to other rights, such as property rights. In the setting of competing rights, a constitutional rights lawsuit is not unusual (Feris 2008:32). Rights may be reduced in accordance with any other provision of the Constitution, according to Section 36(2) of the South African Constitution. As a consequence, rights may constrain one another. Nonetheless, this raises the question of the scope of the environmental right. When may it be used to restrict another right, and vice versa? In *Re Kranspoort Community* 2000 (2) SA 124 (LCC), the Kranspoort Community sought land rights restoration under the Restitution of Land Rights Act. The landowner contested the claim, and his objections included environmental concerns. It was then decided that the region was ecologically sensitive and that its usage at the time aided in the preservation of the ecology. The farm's environmentally friendly operation would be unaffected by restoration.

Environmental concerns were contrasted against section property rights, such as rights derived from restoration. In the event of a genuine land claim, the Court has broad discretion to give relief. When considering whether or not to award relief, the court may take into account a variety of issues, including the feasibility of such restoration. Although the term 'feasibility' is not defined in the Restitution of Land Rights Act, the Court held that the test to be applied is whether the claimant's restoration of the right in land in question will be possible and practicable, taking into account: (a) the nature of the land and the surrounding environment at the time of dispossession; (b) the nature of the claimant's use of the land at the time of dispossession; and (c) the changes that have occurred since. When the chance to participate in this process occurs, it should be seized with both hands.

Conclusion

The environment and human rights are inextricably linked; human rights cannot be exercised in the absence of a secure, unpolluted, and healthy natural setting, and responsible environmental management is impossible in the absence of a foundation built on the recognition and protection of human rights. The environment in which we live is very important to each individual human being. The full enjoyment of a broad variety of human rights, such as the rights to life, health, food, water, and sanitation, is contingent on the existence of an environment that is risk-free, clean, healthy, and environmentally sustainable. Environmental rights as human rights must be respected. Each state should have these rights protected by the constitution in order to ensure sustainable development and protection of human life and dignity. States should endeavour to provide citizens with environmental rights information; improve global and regional environmental cooperation; create and implement national and international environmental legislation.

A rethinking of our connection with the natural world is required to guarantee that everyone has access to a clean, healthy, and sustainable environment. As a result, states should strengthen their environmental management policies and regulations; they should build the capacity of civil society and government entities; they should provide additional funding for training and education of social partners; and they should establish tripartite social dialogue forums on environmental protection that include civil society. States must collaborate with civil society, companies, and other stakeholders to promote efforts to implement environmental rights. They must take immediate environmental action, backed up by proper funding, and advocate for a fair transition to a sustainable, human-rights-based economy. Businesses should include environmental issues into human rights due diligence procedures, fully accounting for how their operations' environmental consequences might potentially harm human rights. Furthermore, governments must also ratify and update existing laws to protect the right to a healthy environment, including holding enterprises, especially extractive industries, accountable.

References

AFRICAN UNION, (1981) *African Charter on Human and Peoples' Rights of 1981*. [Online]. Available from: https://au.int/sites/default/files/treaties/36390-treaty-0011_-_african_charter_on_human_and_peoples_rights_e.pdf

BASIRI, M. A. and NAJAFI, D., (2010) *Human Rights and Environmental Ethics*. [Online]. Available from: https://humanrights.mofidu.ac.ir/article_21246.html?lang=en

BOYD, D. R., (2011) *The Environmental Rights Revolution: A Global Study of Constitutions, Human Rights, and the Environment*. Toronto, UBC Press.

BUHMANN, K., JONSSON, J. and FISKER, M., (2019) Do No Harm And Do More Good Too: Connecting The SDGS With Business And Human Rights And Political CSR Theory. *Corporate Governance: The International Journal of Business in Society*, 19(3), 389-403.

CHOMA, H. (2008) The Environmental Rights Entered in the Constitutions: A Critique. *US-China Law Review*, 5(1).

COUNCIL OF EUROPE, (1950) *European Convention for the Protection of Human Rights and Fundamental Freedoms of 1950.* [Online]. Available from: https://www.coe.int/en/web/human-rights-convention/the-convention-in-1950#:~:text=The%20Convention%20for%20the%20Protection,force%20on%203%20September%201953.

CULLET, P., (1995) Definition of an Environmental Right in a Human Rights Context. *Netherlands Quarterly of Human Rights,* 13(1), 25-40.

DE VILLIERS, C. and VAN STADEN, C. J., (2006) Can Less Environmental Disclosure Have A Legitimising Effect? Evidence from Africa. *Accounting, Organisations and Society,* 31(8), 763-781.

DE WET, E. and DU PLESSIS, A., (2010) The Meaning of Certain Substantive Obligations Distilled from International Human Rights Instruments for Constitutional Environmental Rights in South Africa. *African Human Rights Law Journal,* 10(2), 345-376.

DU PLESSIS, A., (2008) Public Participation, Good Environmental Governance And Fulfilment Of Environmental Rights. *Potchefstroom Electronic Law Journal/Potchefstroomse Elektroniese Regsblad,* 11(2), 1-34.

DUGARD, J. and ALCARO, A., (2013) Let's Work Together: Environmental and Socioeconomic Rights in the Courts. *South African Journal on Human Rights,* 29(1), 14-31.

FERIS, L., (2008) Constitutional Environmental Rights: An Under-Utilised Resource. *South African Journal on Human Rights,* 24(1), 29-49.

FRANCIONI, F., (2010) International human rights in an environmental horizon. *European Journal of International Law,* 21(1), 41-55.

HUGHES, E. L. and IYALOMHE, D., (1998). *Substantive Environmental Rights in Canada.* [Online]. Available: https://rdo-olr.org/wp-content/uploads/2018/01/olr_30.2_Hughes_Iyalomhe.pdf

HUNTJENS, P., (2021) *Towards a Natural Social Contract: Transformative Social-Ecological Innovation for a Sustainable, Healthy and Just Society.* London, Springer Nature.

IMPERATIVES, S., (1987) *Report of the World Commission on Environment and Development: Our Common Future.* [Online]. Available from: https://sustainabledevelopment.un.org/content/documents/5987our-common-future.pdf

INTERNATIONAL LABOUR ORGANISATION, (1989) *Indigenous and Tribal Peoples in Independent Countries Convention 169 of 1989.* [Online]. Available from: https://www.ilo.org/dyn/normlex/en/f?p=NORMLEXPUB:55:0::NO::P55_TYPE,P55_LANG,P55_DOCUMENT,P55_NODE:REV,en,C169,/Document

KIDD, M., (2010) Public Interest Environmental Litigation: Recent Cases Raise Possible Obstacles. *PELJ,* 13, 27-30

KOTZÉ, L. J., (2007) The Judiciary, the Environmental Right and the Quest for Sustainability in South Africa: A Critical Reflection. *Review of European Community & International Environmental Law,* 16(3), 298-311.

KOTZÉ, L. J. and DU PLESSIS, A., (2010) *Some Brief Observations on Fifteen Years of Environmental Rights Jurisprudence in South Africa.* [Online]. Available from: https://www.researchgate.net/publication/236165986_Some_Brief_Observations_on_Fifteen_Years_of_Environmental_Rights_Jurisprudence_in_South_Africa

LEE, K, et al., (2020) Youth Perceptions of Climate Change: A Narrative Synthesis. *Wiley Interdisciplinary Reviews: Climate Change,* 11(3).

LYSTER, R., (1992) The Protection of Environmental Rights. *S. African LJ,* 109.

MALONE, L. A. and PASTERNACK, S., (2002) Exercising Environmental Human Rights and Remedies in the United Nations System. *Wm. & Mary Envtl. L. & Pol'y Rev.*, 27.

MAY, J. R. and DALY, E., (2016) *Environmental Constitutionalism*. Cheltenham, Edward Elgar Publishing Limited.

MOYSIADIS, V. et al., (2021). *Smart farming in Europe*. [Online]. Available from: https://www.sciencedirect.com/science/article/abs/pii/S1574013720304457

MURCOTT, M. J., (2021) Innovative Regulation of Meat Consumption in South Africa: An Environmental Rights Perspective. *Potchefstroom Electronic Law Journal/Potchefstroomse Elektroniese Regsblad*, 24(1).

OHCHR, (2023) *Special Rapporteur on the Issue of Human Rights Obligations Relating to the Enjoyment of a Safe, Clean, Healthy and Sustainable Environment*. [Online]. Available from: https://www.ohchr.org/en/special-procedures/sr-environment

OHCHR, (2023). *Human Rights Council Resolutions on Human Rights and Climate Change* [Online]. Available from: https://www.ohchr.org/en/climate-change/human-rights-council-resolutions-human-rights-and-climate-change

ROSSOUW, N. and WISEMAN, K., (2004). Learning from the Implementation of Environmental Public Policy Instruments after the First Ten Years of Democracy in South Africa. *Impact Assessment and Project Appraisal*, 22(2), 131-140.

SAFILL, (2004) *BP Southern Africa (Pty) Ltd v. MEC for Agriculture, Conservation and Land Affairs* 2004 (5) SA 124 (WLD). [Online]. Available from: http://www.saflii.org/za/cases/ZAGPHC/2004/18.html

SAFILL, (2005) *De Kock v. Ministry of Water Affairs and Forestry* (CCT 30/05) *Ferreira* v *Levin* (CT5/95). [Online]. Available from: https://www.saflii.org/za/cases/ZACC/2005/12.html

SAFILL, (2007) *Petrol Retailers Association of South Africa (Pty) Ltd v. Director General Environmental Management Mpumalanga and Others*. [Online]. Available from: https://www.saflii.org/za/cases/ZACC/2007/13.html

SAFILL, (2004) *Re Kranspoort Community 2000 (2) SA 124 (LCC)*. [Online]. Available from: https://www.studocu.com/en-za/document/university-of-the-witwatersrand-johannesburg/property-law/in-re-kranspoort-community-2000-2-sa-124-lcc/28002004

SAFILL, (1996) *Welfare v Woodcarb (Pty) Ltd* 1996 (3) SA 155 (N). [Online]. Available from: https://cer.org.za/virtual-library/judgments/high-courts/minister-of-health-and-welfare-v-woodcarb

SHELTON, A .L. and PIPPITT, H. A., (2007) Fixed versus dynamic orientations in environmental learning from ground-level and aerial perspectives. *Psychological research*, 71, pp.333-346.

SOUTH DURBAN COMMUNITY ENVIRONMENTAL ALLIANCE, (2023) *About*. [Online]. Available from: https://sdcea.co.za/

SOUTH AFRICAN GOVERNMENT, (1989) *Environment Conservation Act 73 0f 1989*. [Online]. Available from: https://www.gov.za/sites/default/files/gcis_document/201503/act-73-1989.pdf

SOUTH AFRICAN GOVERNMENT, (1998) *National Water Act 36 of 1998*. [Online]. Available from: https://www.gov.za/documents/national-water-act

SOUTH AFRICAN GOVERNMENT, (1998) *National Environmental Management Act 107 of 1998*. [Online]. Available from: https://www.gov.za/documents/national-environmental-management-act

SOUTH AFRICAN GOVERNMENT, (2004) *National Environmental Management: Air Quality Act 39 of 2004*. [Online]. Available from: https://www.gov.za/documents/national-environment-management-air-quality-act

SOUTH AFRICAN GOVERNMENT, (1998) *Marine Living Resources Act 18 of 1998*. [Online]. Available from: https://www.gov.za/documents/marine-living-resources-act-27-may-1998-0000

SOUTH AFRICAN GOVERNMENT, (2004) *National Environmental Management Biodiversity Act 10 of 2004*. [Online]. Available from: https://www.gov.za/documents/national-environmental-management-biodiversity-act-0

SOUTH AFRICAN GOVERNMENT, (2004) *National Environmental Management Air Quality Act 30 of 2004*. [Online]. Available from: https://www.gov.za/documents/national-environment-management-air-quality-act

SOUTH AFRICAN GOVERNMENT, *Local Government: Municipal Structures Act 117 of 1998*. [Online]. Available from: https://www.gov.za/documents/local-government-municipal-structures-act

TREVOR, N. and PATRICK, B., 2020. South Africa's shrinking sovereignty: Economic crises, ecological damage, sub-imperialism and social resistances. *Вестник Российского университета дружбы народов. Серия: Международные отношения*, 20(1), pp.67-83.

UNITED NATIONS, (1948) *Universal Declaration of Human Rights of 1948*. Geneva, United nations.

UNITED NATIONS, (1972) *Stockholm Declaration of the United Nations Conference on the Human Environment of 1972*. [Online]. Available from: https://www.un.org/en/conferences/environment/stockholm1972#:~:text=The%20Stockholm%20Declaration%2C%20which%20contained,and%20the%20well%2Dbeing%20of

UNITED NATIONS, (1966) *The International Covenant on Economic, Social and Cultural Rights 6 of 1966*. [Online]. Available from: https://www.ohchr.org/en/instruments-mechanisms/instruments/international-covenant-economic-social-and-cultural-rights

UNITED NATIONS, (1989) *Convention on the Rights of the Child of 1989*. [Online]. Available from: https://resourcecentre.savethechildren.net/document/united-nations-convention-rights-child-0/#:~:text=UN%2C%20United%20Nations,The%20United%20Nations%20Convention%20on%20the%20Rights%20of%20the%20Child,%2C%20French%2C%20Russian%2C%20Spanish.

UNITED NATIONS, (1966) *International Covenant on Civil and Political Rights of 1966*. [Online]. Available from: https://www.coe.int/en/web/compass/the-international-covenant-on-civil-and-political-rights#:~:text=This%20Covenant%20was%20adopted%20by,Universal%20Declaration%20of%20Human%20Rights.

UNITED NATIONS, (2020) *Human Rights and the Environment*. [Online]. Available from: https://unsdg.un.org/sites/default/files/2020-03/Human-Rights-and-the-Environment.pdf Date visited, 10 March 2023.

UNITED NATIONS, (2022) *General Assembly Adopts Landmark Resolution Recognizing Clean, Healthy, Sustainable Environment as Human Right*. [Online]. Available from: https://press.un.org/en/2022/ga12437.doc.htm

UNITED NATIONS, (2023) *The 2030 Agenda for Sustainable Development*. [Online]. Available from: https://sustainabledevelopment.un.org/content/documents/21252030%20Agenda%20for%20Sustainable%20Development%20web.pdf

Karl Marx Justice in Environmental Discourse in South Africa

Lele Dominic Dummene

Introduction

The contemporary world is filled with inequalities and exploitation of rights, hence, justice is vital to eradicate the discrimination, exploitation, and deprivation of rights in society and institutions. Justice can be viewed and achieved from different perspectives, such as environmental justice, human rights justice, economic justice, social justice, political justice, and many other forms of justice that can be identified and described. These forms of justice are employed to address issues of inequalities, deprivation, and exploitation in society or institutions. Karl Marx tried to describe what justice entails and how it should be achieved between individuals in society or institutions. However, Marx's position on justice is debated because his views are often viewed from his critique of capitalism. Although Marx did not categorically speak about justice, he perceived justice as fairness and equality in the economic setting; thus, necessitating economic justice.

The distribution of environmental resources has caused a lot of crisis, inequality, and injustice among individuals and communities (Mcdonald 2002; Bullard 2005; Regan 2012). Environmental resources in our communities are being commercialized and politicized by the elites and powerful for private use; hence, this causes inequality and injustice in the environmental and economic inequalities in communities (Masters and Kisiangani, 2010). When discussing justice in the distribution of environmental resources, we think of environmental justice, human rights, and social justice (Taylor 2017:1). This is because these forms of justice convey elements of the environment and concerns for humans. In this paper, Karl Marx's view of justice (economic justice) is explored and employed to investigate and proffer solutions to environmental issues, such as the distribution of environmental resources. Karl Marx's view of justice is mostly seen as economic justice- bringing justice, equality, and fairness to the economy; thus, we lose the depth of insights and significance of Karl Marx's justice to environmental discourse. This chapter discuss some of the struggles and injustices in the distribution of environmental resources in South Africa. The chapter also present conceptions of environmental and social justice. Karl Marx's justice (economic justice) in this chapter demonstrates economic equality in the distribution of environmental resources to offer solutions to environmental issues.

Environmental Justice Struggles in Apartheid and Post-Apartheid South Africa

Environmental issues in South Africa can be traced back to the apartheid period. The apartheid environmental issue focused on the struggle against environmental racism, while the post-apartheid environmental phase marks contemporary environmental issues such as hydraulic fracturing, pollution, and health effects from oil and chemical industries (Bullard 1994; Khan 2002). During the apartheid period, environmental issues were neglected and silent. Environmental activism was dormant and silent against the issues of the environment (Death 2014). The apartheid phase was dominated by environmental segregation or environmental racism which is defined as:

> racial discrimination in environmental policymaking and the enforcement of regulations and laws, the deliberate targeting of people of colored communities for toxic waste facilities, the official sanctioning of the life-threatening presence of poisons and pollutants in our communities, and a history of excluding people of color from leadership in the environmental movement (Di Chiro 1995:304).

An example of environmental racism in the apartheid period was when some black South Africans were forcefully driven from their indigenous lands (Mcdonald 2002:1). In South Africa's environmental context of today, the question is, has environmental racism ended with the apartheid period? The process of hydraulic fracturing for Shale gas which has just been proposed in South Africa is situated in the KwaZulu-Natal region (Midlands Conservancies Forum 2016), where there are mostly blacks. This exposes the continuous environmental racism in contemporary South Africa, almost three decades after the demise of the apartheid system.

Another environmental racial oppression in South Africa was when "whites-only policies in national parks meant that black South Africans could not enjoy the country's rich natural heritage and draconian poaching laws kept the rural poor from desperately needed resources" (Mcdonald 2002:2). Environmental racism during the apartheid period meant that the blacks were deprived of their indigenous ancestral lands to build parks and game reserves for the whites. Thus, the blacks lost their roots, religion, ancestral heritage, and lands to capitalism and environmental and social oppression. The blacks lost it to environmental injustice and social injustice. It also means that despite being driven from their ancestral lands due to environmental racism and oppression, they were also deprived of the joys (socialization) of entering the parks because they were not allowed to be in the parks and game reserves. As a result, there was not much attention given to environmental issues because it favors the minority in power and the apartheid government.

During the apartheid period, the approach to environmental justice was characterized by the preservation and conservation of species (Khan 2002:15). However, this was rooted in environmental racism because blacks were not involved in the conservation of the species. The conservation process involved mainly the educated, elites, and white minority, while the blacks were alienated because the whites assumed that the blacks lacked knowledge of conservation and also of their colour, social, educational, and environmental experience. This is seen in the activities of the Western Districts Game Protection Association and the Transvaal Game Protection Association (TGPA) where membership is for the affluent (Pringle 1983:63). This membership for affluent by the game associations was to support the fact that the whites are more exposed and that Africans (black South Africans) were not exposed; thus, they would be tempted to hunt the species for consumption. This was rooted in the assumption and stereotyping that Africans are environmentally destructive. This assumption and stereotyping are seen as part of environmental racism (Carruthers 1995:31).

The exclusion of black South Africans from the environmental movement continued during the apartheid period. However, there was a surprising emergence of black environmental social movements during this period of environmental racism. The emergence of the Native Farmers Association (NFA) advocated for access to land and soil conservation, which was a necessity for blacks (Khan 2002:19-20). However, the efforts of the NFA were not fruitful as the whites and government were against their policies and goals. The government policies on the environment were also biased to favor the white minority. This ushered environmental racism into the political domain. Under the apartheid regime, environmental racism moved into politics, and environmental issues were politicized. For example, some of the government policies to support agriculture were in favor of the whites (Khan 2002:19). During the apartheid period, laws were passed that disempowered blacks by not letting the blacks participate in environmental decision making (Khan 2002). This affected the spiritual, emotional, social, environmental, health, and physical well-being of the blacks. These government policies and incidences of environmental racism hindered the economic, environmental, and social aspects of black communities in South Africa. This also exposes the injustice and inequalities in environmental discourses in South Africa that have led to economic injustice and inequalities; thus, Karl Marx's justice is needed to address the economic injustice and inequalities in environmental discourse in South Africa.

The post-apartheid environmental issues in South Africa are contemporary environmental issues. The post-apartheid environmental issues involve the struggle against environmental capitalism in South Africa. The post-apartheid environmental issues are climate change, waste, pollution, carbon emission, hydraulic fracturing, deforestation, work hazards, and the rise of environmental capitalism that brings economic inequalities and injustices in the environmental discourse. Unlike the apartheid phase, the post-apartheid period saw much activism for the environment from grassroots and black communities against contemporary environmental issues. For example, there were protests and demonstrations against plans to site a nuclear power station against a toxic waste recycling plant (Khan 2002:28). Community-based organizations in both rural and urban areas also took up green campaigns and projects in Durban areas.

The post-apartheid period saw the redefinition of the environment to include everyone irrespective of race. This period also saw academics, business unions, and non-profit organizations taking up environmental campaigns in their respective sectors (Mcdonald 2002:2). This was evident as trade unions began to incorporate environmental policies into industrial policies, such as workers-health and occupational safety. In the post-apartheid period, communities also stood up against environmental racism. This was displayed by the Richtersveld Northern Cape farmers refusing to be evicted from their ancestral land for the development of national parks. This period also saw the emergence of new movements and organizations for the environment challenging environmental practices and policies that existed in the apartheid period and they also expressed great concern for the poor and marginalized in rural areas (Mcdonald 2002; Khan 2002).

One of the new organizations that emerged during the post-apartheid period in 1988 was Earth-life Africa. Earth-life Africa was concerned with the creation of a safe and healthy environment for all, especially for the poor (Khan 2002:30). A major approach adopted by Earth-life Africa to realize its goals was to form alliances with unions, and local, and international environmental organizations. This was seen in their alliance with Chemical Workers Industrial Union and Greenpeace International to take up actions against Thor Chemicals, which had poisoned the drinking water of a community in KwaZulu-Natal (Khan 2002; Death 2014).

In South Africa, the majority of mining industries belong mostly to whites and a few blacks with strong political affiliations (Masters & Kisiangani 2010). For example, Reichardt (2008) note that "key figures in the mining are Patrice Motsepe of African Rainbow Mineral, Mane Dipico of De Beers, Tokyo Sexwale of Mvelaphanda, and a host of others with prominent affiliations to the ANC" (10). Other mining industries that have occupied the mining space are Anglo America, Xstrata, BHP Billiton, Ehlobo Group, Batho Barena Consortium, and recently Rhino Oil and Gas and Sungu Sungu (Callinicos 1980; Jones 1995; Terreblanche; 2003; Bond 2005; Masters & Kisiangani, 2010:17). These are mostly white-owned mining industries and a few black elites and other races with strong political ties with ANC ruling political party in South Africa (Masters & Kisiangani 2010:17). This buttresses the point on how the environment is linked to the economy. It also shows the unjust distribution of environmental resources which shows economic injustice and inequality.

The effects emanating from this show that environmental resources are being commoditized by a few individuals and groups in South Africa. It also buttresses the struggle for the environment and its resources and exposes the corruption in the government by giving access to resources to a few individuals. This analysis of environmental struggles in South Africa also highlights the widening poverty and unemployment gap in the economy. In essence, this analysis shows the power tussle for environmental resources, empowerment of few elites, marginalization, inequality, injustice, and limitation of the majority to environmental resources in South Africa. This analysis shows the inadequacy in the governance of natural resources in South Africa. It shows the lack of implementation of the National Environmental Management Act (NEMA) 1998 that outlined principles of environmental governance and sustainable development of the environment. Hence, from these expositions of the environmental struggles in South Africa, it emphasizes the fact that environmental issues and injustice necessitates economic issues and economic injustice; thus, there is a need for justice, not just environmental and social justice but economic justice which Karl Marx echoed in his criticism of capitalism. The following subheadings highlight the various kinds of justice that can be employed to address the environmental inequalities and injustices in South Africa.

Conceptions of Social Justice

There are various explanations and definitions of justice and what it entails. Some authors define justice based on social welfare and societal issues while others apply the concept of justice to issues outside societal issues such as personal issues, institutions, states, culture, and personal identity (Prigoff 2003; Reisch 2007:68). In explaining the concept of justice, some authors conceive justice as social justice. Social analysts such as John Stuart Mill, Leslie Stephen, and Henry Sidgwick introduced the term social justice in the society and political arena. The term was used alongside distributive justice at a time when economic and social institutions were under ethical scrutiny and when the responsibility of the state was increasing and challenging. Barry (2005) highlighted that social justice entered into social and political discourse from capitalism, which was seen as unjust to the people in society; thus, the concept of social justice was introduced to advocate for social and economic justice. The modern conception of social justice started in the 18th century as a child of the Industrial and French Revolutions (Jackson 2005; Brodie 2007:95). The term became popular in the 19th century as states and institutions began to advocate for social goals (Premdas 2016; Fleischacker 2004). The term was further adopted in the 20th century when liberal democracies and socialism grew stronger (Brodie 2007:95; Reisch 2007; Ilcan & Lacey 2013). Social justice was adopted by liberals to critically analyse land ownership, private properties, and inherited wealth to charge the state to implement laws and structures that will bring about distributive justice (Miller 1999:3). From this, we can deduce and imply that social justice is an ideal concept in the distribution of social, economic, and environmental resources and enacting justice.

Social justice analysts argue that for social justice to be achieved, it requires a strong state and institutions in which economic and social differences between social classes and groups will be reduced (Jansson 2005:24). The state and institutions facilitate distributive justice, with appropriate consideration of needs, citizenship, and rights. Thus, outside strong state and institution roles, social justice will be elusive (Dobson 2003; McCarthy 2010; Ekanga 2005). The second part of Miller's conception of social justice also means that social justice principles appeal to the state and institutions to implement policies and laws that foster justice. To extend this point on social justice, Rawls (1971:7) notes that the state and institutions are the conveying objects of justice. This is because the institutions and state are the avenues through which justice is administered. The state and institutions define and defend the rights and duties of the people by upholding human rights of equity, equality, and fairness in all aspects of society (Theoharis 2007:223). An extended explanation of social justice and its relation to state and institution is that social justice applies to people (individuals) who share national identities and live in a society and institution with bonds of solidarity that override personal interests in the distribution of societal resources (Miller 1999:18).

For Miller (1999:1), social justice addresses how the good and bad of life should be distributed among members of society. When state policies and individuals are condemned for being unjust in society, it implies that the policies favor a few in society and some individuals(s) enjoy fewer advantages than others. Hence, social justice negates individualistic principles toward the distribution of societal resources. It aims to empower citizens who are deprived by the competitive market (Premdas 2016). In the same light, Ekanga (2005) posits that social justice is about fairness and equality of opportunity. Social justice urges people to be responsible for their actions and consequently to approve or condemn their actions. Social justice is also employed to be a fulfilment of deficiency. This implies that those who cannot help themselves need to be helped. Hence, the need becomes a basis and part of social justice. This aspect of social justice comes from a Judeo-Christian tradition that holds firm the values of universal love, charity, altruism, cooperation, and self-sacrifice. The '*need*' side of social justice arises from or relies on fairness and equality (Ekanga 2005:89). This means that from the Judeo-Christian perspective, everyone is treated fairly and seen as equal and living in a community of oneness.

In the conceptualization of social justice, Premdas (2016:453) highlights two variants of social justice which could be conceived as the two phases of social justice. The first phase of social justice deals with issues of marginalization, oppression, exploitation, and discrimination as illustrated in environmental racism above. Thus, social justice addresses these issues to justify the need for redistribution of resources and the adjustment of social and political institutions to restore rights, equality, equity, and justice to the marginalized and exploited as in the case of environmental racism explained above in South Africa and the world. The second phase concerns distributive justice. The distributive dimension of social justice "refers to a demand for the equal allocation of both material and symbolic goods in society" (Premdas 2016:457). Another aspect of the distributive dimension of social justice is the demand for just compensation by affected and marginalized groups. This second phase of social justice addresses reforms and the just distribution of opportunities and resources for everyone.

In essence, this phase of social justice could be employed to address the reform of government and institutional policies that are not discriminating against people. This phase of social justice should be employed to address the environmental policies enacted against blacks in South Africa. This second phase of social justice emphasized by Premdas (2016) is also applicable to seeking compensation for affected communities and individuals due to environmental hazards from the distribution of environmental resources. This second phase is also related to environmental justice as they both seek fairness and compensation to affected and exploited laborers, individuals, and communities. It also relates to Marx's view of justice (economic justice) as they both call for fairness and compensation of workers who received fewer wages that do not equate to their skills and talents. In essence, social justice is needed in environmental discourse as it calls for fairness and equality in the distribution of environmental resources.

Karl Marx's Concept of Justice (Economic Justice)

Before the exposition of Karl Marx's view of justice; it is important to state clearly that this part of Marx's view of justice does not focus on his critique of capitalism; rather it highlights and discusses the ideas of justice embedded in his critique of capitalism. Highlighting Marx's view of justice is significant in the distribution of environmental resources as it connects with environmental justice and social justice which condemn inequalities and injustices in the distribution of resources. The adherent of Marxism argued that Marx did have ideas of justice in his critique of capitalism. Scholars such as Van de Veer (1973), Husami (1980), and Stoian (2014) hold that justice is a part of Marx's condemnation of capitalism; thus, they argue that Marx's definition of justice has an implicit and explicit substantive conception of justice. This means that Marx's view of justice is linked to the broader view of justice. Marx's idea of justice denotes economic equality-which gives the right to every individual in the society to receive the same amount of resources regardless of occupation, skills, and work. This is the conceptual definition of Marx's view of justice that will be used for this work. It is the conceptual definition because; justice in Marx's idea is to remedy the exploitation of workers. In this view, Marx was articulating economic justice - which remedies economic inequality, and social injustice, and eliminates environmental injustice. It is also the conceptual definition because it expresses the idea of equality (fairness and justice) which is also expressed in environmental and social justice.

The contextual significance of Marx's view of justice in this work is that Marx was at the forefront of the early societal activists (movements) who advocated for justice and fair distribution of societal resources (Stewart & Zaaiman 2015). Thus, it is important to lean on Marx's paths in attaining justice in the distribution of environmental resources, as he was able to speak out against injustice and marginalization in a strong state of government, unlike this contemporary liberal and democratic society and governance. Hence, the environmental social movements of today are the modern Marxists, advancing fairness and justice in the distribution of environmental, economic, and societal resources.

To comprehend Marx's view of justice, we must understand it from his theory of class. Marx explained two types of classes - the bourgeoisie (the rich or capitalist class) and the proletariat (the poor or labourers) who are exploited by the bourgeoisie (Stewart & Zaaiman 2015; Chellan 2016:3). Furthermore, Marx posited some criteria of 'class', namely; the ownership of property and capital and the second criterion is based on class-consciousness in lifestyle, norms, and beliefs. This means that each class shares a perception of their class position which is vital in the way that affects their activities. For example, those who own the means of production automatically know the class they fall into and their lifestyle, beliefs, and values reflect their class. This is also the same in the case of those who do not own the means of production (the poor). Marx also explained that each class undergoes a class formation in which each class develops a shared economic interest which implies the same economic level. Marx further asserted that the economic characteristics of each class will also determine the political characteristics of the class and its members.

Marx's view of justice is also conveyed when he faults capitalism on the basis that it encourages alienation which he sees as unjust. Alienation to Marx means that the workers are seen as alien objects- that which is outside and that the worker does not work creatively; the workers work to satisfy the capitalist needs. The capitalist also alienates the workers by deciding what to produce and how the product should be distributed (Evans 1975:92). Lange (1968) and Macpherson (1962:56) point out that alienation is displayed when workers are deprived of the right to demand equal wages from production. So it is seen that through Marx's lens, the people (workers) are alienated from the resources (economic, social, and environmental resources), and that in itself is injustice. Hence, in this sense of alienation, there is justice in Marx's critique of capitalism. This justice expressed by Marx links to the ideas of justice in social and environmental justice and to the broader views of justice. The exploitation of workers here can also be linked to the forceful exploitation of black South Africans from their ancestral lands (environmental racism). Thus, there is a need for Marx's view of justice to avert environmental racism and exploitation of environmental resources.

According to Daly (2000:355), Marx's condemnation of "capitalism is not only a moral injustice but an ontological injustice, a violation of the worker's humanity. It is coercion into alienation, fetishism, and idolatry". On that basis, Marx viewed capitalism as a violation as the workers are forced to sell their essential human skills (labor power) and thus, worship the owners of production. It is a moral injustice and ontological injustice because the workers lose their essence and dignity as human beings and see themselves as mere machines used for production. This aspect of ontological injustice which denotes the loss of a sense of human dignity also connects to the environmental racism above where the black South Africans also lose their sense of human dignity when they were driven from their ancestral homelands. This connection shows the link between Marx's view of justice (economic justice), social, and environmental justice as the concepts advocate for the reinstatement of justice in human dignity, economic, social, and environmental situations.

To capture justice in Marx's thoughts, Yenigun (2013:308) emphasise that if there was no justice in Marx's thinking, "why should Marx want us to care about terms/words such as alienation, dehumanization, self-realization, free development or emancipation"? Yenigun sees justice in Marx's use of these terms, especially through his critique of capitalism. This is because these terms denote injustice and they are employed to condemn unjust situations and acts. The terms development, emancipation, and transformation were used by Marx to awaken the exploited laborers in his condemnation of capitalism. These terms reflect in the explanations of environmental and social justice as the terms are used to convey ideas of justice. Thus, this shows the link between Marx's justice (economic justice), and social, and environmental justice discussed in this work. These terms used by Marx can also be used in environmental discourse to awaken those deprived of their environmental rights and to advance the need for justice in the distribution of environmental resources. The laborer employed to produce it creates the value of a product.

However, the capitalist rewards the laborer with a little part of the value; by doing this, laborers are deprived of their just wages equal to the value of the products created. In pointing this out, Marx shows that the wages paid to laborers do not equate to the surplus profit accumulated by the capitalists which is clear proof of the exploitation of the laborer's labor power and talent which implies injustice (Hancock 1971:65). Situating this understanding in environmental discourse, it means that the compensation given to affected communities and individuals cannot be equated to the surplus profits made from the sales of environmental resources. Marx's position also shows that the people living in the environment are not given a fair share of environmental resources, just as in the case of environmental racism in South Africa. Thus, Marx's call for justice (economic justice) is in line with the call for justice expressed in environmental and social justice that will necessitate the fair distribution of environmental resources (Rashid 2002:448).

Environmental Justice

The concept of environmental justice is very broad and there is no specific definition of environmental justice. However, there are similarities in all its explanations. Environmental justice arose when the First National People of Color Environmental Leadership Summit was convened in 1991 in Washington, where delegates from North and South America were present. The principles of environmental justice were laid out in the Summit which brought many people together in agreement for a new approach to the environment (Di Chiro 1995:307). Before the birth of environmental justice principles in the Summit, environmental justice entails justice and equity concerning the distribution and redistribution of environmental benefits and burdens and ensuring that affected communities do not suffer disproportionately from environmental hazards (McCarthy 2010:242). However, the Summit "broadened the environmental justice principles beyond its anti-toxics focus to include issues of public health, worker's safety, land use, transportation, housing resource allocation, and community empowerment" (Khan 2002:27). This means that environmental justice does not only focus on issues related to the environment but it also encompasses the general welfare and justice for the people in the society.

Bullard (2005) notes that the framework of environmental justice seeks to prevent environmental threats. These environmental threats involve unsafe industrial and housing issues; land degradation and health issues (Bullard 2005:23). This aspect of environmental justice shows the link between the environment, social, and economic issues. It also shows that the term environmental justice is generic and can be applied to various aspects of life and issues of inequalities, threats, and exploitation. The framework of environmental justice that cut across various aspects of life in society includes:

> The principle is that all individuals have a right to be protected from environmental degradation. The public health model of prevention is the preferred strategy: it focuses on eliminating a threat before harm occurs. It rests on the precautionary principle for protecting workers, communities, and ecosystems. It shifts the burden of proof to polluters and dischargers who harm, discriminate, or

who do not give equal protection to racial and ethnic minorities. It redresses disproportionate impact by targeting action and resources (Bullard 2005:23-29).

In situating the emergence of environmental justice in the context of South Africa, Khan (2002) pointed out that the history of the environmental justice movement in South Africa started in the 1990s. He stated that in South Africa there is "a history of racial discrimination, institutionalized black poverty, and political powerlessness that are central to the environmental discourse" (Khan 2002:27). This quote implies that environmental issues/burdens (negative impacts from the environment) in South Africa were associated with the blacks and carried out within the black communities due to racial discrimination and political deprivation among the blacks. Hence, the blacks were a targeted group of environmental racism and the blacks were victims of the effects of political ecology. Hence, environmental justice in South Africa was a result of blacks advocating for their civil rights. In a comprehensive conception and definition of environmental justice to address issues of environmental, social, health, political, and economic injustices, the Environmental Justice Network Forum (EJNF) (1997) posits that:

> Environmental justice is about social transformation directed towards meeting basic human needs and enhancing our quality of life-economic quality, health care, housing, human rights, environmental protection, and democracy. In linking environmental and social justice issues, the environmental justice approach seeks to challenge the abuse of power which results in poor people having to suffer the effects of environmental damage caused by the greed of others. This includes workers and communities without firewood, grazing, and water.

This definition of environmental justice by EJNF tacitly covers all aspects of society where injustices and inequalities exist among the people. Again, this definition also supports the generic nature of environmental justice. It is suitable because it outlines the need for all kinds of justice. The definition of environmental justice by EJNF above comprises the need and importance for environmental justice; it also covers Marx's view of justice (economic justice) and the definition of environmental justice above also includes issues of social justice- when it addresses the need for social transformation and basic human needs. Thus, we can see how the three types of justice are connected and each of them (social justice, economic justice, and environmental justice) can be employed to address issues in their respective domains.

Marx's Justice, Environmental Justice, and Social Justice: The Connection

Environmental injustice necessitates social and economic injustices, and achieving environmental justice implies social and economic justice. The ideas of justice in Marx, environmental justice, and social justice are connected in their conceptualization as they portray and adhere to objective views of justice. Due to inequalities in the distribution of environmental benefits and damages which affects mostly the poor and marginalized, it is impossible to exclude environmental issues from social and economic issues; they are inseparable. This is because environmental issues always lead to the emergence of human rights and environmental movements/organizations, which hold a joint concern for environmental and social justice. This is evident in Brazil where the Green Environmental Movements "jointly campaign for the rights of indigenous forest dwellers and against commercial deforestation" (Agyeman 1978). In the same way, the dumping of nuclear waste in Benin has caused the emergence of human rights and environmental organizations that focus on social and environmental justice. So also the environmental struggles in the apartheid and post-apartheid period have caused the emergence and mobilization of environmental organizations and human rights activism. Thus, the three types of justices are linked as they are all concerned with social, economic, and environmental justice and they all disapprove of commercial/economic exploitation of environmental resources (Regan 2012).

Another relationship between the three types of justice is that they are all transnational concepts of justice; they all appeal to objective views of justice. This means that they are not specific and focused on a particular region or country but they can be applied in any region or country (Salazar and Alper 2009). This is seen as the environmental social movements and human rights activists in New York, Pennsylvania, Germany, and South Africa can employ the concepts of social justice, environmental justice, and economic justice (Marx's view of justice) to address inequalities and injustices in the distribution of environmental resources in their various countries. Social justice and economic justice stand on three kinds of justice, (a) the distribution of societal benefits and burdens (distributive justice), (b) the assertion of a right to participate in public decisions (participative justice), and (c) the demand for public acknowledgment and compensation of affected group (recognition justice). In the same way, environmental justice also stands on these three kinds of justice. Environmental justice (a) seek a redistribution of environmental benefits and burdens (same as distributive justice), (b) environmental justice demands access to decision-making processes on the environment (same as participative justice) and (c) environmental justice calls for recognition, and compensation of environmental affected group (same as recognition justice). On that basis, the three justices are tacitly connected and can be employed in addressing and advocating for justice in the distribution of environmental resources (Schlosberg 2003; Gilbert 2004; Salazar and Alper 2011).

Holifield (2013) point out that the environmental justice program incorporate distributive justice - which is the distribution and redistribution of lands and environmental resources among everyone. It incorporates procedural justice that gives rights to citizens to partake in decision-making processes. This reaffirms the relationship between the three justices as they all use the term "distributive justice". In addition, Bullard (1996) and Bullard and Johnson (2000) argue that environmental justice works to eliminate unfair, unjust, and inequitable conditions and decisions for the people. This also buttresses the relationship between environmental justice, economic justice (Marxist justice), and social justice as they all advocate for the liberation of the marginalized and seek just compensation for the affected group and individual in society.

Conclusion

Marx's view of justice (economic justice) is vital when discussing the distribution of environmental resources. Sometimes environmentalists and environmental organizations fail to draw on the ideas of Karl Marx in environmental debates; thus, limiting their ideas to environmental and social justice. The expositions of economic justice (Marx's view of justice) above have shown the significance of Marx's thoughts on societal issues such as environmental issues in our modern society, even though some social scientists will think Marx is outdated, his ideas are still relevant in addressing contemporary issues. The three concepts of justice are important in the contemporary and the life of every individual when discussing environmental issues and other related issues. From the conceptualization of the three ideas of justice above, it is seen that linking environmental justice, Marx's concept of justice, and social justice is very vital and suitable. The concepts explain how, why and what motivates environmental organizations and activists to mobilize against environmental inequalities and injustices as they seek equal distribution of environmental resources. This also necessitates economic, social, and environmental justice thereby providing a holistic approach to environmental, social, and economic activism and justice.

References

AGYEMAN, J., (1978) Black People in a White Landscape: Social and Environmental Justice. *Built Environment*, 16(3), 232-236.

AGYEMAN, J., (2005) Alternatives for Community and Environment: Where Justice and Sustainability meet. *Environment: Science and Policy for Sustainable Development*, 47(6), 10-23.

ATKINSON, A., (1991) *Principles of Political Ecology*. London, Belhaven.

BARRY, B., (1999). Sustainability and Intergenerational Justice. In Dobson, A. (ed.). *Fairness and Futurity: Essays on Environmental Sustainability and Social Justice*. Oxford, Oxford University Press.

BARRY, B., (2005) *Why Social Justice Matters*. Cambridge, Polity Press.

BOND, P., (2005) *Elites Transition, From Apartheid to Neoliberalism in South Africa*. Pietermaritzburg, University of KwaZulu-Natal Press.

BOSE, A., (1980) *Marx on Exploitation and Inequality: An Essay in Marxisan analytical Economics*. Delhi, Oxford University Press.

BOTTOMORE, T., (1988) Interpretations *of Marx*. United Kingdom, Basil Blackwell Inc.

BROAD, R., (1994) The Poor and the Environment: Friends or Foes? *World Development*, 22, 811-822.

BRODIE, J., (2007) Reforming Social Justice in Neoliberal Times. *Studies in Social Justice*, 1(2), 93-107.

BRAUN, B., (2005) Writing Geographies of Hope. *Antipode*, 37, 834-841.

BRYANT, R. L., (1997) Beyond the Impasse: The Power of Political Ecology in Third World Environmental Research. *Area*, 29(1), 5-19.

BULLARD, R. D., et al. (2005) Globalization, Marginalization and Contemporary SocialMovements in South Africa. *African Affairs*, 104(417), 615-634.

BULLARD, R. D. & JOHNSON, G. S. (2000). Environmental Justice: Grassroots activism and its impact on Public Policy Decision Making. *Journal of Social Issues*, 56(3), 555-578.

BULLARD, R. D., (1996) *Unequal Protection: Environmental Justice and Communities of Color.* San Francisco, Sierra Club.

BURKE, J. P., CROCKER, L. and LEGTERS, L. H., (1981) *Marxism and the Good Society.* New York, Cambridge University Press.

CALLINICOS, L., (1980) *Gold and Workers 1886-1924.* Johannesburg, Ravan Press.

CARRUTHERS, J., (1995) *The Kruger National Park: A Social and Political History.* Scottsville, University of Natal Press.

CHELLAN, N., (2016) *Capital: An Energy Perspective.* Cambridge, Cambridge Publishing.

DALY, J., (2000) Marx and Justice. *International Journal of Philosophical Studies*, 8(3), 351-370.

DEATH, C., (2014) Environmental Movements, Climate Change, and Consumption in South Africa. *Journal of Southern African Studies*, 40(6), 1215-1234.

DEPARTMENT OF MINERALS AND ENERGY, (2007) *Mineral and Petroleum Resources Development Amendment Bill (Government Gazette No. 29822 of 19 April 2007).* Cape Town, Government Printer.

DI CHIRO, G., (1995) Nature as Community: The Convergence of Environmental and Social Justice. In W. Cronon. (ed). *Uncommon Ground: Toward Re-inventing Nature* New York: W.W. Norton.

DOBB, M., (1960) *Political Economy and Capitalism.* London, Routledge and Kegan Paul.

DOBSON, A. (2003) *Citizenship and the Environment.* Oxford, Oxford University Press.

EDWARDS, S. and FRASER, E., (1969). *Selected Writings of Pierre Joseph Production Proudhon.* London, Macmillan & Co Ltd.

EKANGA, B., (2005) *Social Justice and Democracy: The Relevance of Rawls' conception of Justice in Africa.* Germany, Peter Lang GmbH.

EVANS, M., (1975) *Karl Marx.* London, George Allen and Unwin Ltd.

FLEISCHACKER, S., (2004) *A Short History of Distributive Justice.* London, Harvard University Press.

FORSYTH, T., (2008) Political Ecology and the Epistemology of Social Justice. *Geoforum*, 39(2), 756-764.

GEWIRTZ, S., (1998) Conceptualizing Social Justice in Education: Mapping the Territory. *Journal of Education Policy*, 13(2), 469-484.

GEZON, L. L., (1997) Political Ecology and Conflict in Ankarana, Madagascar. *Ecology*, 36(2), 85-100.

GILBERT, L., (2004) At the Core and on the Edge: Justice discourses in Metropolitan Toronto. *Space Polity*, 8(2), 245-260.

HANCOCK, R., (1971) Marx's Theory of Justice. *Social Theory and Practice*, 1(3), 65-71.

HECHT, S. B. and COCKBURN, A., (1992) Realpolitik, Reality and Rhetoric in Rio: Environment and Planning. *Society and Space*, 10(3), 367-375.

Hobbes, T. (1996) *Leviathan.* Cambridge, Cambridge University Press.

HOLIFIELD, R., (2009) Actor-Network Theory as a Critical Approach to Environmental Justice: A Case against Synthesis with Urban Political Ecology. *Antipode*, 41(4), 637-658.

HOLIFIELD, R., (2013) Defining Environmental Justice and Environmental Racism. *Urban Geography*, 22(1), 78-90.

HUSAMI, Z., (1980) Marx on Distributive Justice. In M. Cohen., T. Nagel. and T. Scanlon. (eds.). *Marx, Justice and History*. New Jersey, Princeton University Press.

IEA, (2014) *IEA- Energy Security*. [Online]. Available from: http://www.iea.org/topics/energysecurity/

ILCAN, S. and LACEY, A., (2013) Networks of Social Justice: Transnational Activism and Social Change. *Studies in Social Justice*, 7(1), 1-6.

JACKSON, B., (2005) The Conceptual History of Social Justice. *Political Studies Review*, 3(1), 356-373.

JANSSON, B., (2005) *The Reluctant Welfare State*. Belmout, Brooks.

JONES, J., (1995) *Through Fortress and Rock: The Story of GENCOR 1895-1995*. Jeppestown, Jonathan Ball.

KHAN, F., (2002) The Roots of Environmental Racism and the Rise of Environmental Justice in the 1990s. In D. A. McDonald. (ed.). *Environmental Justice in South Africa*. Cape Town, University of Cape Town Press.

LANGE, O., (1968) Marxian Economics and Modern Economic Theory. In H. David. (ed.). *Marx and Modern Economics*. New York, Modern Reader Paperbacks.

MACPHERSON, C. B., (1962) *The Political Theory of Possesive Individualism*. London, Oxford University Press.

MASTERS, L. and KISIANGANI, E., (2010) *Natural Resources Governance in Southern Africa*. Braamfontein, African Institute of South Africa.

McCARTHY, J., (2010) Social Justice and Urban regeneration Policy in Scotland. *Urban Research and Practice*, 3(3), 241-256.

McDONALD, D. A., (2002) *Environmental Justice in South Africa*. Cape Town, University of Cape Town Press.

MIDDLETON, J. D., (2003) Health, Environmental and Social Justice, Local environment. *International Journal of Justice and Sustainability*, 8(2), 155-165.

MIDLANDS CONSERVANCIES FORUM, (2016) *We Can't Drink Gas (Neither can Humans). No Mining the KZN Midlands*. [Online]. Available from: http://www.midlands conservancies.org.za/prpagefracking.php

MILLER, D., (1999) *Principles of Social Justice*. Cambridge, Harvard University Press.

PREMDAS, R., (2016) Social Justice and Affirmative Action. *Ethics and Racial Studies*, 39(3), 449-462.

PRIGOFF, A. W., (2003) Social Justice Framework. In J. Anderson. and R. W. Carter (eds.). *Diversity perspectives for Social Work practice*. Boston, Allyn & Bacon.

RAWLS, J., (1971) *A Theory of Justice*. London, Harvard University Press.

RASHID, H., (2002). Making Sense of Marxian Concept of Justice. *Indian Philosophical Quarterly*, 29(4), 445-470.

REGAN, B. E., (2012) *Environment as a form of Social Control: Implications of Native American Reservations and the Prison Industrial Complex in the United States*. New York, University of Connecticut Press.

REICHARDT, M., (2008) *Black Empowerment-Slaying South Africa's Sacred Cow*. [Online]. Available from: http:www.ethicalcorp.com/content.asp?contentID=5998

REISCH, M., (2007) Social Justice and Multiculturalism: Persistent Tensions in the History of U.S. Social Welfare and Social Work. *Studies in Social Justice*, 1(1), 67-92.

RICHARDS, P., (1985) *Indigenous Agricultural Revolution*. London, Hutchinson.

RYAN, A., (1993) Justice. New York, Oxford University Press.

RYAN, C. C., (1980) Socialist Justice and the Right to the Labour Product. *Political theory*, 8(4), 503-515.

SALAZAR, D. J. and ALPER, D. K., (2011) Justice and Environmentalism in the British Columbia and U.S. Pacific Northwest Environmental Movements. *Societal and Natural Resources*, 24(8), 767-784.

SCHLOSBERG, D., (2003) The Justice of Environmental Justice: Reconciling Equality, Recognition and Participation in a Political Movement. In A. Light. and D. De-Shaht, (eds.). *Moral and Political Reasoning in Environmental Practice*. Cambridge, MIT Press.

SCHERER, K. R., (1992) *Justice: Interdisciplinary Perspectives*. Great Britain, Cambridge University Press.

STEWART, P. and ZAAIMAN, J., (2015) *Sociology: A South African Introduction*. Cape Town, Juta & Company (Pty) Ltd.

STOIAN, V., (2014) *Property owning Democracy, Socialism and Justice: Rawlsian and Marxist Perspectives on the content of Social Justice*. Budapest, Central European University Collection.

TAYLOR, D. E., (2000) The Rise of the Environmental Justice Paradigm: Injustice Framing and the Social Construction of Environmental Discourses. *American Behavioral Scientist*, 43(4), 508-580.

TERREBLANCHE, S., (2003) *A History of Inequality in South Africa, 1652-2002*. Pietermaritzburg, University of Natal Press.

THEOHARIS, G., (2007) Social Justice Educational Leaders and Resistance: Toward a theory of Social Justice Leadership. *Educational Administration Quarterly*, 43(2), 221-258.

TUCKER, R. C., (1969) *The Marxian Revolutionary Idea*. New York, Norton and Company.

VAN DE VEER, D., (1973) Marx's view of Justice. *Philosophy and Phenomenological Research*, 33(3), 366-386.

WALKER, P., (2005) Political Ecology: Where is the Ecology? *Progress in Human Geography*, 29(1), 73-82.

WALZER, M., (1983) *Spheres of Justice: A Defence of Pluralism and Equality*. New York, Basic Books.

WHITE, S., (1996) Needs, Labour and Marx's Conception of Justice. *Political Studies*, 44, 88-101.

WOOD, A. W., (1972) The Marxian Critique of Justice. *Philosophy and Public Affairs*, 1 (3), 244-282.

WOOD, A. W., (1984) Justice and Class Interests. *Philosophica*, 33(1), 9-32.

YENIGUN, H. I., (2013) Marx's Justice? Tracing the "Ethical" in Marx's Thought. *Human and Society*, 3(6), 305-322.

ZIMMERER, K., (1996) *Changing Fortunes*. Berkeley, University of California Press.

PART IV:

HUMAN RIGHTS, RELIGION AND CULTURE

Divergent' or Convergent:
The Battle of Culture, Religion and Human Rights

Tendayi Dzinoreva, Francis Machingura and *Pearl Gambiza*

Introduction

In a world where religion, human rights and culture guide people's actions, behaviours and interactions, it is difficult to draw the line between what is the superior of the three. There are various contestations around religious and cultural values versus human rights especially where discipline for young people is concerned or where there is serious moral degradation in society or in a situation where African countries have been victims of neo-colonialist machinations. Human rights have caused serious threats to the diversity of cultural, political, social and religious values leading to cries of suppression of the African cultural, political, social, religious value system by 'westernised ideologies' (Teerikangas & Hawk 2002). When we talk of religion, we imply religion in general. That there is a dialectical relationship between culture and human rights, religion and culture, and culture and religion is of no question. The Universal Declaration of Human Rights (UDHR) as a global system is steeped in the religious and cultural systems of all nations, including Zimbabwe. Understanding the interrelatedness of these three elements is vital in shaping a generation of global citizens who are tolerant, humane and respectful of one another. Culture, religion and human rights are interdependent and should therefore be viewed as complementary rather than contrasting systems of human life. Acknowledging the interwoven nature of cultural, religious and human rights systems could be the basis for unity, love, respect and Ubuntu thereby reducing instances of violation and abuse. There is a systematic and systemic way in which culture, human rights and religion feed off and into each other. They cannot do without the other when it comes to the socialisation of humanity. On that basis, this chapter analyses cases where culture, religion and human rights intersect from the perspective of major religions (mainly Christianity and Judaism) and African culture (with examples from Zimbabwe) and human rights associated frameworks.

Human Rights, Culture and Religion: Systems Thinking Approach

The growing complexity of the world has created steadily more interconnected ways of thinking. Globalization has grown our social systems in novel complex ways. The interconnectedness has to some extent benefited or disadvantaged some communities and nations whereby cultures, mannerisms, thought processes of the powerful western nations were popularised at the expense of the developing Africans nations. Globalisation has largely benefited the powerful nations. It tends to benefit the political, economic and cultural interests of the powerful western countries and, now, the eastern bloc. African nations have become perennial victims of the powerful. With these complex and rapidly growing systems, it is important to understand the world from an interconnected lens. Systems thinking consists of "three kinds of thing elements (in this case, characteristics), interconnections - the way these characteristics relate to and/or feed back into each other" (Ross & Jon 2015:2-3). Thus, the acknowledges that parts are interrelated and interdependent and are constantly interacting. Kim (1999) provides three important features of understanding systems thinking whereby:

> each system has a purpose; all parts must be present to carry out its purpose optimally; The order in which the parts are arranged affects the performance of the system and Systems attempt to maintain stability through feedback (Kim 1999:3).

Culture, religion and human rights are all interconnected parts of a larger system which aims at guiding human behaviour and human interaction. The three elements are interconnected but have to be arranged in a way that does not cause disruption. Religion and culture guide the localised diverse patterns of human behaviour which then feed into the larger system that defines h human rights. The systems thinking approach is fundamentally premised on the Iceberg model which views reality from a multi-level perspective of events, patterns and systemic structures. Events are the tip of the iceberg which is a result of deeper patterns and systemic structures. The general complexities caused by the three separate systems governing human interaction can only be better understood if we dig deeper and understand the interrelatedness between culture, religion and human rights.

War, abuse of all forms and behaviour among many could be lessened if people consciously interlink the various patterns and systemic structures that arise out of the collective relationship between religion, culture and human rights. These three elements are critical in creating a powerful synergy for controlling and regulating human behaviour within the confines of human rights, culture, religion and globalisation. Elsawah, Ho and Ryan (2021) assert that systems thinking are a promising avenue for solving complex problems faced globally. Thus, systems thinking can be employed in solving behavioural and interactional challenges leading to war, abuse, corruption and many other societal issues. As a result, human rights have to be interrogated from a systems thinking perspective.

Human Rights in the Eyes of the Systems Thinking

Human rights are enshrined in the 1948 Universal Declaration of Human Rights (UDHR). To support the UDHR are major regional frameworks which includes the European Convention for the Protection of Human Rights and Fundamental Freedoms (1950), the American Convention on Human Rights (1969), the African Charter on Human and Peoples Rights (1981), the Arab Charter on Human Rights (2004), and the Association of Southeast Asian Nations (ASEAN) Human Rights Declaration (2012). There are 30 human rights in the UDHR clustered around dignity and equality, basic rights, individual rights, social rights and societal order (McFarland 2015). Habermas (2006:155) defines human rights as "the universal language in which global relations can be normatively regulated". Human rights can further be regarded as tools for emancipation and liberation in the face of dispossession, repression and persecution among other forms of abuse of human dignity as happened to most third world nations. The regime of human rights as enunciated in the 1948 UDHR came into place when most African nations were not independent and the situation has continued to favour powerful western nations that oppressed nations. Yet there are rights that are uniquely African related. This is because human rights are grounded in universal human dignity that most Africans also understand and appreciate.

The belief to drive, sustain, and inspire the faith in human dignity and its associated values of liberty, equality, and solidarity proclaimed in Article 1 of the 1948 Universal Declaration of Human Rights (UDHR) (Fortman 2011:1). The concept of equality seem not to speak or include Africans in cases where African leaders have topped the list in terms of being dragged to The Hague or International Criminal Court for breach of human rights. This has excluded leaders of powerful nations such as George W Bush, Tony Blair and Barack Obama who have violated or invaded or facilitated the invasions of other nations using false allegations so as to engineer and safeguard their own interests. The same International Criminal Court has never gone against Arab nations or Arab or Asian national Leaders. Africans are viewed or portrayed as tails of the world and never solution creators or givers. It is interesting that, violations of human rights are as a result of the diversity of cultures and religions that infringe on the rights of people. Therefore, to remedy their infringement, there is a need for action towards socio-cultural and religious receptivity and diversity. The choice listed in the UDHR must be left to the morality of a community and Africans included. Human rights are sustained by individualism but the moral grounds for conviction in cases where violations have been made, entirely rest on the view of those concerned. Secondly, the ratification of treaties is voluntary and not all nations are forced to agree to these human rights charters, thus making it difficult to enforce human rights on all.

Implicitly, responsible individualism is what matters in the process of upholding human rights. There are arguments regarding individualism as the root for the disregard of human rights. The belief that individualism in itself reasonable grounds for upholding human rights is considered a fallacy because it is this same individualism which is insufficient for acknowledging other people's needs (Mirmoosavi 2010; Fortman 2011). This is the opposite of social, religious and cultural rights which are based on community responsibility which is for the fulfilment of everyone's basic needs. This also confirms that the regime of human rights parrots mostly colonising western ideas and ideologies rather than African ideas. Although human rights are universal in nature, their application differs based on religious and cultural norms of the concerned people, especially Africans. The cross-cutting elements of the human rights framework are equality and non-discrimination (Ghanea 2011). Responsibility and non-discrimination in addition to being rights in themselves also inform other human rights. Therefore the African culture and religious world view is critical in understanding human rights.

Unhu/Ubuntu in the African Culture Perspective

The diversity of cultures worldwide causes many divergent thoughts around what is normatively acceptable. The African value system will be employed as a reference point in this discussion. Serrat (2008:4) views culture in its broadest sense as "the totality of society's distinctive ideas, beliefs, values and knowledge." Africans are tied together in the philosophy of *Unhu/Ubuntu*. This belief that people who live in a community or society are bound by similar thoughts and ideas is what shapes many societies today. African philosophy is a belief that African thought is unanimous. Bell (2002:59) discusses African philosophy as the thought that "Africans do not think of themselves as discrete individuals, but rather themselves as part of a community." The UDHR lacked that aspect of the role of communities vis a vis the celebrated human rights. African beliefs and practices (culture, religion, politics and economics) do not leave anybody behind. Such beliefs are underpinned by Mbiti's (1969:108) famous quote "I am because we are; and since we are, therefore I am." *Unhu/Ubuntu* philosophy is by nature a community binding philosophy based on the understanding that individuals only exist within a community framework, thus Mbiti (1969:108) declares that "the individual owes his existence to other people....He is simply part of the whole....whatever happens to the individual happens to the whole group and whatever happens to the whole group happens to the individual." The concept of *Ubuntu/Unhu* is tied to one's personal identity and is intrinsic within the community-oriented outlook. Human rights then become communarian and people oriented. This communal approach to ways of living is augmented by Tutu (2004:25):

> a person is a person through other persons. None of us comes into the world fully formed. We would not know how to think, or walk, or speak, or behave as human beings unless we learned it from other human beings. We need other human beings in order to be human.

Individual judgements of what is right or wrong have no place within society unless they are grounded within socially acceptable norms, beliefs, practices, scriptures, standards and values. Therefore, one who fails to uphold *Unhu/Ubuntu* becomes a social misfit not acceptable to society. Within any socio-cultural system are rules, norms, values and ideologies that guide day to day living with reference to relationships, interactions, language, dress and roles and responsibilities. In the African cultural context, various norms and values are critical in shaping individuals and directing the way of life. *Unhu/Ubuntu* philosophy is one of the guiding philosophies within the African cultural value system. Bangura (2009) asserts that *Ubuntu* is a word from the Southern African Nguni language family meaning humanity. However, it is not peculiar to Zimbabwe, but "*Ubuntu* philosophy is integrated into all aspects of day-to-day life throughout Africa and is a concept shared by all tribes in Southern, Central, West and East Africa amongst people of Bantu origin" (Rwelamila, Talukhaba & Ngowi 1999:338). This entails that there is a common ground or convergence on which most Africans agree based on *Unhu/Ubuntu* philosophy in light of humanity and their right to life.

Ubuntu/Unhu philosophy is an African philosophy, recognised and practised across the various African countries and used to mark African identity. Sibanda (2014:26) posits that *Unhu/Ubuntu* is conceptualised as a symbol of African identity based on "traditional African philosophy which thrives on the vision of a perfect and virtuous individual or an individual who upholds the cultural values and norms of a true African society". The cultural norms and values are embedded within the context of morality and ethics derived from the dualities of good and bad or right and wrong. Samkange and Samkange (1980:89) further discuss *Unhu/Ubuntu* as describing "the attention one human being gives to another, for example, the kindness, courtesy, consideration and friendliness in the relationship between people. It is a code of behaviour or an attitude to others and to life. A person with true *Unhu/Ubuntu* qualities is one who respects and maintains the African cultural standards, expectations, values and norms that protect the African identity. July (2004:135) adds that, "*hunhuism/ubuntuism* is therefore centred on the belief in the goodness and perfectibility of man where emotion, reason and behaviour are regarded as surest guides of man to happier life." *Unhu/Ubuntu* is therefore a social philosophy, which embodies virtues that celebrate the mutual social sharing responsibility, mutual assistance, trust, unselfishness, self-reliance, respect, love and care among many other ethical values. For Samkange and Samkange (1980), the concept of *Unhu* is strongly reinforced by, as well as oriented towards, a collectivist, social morality. It is a philosophy that celebrates life and respect for human rights.

Unhu/Ubuntu is steeped in African moral philosophy which highly regards acceptable behaviour within the context of communal life. Morality is associated with the Latin *moralis* meaning customs and manners (Bell 2002). The term manners or etiquette is defined as socially acceptable and unacceptable behaviour such as swearing, use of foul language and inappropriate dress (Bell 2002:24). Moral values are those values that govern all forms of behaviors and are parameters by which actions are subjugated to levels of acceptance and desirability. Every society has measurements of morality and good behaviour. In linking morality to *Unhu/Ubuntu*, Samkange and Samkange (1980) proffer the following definition for the word *unhu*: Its root *-nhu-* is related to the Ndebele root *-ntu-* which forms the singular noun *muntu* (a person), and *bantu* (the people). Anthropologists are aware that the practice of calling one's own group 'the human beings', 'the people', is not restricted to Africa but is also used, for example, by Amerindians. *Munhu* can mean either an ordinary person or a moral person, that is, one who has morally worthy human qualities. The *hunhu* concept gains its force in contrast with pre-human or animal behaviour. A person has moral attributes not granted to a wild animal. Wild animals 'do not have customs. There is, therefore, a need to separate animalistic behaviour from human behaviour based on reflection within an individual regarding what is socially and morally correct versus individual gratification. Knowledge about what is morally correct or wrong are based on a human being's ability to reason within the standards of his/her social and cultural moral statutes.

Social morality considers whether an action threatens the society's well-being or not. What sustained pre-modern Africa was a strong moral fibre in which all members were answerable to the rest of the community for their moral behaviour, and as Ndondo (2014:3) posits that, "the main force behind its cultural presentation was the philosophy of *Ubuntu*." This entailed an African communitarian way of life which was easily summed up in the popular aphorism 'a person is a person through relationships with other people' (Ndondo 2024:3). This defined the convergence not divergence of how Africans define life. According to Nziramasanga (1999, cited in Ndondo 2014), immorality was a disgrace to the whole African community. The advent of religio-political societies and the general cultural pluralisms brought with it adverse effects on African morality. There is a high incidence of moral degeneration in Zimbabwe today. Morality is under attack and faces great challenges in the face of globalisation and human rights calls. However, Pearce (1990:145) points out that *Unhu/Ubuntu* requires "both that one knows (has learned) custom (tsika) and that one can reflect upon, and take responsibility for one's own behaviour. A higher level of cognitive activity as well as moral self-consciousness is required of *hunhu*." Self-consciousness is usually associated with one's respect for human rights.

The individuals may well be aware of the moral self-consciousness required of *hunhu* but may also be under immense pressure of some need that forces them to neglect the expectations of morality. Social media and globalisation present certain pressures, for instance, fitting in, keeping up with a certain social standard and level of social class, and the desire for belonging which might force individuals to put aside the values required by *unhu (community)*. The issue of morality has long been present in our societies and remains the basis upon which character is judged. No society has the ultimate claim to morality. Humanity has ultimate claim to morality in their different geographic locations. Durkheim (1938, cited in Pearce 1990) contrasts animals to humans and posits that animals cannot be moral agents because in the animal world there are no rules that govern behaviour. With humans, however, "behaviour is everywhere regulated and rules have the character of social fact, being impartially obligatory on everyone according to his/her status and sex" (Pearce 1990:156). Human beings are expected to behave according to the moral standards of society. Whatever one does or exhibits is bound to be judged according to the moral campus of society.

There are various fundamental values critical to *Unhu/Ubuntu* such that a lack of this is considered moral decay. Discipline, morality, altruism, self and social consciousness, responsibility and duty, justice , fortitude, prudence and temperance, willingness to recognise the burdens of judgements and the ability to accept such judgements form the core of *Unhu/Ubuntu* philosophy (Mandela 2006; Khoza 2006; Luhabe 2002). These are only but a chunk of the elements that constitute *Unhu/Ubuntu* philosophy. Sibanda (2014) explains that:

> *Unhu/Ubuntu* defines a good citizen who is able to act upon his/her rational consciousness and according to the expectations of society. The person should be able to uphold norms and values of the family, the community and the society at large. In addition, this person must be able to abide by the country's laws and

statutes, respect him/herself, the elders, as well as youngsters and also respect the leadership of the community, state and world at large.

Unhu/Ubuntu is not a philosophy that forces itself upon people orientations and socialises by setting boundaries within which a full membership and societal integration are achieved. *Unhu/Ubuntu* allows for choice to either be a part of the greater community or live an individualistic life without any judgemental moral standards. People are given the latitude to make decisions and choices about life. There is an interesting intersection between religion, culture and human rights. Nziramasanga (1999) determines that *Unhu/Ubuntu* is captured in the following character traits: good citizenry, well behaved, morally upright person characterised by responsibility, honesty, justice, trustworthiness, hard work, integrity, cooperative spirit, solidarity, hospitality and devotion to the family as well as the community welfare. *Unhu* is closely related to one's religiosity or spirituality or public relations, good citizenry and caring.

The Intersection between Human Rights, Culture and Religion

The UDHR charter takes religion in its preamble as the commitment to the realisation that freedom and equality in "dignity and rights" requires individual self-respect, structural incorporation of respect for each and every human being in the institutions of society and actual day-to-day protection against abuse of power over others. Indeed, right after their Faith-based affirmation of human rights" (Fortman, 2011:4). There is an intricate connection between the three systems that govern human life. Regardless of the seeming individual nature of religion, culture and human rights, there is a thread that runs common among them. However, for Africans, everything is communal including one's religious orientation. The family can have a say in one's religious choices. It is from this understanding that we need to use the systems thinking approach in unpacking the connections that exist among human rights, culture and religion. Mental modes are the beliefs and assumptions about how the world works as blueprints (Ross & Jon 2015). What this implies is that, at religious, cultural and human rights levels; we have rules, values and principles to direct and regulate human behaviour. African Traditional Indigenous systems are shaped around cultural values while religious systems are guided by various regulatory systems such as beliefs, food, dressing, rituals, practices, taboos and customs. Human rights frameworks are global in nature which regulate and balance both cultural and religious systems regardless of colour or creed (article 21). Human rights are the agreed upon (by member states) vision of what we want the world to 'realistically look like.' Similar to African culture and religion, human rights are collectively regarded and are deeply rooted in the principle of humanity. Thus, cultural and religious value systems have a purpose in the broader framework of human rights. Key principles such as respect, love and responsibility among others are all enshrined within human rights.

Cultural and religious diversity are present features of human development and there are always new forms emerging while others fall off. This calls for a unifying framework that responds to as well as incorporates the stagnant and stable features of both culture and religion. People interact easily or have difficulties interacting because of how they understand life and human rights, spirituality and cultural values. Religion, culture and human rights feed into one another. Human rights, culture and religion therefore become the integrated framework for regulating interaction. Globalisation has led to the "world embracing diversity in complex settings while our thinking pattern remains fixed in a 'mono-cultural' view based on traditional [and religious] boundaries and rational thinking" (Teerikangar & Hawk, 2002:8). The long-standing battle leading to divergence between religion, and culture, and human rights lies in some of the discussions such as the LGBTQI discourse. While all other aspects of human rights are embraced by Africans and Christians, the respect for one's sexuality poses challenges in African and Christian communities. The Bible is purported to be clear in its assertions that "that thou shall not judge' (Matthew 7:1-2, Romans 12:2, 14:1-4; Hebrews 12:14; John 3:16; Revelation 3:20; James 1:2-4; Ephesians 2: 8-10; 2 Corinthians 4:6) and 'let he who is without sin cast the first stone' (John 8:7). It is also the same Bible that clearly tells of the story of Sodom and Gomorrah which was destroyed as a result of sexual immorality emanating from sodomy (Genesis 19).

Those engaging in homosexual acts are judged and labelled as perverts or socially unacceptable renegades by Christians based on the Sodom and Gomorrah story. Most Africans subscribe to those views against LGBTQI. The Bible makes the controversy bigger and difficult to address whenever people resort to the Bible to address their differences. Differences to do with life choices and tastes cannot be resolved using biblical texts. Biblical books were written in different contexts to address different issues with contradicting resolutions or positions which do not commensurate with current issues. Interestingly some religions such as Judaism and Christianity use such texts as points of convergence and divergence but with various outcomes. The command not to judge is ignored in this case. It is not surprising that the contradictions inherent in the Bible are used as justification for denying certain groups their right to express their sexuality, beliefs and practices as charged by human rights.

One of the key challenges affecting human rights, culture and religion is that they are absolute on their own with the belief that there are universal moral truths. Human rights offer fundamental freedoms for all humanity at individual level. For instance, article 9, of the Universal Declaration of Human Rights, speaks to freedom of thought, belief and religion. It further allows for freedom to change one's religion or beliefs at any time. Freedom of worship or non-worship then becomes a fundamental human right for all individuals. This is believed to be the absolute moral standard for all. In Judaism and Christianity, the commandments are clear against religious freedom of thought and belief through the limiting commandments, "you shall have no other gods before me. You shall not make for yourself any idol; you shall not misuse the name of God in vain" (Exodus 20:2-7). It is not surprising that some fundamentalist Christians go to the extreme when citing such texts against whosoever does not subscribe to their denominational Christian views.

The same is true of fundamentalist Muslims in Islam who infringe other peoples' rights to freedom of choice and religion by trying to force convergence to adopt their religious and cultural standpoint despite clear divergences. Religion and culture give some kind of social, economic and political hope thereby controlling peoples' behaviour. The Boko Haram, a religio-political terrorist group in Nigeria, well known for its attacks on people of other faith as well as those within its own faith who might want to challenge their religious absolutism. Fundamentalist religious groups are exclusive in their claims to absolute truth such as in Islam leading to violent killings and attacks on those with differing thoughts (Shaaba 2017). Thus, religious absolutism in religion and culture goes against human rights norms and can therefore be the trigger to war and violence. Similarly, cultural absolutism may also be a huge barrier to the acceptance of both human rights and religious norms. As a result, there is a need to reconstruct the fundamentals of human rights, cultural, religious norms and principles.

Some contestations between religion, culture, and human rights derive from the mental modes attached to these concepts. Human rights are perceived as mere basic rights that people have to uphold by virtue of their being human. Human rights are viewed from the perception of humanity and their environment. Cultural and religious values are viewed from the perspective of collective communalism. Human rights have to be shared and agreed upon by communities especially on tolerance and inclusivity. For instance, there are huge contradictions in terms of the treatment of women in both culture and the various religions. Women's control over their sexual reproductive issues is often ignored in some African cultures. Female genital mutilation is a practice that still occurs in some parts of Africa (Fagan 2017) which signals highest levels of disrespecting and mutilating the bodies of women. The human rights then are used to provide protection and emancipation against all forms of chauvinistic behaviour. Another example that clearly articulates the friction points between culture, religion and human rights is that of children's rights. In cultural circles, the child belongs to the community (Mbiti 1969) and is raised by the community to become an acceptable member of the community. African proverbs extend this community responsibility to 'spare the rod and spoil the child.' Jewish Christian's scriptures support or encourage the discipline of children, which have resulted in most cases with the abuse of children. Biblical texts such as Proverbs 6:20, 13:24, 22:6, 12:1, 15: 5, 19:8, 22:15, and 29:15-17 and Leviticus 19:3 are usually cited to buttress the position that disciplining of children has been divinely approved despite mounting cases of children who have suffered under the hands of parents and guardians in the name of discipline though it infringes their rights as minors or children.

Human rights on the other hand view the child as having rights to freedom of expression and thought, and choice (United Nations Convention on the Rights of the Child, 1959). Where children are going astray in African and Christian circles, human rights have often been blamed for negating the role of communities and heeding the biblical teachings on how children must behave. The fact that there is a charter specifically dedicated to the rights of the child (as an individual) is itself a direct challenge to the place of cultural and religious norms where children are expected to act within community agreed rules. A case in point, which shows the polarity between culture, religion and human rights, is that of the use of corporal punishment in disciplining children. In terms of human rights, corporal punishment is an infringement of children's human rights, it is considered abuse. From the perspective of religion and African culture, corporal punishment is the best form of discipline. Zimbabwe is a signatory to both the human rights and the UNCRC charter and is expected to adhere to the laid stipulations. On the other hand, Zimbabwe is guided by the *Unhu/Ubuntu* philosophy in its various interactions as reflected by its inclusion in key government policy frameworks such as the Competency-based Curriculum. In a recent video, the President of the Republic of Zimbabwe, His Excellency Cde E.D Mnangagwa encouraged the use of corporal punishment by arguing that lack of corporal punishment is not an African cultural form of child discipline therefore '*rovai vana mbama kusvika vati tasa* (beat the children until they behave in acceptable ways)' (Pindula.2023). He argued that children's rights were being abused by giving too much power and freedom to children, who were no longer valuing cultural norms such as respect, hard work and responsibility. Therefore, children had to be disciplined through the sjambok, which is the African form of discipline. The utterances by President Mnangagwa indicate a departure from the tenets of the UNCRC Charter, to which the country is a signatory. President Mnangagwa's utterances surprisingly have the support of most Africans in general and Zimbabweans in particular. The same position is held by some Christians who cite biblical texts that encourage the disciplining and, in most cases, canning of children, as the best way of obeying God when it comes to raising children in the right direction. Not disciplining children is regarded as going against the divine will of the creator. As a result of such divergences, we find culture clashing against human rights issues is purely western oriented and has nothing to do with African culture. Thus, battle lines are drawn between what is expected internationally (associated with the West) and that which culture (indigenous) wants to preserve.

On the one hand, human rights are heavily focused and driven towards respecting the most basic fibre of communities, the individual. Yet most Africans focus on the communal position. African religions and cultures are more concerned with upholding community identity. Despite the existing diverging elements between human rights, culture and religion, there are also converging lines. Human rights, culture and religion encapsulate principles of human respect, responsibility and dignity, respect for others and protection of individuals. Despite the challenges, the Church is called upon by "word action and cooperation to commit herself to the defence of the individual and social rights of human beings, peoples, cultures and marginalised sectors of society, together with persons who are in a state of extreme vulnerability (CELAM 1993:165). Culture also speaks to the communal responsibility for one another through the belief that 'I am because we are and we are, because I am' (Mbiti 1969). Although there appears to be a dialectical relationship between religion, culture and human rights, the authors believe that the line that separates these is very thin and difficult to separate the concepts. They influence one another. What is required is a deeper understanding of where the principles of human rights, culture and religion are rooted in. What is interesting is that religion just like culture influences every facet of human life. Human rights are embedded in many of the diverse cultural and religious norms. The differences that do exist need to be respected and explored in the diverse political, cultural and religious groups.

Conclusion

The raging debate around culture, religion and human rights remains ongoing in various circles such as education, social settings as well as in religious groupings. However, in concurrence with many other human rights theorists, the authors believe that " the continuing normative legitimacy of human rights norms depend upon the doctrine's capacity to accommodate a very broad range of culturally based ways of being and belief' (Fagan 2017:319). The lived realities of political, cultural and religious groupings must be considered in the broad framework of human rights. Cultural, political and religious norms must also be revisited to engage with the transformations happening within society. Even though human rights are applied in ways that uphold and retain local cultures and religions; intercultural and interreligious discourse must be promoted to reach global parity. Religious and cultural dominance of the powerful must be discouraged as not all cultural, political and religious practices are entirely compatible with human rights protection. Culture, political, religion and human rights norms must all be viewed as interconnected parts of a larger system and each of these parts must have a purpose relevant to the community that it serves. The Universal Declaration of Human Rights (UDHR) as a global system is universally tipped and steeped in political, religious and cultural systems of all nations, including Zimbabwe. Understanding the interrelatedness of these three elements is vital to shaping a generation of global citizens that is tolerant, inclusive, humane and respectful of one another. Culture, religion and human rights are interdependent and should therefore be viewed as complementary rather than contrasting systems of human life. However, we do not dispute the position that there are those who maintain that they are contradictory. Acknowledging the interwoven nature of cultural, religious and human rights systems could be the basis for unity, love, respect and *Ubuntu* thereby reducing instances of violation and abuse.

References

BALDWIN, J. G., (1983) The Role of the Ten Commandments. *Vox Evangelica*, 13, 7-18.

CELAM, (1993) *Nueva Evangelización, Promoción Humana, Cultura Cristiana.* Santo Domingo, Ediciones MSC.

ELSAWAH, S. HO, A. T. L. AND RYAN, M. J., (2021). Teaching Systems Thinking in Higher Education. *Articles in Advance*, 1-37.

FAGAN, A., (2017) Cultural Harm and Engaging the Limits of a Right to Cultural Identity. *Human Rights Quarterly*, 39, 319-340.

FUKUYAMA, F. (1992) *The End of History and the Last Man.* London, Penguin Books.

KIM, D. H., (1999) *Introduction to Systems Thinking.* Waltham, Pegasus Communications Inc.

KIRMAYER, L. J., (2012) Culture and context in human rights. In M. Dudley, D. Silove. and F. Gale. (eds.). *Mental Health and Human Rights: Vision, Praxis and Courage.* Oxford, Oxford Publishing, pp.95-112.

McFARLAND, S., (2015) Culture, Individual Differences, and Support for Human Rights: A General Review. *Peace and Conflict: Journal of Peace Psychology*, 21(1), 10–27.

MIRMOOSAVI, A., (2010) The Quran and Religious Freedom: The Issue of Apostasy. In B. Fortman. et al. (eds.). *Between Text and Context: Hermeneutics, Scriptural Politics and Human Rights*. New York, Palgrave Macmillan.

ROSS, D. A. and JON, P. W., (2015) A *Definition of Systems Thinking: A Systems Thinking Approach.* [Online]. Available from: https://www.researchgate.net/publication/273894661 _A_Definition_of_Systems_Thinking_A_Systems_Approach

NABUDERE, D. W., (2005) Human Rights and Cultural Diversity in Africa. Entebbe, Association of Law Reform Agencies of Eastern and Southern Africa.

BANGURA, A. K., (2009) *Federalism, Economic Development, Science and Technology for a United States of Africa: An Ubuntu-Clustering Approach.* [Online]. Available from: https:// www.yumpu.com/en/document/view/22797475/federalism-economic-development-science- and-technology-for-a-

BELL, R. H., (2002) *Understanding African Philosophy: A Cross Cultural Approach to Classical and Contemporary Issues*. New York, Routledge.

JULY, R. W., (2004) *The Origins of Modern African Thought*. Trenton, Africa World Press, Inc.

MBITI, J. S., (1969) *African Religions and Philosophy*. London, Heinemann.

NDONDO, S. and MHLANGA, D., (2014) Philosophy for Children: A model for *Unhu/Ubuntu* Philosophy. *International Journal of Scientific and Research Publications*, 4(2), 1-5.

SAMKANGE, S. and SAMKANGE, T. M., (1980) *Hunhuism or Ubuntuism*. Salisbury, Graham Publishing.

PEARCE, C., (1990) Tsika, Hunhu and the Moral Education of Primary School Children. *Zambezia*, 18(2), 1-8.

SIBANDA, P., (2014) The Dimensions of *Hunhu/Ubuntu* Humanism in the African Sense: The Zimbabwean Conception. *IOSR Journal of Engineering*, 4(1), 26-29.

TEERIKANGAS, S. and HAWK, D., (2002) *Approaching Cultural Diversity through the Lenses OF Systems Thinking and Complexity Theory*. Shanghai, International Society for the Systems Sciences at Shanghai.

HABERMAS, J., (2006) *Time of Transitions*. Cambridge, Polity.

FORTMAN, B. D. G., (2011) *Religion and Human Rights: A Dialectical Relationship.* [Online]. Available from: https://www.e-ir.info/2011/12/05/religion-and-human-rights-a-diale ctical-relationship/

SERRAT, O., (2008) *Culture Theory.* [Online]. Available from: https://www.adb.org/ sites/default/files/publication/27578/culture-theory.pdf

GHANEA, N., (2011). *Religion, Equality and Non-Discrimination.* [Online]. Available from: https://www.researchgate.net/publication/329788593_Religion_Equality_and_Non- Discrimination

Influence of African Traditional Religion on the Protection of Women and Children's Rights in Blended Families within Shona Societies

Deliah Nyaradzo Jeranyama

Introduction

An analysis of the conceptualisation of a family unit within the confines of African Traditional Religion (ATR) shows that its philosophical foundation, guiding principles and values that are unique to ATR which almost invalidate the existence of what are known as blended families. Blended families are also called non-traditional families, patchwork families, reconstituted families or new families (Njoroge & Kirori 2018:1). This presents a shift from the traditional family which Baham, Weimer, Braver and Fabricius (2008:2) calls an 'intact family.' Differently put, the blended family structure is generally not well aligned to the dictates of the indigenous religion and has presented some discord, as far as promotion and protection of the rights of women and children are concerned. This chapter discusses how ATR as an indigenous religion of the African people influences the conception and interpretation of a blended family. ATR is grounded on a set of beliefs, practices, philosophical principles and values. Amongst these are the belief in spirit beings and spiritual communication.

While Christianity has been widely adopted across the African continent, the African society continues to have some connection with their indigenous religiosity. Reason being, as Ndemanu (2018:71) puts it, Africans are first and foremost members of traditional religion before they can subscribe or identify with any other religion. Hence traditional religion is the bedrock of all cultures. ATR subscribes to the concept of what Mbiti (1969:26) refers to as the "living dead". The belief originates from the philosophy that death is a transformative process which transitions and elevates one from the physical world and enters the spiritual realm. As such, there are as many labels as there are early ethnographic researchers that have been coined to describe these spiritual beings. Among these labels are the "living dead" coined by Mbiti (1969:26), the "living-timeless" (Banana 1991:33) and "intangible assets" (Mararike 2011:138). The first two labels mirror the status of the dead where the dead are known to be continuously living but in a different state. The belief is that they are in heaven watching over the living (Ndemanu 2018:79). The dead are thus conceived to be in-between the community of the spirits and that of the physical thereby making them bilingual, a characteristic that allows them to speak both the language of the living and that of the dead persons.

Ndemanu (2018:74) has presented another dimension of the notion of the living dead where emphasis on the African people's belief in life after death stretched to the belief in reincarnation which holds that when one dies, they are reborn to another mother, sooner or later. This belief has a huge influence on the traditional family practices and values across Africa. It also influences behaviour, attitude and even perceptions that the African people hold towards women and children in blended families, in some instances, compromising children's rights to education as well as dignity, equality and capacity for property ownership by women. This chapter explore the limits that ATR places on women and children who find themselves in blended families.

Conceptualisation of Blended Family According to ATR

The family unit can be understood from the perspectives of both an African Traditional Religion and the western view that is highly influenced by Christianity which was introduced in Africa during colonialism (Matsika 2000:159), despite Mbiti (1969:229) describing it as old that it can rightly be described as an indigenous traditional, and African religion. He further clearly states that what Christianity brought was the religion and not God. Whilst missionaries came from a society where religion was reflected by church buildings (Nkomazana & Setume 2016: 34) there was little realisation of the readily existent deity who was recognised within ATR which prescribes a set of beliefs among the African people. In that regard, it is crucial to understand what it means to be a blended family in the traditional religion setting and the entry point would be to define it within the boundaries of ATR.

Attention is given to ATR because as Ndemanu (2018:71) observed, African Traditional Religion is embedded in the people's way of thinking and knowing to such an extent that it is nearly impossible to disconnect oneself from it without stripping off their cultural identity. He goes on to say Africans are first and foremost members of traditional religion before they can subscribe or identify with any other religion. Hence, according to ATR standards, family can be nuclear or extended and in Africa the concept of nuclear family is hardly subscribed to. That being the case. When one speaks of the family in an African context, they are referring not to the nuclear family but the extended family (Gyekye, 1996). This extended family has a wider circle of members who include children, parents, grandparents, uncles, aunts, brothers and sisters who may have their own children and other immediate relatives (Mbiti 1969:107). While he identifies and breaks down the composition of family members, Shorter (1998:18) goes on to include the deceased members of the family and those who are yet to be born. This family's foundation is found on kinship and when several nuclear families are combined, they form a clan. This clan has final authority on matters of security, observation of customs as well as marriage. Unlike some traditions, a family is considered to be complete when there are children. In the absence of children, a family remains incomplete and family elders always make an effort to find out the reasons behind the absence. This is because children are regarded not only as assurance of continuity of the society but as a sign of approval of a union by the ancestral community. Mbiti (1969:110) has also reported that in many African societies, God commanded people to get married and bear children, from the very beginning of human life and hence, divorce has always been a solution whenever a marriage failed to produce children.

These traditional views and ideas have very much influenced how the African people in general, and the Shona society in particular, conceptualise blended family or step families which are also known as reconstituted families. To begin with, stepfamilies are not unique to traditional society but instead have been recognised in historical times. The only significant change is how they are now constituted. In the past when a woman died, her niece would be given to the man who would have lost a wife so that she bears children for him and this would create a step family. This was a constituted step family, unlike in the 21st century where most stepfamilies emerge as a failure or collapse of the previous family, either by death, divorce or in situations when a man simply impregnates a woman and denies responsibility. Within that traditional setting, a step family would become unconstitutional when a woman would then bring a child from a previous relationship or marriage. Automatically, in this family are children with one of the parents being biological, while the other is not.

Due to the traditional conceptualisation of what makes up a family unit, the child who comes in with their mother into a new family would, and still attracts labels such as *gora* ('wild cat which has gone astray') or *mubvandiripo* (Chitauro-Mawema 2003:137). These labels are also only applicable to the children who are brought in by the woman into a step family. Due to this existing setup, complexities arise when the two parents who would have decided to come together still have to deal with two other parents outside this family but who potentially have an influence within this blended family. This is why traditionally, there are some invisible boundaries that prescribe the management of stepfamilies. In some cases, they interfere with the promotion and protection of economic, social and cultural rights of women and children in Zimbabwe.

Perceptions of Women and Children in Blended Families

The government of Zimbabwe acknowledges the international and regional frameworks that are in place to protect and promote the rights of women and children. As a way of showing its commitment to ensuring upholding these rights, Zimbabwe has at least signed, ratified and domesticated frameworks such as the United Nations Convention of the Rights of the Child (UNCRC), African Charter on the Rights and Welfare of the Child (ACRWC) the Convention on the Elimination of All Forms of Discrimination Against Women (CEDAW) and the Sustainable Development Goals. More commitment is shown by the presence of the Children's Act which makes provision for the protection, welfare and supervision of children. The Constitution of Zimbabwe also provides for the protection of children, just as it aims at promoting gender equality and protect women. A Gender commission was also established in terms of section 245 of the Constitution to promote gender equality. Zimbabwe also has a social welfare department that functions within the public services and labour ministry.

All these complement each other to curb economic and social vulnerabilities that women and children are susceptible. They are also important in understanding the issues discussed in this chapter because women and children are part of the constituents of a family (nuclear or extended). Despite the effort, ATR has a strong influence on how society generally perceives blended families. It is not fully accepted as a constituted unit because of the general belief that a family consists of members of the spirit community, yet, in a blended family, there are more than one clan involved that automatically means there are additional spirits involved in this family. This section will therefore focus on how these perceptions have violated or limited the enjoyment of economic, social and cultural rights and benefits by women and children in blended families. These perceptions are embedded in the concept of othering which Lister (2004:101) defines as "process of differentiation and demarcation, by which the line is drawn between 'us' and 'them' – between the more and the less powerful – and through which social distance is established and maintained." This concept emphasizes on desirable and undesirable attributes between the in-group and the out-group. It also provides a clear demarcation which is drawn between this newcomer stepping into an already established family and those who were there before this newcomer joined the family. Othering has been defined as the process through which a person or group is turned into somebody different from us, an "other" from whom it is possible to distance ourselves (Wuthnow 2017:258). The other is therefore the stranger who is perceived inferior, stigmatised and very much less respectable. As an imposed state of difference, Otherness relies on binary, dualistic thinking, making divisions into two opposing categories such as 'I' and 'You,' 'We' and 'Them,' 'Self' and 'Other' (Udah 2019:12). It is a very subtle form of acceptance of the given identity. This non-communicated acceptance legitimizes the exclusion, marginalization, subordination and exploitation. This creates on opportunity for the propagation inequalities and group-based domination (Powell & Menendian 2016:17).

Manifestation of Compromised Rights of Women and Children

Most African women are denied the equal enjoyment of their human rights, in particular by virtue of the lesser status ascribed to them by tradition and custom, or as a result of overt or covert discrimination (Ssenyonjo 2007:39). While in a traditional family setting, there are no documented rights to guide processes and decisions, the concepts of access, control and ownership are clearly understood. These therefore feed into and influence implementation of economic, social and cultural rights which guarantee humans the conditions needed to live a life of dignity where every individual can achieve wellbeing, realise their potential and have opportunity to find happiness and fulfilment. It is however evident that women and children continue to have their rights compromised because there tends to be a clash of tradition and human rights laws and frameworks that have been put in place to ensure promotion and protection of the rights of women and children who find themselves in a blended family setting.

Traditionally this category of rights has been often marginalized rather than prioritized (Oloka-Onyonga 2003:829). One other factor that contributes to this misalignment is that the constitution of family in the general African setting does not fully welcome and acknowledge the legitimacy of blended families partly because in the Shona society, a woman who decides to remarry is expected to leave her children from the previous union with her parents. However, due to the global human rights best practices, women tend to take their children with them and these children whether male or female are not fully accepted and get to be labelled as *mubvandiripo,* which means a child who was already born before his/her mother married her husband. The term is widely used across many Shona societies as there is no noun for a step-child. It not only identifies this child with their past or previous family but also goes on to drag this past into their present while at the same time subtly detaching them from their present. This section thus focuses on the nature of the rights of women and children (particularly those who step into a family with their mother) that are violated by ATR beliefs, practices and values as they are informed by the belief in the existence of a spiritual world.

Losing Out on Access and Ownership of Inheritance

In any African traditional family, access to family property is controlled through membership (du Plessis 2011:57) and this has remained unchanging despite the new global order and the new role of financial planners and estate planning strategies. Children in blended families tend to be left out on access and ownership of property battles. From an African perspective, tradition requires that when an individual passes on, their wealth is distributed among their immediate and extended family members. This process is not very open to discuss issues that Herzberg (2022: 54) identified as important to consider when handling estates and finances in a blended family. These include how property is owned, how to title assets owned pre-marriage, management of current expenditures, fair treatment of children involved, avoiding unintentionally disinheriting children as well balancing the needs of the spouse and biological children.

In blended families where stepchildren who were brought in by the woman are involved, they tend not to be considered for this traditional practice and this exclusion is based on the fact that they do not belong and not much effort is put towards addressing the issues raised by Herzberg (2022:54). This is despite their mother having contributed to the accumulation of the wealth. At this point, culture dictates how the process is handled. As such, these children lose out. So in other words, the nature of this assigned identity compromises their social security. Their investments towards the building up of immovable properties within the blended family also goes unnoticed. Within that context, the only avenue for these stepchildren to be rewarded is by having access to that wealth which their mother is allocated, otherwise, there is no room for stand-alone benefits. Again, ATR has remained silent when in as far as what transpires if the mother passes on first and leaves stepchildren in the blended family. There is generally no clear principle or guideline to inform the distribution of inheritance amongst step siblings and this seems deliberate, from an ATR perspective, because already the idea of a blended family tends not to acknowledge the legitimacy of a stepchild in a blended family.

The authenticity of this blended family remains contested, not verbally, but through attitudes and behaviours that are directed towards it. This echoes the labels that such children get which already earmark them as more or less like a parasite that can only benefit from its prey. These labels include *gora* ('wild cat'), *chemudondo* ('the thing of the forest'), *vasina musha* which means without home (Chitauro-Mawema 2003:137). Shona literature has also identified these stepchildren as *mudzingwa* ('the one who was rejected') and this name appears in a Shona novel Gararirimo by Zvarevashe (1976:19). Women also face this loss because they are not spared from the derogatory labels, which are meant to explain how they ended up being single parents before they established a blended family. Chitauro-Mawema (2003:136) has also noted some of the labels as *nzenza* ('one easily carried away') and *pfambi* ('prostitute'). On the other hand, the children who belong to the husband do not face the same predicament. What this also implies is that stepchildren brought in by women are perceived as less important because they will always carry that tag of an outsider. More so, there is no solid legal ground on which they can stand and demand that treatment which they may consider fair. This is because, according to ATR, everything that is owned by an individual is strongly attached to their spiritual world and hence these children are not considered to be full members of this family because they do not belong to the clan of the household head. In that context, there is so much fear of upsetting ancestors who are believed to question the stepchildren's eligibility as heirs of the deceased's estate.

Exploitation and Emotional Abuse

There is also a very subtle element of soft, unintended, unacknowledged and at times unnoticed exploitation of stepchildren during their stay in a blended family. According to the principles of ATR, all these should be sanitised by a subtle admission which is expressed by the stepfather's gesture of giving a token to the stepchildren. This was confirmed by Zvarevashe (1976:18) who portrayed a stepchild (Togarasei) receiving a beast from his stepfather (Gararirimo) as a token for the household chores he had done. The fact that in a blended family where there are other children, only the stepchild from the woman's side gets to be rewarded for having done some chores that the rest of the children in the house have been doing shows that there is some acknowledgement of having exploited a child as well as a reminder that this child does not fully belong, according to traditional society standards. It also seems that this temporary belongingness facilitates some degree of exploitation.

From the ATR perspective, the interpretation of the acts of reward is more spiritual in the sense that it is taken as a token which serves to calm any potential fury from the stepchild's ancestors who are believed to have the capacity to punish the stepfather for exploiting their own without any recognition. In that context, fear of the potential negativities from the spirit community interferes with the promotion rights of children. While this could be done as a mechanism to prevent conflict between the living and the dead, the whole concept leaves room for stepchildren to be exploited with an attitude that they shall still get a token of appreciation anyway.

Further, emotional abuse here entails all behaviours that are meant to humiliate, manipulate, control and intimidate an individual. All these have been known to manifest through the different forms of stigma that women and children in blended families are subjected to. These could be in the form of public, systematic and self-stigma as well as discrimination. All these tend to manifest in the attitudes that the society in general and family members give. Public discrimination is embedded in devaluation by others while systematic stigma facilitates reduced access to resources within the family setting. When these are continuously experienced, the affected individuals get to a point when they internalise the negative stereotypes. All these types of stigma faced by women and children in blended families are experienced as a function of 'othering'.

Stigma always follows step children due to a number of factors that include being perceived as a product of promiscuity who is also an unbranded and uncelebrated person. Promiscuity invites negative perceptions on an individual, despite the factors that may have led to that promiscuity. That being the case, a stepchild who is brought into a blended family by the woman is judged negatively from the onset. In many instances, the negativity spills to their mother who was either never married or was divorced. She is thus judged for having children and this is heavily dependent on the circumstances surrounding the children's conception. In that context, *the* child is judged for the decisions that were made by their mother or the circumstances the mother found herself in yet in some cases the mother would not have made any decision but was just a victim of circumstances. Further legitimisation of the emotional abuse is also visible when a woman in a blended family is blamed for being a husband snatcher, especially when her husband was a divorcee before they established a blended family. These accusations can emerge from the husband's family and this may result in this blended family never getting approved.

As prescribed by culture, when a woman brings a child into a blended family, this child is generally expected to move out of the blended family and go back to their maternal grandparents when they reach an age of maturity. When this happens, the mother may not be able to protect them as they would have also been put in a position to choose between her marriage to her husband or her children. In some instances, a woman is already expected to leave those children who would have matured enough to be able to survive in her absence. As a result, because of the value and respect that society in general attaches to a married woman, women tend to compromise their love for their children so that they maintain the 'married' status. This implies that a child may get to be exposed to two different family units when they enter a blended family (experiencing a family for the third time), which they will have to leave again when they move in with the maternal grandparents. In other words, a woman can get married and bear children, gets divorced or widowed, moves back to her parents' house with her child, remarries and establishes a blended family and finally has her child going back again to the maternal grandparents. This repeated displacement obviously interferes with the development of the child just as it affects the mother who finds herself in a position where she cannot save herself or her child. This final destination does not provide a full sense of relaxation to both the mother and the child as cultural expectations offload the burden and pressure to compensate the grandparents for taking care of their grandchild in the form of *chiredzwa/maredzwa*. Within the Shona traditional society, the maternal grandmother is a very critical pillar in the life of every child who joins a blended family with their mother, despite gender or age and this payment of *chiredzwa/maredzwa* is a process that cannot be escaped.

Identity Crisis

The right to identity facilitates smooth promotion and protection of other child rights such as the right to education and the right to a family environment. Nevertheless, children who are brought into the blended family by the woman find themselves assigned numerous identities, which are dictated by those around them thus creating a situation where they have to embrace the given identity, and this may suppress who they are. For instance, in situations when they are deemed as part of their stepfather's family, this child genuinely commits to this family but again a situation arises again when they are excluded and left out of some decision-making processes. This arrangement of being welcomed at the convenience of other stakeholders patronises these stepchildren to such an extent that a sense of inadequacy is instilled in them. This affects relations with the stepfather's extended family as well as siblings that are born out of this union. It is never clear at which point should this stepchild drop their commitment to this blended family or to what extent they should invest in it. This also disturbs family stability which Mafumbate (2019:8) presents as a critical aspect for continuity.

This investment is not necessarily financial but can be of an emotional nature which involves feelings such as trust, love and even confidence. The stepchild is therefore never sure how much of these feelings can they give away without getting hurt if there is no reciprocation. A closer look at this dilemma shows that a stepchild's identity crisis can be induced especially when it is cultivated by the stepfather's family. It then breeds mistrust in the sense that the stepchild tends not to be sure how much of their commitment should they invest when they do not have a clear projection of how much positive feedback they shall also get in return (Adjiwanou, Boco & Yaya 2021:635). This is because there seems to be no guarantee that positivity earns them some positive feedback. Within this context, stepchildren are therefore ready to be either good or bad people, depending on how much positive or negative energy is directed to them. In other words, the kind of person that this child turns out to be is to some extent shaped by the energy directed to them so much such that in the process of assigning an identity to them, a new monster is being created.

This also triggers stepchildren's urge to dig up their true identity because they would be constantly reminded of their status. The moment that child understands that they do not belong and they are only temporarily welcomed for a certain period of time, it brings discomfort and so much desire to know who they really are. At this point, they stop at nothing and at times the speed with which they demand for answers creates so much tension between them and their mother. All that a stepchild will be hoping to do is to find closure and fill the void that comes with the inconsistent reactions to their being part of the family. In other words, this will be a search for a space where they feel permanently recognised and accepted. This is also closely related to the belief that the ancestors guarantee security and progress in an individual's life. Consequently, the stepchild will be in search of some guaranteed security and positive progress in all aspects of life as a way to fix that feeling of being a social misfit. They therefore take a risk of trading already established relations in exchange for potential relationships with their paternal relatives or ancestors. This is because at this point, the only important things for them would be to establish who they really are.

Missed Opportunities

There is a risk of missing out on opportunities by stepchildren, particularly those brought in by a woman, because of the nature of their identity which creates some fluid borders that are used as and when they are convenient for some family members. This is in line with what Sanni (2014:2) puts across regarding identity and contexts. The different social contexts that these children find themselves in tend to have a bearing on their belonging. When a sisterly responsibility arises among siblings, a female stepchild may be assigned the responsibilities of a sister but when the same responsibility arises in a marriage negotiation setting, she does not qualify. While the constitution of Zimbabwe demonstrates commitment to curb gender gaps, the patriarchal nature of the society tends to be a hindrance in some instances especially where cultural values take precedence on the decision-making table. This also applies to policies that have been formulated to protect both women and children in general which subtly get overtaken by cultural principles, values and norms. In that sense, a decision can easily be reached on the grounds of cultural principles thereby overlooking these national frameworks.

It appears that the dominant identity amongst them all or that identity which is chosen as more defining than the rest carries all the weight in deciding eligibility for potential benefits. For example, an opportunity may arise for a stepchild to access a piece of land in the stepfather's village where he grew up. It is at this point when the finer details of their identity can jeopardize the opportunity. This clearly demonstrates how cultural values regulate decisions because according to ATR every decision to include or exclude an individual is zeroed down to whether there is any relationship by bloodline. In that regard, despite some degree of being acceptable to the extended family members within a blended family, bloodline takes precedence regardless of stepchildren carrying some equally legitimate title such as 'brother' or 'sister'. Some opportunities are missed out on the basis of who is bringing them. If the opportunity is coming from the stepfather's family, there are chances of that further scrutiny in order to discriminate stepchildren from their siblings. This finding also emerged from a similar study by Adjiwanou, Boco and Yaya (2021:634) that since a stepfather may not expect anything from his stepchildren, he may take advantage of his own children instead of the stepchildren. This therefore means the approach of stepfathers in most parts of Africa could be informed by this way of thinking.

Generally, all these can be experienced as a function of othering. The fact that, more often than not, stepchildren are not consulted in decisions that affect their lives has some negative consequences. One of them is that priority is often given to the needs of the other siblings as they will be in the interest of the rest of the stepfather's extended family. In many cases, these opportunities are not material in nature but also take the form of attention and love. Findings from a similar study by Adjiwanou, Boco and Yaya's (2021:643) have shown that children living with stepfathers are less likely to attend school compared to children living with both biological parents. This confirms previous findings from a study in Mozambique on stepfamily arrangements and child wellbeing by Lopus (2017:897), where it was realised that children's school enrolment was higher among children who lived with their biological fathers, whereas children who lived with stepfathers, other types of adult male non relatives, or no adult males fared substantially worse. It is however not clear if this is a conscious decision or it just happens without any pre-meditation. As a result, one may argue that this could just be a perception or a preconceived idea that stepchildren fabricate to compensate for their high expectations which are often not met. This also shows the possibility of mainly benefiting either as an afterthought or from the last portion of the grab.

Pre-Determined Cultural Boundaries

By virtue of being a member of traditional religion, we are bound to subscribe to some readily set boundaries that we cannot cross. While these boundaries do apply to everyone, women and children in blended families often experience the negativities embedded in these cultural boundaries mainly because most African societies are governed by patriarchal values which emphasise dominance and superiority of men over women. This is the most common setting despite many families subscribing to Christianity. Their participation in many aspects of life is therefore very limited. The primary boundary which culture draws for women and children in blended families is the labels that are attached to them as a way of identifying them. The broad Shona culture allows the use of labels such as *mubvandiripo*/gora and *mvana* (Chitauro-Mawema 2003:135) amongst many others because they carry a lot of meaning to both *the* woman and the child and those around them. The former is known to have been coined from the general cultural expectation of how a family should live, and so, the moment a child grows outside the family unit setting, the name is applicable whenever the mother decides to start another family with another man. Hence, the label seemingly provides some justification of anything that shall befall them in their journey of life, just as it is believed that whatever would have made the mother to raise the child alone warrants the mixed bag of what life shall present to her and her children in the future. It is also critical to note that, whilst terms such as stepchild and single parent are actually legal, the dignity that is embedded in the Shona label is far much lesser than that carried by the English nouns.

The conceptualisation of identity among the Shona, just as in any African society, clearly points to three main parameters that define identity. These are bloodline which results in someone belonging to a clan as well as totem animals and behaviour which is likened to an animal's, thereby giving a person a totem. Within this understanding, relations emerge when people share the same totem animal. Each clan has some specific behaviours that they portray which are a symbol of the animal they represent thereby connecting them to these totem animals spiritually. This is very visible from totem poetic praises. For example, those who belong to the Soko clan are praised as: *Soko Mukanya* (Soko, the pompous one) *Makwiramiti* (tree-climber) *Vanopona nezvekuba* (Those who survive by stealing).

From this standpoint, a totem clearly distinguishes who is who and what they can and cannot do. It is also something that cannot just be assigned to an individual. This comes from the understanding that there is more that comes with a totem as it connects one to their ancestors and clan. In this case, the totem is the first connector which can then not be separated from the clan. So anyone who carries the family name and thus, the totem, can communicate with the ancestors and yet *mubvandiripo* can never connect to the family ancestors. Hence, whenever a traditional ceremony or family meeting (*dare*) is ongoing, stepchildren, particularly *mubvandiripo*, are silently reminded that they cannot partake in the important round hut (also known as rondavel) gatherings. Most Shona families gather in a round hut for all important family discussions and this child has no legitimate space in this hut no matter how old they may be. The main reason for this act of discrimination is that this child is not related by bloodline so they cannot be part of any discussions that are deliberated in the round hut and the closest they can be would be the round hut's perimeter wall otherwise known as *muberere*.

The emphasis goes beyond being the inclusion and exclusion criteria but also serves as markers of acceptance levels of the individual. Despite such clear boundaries, issues that directly affect the stepchild are still discussed in their absence. As an extension to this boundary, a stepchild does not hold full participating rights within the family as they cannot actively participate in important family meetings including those that involve recognition tokens (*zvirango*). This recognition often comes in the form of some specific meat parts that are given to an individual if an animal is slaughtered for any ritual. In some instances, it comes in the form of respect that one commands at a family traditional gathering. As such, there seems to be unanimous agreement that, should children attend these family meetings, they only do so just to listen but otherwise cannot contribute. This is because these family meetings (*matare*) involve family spirits so the belief is that they will question who this foreigner is who is participating in their family issues.

Within that context, ATR does not permit stepchildren to fit into the communication protocol known as "*kusumana*". This is a communication model that is common among the Shona people which sometimes takes place in the round hut. All family members will be present and communication is channelled from the youngest to the eldest whereby the youngest is asked to tell that individual who is older than they are and the chain goes on. This is generally done for two main reasons; the first being to ensure that family members get to know each other by name through knowing the family hierarchy as well as to instil discipline and respect for one's elderly family members. As such, stepchildren fail to fit in because they cannot be recognised in this family hierarchy, which makes people qualify to be involved or consulted in the decision-making process. When a decision is to be made, the same hierarchy is used to hear each and every person's thoughts, be it contributions, concerns or fears, starting with the eldest to the youngest. Within this model, a stepchild can therefore not be asked of their thoughts on whatever matter is under discussion. This is not because they do not have an opinion but it is sorely because they cannot give that opinion which they may have otherwise if they do, then they would be contributing to building a home which is not theirs. Whilst the effects are highly unintended, this act certainly bruises their ego and dignity.

Further, stepchildren are known to be unfit to participate in any proceedings that do take place at the earthen flat clay-pot shelf, which is known as "chikuva/huva" in their stepfather's house. This shelf is a very important place in every traditional kitchen, as it is believed to be the sacred place or alter where the ancestors dwell (Mahohoma 2020:7). Hence, this is the place where rituals are done and even if a child or family member gets ill, they are placed there and totem poetic praises are made in communication with the ancestors. Even when someone intends to venture into something, they take a wooden plate with snuff (*bute*) and then place it on the *chikuva* and ask for blessings from the ancestors. In this regard, stepchildren can therefore not be placed on this sacred place, neither can they perform any ancestral communication (referred to as *kuomberera*) there because his or her ancestors do not dwell there.

There is respect for traditional beer since it is believed to be a vehicle for communication between the living and the spirit community. Generally, the beer is served from clay pots and which are allocated to both relatives and commoners. In accordance to ATR, stepchildren cannot drink beer from the pot meant for relatives. They only drink from the pot for commoners which is referred to as "*hari yemhondoro*" or "*kahari kasina zita kekusereredza mhepo*" by some. This *mhondoro*, according to Gundani (2011:311) is a cult of royal ancestors. In that context this separate beer pot is made reference to at family events which involve traditional beer brewing. Hence there would be specific beer clay pots that are allocated to specific family members but there is also a clay pot that is allocated to all other individuals present. Whilst remembering that ancestors constitute family according to ATR, when the family decides to brew some beer for its ancestors, a stepchild's spirit will still be acknowledged through this unnamed pot and when some beer is poured on the ground a typical poem only to acknowledge the stepchild's spirit, among other spirits.

Conclusion

This chapter has explored African traditional religion's shortcomings in the context of rights of women and children. While we cannot completely point to it as compromising, it can be practised in a manner that is detrimental to both the psychological wellbeing of women and children. This compromises particularly SDG 3 whose emphasis is on ensuring healthy lives and wellbeing for all at all ages. This would be critical in establishing communities that are not only confident but also empowered and meaningfully included in the decisions that directly affect their lives. Following the realisation that gender does affect women and the stepchildren they bring into the blended family differently, it would be of relevance to bridge the identified gender gap and strengthen the effort towards bridging the existing gaps.

One potential means of achieving that would be to begin by engaging the traditional leadership and justice systems and try to harmonise the management and distribution process of wealth by revisiting the cultural principles which can be potentially toned down when stepchildren are involved. Since blended families are legally recognised, this would then create a safe zone for stepchildren by allowing the state to take over when it is realised that stepchildren have been genuinely put to a disadvantage. This could be spearheaded by the relevant government departments. There is also adequate evidence that the concept of a blended family is not completely accepted within the confines of the Shona cultures. This particularly applies to the bringing in of stepchildren by a woman into the newly established family unit.

Within this context, it could also be worthy for the Social Welfare department to conduct a full needs assessment and develop a tool that can be adopted and used to mainstream stepchildren into blended families. A desk can also be established for the purposes of rendering family counselling, psychosocial support and any other mental-health related services as a strategy to deal with the self-esteem and confidence issues that come with their identity struggles. It also becomes a way of protecting individuals who find themselves as stepchildren in any cultural context within the Zimbabwean borders. The government of Zimbabwe through the Ministry of Justice, Legal and Parliamentary Affairs could also consider ways of balancing both policies that govern the protection of women and children in general so that they become applicable in the cultural setting where administration of estates and management of inheritance as well as finances are also implemented. This would be a signal of commitment towards creating a safe space for the women and children whose cases may never reach the courts.

References

ADJIWANOU, V., Boco, A. and Yaya, S. (2021) Stepfather Families and Children's Schooling in Sub-Saharan Africa: A Cross-National Study. *Demographic Research,* 44(27), 627-670.

BANANA, C. S., (1991) *Come and Share: An Introduction to Christian Theology.* Uppsala, Swedish Institute of Missionary Research.

BAHAM, M. E, et al., (2008) Sibling Relationships in Blended Families: *The International Handbook of Stepfamilies,* Arizona: John Wiley and Sons, Inc.

CHITAURO-MAWEMA, M. B., (2003) Mvana and Their Children: The Language of the Shona People as it Relates to Women and Womens' Space. *Zambezia,* 30(2), 135-153.

GUNDANI, P., (2011) Shifting Contexts and Identities. *Missionalia Southern African Journal of Missiology* 39(3), 306–315.

GYEKYE, K., (1996) *African Cultural Values: An Introduction.* Legon, Sankofa Publishing Company.

HERZBERG, P., (2022) Navigating Estate Planning for Blended Families. *Journal of Financial Planning* 35 (1) 50-53.

IDOWU, E. B., (1973) *African Traditional Religion: A Definition*. London, SCM Press Ltd.

LISTER, R., (2004) *Poverty*. Cambridge, Polity Press.

LOPUS, S., (2017) Relatives in Residence: Relatedness of Household Members Drives Schooling Differentials in Mozambique. *Journal of Marriage and Family*, 79(4), 897-914.

MAFUMBATE, R., (2019) An Undiluted African Community, Values, the Family, Orphanage and Wellness in Traditional Africa. *Information and Knowledge Management*, 9(8), 7-13.

MAHOHOMA, T., (2020) Experiencing the Sacred. *Studia Historiac Ecclesiastiacae*. 46(1).

MAGESA, L., (1997) *African Religion: The Moral Tradition of Abundant Life*. New York, Orbis Books.

MARARIKE, C. G., (2011) *Survival Strategies in Rural Zimbabwe: Role of Assets, Indigenous Knowledge and Organizations*. Harare, Best Practices Books.

MATSIKA, C., (2000) *Traditional African Education: Its Significance to Current Educational Practices with Special Reference to Zimbabwe*. [Online] Accessed from: https://scholarworks.umass.edu/dissertations_1/5394 [Accessed 15 June 2023].

MBITI, J. S., (1969) *African Religions and Philosophy*. London, Heinemann.

NDEMANU, M. T. (2018) Traditional African Religions and their Influences on the Worldviews of Bangwa People of Cameroon: Expanding the Cultural Horizons of Study Abroad Students and Professionals. *Frontiers: The Interdisciplinary Journal of Study Abroad* 1(30), 70-84.

NJOROJE, M. and KORORI, G., (2018) Blended Family Dynamics and Academic Performance Outcome of the Child in Kenya: Case of Kabete Sub-County in Kiambi County. *Journal of Culture, Society and Development*, 41, 18-25.

NKOMAZANA, F. and SETUME, S, D., (2016) Missionary Colonial Mentality and the Expansion of Christianity in Bechuanaland Protectorate, 1800 to 1900. *Journal for the Study of Religion*. 29(2), 29-55.

OLOKA-ONYANGO, J., (2003) Reinforcing Marginalized Rights in the Age of Globalization: International Mechanisms, Non-State Actors and the Struggle for Peoples' Rights in Africa. *American University International Law Review* 18(4), 851-913.

POWELL, J. and MENENDIAN, S., (2016) The Problem of Othering: Towards Inclusiveness and Belonging. *Othering and Belonging*, 1, 14–39.

SANNI, J. S., (2016) Religion: A New Struggle for African Identity. *Phronimon*. 17(2), 1-13.

SHORTER, A., (1998) *African culture: An overview Socio-cultural Anthropology*. Nairobi, Paulines Publications.

SSENYONJO, M., (2007) Culture and the Human Rights of Women in Africa: Between Light and Shadow. *Journal of African Law*, 51 (1), 39-67.

UDAH, H., (2019) Searching for a Place to Belong in a Time of Othering. *Social Sciences* 8(297), 1-16.

WUTHNOW, R., (2017) *Othering: Cultural Diversity and Symbolic Boundaries in American Misfits and the Making of Middle-Class Respectability*. [Online]. Available from: http://www.jstor.com/stable/j.ctt1vwmhfj.12

ZVAREVASHE, I. M., (1976) *Kurauone*. Salisbury, College Press.

Critical analysis of the Freedom of Thought, Conscience and Religion: A case of Zimbabwe

Tauya Chinama, Edward Muzondo and *Isaac Mutelo*

Introduction

Religious tolerance promotes social cohesion through mutual understanding and respect, the need to uphold human rights especially freedom of belief and conscience and economic growth through collaboration and mutual support. Religious tolerance is important to the Zimbabwean which has rich cultural, ethnic and religious diversity. Although there have been challenges, Zimbabwe remains a pluralistic state in which various faith traditions coexist harmoniously. Granting that Zimbabwe is predominantly Christian, religious freedom without discrimination based on religious belief is guaranteed at least legally (Ndoro 2017). Article 60 of the Zimbabwean Constitution stipulates "freedom of thought, opinion, religion or belief; and freedom to practise and propagate and give expression to their thought, opinion, religion or belief, whether in public or in private" The provision is meant to protect everyone to express and hold religious or nonreligious belief without unwarranted interference. However, major challenges include sectarianism and tensions among different religious groups and faith traditions, political interference and lack of awareness and exposure to other religious and worldviews which often leads to misunderstandings and intolerance. Efforts that have been made to promote religious tolerance include legal protection especially through constitution, interfaith dialogue strategies and ecumenism. This chapter analyses the freedom of thought, conscience and religion as instituted in Article 18 of the Universal Declaration of Human Rights with reference to Zimbabwe. Current impediments against respect for human rights due to religious intolerance are examined and initiatives for improving religious tolerance and observance of human rights in Zimbabwe. Although there are efforts being made by the government, civil society, religious adherents and non-believers to promote a culture of acceptance and respect for diverse beliefs, there is need for more initiatives and programmes.

Religious Tolerance

Religious freedom is a complex issue in human rights law and practice which has continued to be debatable (Robertson 2004). It encompasses related civil liberties and claims and can be viewed from divergent perspectives, which include freedom from discrimination based on one's religion, freedom to practice a religion unconstrained, freedom from living in the social order that gives inclination to a specific religion, and freedom to enjoy civic respect for one's religion (Galtung 1996;

Salomon 2009). From a historical perspective, Clark et al (2012) note that the existence of religious inspired violence due to intolerance on the part of some religions toward members of other religious groups. It includes a series of violence, oppression, torture and war. Anat Scolnicov (2011) identified the difference between the principle of religious toleration and the idea of religious freedom. It is important to articulate the justifications for a right to religious freedom and how this right should be coherently understood. Religious freedom is crucial to Zimbabwe which is regarded as a diverse and pluralistic society. According to statistics, "74.8% identify as Protestant, 7.3% identify as Roman Catholic and 5.3% identify with another denomination of Christianity. Approximately 2.1% of Zimbabweans identify with another faith, such as traditional beliefs or Islam, and 10.5% do not identify with any faith" (Evason 2017). While the percentages have changed and may understate the number of people of other philosophies and minor faith traditions in Zimbabwe, they show the importance of religious tolerance in a pluralistic and multicultural context.

The number of those who do not identify with any faith tradition or religion is high in Zimbabwe as compared to other countries in Africa partly because "many found it draining to be part of organized religion or denominations, of late citing the poor economic performance of the country, which has led a number of religious officials to turn entrepreneurs than pastors, congregants being the clients in their enterprise" (Chinama 2023). This requires that such a context allow different religions, faith traditions and the non-religious to flourish and dialogue. While the basis for the right is individualistic, it is related to a demand for the co-existence of religious and non-religious groups. Furthermore, some religions might expect group or institutional determinations to supersede individual autonomy. A vital constitutive part of many religions lies in the ability of the group or its institutions to make binding determinations for its members, and in some cases, the group can stand in conflict not only with non-members but also with its members and its dissenting subgroups. At times religious intolerance is manifested in limiting freedom of expression about religion, including the offence of blasphemy, defaming a deity or the sacred (Robertson 2004). The legal control against blasphemy, which still exists in some jurisdictions, can present problems for the doctrine of human rights. Inevitably, a law that places limits on freedom of expression on religious issues is a restriction on freedom of speech, leading to the conclusion that the latter is not absolute freedom. Moreover, the Constitution of Zimbabwe Amendment (No. 20) Act of 2013 in the preamble has a clause that states:

> Acknowledging the supremacy of Almighty God, in whose hands our future lies, resolve by the tenets of this constitution to commit ourselves to build a united, just and prosperous nation, founded on values of transparency, equality, freedom, fairness, honesty and the dignity of hard work. And imploring the guidance and support of almighty God.

The above-mentioned clause gives an impression that Zimbabwe is a quasi-theocratic state of the Christian persuasion, hence discriminating against nontheistic religions such as Buddhism and the nonreligious/humanists. Mostly, at public gatherings in Zimbabwe Christian prayers are said disregarding religious plurality.

For instance, in the 2018 harmonized elections President Emerson Dambudzo Mnangagwa of the Zimbabwe African National Union Patriotic Front (ZANU PF) would often say 'the voice of people is the voice God' while Nelson Chamisa of Movement for Democratic Change Alliance (MDC-A) now the president of Citizens Coalition for Change (CCC), the runner up and main opposition leader used to say '#God Is in It'. Furthermore, some Christian pastors and gospel artists detest indigenous traditional religion in their songs. All this is predicated on the religious intolerance of some sought.

Understanding Human Rights in Context

According to Karagiannis (2018), the contemporary understanding of human rights emanated from landmark documents such as the English Bill of Rights (1689), the United States Bill of Rights (1791) and the French Declaration of the Rights of Man and the Citizen (1789) included provisions for the protection of human rights. The cause of human rights was advanced further after the first half of the twentieth century partly because of the two world wars which resulted in the need for peace, harmony and solidarity. The Universal Declaration of Human Rights, adopted by the United Nations General Assembly in 1948, is generally considered to be the founding document of the international human rights regime (van der Ven 2010). Article 18 of the Universal Declaration of Human Rights made it clear that "everyone has the right to freedom of thought, conscience and religion; this right includes freedom to change one's religion or belief, and freedom, either alone or in community with others and in public or private, to manifest one's religion or belief in teaching, practice, worship and observance." While the Universal Declaration of Human Rights (1948) is rightly acclaimed for its deep-rooted, lucid formulation on human dignity, freedom and equality, the roots of these rights go much further back. One finds noteworthy elements of them in all the major religions, from the Mesopotamian heritage among which the Epic of Gilgamesh and the Code of Hammurabi, the earliest Hindu and Buddhist texts, Confucian doctrine, the Jewish Bible, the New Testament, and the Qur'an to Christian patristics and scholasticism, which were deeply influenced by Greek and Roman philosophy.

Clapham (2015) articulates how different people perceive human rights in the contemporary world. For some, invoking human rights is a profound, morally justified demand to rectify all sorts of injustice, while for others it is no more than a slogan to be treated with doubt or even hostility. Several reports have exposed human rights abuses and violations in Zimbabwe. For example, the 2022 Country Reports on Human Rights Practices (Zimbabwe) cites human rights abuses such as "unlawful or arbitrary killings, including an extrajudicial killing; torture and cases of cruel, inhuman, or degrading treatment or punishment by the government; harsh and life-threatening prison conditions; arbitrary detention; political prisoners."

In some cases, religious and political authorities perceive human rights advocates with suspicion and contempt. Legal representatives sometimes consider that human rights epitomize almost a term of art, representing only those claims that have been or can be upheld as legal rights by a national or international court. Yet in some cases the application of human rights law in court is almost always questioned, with both parties to a dispute demanding that human rights law be applied in their courtesy. The language of human rights is positioned to criticize, defend, and reform human conduct. Human rights have a pedigree of a notable struggle against oppression and the promise of a reasonable future in Zimbabwe and beyond. However, there is a utopian view of human rights, Samuel Moyn (2010) notes, that when people hear the phrase 'human rights,' they think of the highest moral precepts and political ideals. They perceive indispensable liberal freedoms and extensive principles of social fortification.

Freedom of Thought, Expression, Belief and Religion

There is a relation between norms and social reality. Although an important function of norms is to deny the existence of the prohibited, the reality is more often the opposite; the prohibition of a particular behaviour is sometimes taken as *prima facie* evidence of its existence (Sands et al 2007). Religious norms, when they are understood to demarcate the highest ideals, are particularly counterfactual. In some cases, the common violation of the ideal may highlight the extraordinary character of total obedience. And, just as total obedience may seem extraordinary and therefore sacred, so can extreme transgression or deviation. Some religious traditions include, particularly among their mystics, practices that are sacred precisely because they are unusual or even transgress. The religious meanings and realities of homoeroticism, therefore, are rarely if ever fully visible. Homoeroticism is especially susceptible to negative interpretation because as non-procreative sex it stimulates what has sometimes been termed 'excessive' forms of pleasure, play, and intensity that are as dangerous.

Regarding the question of rights, the Social Contract of Jean-Jacques Rousseau published in 1762 developed the idea that an individual may have a private will (volonté particulière) and that his/her private interest (*intérêt prive*), which may dictate to him/her very differently from the common interest. Rousseau considered that whoever refuses to obey the general will be compelled to it by the whole community; this only forces him/her to be free. For Rousseau; a human person loses by the social contract his/her natural liberty and an unlimited right to all which tempts him/her, and which he/she can obtain; in return acquires civil liberty and proprietorship of all they possess. In the 19th century, natural rights became less relevant to political change, and thinkers such as Jeremy Bentham (1843) ridiculed the idea that "all people are born free" as "absurd and miserable nonsense". Bentham dismissed natural and imprescriptible rights as "nonsense upon stilts, declaring that wanting something is not the same as having it. In Bentham's terms; hunger is not bread". For Bentham, real rights were legal rights, and it was the role of lawmakers, and not natural rights advocates, to generate rights and determine their limits.

Bentham considered that one was asking for trouble, inviting anarchy even, to suggest that the government was constrained by natural rights. The contemporary scholar Amartya Sen (1999) has recalled Bentham's influence and highlighted a validity critique whereby some see human rights as pre-legal moral claims that can hardly be seen as giving acceptable rights in courts and other institutions of execution, Sen warns against puzzling human rights with legislated legal rights (Sen 1999). He also points to a further retort to human rights discourse; it has been claimed by some that human rights are alien to some cultures which may prefer to rank other principles, such as respect for authority, Sen calls it, the cultural critique. Karl Marx (1843) responded to the proclamation of rights in the Constitutions of Pennsylvania and New Hampshire and the French Declaration by ridiculing the idea that rights could be useful in creating a new political community. For Marx, these rights stressed the individual's egocentric fixations, rather than providing human freedom from religion, property, and law. Marx had an idea of an imminent community in which all needs would be gratified, and in which there would be no clashes of interests and, therefore, no role for enforcement of rights (Marx 1843). Marx also highlighted the conundrum that if rights can be limited for the public good then the proclamation that the aim of political life is the protection of rights becomes complex.

Today, freedom of thought and expression is a guaranteed fundamental human right contained in several international, regional and national human rights instruments and Constitutions. Freedom of thought and expression guarantees one the right to hold certain opinions and express them freely through speech, published articles or books, works of art, social media, internet, radio broadcasting or television without unjustified interference (Equality and Human Rights Commission 2023). The Universal Declaration of Human Rights under Article 19 states that "everyone has the right to freedom of opinion and expression" and to "impart information and ideas through any media and regardless of frontiers." Similarly, article 60 of the Zimbabwean Constitution guarantees freedom of thought and opinion and the freedom to give expression to one's thought or opinion both in public and in private. Robertson (2004) notes that in most Constitutions clauses on freedom of conscience are frequently linked to religious freedom or freedom of thought, and the concept has several dimensions. Above all, freedom of conscience is guaranteed that no one will be victimized against or maltreated for any belief that one has declared openly. In Zimbabwe, the government has continued to monitor public events; prayer rallies, religious gatherings, and faith based organizations, religious official, and faith based organisations who are critical of the government are often targeted by security services (United States Department of State 2022). For example, in 2021 Talent Farai Chiwenga, founder of Apostle T.F Chiwenga Ministries was targeted by the government for using his sermons to criticize the impunity for government officials who committed human rights abuses (United States Department of State 2022). There is little point to freedom of conscience if this has to be only exercised in private, and when public expression of one's beliefs is often implicitly guaranteed where the right is recognized. Moreover, while the non-religious/humanists in their diversity are also entitled to the same freedom in Zimbabwe, one rarely finds them featured in the public arena. Chinama (2023) notes that:

> …many people in Zimbabwe do not know about humanism as a non-religious life stance. One reason for this is that in the Zimbabwean education curriculum, one rarely finds any allusion to humanism, or anything to do with being non-religious. Instead, the formal school system is dominated by Christianity, because Christian missionaries originally introduced it. When humanism is mentioned, it is usually

associated with *ubuntu/unhu* which is an ethical theory known for governing human conduct in the traditional African societies, or probably because of the lack of a better English term to refer to *Ubuntu/unhu.*

Non-Religious people opt for human rights; prefer direct, active, subjective rights that are rooted in the dignity of the human person in a democratic context. They are also mistrustful of certain moral claims of religions because of the way they easily tend to erase from their collective memory the many forms of religious violence or conflict, religion-related abuse, religion-motivated terrorism, and genocide perpetrated in their name of religion. Van der Ven (2010) claims that the Universal Declaration of Human Rights of 1948 broke with the tradition of religious foundations, however, watered down the references to a deity, natural law, or natural rights may have become over the years. For the Universal Declaration of Human Rights, the national scale had to be extended to encompass the whole world, so religious language inevitably became an obstacle to a universal foundation. Besides, the growing number of groups that had turned their backs on religion of any kind, including the elite of the radical Enlightenment, made a universal religious foundation problematic.

MacArthur Mkwapatira (2018) argued that it is no longer possible for religion to dominate and control politics, business and social life. Non-Religious/humanists in Zimbabwe are growing in numbers and are organising themselves and challenging the status quo by forming synergies such as *Humanists Zimbabwe,* which is responsible for pursuing the humanist agenda. Some humanists in Zimbabwe have managed to go on print media, radio and television shows; the likes of Shingai Rukwata Ndoro, Takudzwa Mazwienduna, Lynda Caroline Tilley, Tauya Chinama, Monica Zodwa Cheru, Mxolisi Masuku, MacArthur Mkwapatira, Prosper Mtandadzi and Mneka Shaura Mbanje among others. This has helped to clear some misconceptions people have, including the misconceived belief that being nonreligious/humanist is just a euphemism for devil-worship (Satanism). With the use of the humanist label, they have shown that their lives have a purpose and that purpose is to pursue happiness and the betterment of society through the use of reason and science (Mkwapatira 2018).

Furthermore, a number of Zimbabweans have already emigrated inwardly without renouncing external religious membership, a fact contained in the statistics of the country that about 10.5% do not identify with any faith (Evason 2017). When one speaks about religion today, in this case, Christianity in Zimbabwe, one is speaking about a complex diversity of beliefs, rites, and community leadership forms in an era of ever-growing agnosticism and pragmatic atheism. However, neutrality towards religion is manifested differently in different legal systems; Obama in his inaugural speech adopted a middle way, a delicate balancing act when he said "We progressives… might recognize the overlapping values that both religious and secular people share when it comes to the moral and material direction of our country… We are a nation of Christians and Muslims, Jews and Hindus, and non-believers" (Obama 2008). Obama was expressing his adherence to a conception of the American nation as not strictly speaking Christian, but pluralist, open to all religions, whether monotheistic or not. Above all, it is inclusive enough to accept without restriction those who, because of atheism or indifference, reject any religion. Such a stance somehow advocates the need to put nonbelievers on the same footing as religious, and Zimbabwe can learn a lot from such a conception.

Henk ten Have (2017) notes that philosopher and biologist Julian Huxley, the first Director-General of the United Nations Educational Scientific and Cultural Organization, had an appealing idea that scientific progress contribute to peace, security, and human thriving, it is not only indispensable to cooperate, but also to know each other's cultures and traditions. He related science to standards that are promoting the value of humanity based on the idea that human progress is primarily driven by cultural evolution. Education is of principal importance since it means learning from each other; science is equally significant since knowledge helps to better daily life for everybody. Recognizing variances is crucial but at the same time, it should lead to pinpointing what is fundamental for every human being. For instance, Igwe (2015) notes that throughout Zimbabwe, nonreligious/humanists often feel quite helpless in the face of the overwhelming influence of the religion which might make one question the future for humanism in Zimbabwe. Nevertheless, some non-believers in Zimbabwe have continued with their campaign for an open, secular and freethinking society based on the belief that their views are important to nation-building and progress (Igwe 2015).

Strategies to improve Religious Tolerance

The practice of different religions and faith traditions in the spirit of mutual understanding, tolerance and dialogue exists in Zimbabwe although it needs to be strengthened. Ways to strengthen religious tolerance in Zimbabwe includes intermarriages, interreligious dialogue, ecumenism and through bodies such as the Zimbabwe Council of Churches. Devor (2009) notes that; families are now experiencing their own pluralism as they marry people of different religious backgrounds. The timeworn recommendation restricting courtship and marriage to members of one's faith tradition is less and less common, though some Seventh Day Adventists and African indigenous churches elders in Zimbabwe still discourage the practice. Interreligious partnerships and partnerships between nonreligious and religious people are also becoming a norm in Zimbabwe. For instance, Crespin-Boucaud (2019:15) found that in Sub-Saharan Africa, while "28% of interfaith unions are realized, … most interfaith unions hence involve a spouse who identifies as Muslim, Christian or nonreligious and a spouse who belongs to the group or other faith". As such, the proliferation of intermarriages is likely to continue promoting tolerance among religions and also non-religious in Zimbabwe. Secondly, interfaith and interreligious dialogue have fostered constructive and positive cooperation and dialogue among religions, faith traditions, and non-believers both at individual and institutional levels in Zimbabwe (Office of International Religious Freedom 2021).

The promotion of common understanding, peaceful co-existence and dialogue has enabled different individuals and groups to accept each other and collaborate. Several organisations that promote interreligious dialogue and solidarity exist in Zimbabwe. This includes the Zimbabwe Interreligious Council (ZIRC) which "convenes Christians and Muslims to promote peace, reconciliation, good governance and holistic human development through interfaith action and collaboration" (Office of International Religious Freedom 2021). Mannion (2007) contends that the Christianity itself already has adequate resources to promote tolerance and diversity. Historically, Christianity has not only addressed internal issues about doctrine, theology, self-understanding and inter-denominational relations, but it has also engaged with wider social issues and concerns including the question of the relationship with people of other faiths traditions. Moreover, the World Council of Churches has continued its work in Zimbabwe through the Zimbabwe Council of Churches. Apart from its primary aim to "enhance the spiritual, moral, social, economic, and political welfare of the people of Zimbabwe through collective action", the Zimbabwe Council of Churches works to "promote Christian unity, inter-faith dialogue, social justice, human rights, national healing and reconciliation, and economic development" (Adequate Travel 2023).

Conclusion

Religious tolerance is important in a diverse and multicultural society like Zimbabwe since it fosters harmony, social cohesion, peaceful coexistence, interfaith dialogue, economic growth and democratic principles. In Zimbabwe, religious tolerance has helped create an inclusive and peaceful society where citizens generally embrace diversity and respect the views and beliefs of others. This has fostered a harmonious culture and co-existence where citizens collectively thrive and contribute to the common good. Although efforts are being made to promote religious tolerance, challenges such as sectarianism, political interference, mistrust and misunderstandings caused by lack of awareness of other religious/nonreligious and worldviews persists. Zimbabwe ought to be open to plurality in all spheres of life through formulating a 'Tolerance Act' to guide the process. Moreover, the government, civil society, religious organisations and non-believers ought to collaborate in the spirit of mutual understanding, respect and acceptance in ensuring that religious tolerance is fully embraced and appreciated.

References

ADEQUATE. T., (2023) *Zimbabwe Council of Churches in Zimbabwe: History, Facts, & Services.* [Online]. Available from: https://www.adequatetravel.com/placeguide/Zimbabwe/zimbabwe-council-of-churches-in-zimbabwe-history-facts-services

BENTHAM, J., (1843) 'Anarchical *Fallacies; being an examination of the Declaration of Rights issued During the French Revolution.* Edinburgh: William Tait.

CHINAMA, T., (2023) *Humanism in Zimbabwe.* [Online]. Available from: http://freethinker.co.uk/2023/02/humanism-in-zimbabwe/

CLAPHAM, A., (2015) *Human Rights: A Very Short Introduction.* Oxford, Oxford University Press.

CLARK, K. J., (2012) *Abraham's Children: Liberty and Tolerance in an Age of Religious Conflict.* New Haven, Yale University Press.

CRESPIN-BOUCAUD, J. (2019) *Interethnic and Interfaith Marriages in sub-Saharan Africa.* [Online]. Available from: https://shs.hal.science/halshs-01834808v2/document

EQUALITY AND HUMAN RIGHTS COMMISSION, (2023) *Article 10: Freedom of Expression.* [Online]. Available from: https://www.equalityhumanrights.com/en/human-rights-act/article-10-freedom-expression#:~:text=Everyone%20has%20the%20right%20to,authority%20and%20 regardless%20of%20frontiers

GALTUNG, J., (1996) *Peace by Peaceful Means: Peace and Conflict Development and Civilization.* Thousand Oaks, Sage.

HUXLEY, J., (1946) *UNESCO, Its Purpose, and Its Philosophy.* [Online]. Available from: https://unesdoc.unesco.org/ark:/48223/pf0000068197

IGWE, L., (2015) The Challenge of Atheism in Contemporary Zimbabwe. [Online]. Available from: https://www.maravipost.com/the-challenge-of-atheism-in-contemporary-zimbabwe/

KARAGIANNIS, E., (2018) *The New Political Islam: Human Rights, Democracy and Justice.* Philadelphia, University Pennsylvania Press.

MARX, K., (1843) On the Jewish Question. In M. R. Ishay. *(*ed.). *The Human Rights Reader: Major Political Essays, Speeches, and Documents from the Bible to the Present.* London, Routledge.

MKWAPATIRA, M., (2018) *The Rise of Secularism in Zimbabwe.* [Online]. Available from: https://medium.com/humanist-voices/the-rise-of-secularism-in-zimbabwe-5dc79cb283cd

MOYN, S., (2010) *The Last Utopia: Human Rights in History.* Massachusetts, Harvard University Press.

NDORO, S. R., (2017) *Zimbabwe is not a 'Christian nation'.* [Online]. Available from: https://www.sundaymail.co.zw/zimbabwe-is-not-a-christian-nation-2

OBAMA, B., (2009) *Inaugural Address,* [Online]. Available from: www.whitehouse.gov/blog/inaugural/address

ROBERTSON, D., (2004) *A Dictionary of Human Rights.* New York, Europa Publications.

ROUSSEAU, J. J., (1947) *The Social Contract, or Principles of Political Right.* New York, Hafner.

SALOMON, G., (2009) Peace Education: Its Nature, Nurture and the Challenges It Faces. In J. de Rivera (ed.). *Handbook on Building Cultures of Peace.* New York, Springer Science Business Media.

SCOLNICOV, A., (2011) *The Right to Religious Freedom in International Law: Between Group Rights and Individual Rights.* London, Routledge.

SEN, A., (1999) *Development as Freedom.* New York, Knopf.

US DEPARTMENT OF STATE, (2021) *Office of International Religious Freedom Report.* [Online]. Available from: https://www.state.gov/wp-content/uploads/2022/04/ZIMBABWE-2021-INTERNATIONAL-RELIGIOUS-FREEDOM-REPORT.pdf

US DEPARTMENT OF STATE, (2022) *Country Reports on Human Rights Practices: Zimbabwe.* [Online]. Available from: https://www.state.gov/reports/2022-country-reports-on-human-rights-practices/zimbabwe/#:~:text=Significant%20human%20rights%20issues%20included ,arbitrary%20detention%3B%20political%20prisoners%3B%20arbitrary

VAN DER VAN, J. A. et al., (2010) *Human Rights or Rules?* Leiden, Koninklijke Brill.

Ritual Killings: Desire for Prosperity, Cultural Falsity and Implications on Creeping Human Rights Laws in Southern Africa

Taruvinga Muzingili, Muzondo Edward, Kudzai Mwapaura
and *Noel Garikai Muridzo*

Introduction

While the issue of ritual killing has been in existence in antiquity, today, this menace has become a phenomenon that the entire world, especially African, is grappling with. Listening to the mass media, cases of ritual killing among other crimes against humanity are becoming prevalent (Oyewole 2016). Given the call for the efforts that are being put in place to amplify human rights, one would have expected such acrimonious acts to be ebbing. Regrettably, some religious, business people and political leaders have been caught in the act (Bailey 2010). Whatever the motive, ritual killing is considered as a serious violence of human rights that has unquestionable implications on human rights and society moral standing. While the perpetrators of ritual killings are sometimes convicted, legal instruments in Southern Africa, so often bequeath every murder case on the same level with little attention differentiating murder types for proper justice. This chapter unravels reasons for ritual killings in Southern Africa. Apart from human rights perspective, the chapter debates the morality of ritual killings, basing the argument on how such acts defy the collective nature of social friendships, solidarity and inherent human dignity. While this chapter is focused on ritual killings in the context of human rights, it can be erroneous to ignore ramifications of such acts on people's psychosocial life.

Conceptualising Ritual Killings

The term 'ritual killing' is a social menace whereby human beings are offered as an object of sacrifice to a deity or god to appease or request for a favour (Maganga & Tembo 2015). From biblical, economic, social or cultural perspectives, ritual murders involve killing of a living creature as a ritual offering to a god or spirit, usually in expectation of a return in the form of good fortune. So often, reports show that whole or severed parts of human beings, such as the head, genitals, breasts, eyes, intestine, arms and legs as well as exhumed dead bodies or its severed parts are used (Vincent 2008:43-53). Among African societies, ritual murder involves removing the required body parts from the victim while the person is still alive (Labuschagne 2004:191-206). Ethically, ritual killing and other related practices is a crime against humanity, public peace and peaceful co-existence. This barbaric act wherever it exists, indicates the breakdown of moral and ethical standards set by collective human beings in their quest to live life characterised by empathy, love, peace, dignity and respect. Fontaine (2011:2) defines ritual killing as "a religious performance and embodies authority; its aim is public, the personnel that perform it and, ideally, their actions, are specified and cannot be varied without weakening its efficacy". Thus, such an act involves the sacred. It is a truism of anthropology that appears to invoke the highest cultural legitimacy, activating spiritual powers, whether they be of gods, spirits, or ancestors, in order to achieve a beneficent result.

Some studies have shown that ritual killing, expressed in various forms, be direct killing, systematic rape, or human trafficking, constitute substantial division and ill-will directed to those who have not acted this way themselves, thereby denigrating their special capacity to exhibit the opposite traits of identity and solidarity (Rannditsheni et al 2016). From both legal and moral arguments, the actor of ritual killings treats others as separate and inferior. In both legal and moral spheres, it is important to differentiate between ritual killing and a general murder. Ritual killing is a form of murder although not all murder cases can be regarded as ritual killing (Cimpric 2010). Murder is a situation whereby someone snuffed out life from another person either intentionally or accidentally. Many times, people commit murder for revenge or to cover an evil act while ritual killing is a deliberate action of killing for the purpose of rituals (Vincent 2008). Ritual killing is highly premeditated but not all murders are premeditated. Therefore, ritual involves killing or severing the body part of abducted persons for the purpose of using it as an object of ritual sacrifice to acquire ritual-money, favour, fame, success, power and protection.

Ritual Killings: Human Rights and Social Moral Lens

The United Nations (UN) has been at the forefront in the recognition and promoting global, regional and arrangements for the protection of human rights. Regardless of social, political, cultural and technological orientation, human beings have the right to something (Ashby 2015). For example, article one in the Universal Declaration of Human Rights reads: "all human beings are born free and equal in dignity and rights. They are endowed with reason and conscience and should act towards one another in a spirit of brotherhood." At continental level, the African Charter on Human and People's Rights under article five states that:

> Every individual shall have the right to the respect of the dignity inherent in a human being and to the recognition of his legal status. All forms of exploitation and degradation of man particularly slavery, slave trade, torture, cruel, inhuman or degrading punishment and treatment shall be prohibited.

Therefore, all agents of humanity have a stringent duty to treat every human being in a certain way that obtains fulfilment of one's inherent and intrinsic desire for existence. This duty should be predicated upon the quality one shares with (nearly) all other human beings and that must be contented, even if not doing so would result in marginal gains in intrinsic value or in somewhat fewer violations of this same duty in the long run (Scurlock 2006). In discussing the value of human rights, it must be construed that a human right is a moral right against others, that is, a natural duty that ought to be taken into account by morally responsible individuals or agents. This is, regardless of whether they recognise that they ought to. Regardless to debates surrounding human rights debates, the definition of human right, be enshrined in legal framework or embedded in cultural morality, human beings should not be treated in variance.

Human beings, regardless of diversity associated with their tribe, creed, sexual orientation, political status or economic status, should be deemed equal. Article two of the Universal Declaration of Human rights states that "everyone is entitled to all the rights and freedoms set forth in this Declaration, without distinction of any kind, such as race, colour, sex, language, religion, political or other opinion, national or social origin, property, birth or other status." The African Charter on Human and People's Rights (article 2) further elaborates that:

> Every individual shall be entitled to the enjoyment of the rights and freedom recognised and guaranteed in the present Charter without distinction of any kind such as race, ethnic group, colour, sex, language, religion, political or any other opinion, national and social origin, fortune, birth or other status.

It is, therefore, important to underscore that, in understanding ritual killings, one needs to be reminded that human rights are to treat an individual as having dignity, roughly, as exhibiting a superlative non-instrumental value. Thus, ritual killings constitute a serious human rights violation which infers failure to honour people's special nature, often by treating them merely as a means to some ideology such as racial or religious purity or to some prudentially selfish end. Using this framework, one would distinguish the violation of a right from a justifiable limitation thereof, roughly in terms of the reason for which the right has not been observed (Clark 2009). Perpetrators of ritual killings, apart from their demonstration of moral limitation, they degrade human dignity including their right to enjoy life freedoms, aspirations and blossoms. Such acts also contradict the plausibility of continental instruments such as article six of African Charter on Human and People's Rights, which state that "every individual shall have the right to liberty and to the security of his person. No one may be deprived of his Freedom except for reasons and conditions previously laid down by law" Thus, ritual killing undermines the respect for the dignity of persons as individuals with the capacity for friendly relationships *inter alia* human identity and camaraderie which accounts naturally for rights to liberty.

This theoretical framework, in which human dignity is the foundational value of human rights, has become the dominant view among moral philosophers, jurisprudential scholars, United Nations theorists, and others (Hall 2011). The article three of Universal Declaration of Human Rights succinctly avers that "everyone has the right to life, liberty and security of person." In the same context, article five states that "no one shall be subjected to torture or to cruel, inhuman or degrading treatment or punishment." Thus, ritual killing entails human rights violations which constitute a serious degradation of people's capacity for friendliness, understood as the ability to share a way of life and care for others' quality of life. Apart from legal accountability, committing a murder within Afrocentric collective values is a sign of human degradation, which indicates exhibition of extraordinarily unfriendly behaviour toward another person (Hall 2011; Saralyn 2012). Whatever the reasons, be political, economic and cultural, ritual killing is a human rights violation which gravely indicates disrespecting people's capacity for communal relationship, conceived as identity and solidarity, which disrespect principally takes the form of a significant degree of anti-social behaviour (Clark 2009).

While Southern African countries have legal frameworks which treat ritual killing, like any murder case, the observation is that the topic is treated with pacifism in human rights debates, yet there is no justification for such violence to other human beings. With the current increase in cases of ritual killing, it is natural for this chapter to suggest that the existing legal frameworks in southern Africa have not shown a serious impermissibility to such human rights violations. As argued by (Comaroff & Comaroff 1999), so often, the victims of ritual killing are innocent people in the community. Thus, the rationale for those committing such violence can be considered as retributive and aggressive beyond the pale of human communal relationships. Within human rights discourse, there is no deserved principle of permitting punishment, coercion and death to someone who is part of humanity.

Historical Perspective of Ritual Killings

While ritual killings are gaining momentariness, its historicity cannot be understood without some reflection on biblical times. The historical development of sacrifices and offerings in the Old Testament (OT) is extensive (Bvunabandi 2008:280). These sacrifices were considered as supreme activities or acts in the Jewish culture. Even today, this ghastly practice has been part of many societies and took place in most regions around the world. For example, the bible records several instances of Israelites sacrificing their sons and daughters to idols in religious ritual (Jeremiah 7, 18 and 32). More so, at some point the children of Israel were also involved in this nefarious act. Even in the so-called Great civilization of the world-Babylon, Egypt, China, Greece, and even the precursor to the Romans, all took part in ritualised killings (Scurlock 2006). In ancient Egypt and China, for instance, slaves were often buried alive, along with the body of their owner, to serve him in the afterlife.

Mass human sacrifices were particularly a feature of ancient states whose dead leaders required their courtiers and followers to accompany them into the afterlife. The tombs of the first dynasty of Egyptian pharaohs (3100-2890 BC) were each surrounded by the graves of their courtiers. In the royal tombs of ancient Mesopotamia, the courtiers - guards, musicians, handmaidens and grooms - died at their posts in the tomb, having taken a lethal draught of poison. Some of the largest mass sacrifices accompanying dead rulers are the royal tombs of the African kingdom of Kerma, around 1500 BC. The case of "Abobakus" in the ancient Yoruba Kingdom is a typical picture of ritual killing (Scurlock 2006). Whether ritual killings were done on religious grounds, it can be seen that there is a sense that they activated the legitimacy powers from the deity for protection from any unfortunate human circumstances.

Specifically, a plethora of chronicles of ritual killings are found in the biblical texts (2 Kings 6:26-29 and Lamentations 4:10). Further, all firstborn sons of humans, including of cattle and sheep, were given to God on the eighth day after birth (Exodus 22:29-30). In Genesis (22:2), God commands Abraham to take Isaac, his only son, and sacrifice him as an offering at Mount Moriah. Human beings were also killed in Mesopotamia in disparate circumstances to avert divine wrath (Scurlock 2006). Many other biblical texts demonstrate that human sacrifice, which also constitutes ritual killings, occurred in ancient Israel. The book of Deuteronomy, indubitably confirms the practices of the Canaanites in which parents burnt their sons and daughters in the fire as sacrifices to their gods (Deuteronomy 12:31; 18:9-12), which justified the extirpation from the land. To consolidate their political and quasi-spiritual dominance, some of the ancient Israel kings are implicated in local rituals of sacrificing their sons and daughters, which in the eyes of God was detestable (2 Kings 16:3; Jeremiah 19:4-5). Still in the context of biblical times, God as the architect of ritual murder is further problematized by reading the Gospels both of which present Jesus as the Son of God (Matthew 11:27; 16:15-17; Mark 14:61-62; Luke 3:21-22; John 17:1) whom He allowed to die on the cross as an atonement or substitution for the sinful world (Galatians 3:13). This is further problematised in Jesus as the sacrificial lamb (Matthew 27:46; Sandy 1991:447- 460). In the context of these biblical narratives, in modern day, ritual killings have taken new dispensation. Today, universal human rights dictates are regarded as precursors of human dignity, worth and liberty, regardless of their religious orientation.

Discussing ritual killing without social rhetoric can be considered prejudicial. Human killing or sacrifice has been common within social and cultural space in Southern Africa, like throughout the African continent. Narratives of witchcraft and human sacrifice are inseparable in Africa. Conceptually, witchcraft is "the use of magic powers, especially evil ones" (Ashby 2000:1371). For Manala (2004:1492) the concept of witchcraft refers to the use by some people of evil magic powers to harm or cause misfortune to others. African and European belief in witchcraft is extensively documented (Leistner 2014). While people struggle to problematize witchcraft in the context of ritual killings, African authors see its locus in murder cases. The proliferation of the belief in witchcraft is not only widespread across sub-Saharan African countries (Cimpric 2010), but also very disturbing in the discussion of murder cases. In some Southern African countries like Tanzania, studies have discovered that thousands of elderly people, especially women, have been accused of witchcraft and then beaten and/or killed (Cimpric 2010:13). In this case, ritual killing is ignited in twofold: a witch being murdered or someone being killed by a witch. Furthermore, some scholars consider ritual murder as a pandemic because of its perennial effects on the welfare of most communities (Rannditsheni et al 2016). It is a common practice among Africans and an acknowledged problem in the contemporary dispensation (Maganga & Tembo 2015). Ritual or *muti* murders are a form of human sacrifice practised by some African tribes (Munthali 2005:29), which needs attention from legal, moral and psychosocial perspectives.

Drivers for Ritual Killing

African belief systems are complex and mysterious (Magosa & Rugwiji 2018). Numerous factors are assumed to precipitate the killing of humans for ritual purposes among African societies. Arguably, the reasons for such killings are based on selfishness, greed and to some extent on laziness. Some ritual killers attempted to make shortcuts to prosperity. Others engage in ritual killings for voracious desire to remain in political power. Various Constitutions of Southern African countries are famously considered progressive for explicitly entitling citizens with economic prosperity. Specifically, in Zimbabwean and South African constitutions, people have rights against the state to resources such as housing, healthcare, food, water, social security and education. Whether related to state failure to provide economic stability to its citizens, society today has increasingly become materialistic in nature. In such a context, money or having luxurious properties are some of the yardsticks for measuring how successful one is. In their quest for financial prosperity, many people have gone into moneymaking rituals which require use of human parts or blood (Dombo 201; Hall 2011). This singular act accounts for many cases of ritual killing in Southern African countries.

Arguably, it will be an understatement that some African countries have failed to economically satisfy their citizens. For example, economic indices such as poverty, unemployment, poor infrastructure, ailing health care services, high inflation rate and other indices are pointers to the fact that the government has refused to live up to expectations in Africa (Setsiba 2013). The failure of government has led many people to self-help for survival, which some have triggered inglorious acts of ritual murder in the expectation of financial prowess. Some people took to kidnapping as means of beating the harsh economic reality of the day (Kasooha 2009). The observations are that people are tools in the hand of power hungry politicians and pastors that are demanding body parts from their customers for one fetish portion or the other (Patrick 2009). Shumba (2013) reports that machete-wielding thugs killed a Bulawayo (Zimbabwe) man and then ripped out his heart in a suspected ritual killing in order to gain economic prosperity. Parts of dismembered remains of the victim, identified as Edmore Rundogo, were found in Maun, about 500 km from Botswana's second city of Francistown (Magosa & Rugwisi 2018). It is this legendary belief of connecting the dead/the supernatural with the living which motivates human societies all over the world to engage in ritual murder in order to gratify the gods who in return would 'bless' and enrich the offerer (Magosa & Rugwisi 2018).

Zimbabweans have not been spared from ritual killing associated with desire to gain wealth. For example, Kavirimirwa (2014) reports that villagers and pupils of Mhondoro-Mubaira were living in fear following a spate of suspected ritual killings. In this case, Kavirimirwa reiterates that the attacks on pupils took place in Morowa village under Chief Nyamweda in December 2013, with suspected cases of selling human parts for sacrifices. In another gruesome incident, Rupapa (2017) reports a 16-year-old Moreblessing Murove was fatally axed and her body parts were mutilated in another suspected case of ritual murder. Rupapa (2017) also writes about a 42-year-old Harare woman who is being interrogated on charges of ritual murder of a Grade 1 pupil in Norton. Rupapa reaffirms that Chaitwa and Garande reportedly kidnapped and killed Perfect Hunyani, whose body parts were missing when the body was recovered. Cases of ritual killing have also been heard as being practised among the Ngombe people of Zambia, who believe that a novice diviner must first kill a near relative before the basket will divine properly (Zuesse 1975:168). Similar cases are also conveyed from other destinations such as Kenya, Namibia, Lesotho, Liberia and Mozambique (see Bukuluki 2014:1; Mokotso 2015:210), among others. Majority of these cases are linked to ritual killings for economic prosperity. The observation is that an individual is asked by diviners to kill before they become healthy. These acts, apart from poverty, are linked to materialistic behaviours which are characterising the modern day society.

It is further observed that ritual killings originated as a result of man's insatiable quest for power and material things. Literature shows that, due to modernization and industrialization, people's greed to acquire all and have everything under his control increased (Obineke 2008). In countries like Botswana, Burke explains witchcraft in terms of two words: *boloi* and *dipheko* (Burke 2000). The term *boloi* in which an individual manipulates materials for personal gain or to harm someone. In such a context, power is a force seen or unseen that enables people to accomplish tasks. Power in this context can be physical, spiritual, and political. The quest for power by human beings, especially Africans is a major factor fuelling the incessant cases of ritual killing (Rimoldi 2005). The current trends in Southern Africa is that the quest for prestige and accolades that accompany power and position have increased the insatiable quest to feed their evil desire. While various Bill of Rights accords citizens the rights to form political parties, to support a political party of their choice, to vote in regular elections, and to run for public office, some individuals resort to rituals to outcompete the enemies (Labuschagne 2004). Some political individuals are part of ritual killing networks. From political reasons, the observation is that politicians can find some conduct the acts on their behalf, while promising the perpetrators the financial gains.

Studies have shown that some strong political individuals honoured the gods by giving them something to eat in exchange for potency (Bvunabandi 2008). It is argued that the ritual by Africans of venerating and or appeasing the ancestors by brewing traditional beer probably arose as a result of such an ideology (Anderson 1993). In view of the philosophy explained above, it is plausible that as the quest for power to outshine one another heightened, a more complex method of acquiring potency arose. For example, reports are that some spate of killings of people with albinism in Northwest Tanzania placed the country in the international limelight in 2007 (Schühle 2013:27). It is believed that the bones of people with albinism were a necessary ingredient in power and wealth-generating magic potions. Thus, this provoked more killings which had no precedents in Tanzania or the local Sukuma culture (Schühle 2013). In the context of Swaziland, ritual murders are also perpetrated for the quest of political and economic power (Laing 2010). According to Laing (2010), these murders mainly target albino killings, where skin pigmentation is considered to be a source of lucky charm to consolidate political or economic power.

Moreover, it is believed that, among many African societies, issues related to diseases or sickness cannot just happen (Kellaway, 2003). From a cultural perspective, it has a cause, and usually witchcraft and food poisoning are cited. The belief is that people with evil powers could cause other people they see as their enemies or who are disrespectful toward them to become sick as a way of punishment (White 2015). In some African communities, one could become sick through invocation of curses in the name of the river deity, *Antoa*, upon an unknown offender (White 2015:2). These communities are just one illustration among numerous others across Africa in which narratives of witchcraft and cultural practices are common. For example, one of the tenets in African witchcraft is that one can fly in a winnowing basket (*rusero* in Shona) to various parts of the world and back within a few hours of the night. In fact, it takes several hours for a modern aircraft to travel to any of the above destinations (Magosa & Rugwiji 2018). It is believed that these witches can kill someone during the nights. It is believed that this accounts for some people who die in their sleep. In those scenarios, it is also reported that they can eat the soft tissue of the dead person for protection from their enemies.

In Zimbabwe, Chivasa (2021) analysis showed that *kutanda botso* ritual has a dual role: firstly, the fear of negative consequences deters the possible perpetrators from such acts of violence. Secondly, it symbolises the social values of motherhood by extolling and venerating it as an important and admirable position that should be treated with reverence and respect. Mothers deserve to live in nonviolent spaces and social relationships. The fear of *kutanda botso* in Shona social life is not rooted in law enforcement agencies but in internalism in which an individual must weigh the consequences of their actions and then decide whether or not to commit acts of violence against their biological mother. Maroro (2018) singled out some of the acts of violence that might warrant engagement in *kutanda botso*. These acts include, but are not limited to, physical and verbal abuse, rape, assault or murder. While this act is not linked directly to ritual killings, some believe that a child can become mentally ill, and can commit ritual killing for mental stability. Such criminal acts, even based on social or cultural reasons, are against human rights in Zimbabwe. For example, Zimbabwe constitution Amendment (No. 20) section 53 states that "every human being has freedom from torture or cruel, inhuman or degrading treatment or punishment."

One biblical view is that God forbids human sacrifice in any form. Apart from the account of God instructing Abraham to sacrifice his son Isaac as a means of testing his love for God, there was no such account where God requires that human beings be sacrificed unto him (Romiti 2009; Fontaine 2011). In fact, God frowns at killing in any form- murder, ritual killing, manslaughter and any form of termination of human life under whatever circumstances. In Ex 20:13 God explicitly warned the Israelites in the Ten Commandments when he said "Thou shalt not kill". However, some so-called pastors, bishops and other church people are involved in ritual killing to get fame, position and power (Oyewole 2016). In a situation where an aspiring president of a nation kills people for ritual to take position, in such a nation ritual killing is inevitable (Oyewole, 2016). In countries like South Africa, others blame *muti* murders on Satanism. For example, Hamilton (2016) reports that human sacrifice, animal slaughter and child pornography are some of the terrifying claims made against Satanism. Hamilton further states that some cults within Satanism have confirmed that they do practise ritual killing. Rotimi (2006) reports the incidence of a priest who sacrificed his son to appease gods. Clearly, murders based on religion cannot be accepted. Paragraphs 138 and 139 of the 2005 World Summit Outcome Document highlights the responsibility of governments to protect their own citizens from genocide, war crimes, ethnic cleansing and crimes against humanity and accepted a collective responsibility to encourage and help each other uphold this commitment contravenes various legal instruments. For example, this raises some questions on the purity of some religious sects. Some ritual murders associated with Satanism may find solace in the article eight of the African Charter, which states that "freedom of conscience, the profession and free practice of religion shall be guaranteed. No one may, subject to law and order, be submitted to measures restricting the exercise of these freedoms." However, this article does not promote the acts of murder or ritual killing as indicated in the article ten of the same charter which provides clarity on religious freedom by noting that "every individual shall have the right to free association provided that he abides by the law." In modern day, religious sects should be part of human rights promotion movements, not violators.

Creeping Legal Frameworks on Ritual Killing in Southern Africa

Besides enduring psychosocial trauma and financial burden for the burial, current legal instruments in Southern African are not doing enough to end this problem. The worrying phenomenon is that in most cases the murderers, although known, are not arrested, or are released shortly after arrest due to lack of evidence (Rannditshen et al 2016). This is antithetical with the Universal Declaration on Human Rights, specifically article seven which states that:

> All are equal before the law and are entitled without any discrimination to equal protection of the law. All are entitled to equal protection against any discrimination in violation of this Declaration and against any incitement to such discrimination.

While law also protects the perpetrators as human beings, this state of affairs explains the complexity of the mammoth task to apprehend ritual murder Southern African countries. For example, cases of crime in Swaziland were reported which included killing for ritual purposes. Evidence shows that the three accused persons were recently charged with the ritual murder of a four-year-old girl (Langwenya 2013). It is further stated that the court found that the prosecution had failed to prove its case beyond reasonable doubt, since the evidence of the accomplice witness on which the prosecution had relied had been discredited by the defence.

In Zimbabwe, the issue of witnesses is difficult to solve for several reasons such as; vulnerability of the victims, intimidation and by the virtue that some of these acts are done in secrecy. Sections 47(2) of the Criminal Law Code in Zimbabwe provide that when a court is deciding the appropriate sentence for murder, it must regard as aggravating in case of murder the factors there set out, although it may regard other factors as aggravating in addition to those laid down. Among the factors which a court must regard as aggravating are if the murder was committed in the course of committing an act of terrorism or kidnapping or rape – and this includes situations where the murder was committed during the commission of an act constituting an essential element of such a crime (whether or not the accused was charged with or convicted of the crime). Section 48(2) of the 2013 Zimbabwe Constitution now provides that the death penalty may be imposed only for murder committed in aggravating circumstances. While the issue of death penalty is debatable, the same constitutions provide that the law providing for such penalty must permit the court a discretion as to whether or not to impose the penalty. While legal instruments are important, they have failed to adequately attend to issues of ritual killings. No urgent measures are being taken in legal reforms on issues of witnesses, evidence and sentences. More so, the protection of remaining families' members has not been guaranteed by Southern African laws. In an attempt to apprehend ritual murder in Southern Africa, the following recommendations should be considered:

- There is a need for stiffer jail sentences and/or heavy fines for those involved in ritual murder cases (Magosa & Rugwiji 2018).
- Communities should be empowered on economic and entrepreneurial skills for self-sufficiency. This will help in reducing the desires for quick success or prosperity.
- Intensification of DNA programme for evidence gathering. This will help in solving the problem of failure to prove the judicial system beyond any reasonable doubt.
- Whistle-blowers are invisible law-abiding citizens whose main function is to disseminate information which provides details towards the arrest of suspected ritual murderers. They should not be known and the law-enforcement institution should not mention them as their link persons.
- Human rights activism against *muti* murder should be intensified. This should incorporate some members of society to participate in a solidarity campaign against the practice.

Conclusion

The moral-legal interpretation of ritual killing shows greediness, jealousy, selfishness and lack of collective consciousness. Those who commit ritual killings lack humanness by honouring friendly relationships (of identity and solidarity) with others who have dignity by virtue of their inherent capacity to engage in such relationships. The act constitutes human rights violations which poses a serious degradation of human capacity, often taking the form of very unfriendly behaviour that is not proportionate and counteractive to community solidarity. This is a limited justification to murder someone for cultural pleasure, desire for political and economic prosperity. In the context of major human rights clusters, ritual murders undermine human dignity, worth and intrinsic value of humanity. Further, human rights violations are well understood as failures to treat people as important beings of social, political and cultural ecosystem. This conception of human rights violations in the form of ritual killings, straightforwardly accounts for many deficiencies in Southern African Constitutions. Ritual killing has been in existence for a very long time ago though the rate at which this menace is going now is becoming alarming.

Ritual killing can be curbed if not eliminated through joint efforts. The Southern African Development Community must eradicate the wanton shedding of blood and termination of human life for the sake of fame, falsity and greediness.

References

ASHBY, A., (2015) Witchcraft, Justice and Human Rights in Africa: Cases from Malawi. *African Studies Review,* 58(1), 5-38.

BAILEY, C., (2010) *Muti Killings Is a Way of Life on Rural Areas.* [Online]. Available from: http://www.iol.co.za/news/south-africa/

BURKE, C., (2000) They Cut Segments into Parts: Ritual Murder, Youth, and Politics of Knowledge in Botswana. *Anthropology Quarterly,* 73(4), 204-214.

BVUNABANDI, S., (2008) *The Communicative Power of Blood Sacrifices: A Predominantly South African Perspective with Special Reference to Epistle of Hebrews.* Pretoria, University of Pretoria

CHAVASA, N., (2021) The Kutanda Botso Ritual as a Means of Preventing Femicide Targeting Biological Mothers in Shona Communities of Zimbabwe. *Journal of International Women's Studies,* 22(1), 473-485.

CIMPRIC, A., (2010) *Children accused of Witchcraft: An Anthropological Study of Contemporary Practices in Africa.* Dakar: UNICEF WCARO.

CLARK, J., (2009). *Albinos in Africa—Murder for Magic, A Human Rights Nightmare.* [Online]. Available from: http://blogs.howstuffworks.com/

COMAROFF, J. and COMAROFF, J. L., (1999) Occult Economies and the Violence of Abstraction: Notes from the South African Postcolony. *American Ethnologist,* 26(3), 279-30.

DOMBO, V., (2011) Community Presented Unity Front against Ritual Killing. *Limpopo Times,* 1-2.

FONTAINE, J. L. (2011) *Ritual Murder?* London, Open Anthropology Cooperative Press.

HALL, E., (2011) *Murders Inquiry Highlights Trade in body Parts.* San Diego, Academic Press.

HUMAN SCIENCES RESEARCH COUNCIL, (2010) *Tsireledzani: Understanding the Dimensions of Human Trafficking in Southern Africa.* Pretoria, Human Sciences Research Council.

KASOOHA, I., (2009) Girl Beheaded in Ritual Murder. *New Vision,* 16, 52-59.

KAVIRIMIRWA, F., (2014) *Ritual Murders Shock Mhondoro.* [Online]. Available from: https://www.herald.co.zw/ritual-murders-shock-mhondoro/

KELLAWAY, J., (2003) *The History of Torture and Execution: From Early Civilization through Mediaeval Times to the Present.* Canada, Lyons Press.

LABUSCHAGNE, G., (2004) Features and Investigative Implications of Muti in South Africa. *Journal of Investigative Psychology and Offender Profiling,* 1(3), 191-206.

LAING, A., (2010) *Albino Girl, 11, Killed and Beheaded in Swaziland for Witchcraft.* [Online]. Available from: https://www.telegraph.co.uk/news/worldnews/africaandindianocean/swaziland/7956458/Albino-girl-11-killed-and-beheaded-in-Swaziland-for-witchcraft.html

LANGWENYA, M., (2013) *A Review by Afri-MAP and the Open Society Initiative for Southern Africa.* Johannesburg, Open Society Foundation.

LEISTNER, E., (2014) Witchcraft and African Development. *Journal of African Security Review,* 23(1), 53-77.

MAFOHLA, F. W. T., (1926) The Ngozi of Chinyowa. *NADA,* 4, 104-106.

MANALA, M. J., (2004) Witchcraft and its Impact on Black African Christians: A Lacuna in the Ministry of the Hervormde Kerk in Suidelike Afrika. *HTS,* 60(4):1491-1511.

MASANJA, M. M., (2015) Albinos' Plight: Will Legal Methods be Powerful enough to Eradicate Albinos' Scourge? *International Journal of Education & Research,* 3(5), 231-244.

MASOGA, A. and RUGWIJI, T., (2018) *A Reflection on Ritual Murders in The Biblical Text from An African Perspective.* [Online]. Available from: http://www.scielo.org.za/scielo.php ?script=sci_arttext&pid=S2305-445X2018000100017

MUNTHALI, R. C., (2005) *Trauma Ritual Murders in Venda: A Challenge to Pastoral Care.* Pretoria, University of Pretoria.

MURORO, G. C., (2018) Demystifying African Cultural and Religion Practices: Our Cultural Heritage. [Online]. Available from: http://mbuyavachinjanjamuroro.blogspot.com/ 2018/04/kutandabotso.htm (Accessed 08 April 2023).

OBINEKE, C. L., (2008) *The Implications of Ritual Killing and Security in Nigeria.* Nsukka, University of Nigeria.

OYEWOLE, S., (2016) Kidnapping for Rituals: Article of Faith and Insecurity in Nigeria. *Africology: The Journal of Pan African Studies,* 9(9).

PARKER-PEARSON, M. (2023) *The Practice of Human Sacrifice.* [Online]. Available from: https://www.bbc.co.uk/history/ancient/british_prehistory/human_sacrifice_01.shtml

PATRICK, W., (2023) *Why ritual killings thrive in Nigeria.* [Online]. Available from: https://www.thepointng.com/why-ritual-killings-thrive-in-nigeria-fcid/

RANNDITSHENI, A. E., MASOGA, M. A. and MAVHANDU-MUDZUSI, A. H., (2016) Some Perspectives on the Impacts of Ritual Murders in the Vhembe District of South Africa: An Interpretative Phenomenological Approach. *Journal of Social Science,* 48(3), 239-245.

RIMOLDI, E., (2005) Human Sacrifice and the Loss of Transformative Power. *Social Analysis,* 49, 94-108.

ROTIMI, W., (2006) *Human Sacrifice: Priest Kills Son to Appease Gods.* Durban, Westville Press.

RUPAPA, T., (2017) *Court denies Ritual in Murder Suspect Bail.* [Online]. Available from: https://www.herald.co.zw/court-denies-ritual-murder-suspect-bail/

SARALYN, S., (2012) *The Practice of Ritual Killings and Human Sacrifice in Africa.* Cape Town, University of Cape Town Press.

SCHÜHLE, J., (2013) *Medicine Murder of Peoples with Albinism in Tanzania – How Casino Capitalism Creates Rumorscape and Occult Economies.* Berlin, Center for Area Studies.

SCURLOCK, J., (2006) *The Techniques of the Sacrifice of Animals in Ancient Israel and Ancient Mesopotamia: New Insights through Comparison. Andrews University Seminary Studies,* 44(4), 241-264.

SETSIBA, T. H., (2012) *Mourning Rituals and Practices in Contemporary South African Townships: A Phenomenological Study.* Durban, University of Natal Press.

SHUMBA, P., (2013) *Heartless ... Zim Man's Heart ripped out in Botswana Ritual Murder.* [Online]. Available from: http://www.chronicle.co.zw/heartlesszim-mans-heart-ripped-out-in-botswana-ritual-murder

TANNER, R., (2010) Ideology and the Killing of Albinos in Tanzania: A Study in Cultural Relativities. *Anthropologist,* 12(4), 229-236.

WHITE, P., (2015) The Concept of Diseases and Health Care in African Traditional Religion in Ghana. *HTS Teologiese Studies/Theological Studies,* 71(3), 1-7

Towards the Development of a Human Rights Script that Oscillates with Indigenous Knowledge System: Emergence of Post—Decolonial Human Rights Discourse

Aubrey Tshepo Manthwa

Introduction

Law is partly a reflection of the culture of a society. In South Africa, law does not reflect African culture and values, but Western culture and philosophy (Church 1999:96-98). The South African values of *ubuntu* and communalism are often sidelined in the interpretation of human rights. The Western legal culture is often imposed on South African indigenous culture because indigenous culture is often seen as patriarchal (Rautenbach 2018:213). However, the application of these rights to the indigenous people of South Africa is done in a foreign setting. For example, in *Mayelane v Ngwenyama and Another (CCT 57/12) [2013] ZACC 14*, the Constitutional Court treated the right to equality and dignity as part of a requirement for polygamous marriage. The court argued that a second marriage is unlawful if it was not concluded with the consent of the first wife. This is problematic as it meant that the second wife's marriage would be unlawful although she may not have known that there was another woman whose consent was required for the second marriage. A question can be asked as to what kind of equality jurisprudence places the court in a situation where it must choose between two women who find themselves in a predicament that is not of their own making? Under the humanity of customary law based on *ubuntu* and communalism, this would not have happened.

The right to equality has been viewed as an important right in the Bill of Rights; however, there is no consensus on its meaning (Klug 2010:3). This is because different terms have been bandied around to try to remove it from its Aristotelian interpretation of treating people in similar situations the same way to accommodate the historical perspectives of people (Klug 2018:203-204). Terms such as substantive equality and affirmative action to consider the disadvantages people have previously suffered, have already been adopted in South Africa and other legal systems such as America (Klug 2018:213). This chapter maintains that jurisprudence must be developed based on the needs and circumstances of the country and the outcome should reflect its demands (Smith 2008:201). The current human rights script is problematic because it does not embrace the rich diversity contained in the South African indigenous value system. Although patriarchy is used as a problem in indigenous law, justifying reliance on Western conceptions of human rights: patriarchy is rather a Western creation. The chapter will also consider gender equality within succession to traditional leadership to highlight important considerations that are overlooked and may not achieve the desired end of achieving equality in the end.

History of Gender Discrimination

Grosfoguel (2013:85) provides an account of how women were mutilated in the middle of the 16th century. The sins of the women were the passing of knowledge from one generation to the next. These women mastered indigenous knowledge from ancient times. Their knowledge covered different aspects of life, such as astronomy, medicine and biology. They were empowered by the gift of ancestral knowledge, and organised life based on communal living to secure the interests of the family economically and politically. However, these women were persecuted in the mediaeval era because of the knowledge they possessed. The persecution was intensified in the 16th and 17th centuries, with the rise of colonialism and patriarchal power structures in Europe, resulting in millions of women being burnt alive and accused of being witches (Grosfoguel 2013:86). Women were depopulated because of the indigenous knowledge they possessed which was viewed as a threat to "Christian-centric patriarchy" and to further destroy communal forms of land ownership in favour of individualism Grosfoguel 2013:86). It was important that they depopulated the knowledge carriers to destroy epistemology and the pedagogy of disseminating knowledge, which was transmitted orally. It was important that Christianity was viewed as the central, and any threat to it had to be destroyed. At the centre of the advancement of Christianity were strong patriarchal elements that entailed that man had to be at the forefront of epistemology. Any other culture, religion or knowledge system was regarded as inferior to the masculinity of Western epistemology (Grosfoguel 2013:86).

In ancient Greece, Aristotle compounded the belief that males were active, and females were passive, justifying the differences on biological grounds, seeing women as weaker and inferior in their ability to participate in material matters. According to him, men were born to lead while women were born to be inferior. Consequently, a man must take command of women. This belief has regrettably been perpetuated through cultural and religious bigotry to the extent that one generation after the other, grows up with the cultural belief that such a way of life should be maintained (Lerner 1989:8-11). This stretches to the victims of patriarchy, such as young girls and women, also accepting and defining their roles in society on the narration that they are the weaker sex. Patriarchy can be described as the complete domination of a woman by a man, where the woman must completely succumb to the dictates of the man (Ademiluka 2018:340). The term originated from the Greek *patriarkhes*, which traditionally meant the rule of a father as a leader of a race. Largely referring to the position of the father in relation to his household, it has progressed to refer to the systematic male domination over females. It allows males to occupy material advantages economically, politically and otherwise, placing severe restrictions on females to be in a similar position to compete (Millet 1970: 25). Although the treatment of women as perpetual minors began to develop in Europe, indigenous law has in general acquired the unwanted reputation of being a patriarchal arrangement, largely because precolonial African societies operated under the auspices of the head of the family who, in most cases, happened to be a male. Elements of patriarchy did exist in pre-colonial African societies, however, were exacerbated by contact with colonialism. This was the law received in Africa with its strong patriarchal elements.

Consequently, the right to equality and dignity are blindly given effect to achieve gender neutrality in indigenous law due to its patriarchal elements without considering any other relevant consideration and the space where these rights must operate (Lewis 2014:1139). Since the Convention for a Democratic South Africa, multiparty meetings, traditional leaders have consistently proposed that indigenous law practices such as primogeniture and accession to male chieftaincy be excluded from being subject to the Bill of Rights, particularly the right to equality (Kaganas 1994:409). Regrettably, in some quarters, this has extended to defining gender roles in terms of hierarchies that would see men subvert to the top. The subtext of this is the ignominy that indigenous law traditionally fed into the marginalisation and subjugation of women when, in fact, gender-defined roles were complementary, but are continuously distorted for narrow self-interest. The fight for manhood has continued in the Constitutional era and, regrettably, it has continued along the margins of masculinity. Some traditional leaders, for example, have convinced the executive arm of Parliament to redefine law contents in indigenous law, such as the Communal Land Rights Act 11 of 2004, to empower them and limit female participation in material advantages (Walker 2005:297).

The biggest concern is that the voices of the people who will be ruled by the newly appointed leaders are considered. Section 11(3) of the Black Administration Act 38 of 1927, made African women married under indigenous law, minors of their husbands, which disqualified them from inheriting family property as wives or daughters (Mbatha 2002:264). The problem was not indigenous law but its codified version which excluded the participation of widows, even when they may have been better suited to further the interest of the family and dependents (Mbatha 2003:265). Today, the narrative continues that gender equality is the fundamental problem in indigenous law. Gender equality remains problematic, and the solution to it is to use a carbon copy of the Western standards of human rights than to fashion an African version thereof.

The South African human rights system as enshrined in the 1996 Constitution resembles that of the Canadian Bill of human rights. This means that the country has not been able to develop its own human rights and equality version (Davies 2003:186). This is despite the attitude of the court in the early years of the Constitution which said that the right to equality should be given space to develop on a case-by-case basis (*S v Ntuli 1996 (1) BCLR 141 (CC)* at 19). In *Prinsloo v Van der Linde 1997 (3) SA 1012 (CC),* the Constitutional Court emphasized the importance of developing South Africa's human rights jurisprudence, which includes taking cognisance of the context of rights in determining discrimination. Yet an opportunity was missed in judgments such as *Shilubana v Nwamitwa* to develop it in a way that reflects the African side of the story.

The Constitutional Court endorsed a *Shilubana* as *hosi*, to give effect to the right to equality and dignity of a female. The dispute was between the first applicant, daughter of *hosi* Nwamitwa and the respondent, Mr Nwamitwa, son of *hosi* Malathini Nwamitwa. The eldest daughter was initially not considered for succession to chieftaincy and was ineligible because of her gender. Consequently, *hosi* Fofoza was succeeded by his younger brother *Shilubana* (para 87). This was done in accordance with a resolution taken unanimously by the Valoyi council which resolved to confer Ms Shilubana to the chieftaincy (para 3-4). This was done in accordance with the advocacy by the constitutional dispensation to achieve gender equality. Mr Shilubana instituted proceedings in the High court for a declaratory order that he and not Ms Shilubana should be successor to the chieftaincy. The High court and later the Supreme Court of Appeal ruled in his favour. In the Constitutional Court where the High court and SCA judgement were overruled, an argument was brought that succession to *hosi* is a birth right, a *hosi* is born, not democratically elected.

The decision to approve the royal council decision to elect Ms Shilubana is easy to justify on constitutional grounds, however, unsustainable in terms of indigenous law because it disrupts the lineage. More than anything, state institutions have demonstrated a commitment towards a Eurocentric idea of human rights. The decision is compromised by the heavy reliance on western conceptions of gender equality and failure to afford indigenous law an opportunity to achieve the same end (Ntlama 2020:18). The lack of integrating an African human rights script highlights South Africa's obsession with western genuflection rather than paving its own identity.

South Africa's Aspiration towards Eurocentric Human Rights Discourse

South Africa is suffering from what can be termed 'aspiration' towards a Eurocentric ideal of the nation-state (Comaroff & Comaroff 2004:521). There is thus a need to clown South Africa in a Western image. This can be seen from the number of international treaties that the country ratified in the early 1990s. These treaties were signed with the objective of protecting and advancing gender equality. Amongst them were the International Covenant on Civil and Political Rights. More important was the United Nations' Convention on the Elimination of All Forms of Discrimination against Women (CEDAW). CEDAW has as its principal mandate to have party states enact legislative measures to eradicate all forms of gender discrimination, including all customary practices that are viewed as treating women as subordinates. Discrimination is defined in article 2(g) of CEDAW as:

> discrimination against women as any distinction, exclusion, or restriction made on the basis of sex which has the effect or purpose of impairing or nullifying the recognition, enjoyment or exercise by women, irrespective of their marital status, on a basis of equality of men and women, of human rights and fundamental freedoms in the political, economic, social, cultural, civil or any other field.

While recognising the importance of international treaties, it is imperative to emphasise that the African value system with its communal laws is capable of eliminating all practices that undermine the collective rights of women as endowed in *ubuntu* and communalism. This includes the right to equality and dignity of women as enshrined in the South African Constitution. Within this arrangement, the community have a responsibility to protect African heritage and it is the responsibility of the community to protect people and particularly vulnerable women. Communal laws make provision for this, entailing that one does not have to first look at international laws for solutions to protecting women. It is important that state institutions understand and give effect to the true role of traditional leadership and communities to ensure they do not respond based on a distorted view of gender defined roles.

There is a lot of effort and movement by state institutions that targets their spear at indigenous law as a legal system that is viewed as anti-gender equality. In addition to the obsession to mirror indigenous law in a Western image, there are also in-house organisations that have made it their goal to achieve gender equality, but it is indigenous law that feels the wrath of these organisations the most because human rights organisations can join indigenous law disputes as *amici curiae* to paint a picture of indigenous law as patriarchal. State institutions such as the South African Human Rights Commission (SAHRC), support democracy in accordance with chapter 9 of the South African Constitution and have an interest in the protection of women's rights. The Women's Legal Centre is similarly a non-governmental organisation whose objectives are to protect and advance women's rights in South Africa, and to abolish cultural marginalisation.

Human rights institutions and organisations can join court proceedings as respondents and friends of the court in cases where they believe gender discrimination is a concern (Manthwa 2019:475). Legislation has been promulgated to further the equality goal, for example the Promotion of Equality and Prevention of Unfair Discrimination Act, which prohibits gender discrimination 4 of 2000, gender-based violence and any such practice, including traditional, customary or religious practices, which impairs the dignity of women. Further commitment to gender equality can be seen with the promulgation of the Recognition of Customary Marriages Act, which strongly protects women's right to equality (Higgins, Fenrich & Tanzer 2011:425). As stated earlier, gender defined roles were done for a legitimate purpose, not in furtherance of patriarchy. Distortions of indigenous law should be separated from true law. Hence the need to ascertain the true versions of indigenous law and this can be done by visiting thousands of people who live in the traditional rural areas. These traditional rural areas can assist courts, and ignorant academics especially those of European extract and state institutions in general to understand the value of indigenous value systems. They can assist courts in better understanding the role of traditional leaders in communities. Women today are appointed to traditional leadership to achieve gender equality but if this is not done in ways that recognise the legitimate role played by indigenous law, the aimed outcome may not be achieved. More concerning is the ignorance of the African perspective of gender defined roles in settling disputes.

African Perspectives on Human Rights and Gender Defined Roles

Nhlapo (1995:157) asserts that Africa has an indigenous normative framework in the form of *ubuntu* which was regrettably misunderstood and deliberately overlooked since contact with colonialism:

> The so-called 'African concept of human rights' is therefore actually a concept of human dignity. The individual feels respect and worthiness as a result of his or her fulfilment of the socially approved role. Any rights that might be held are dependent on one's status or contingent on one's behaviour. Such a society may well provide the individual with a great deal of security and protection. He adds that one may even argue that people may well value such dignity more than their freedom to act as individuals. In relatively homogeneous static and small-scale societies, this tendency is likely to be stronger than the tendency towards individualism' (Nhlapo 1995:30).

Mahao (2000:35) further points out that humanness has always been engraved in the African way of living. What is required is that Judges must have the appetite to infuse African jurisprudence when adjudicating on disputes. An example is *Dalindyebo v State*, where an opportunity to develop the African philosophy of ubuntu was wasted in the interpretation of the criminality of a king or queen within the framework of indigenous value knowledge (Ntlama 2019:207). The court could have developed the concept of the 'king can do no wrong' and enabled the infusion of African criminal law into the determination of the guilt of the king. Mahao points out that a person cannot have rights rooted in human rights while he or she lives in wretched conditions. This form of human rights is limiting and deprives the individual of self-worth and respect. In *MEC for Education: Kwazulu Natal v Pillay (2006 (10) BCLR 1237 (CC),* the Court emphasised that "cultural identity is one of the most important part of a person's identity precisely because it flows from belonging to a community and not from personal choice or achievement". Indigenous law protects the dignity of a person but integrates all the collective elements that complete a person, such as his or her collective identity, including his/her relationship with the living dead, moreover with his or her spiritual, physical and cultural and material worth (Mahao 2010:326).

The legitimate purpose served by African value systems and human rights cannot be understood by randomly asking what a rule, concept or doctrine entails, without an understanding of the context to which such rules and doctrines apply (Ndima 2003:328). Decisions that have been made on human rights such as the right to equality and dignity in indigenous law in a Western setting have often been hailed as progressive and perhaps as providing a platform to open further dialogues on other indigenous law practices that may be inconsistent with western human rights (Perumal 2010:103). Human rights may not always serve a purpose in the context of indigenous law because of the limiting nature in which they are applied except to obliterate indigenous law. The concern for indigenous law today is that it has not escaped the reputational damage caused by colonisation, which created the context in which it is widely understood today. Admittedly, to the outsider, at face value indigenous law has elements that appear to be gender discriminatory. For example, Ademiluka argues that indigenous law is patriarchal. In support of his argument, he refers to the fact that women carry their husbands' surnames, which illustrates male domination (Ademiluka 2018:349). This argument illustrates ignorance because the carrying of surnames by women in indigenous law has nothing to do with masculinity. Women from Nguni ethnic groups carry their maiden surnames after marriage. An example of this is the fact that the wives of the former president of South Africa, Mr Jacob Zuma, carry their maiden names. His first wife is addressed as MaKhumalo, which is her maiden surname.

In the contemporary world, women have options of carrying their maiden names after marriage or of carrying double-barrel names. Courts determine the true meaning of practices, so they can give effect to them without distortions. Women have been and remain the custodians of indigenous knowledge systems and their contributions cannot be ignored. An example is the kingdom of Modjadji where women are revered for their ability to make rain for their people. The Modjadji kingdom is well managed. African kings such as Shaka, Moshoeshoe, Mswati, Makhado and Sekhukhune are revered at her site (Ivanovic 2015:41). Courts can force change on constitutional grounds to achieve gender equality. This, however, will not have a buy-in from communities. This is because communities must feel obligated to observe norms. There is thus a need to provide a synopsis of how gender roles were defined free of colonial contamination. To show how, through contact with colonialism, gender roles were impacted. This is important when one considers that the right to equality is the central theme of the existing South African constitutional order (Davies 1999:400).

A broad view of looking at the issue of gender equality in indigenous law is ignored which does not look at the difference between men and women through gendered lenses (Ndima 2013:56). Accordingly, practices such as primogeniture should be understood in terms of the legitimate role they serve. This is based on the social, political and legal organisation of society where the interests of vulnerable members must be protected. Men were anointed with accountability for vulnerable groups, particularly women and children. This does not mean that masculinity played a role. The way the court went about achieving gender equality in cases such as *Shilubana*, is problematic because the court limited the right to equality within the framework of customary law (Ntlama 2012:344). This re-affirmed the position of indigenous law as the subservient legal system to the common law. This depicts indigenous knowledge systems as having internal limitations while the Western human rights in the Constitution are expressed as being tailor made to address the shortcomings of indigenous value systems. This cannot be the basis for bringing about a balance between two competing value systems (Ntlama 2012:344). There is a need and value in adopting an approach that is grounded in the traditions and practices of indigenous culture. This approach can help ensure that the legal system is more accessible and relevant to the people it serves.

Gender defined roles in African law are complementary rather than an advance of masculinity. Within the African set-up, both men and women played significant roles. While a male could be the head of the family, a woman could occupy the important role of mother of the family or queen mother. She had to undergo certain training in accordance with custom before she could be made mother of the family. Acquiring maturity, this training enabled her to embrace the collective families' needs. This, however, is not to strengthen stereotyping that women needed training to acquire maturity. As stated earlier, the ability to occupy the position of head of the family and, in this case, mother of the family, depended on character traits. One who did not have them automatically was presented with opportunities to acquire the necessary skills. Women were traditionally not confined to the kitchen in African law; they assumed more challenging leadership roles in national discourse. There have always been female heroes, such as warrior queen Mmanthatisi of the Batlokwa clan, Mmantshopa of the Basotho and Nongqawuse of the amaXhosa, who contributed immensely to the history of their clans (Mahao 2010:325).

Towards A Pluriversal Approach to Human Rights

There is potential danger in rejecting Western values in the development of human rights jurisprudence as this may limit the scope and potential of a legal system. Western legal systems have developed over centuries, with input from diverse cultures and traditions, and have been refined through trial and error. By disregarding these values, one may risk limiting the scope of the indigenous legal system and potentially missing important ideas and practices that could help improve indigenous society. However, what is important is not to hegemonize human rights but to recognise that human rights from an African perspective also have a role to play. Grosfoguel (2007:212) argues for a departure from the universal claim to morality to a legal and knowledge system that is 'pluriversal', which will allow other systems to participate in forming and shaping law, morality and the idea of civil rights. This is important because colonial culture must be ditched and this is more than about replacing wigged and robed white Judges with wigged and robed black Judges. This requires that one ought to be careful with what is fought for in a struggle. Indigenous people should not merely fight for human rights as if their legal system does not offer them (Cachalia 2018:385). What is emphasized is the recognition of indigenous value systems to play a role in indigenous disputes in court. Appointments of women to traditional leadership is not a problem, nor is any measure to achieve gender equality.

However, such appointments must be conferred while considering their implications in terms of indigenous law. In *Ludidi v Ludidi 2018 ALL SA 1 (SCA)*, the daughter of the late Chief Manzodidi was his only child, the Chief shared a father with Chief Manzezulu, their father was Chief Dyubhele Ludidi. Chief Manzezulu passed away in 1978 and was survived by his wife and only daughter, who was 12 years old when he passed away. Mr Ludidid Ludidi challenged Ms Nolitha Ludidi as the Chief of the *amaHlubi* (the decision) by the member of the Executive Council for Cooperation, Governance and Traditional Affairs, province of the Eastern Cape, MEC, pursuant to her identification as such by the Hlubi Royal family. Mr Ludidi Ludidi wanted the decision to appoint Ms Nolitha Ludidi as inkosi to be reviewed and set aside and for him to be recognised as the *Inkosi* of the *amaHlubi*. The Eastern Cape Local Division dismissed this. The SCA dismissed the appeal, thus recognising Ms Nolitha Ludidi as the rightful Inkosi. As stated above, this contribution is not against the appointment of women to the position of Inkosi. It, however, argues that the implications of such a decision should be considered on the lineage of the families and communal interests. Ntlama (2020:17-18) argues that the purpose behind affirming the appointment of women into traditional leadership is done to achieve gender equality, which in fact has the effect of undermining the rights of women:

> They subject women to the unnecessary pressure of undermining their own privacy and reproductive rights because they will have to make, for example, uncomfortable choices about their private lives, such as to decide whether they will have children or not, or even if they will get married. If they opt for the latter, they cannot marry with the "throne" to the marital family.

When courts only focus on gender equality instead of the duties and responsibilities of communal interests, the court is giving effect to colonial distortions perpetuated by the Black Administration Act. Whereby rigid gender discrimination rules were imposed when indigenous law as a legal and knowledge system was not discriminatory (Claassens & Mnisi 2009:499). After this, the government of the day was reluctant to grant land to women and had marriages automatically defaulting out of the community of property. The focus on gender equality to reform indigenous law by courts has the consequence that succession is given to people who lack family responsibility (Himonga and Nhlapo 2014:168). One should pause to imagine the consequences of having a leader who decides to sell family property for personal gains. This is not in the best interests of the family at large. The decision of who should be head of the family should thus be dependent on one's ability to execute their responsibilities towards family and children. The question can be asked in the wake of judgments such as *Shilubana v Nwamitwa* whether the woman appointed as *hosi*, had over the years acquired the required character traits to lead the clan? If not, what consequences is this likely to befall on the wellbeing of the family property? Himonga and Nhlapo (2014:68) argue that *Shilubana* brings uncertainty to the following scenarios:

> (a) Whether the amendment was not unnecessary since the son of the previous traditional leader was available, ready and able to succeed his father; (b) What the implications of the appointment of a woman to such a position would be where the woman was married to a commoner, with whom she had children, and therefore could not produce a successor to the traditional leadership position; (c) The validity of the court's reliance on the flexibility of living customary law to provide a future solution when the time to succeed the woman came after such conditions of uncertainty had been created.

While judgments such as *Ludidi* are an indigenous law succession dispute, there is nothing African about the solution the court deploys. The court ignores the importance of a lineage in an indigenous law context which is priceless even from an ancestral perspective. Ramose (2007:323) explains the importance of this issue in the following terms:

> The community in African culture is an ethical entity comprising the living, the living dead and the yet to be born. The critical ethical concern is to recognize and abide by the obligation to maintain and preserve harmonious relations within these

three dimensions of the community. For many of the indigenous conquered peoples, a name is an identity card that opens up the genealogy and history of the bearer of that name. As such it is the affirmation of connections and relations with the extended family, the living dead (ancestors) and the community from which the name-bearer originates.

The court did not have to destroy certainty in succession to traditional leadership but could have achieved gender equality without obliterating the African value systems. For example, it could have appointed Ms Shilubana as a queen mother, which could have enabled a situation where there is a return to a male successor to the throne. Similarly, when a king such as Inkosi Dalindyebo has violated human rights by kidnapping and torturing people, he is responsible for protecting, and then this is against indigenous law. The crime cannot be treated as if the problem is a lack of human rights from indigenous law. The problem is the king in this case, but this does not mean indigenous law does not have a mechanism to address his crimes though its human rights script as embodied in *ubuntu*. The problem is the total exclusion of human rights from an indigenous law perspective. Indigenous knowledge system has a normative framework in the form of *ubuntu*, which integrates human rights. The problem is the exclusion of African concepts of human rights from judicial pronouncements. For example, pre-colonial societies had measures of holding kings accountable and ensuring that they protect African concepts of human rights (Ayittey 2010:1185). Courts miss opportunities to integrate the African concept of *ubuntu* in the interpretation of human rights within the framework of indigenous law disputes (Ntlama 2020:209). Traditional courts are available to resolve disputes but parties often refer their disputes to mainstream courts where the focus is on individual than group interests

Conclusion

The African indigenous value system has not escaped its colonial subjugation where it was treated as inferior. Today, human rights such as the right to equality and dignity are imposed into indigenous law disputes. However, the problem is that this is done by accepting these rights in their western setting and no attempt is made to look at the indigenous human rights jurisprudence as encapsulated in the concept of *ubuntu* and communalism. The African indigenous knowledge system has a lot to contribute and it is important to look at a pluriversal system where human rights from an African perspective are allowed to participate and the law is decolonised from being heavily Eurocentric dominated. The concern is the lack of application of communalism and *ubuntu* and an understanding of gender equality from an indigenous law perspective. The interpretation of rights is solely focused on giving effect to human rights from a common law perspective where emphasis is only on the individual.

References

ADEMILUKA, S. O., (2018) Patriarchy and Women Abuse: Perspectives from Ancient Israel and Africa. *Old Testament Essays*, 31(2), 339-362.

AYITTEY, G. B. N., (2010) Traditional Institutions and the State of Accountability in Africa. *Social Research*, 77(4), 1183-1210.

BEKKER, J. C., RAUTENBACH, C. and GOOLAM, N. M. I. (2018) *Introduction to Legal pluralism in South Africa*. New York, Lexis-Nexis.

BENNETT, T. A., (1991) The Compatibility of African Customary Law and Human Rights. *Acta Juridica*, 18, 18-35.

CACHALIA, F. (2018) Democratic Constitutionalism in the Time of the Post Colony: Beyond Triumph and Betrayal. *South African Journal of Human Rights*, 34(3), 375-397.

CHURCH, J. (2005) *The Place Of Indigenous Law in a Mixed Legal System and a Society in Transformation: A South African Experience*. [Online]. Available from: https://www.escr-net.org/sites/default/files/Church.pdf

CLAASSENS, A. and MNISI, C., (2009) Rural women redefining land rights in the context of living customary law. *South African Journal of Human Rights*, 25(3), 491-516.

COMAROFF, J. and COMAROFF, J. L., (2004) Policing Culture, Cultural Policing Law and Social Order in Post-Colonial South Africa. *Law and Social Inquiry*, 29(3), 513-545.

DAVIES, D. M., (2003) Constitutional Borrowing: The Influence of Legal Culture and Local History in the Reconstitution of Comparative Influence: The South African experience. *International Journal of Constitutional Law*, 1(2), 181–195.

DAVIES, D. M., (1999) Equality: The majesty of Legoland jurisprudence. *South African Law Journal*, 116, 398-413.

GROSFOGUEL, R., (2007) The Epistemic Decolonial Turn. *Cultural Studies*, 21(3), 211-223.

GROSFOGUEL, R., (2013). The Structure of Knowledge in Westernised Universities: Epistemic Racism/Sexism and the Four Genocides/Epistemicides of the Long 16th Century. *Journal of the Sociology of Self Knowledge*, 1, 72-90.

HIGGINS, T. E., FENRICH J. G. P. and TANZER, Z., (2011) *Customary Law, Gender Equality, and the Family: The Promise and Limits of Choice Paradigm*. [Online]. Available from: https://www.researchgate.net/publication/292422862_Customary_la w_gender_equality_and_the_family_the_promise_and_limits_of_a_choice_paradigm

HIMONGA, C. and NHLAPHO, T., (2014) *African Customary Law in South Africa: Post-Apartheid and Living Law Perspectives*. Cape Town, Oxford University Press.

IVANOVIC, M., (2015) The Role of Tribal Authorities in Rural Tourism Development in South Africa: The Case of the Kingdom of the Rain King. *African Journal for Physical, Health education, Recreation and Dance*, 1, 37-54.

KAGANAS, F., (1994) The Contest between Culture and Gender Equality under South Africa's Interim Constitution. *Journal of Law and Society*, 21, 409-433.

KLUG, H., (2018) Decolonisation, Compensation and Constitutionalism: Land, Wealth and the Sustainability of Constitutionalism in Post-Apartheid South Africa. *South African Journal of Human Rights*, 34(3), 469-491.

KLUG, H., (2010). Finding the Constitutional Court's Place in South Africa's Democracy: The Interaction of the Principle and Institutional Pragmatism in the Court's Decision Making. *Constitutional Court Review*, 3, 1-32.

MAHAO, T., (2000) '*O Se Re Ho Morwa 'Morwa Towe!'* African Jurisprudence Exhumed. *Comparative and International Law of Southern Africa*, 43(3), 317-336.

MBATHA, L., (2002) Reforming the Customary Law of Succession. *South African Journal of Human Rights*, 18, 259-286.

NDIMA, D. D., (2013) *Re-Imagining and Re-Interpreting African Jurisprudence under the South Africa Constitution.* Pretoria, University of South Africa.

NDIMA, D. D., (2003) The African Law of the 21st Century in South Africa. *Comparative and International Journal of Southern Law*, 35(3), 325-345.

NHLAPO, T., (1995) African Customary Law in the Interim Constitution. In S. Liebenberg. (ed.). *The Constitution of South Africa from Gender Perspective*. Cape Town, University of Cape Town.

NTLAMA, N., (2019) *The Centrality of Customary Law in the Judicial Resolution of Disputes that Emanate from it – Dalisile v Mgoduka (5056/2018) [2018] ZAECMHC.* [Online]. Available from: https://obiter.mandela.ac.za/article/view/11199#:~:text=Abstract,from%20a%20 customary%2Dlaw%20context.

NTLAMA, N., (2020). *The Changing Identity on Succession to Chieftaincy in the Institution of Traditional Leadership: Mphephu v Mphephu-Ramabulana (948/17) [2019] ZASCA 58.* [Online]. Available from: http://www.scielo.org.za/scielo.php?pid=S1727-37812020000100020&script=sci_abstract

PERUMAL, P., (2011) Harmonising Cultural and Equality Rights under the Customary Law-Some Reflections on Shilubana v Nwamitwa 2009 (1) SA 66 (CC) 2010. *Agenda*, 24(84), 101-110.

LERNER, G., (1989) *The Creation of Patriarchy*. Oxford, Oxford University Press.

LEWIS, L., (2015) Judicial "Translation" and Contextualization of Values: Rethinking the Development of Customary Law in Mayelane. *Potchefstroom Electronic Law Journal*, 18(4), 1126-1161.

RAMOSE, M. B., (2007) In Memoriam: Sovereignty and the 'New' South Africa. *Griffith Law Review*, 16(2), 310-329.

SMITH, A., (2008) Constitutionalizing Equality: The South African Experience. *International Journal of Discrimination and the Law,* 9, 201-219.

WALKER, C. (2005) Women, Gender Policy and Land Reform in South Africa, *Politikon*, 32, 297-315.

Domestication of Disability Rights in Southern Africa: Lessons from a Zimbabwean Experience

Muzondo Edward, Taruvinga Muzingili and Tauya Chinama

Introduction

Persons with disabilities represent one of the most marginalised minority groups in the world (United Nations Division of Social and Economic Development 2021), hence their needs and concerns are commonly not taken into consideration, bottled-up and given sub-standard attention. The United Nations Children's Fund (2022) estimates a disability prevalence of 15% of the world population or more than 1 billion people. Further, more than 80% of persons with disabilities live in developing countries and more than half of them are women (United Nations Division of Social and Economic Development 2021). Persons with disabilities (PWDs) have specific human rights, responsibilities and entitlements they should enjoy at an equal level with the non-disabled without any restrictions. These rights do not exist separately from the broader human rights family but they are an offshoot of them. Disability rights are designed to promote, protect and safeguard the welfare of persons with disabilities and they are codified in international, regional as well as national legislations and human rights instruments. These include the Universal Declaration of Human Rights, United Nations Convention on the Rights of Persons with Disabilities, and the Protocol to the African Charter on Human and People's Rights on the Rights of Persons with Disabilities among others.

Notwithstanding the existence of laws that enforce the enjoyment of disability rights in Southern Africa, persons with disabilities are continuously living in subjugated circumstances. Chief among them being difficulties in accessing the physical environment such as buildings, recreational facilities as well as information platforms. In addition, PWDs face attitudinal barriers characterised by social stigma and structural discrimination in political and economic spheres of life. This chapter uses a cogent argumentative approach to analyse the extent to which the government of Zimbabwe domesticates international and regional human rights laws into its own institutional and legislation frameworks on disability. The chapter gives a historical overview of disability rights from a global, regional and local perspectives. It also discusses various models and principles that underpin the rights and welfare of persons with disabilities and conclude by highlighting the prospects that social workers and other helping professionals should consider in order to ensure the maximum realisation of disability rights in Zimbabwe and beyond.

Models of Disability Rights

The way some people understand or misunderstand disability has a strong bearing on the living experiences of persons with disabilities. The conceptualization of disability can be best understood using models of disability. There are two groups of models that define the historical development of disability rights. The first group comprises traditional models such as the religious, charity and the medical models. According to Oliver (1990), traditional models put the blame on an individual with a disability, subjecting them to further tribulations. The second group is made up of contemporary models such as the social and the human rights models of disability. Unlike the traditional models of disability that blame an individual with a disability, modern models put the blame into the environment that disables persons with impairments (Oliver 1990). The following section discusses the influence of models of disability in the development of disability rights and laws in Zimbabwe.

Historically, disability has been partly perceived as a charity or a medical issue. Some people understood disability as an individual's pathology and the blame was in the person with a disability (Mtetwa 2014). The religious model regarded disability as a curse from the gods because of one's or family's sins (Chavhunduka 1993). According to this model, a person with a disability should be exorcised as a way of restoring one's normalcy. On that basis, "if parents give birth to a child with a disability, either the father or the mother should testify for any wrongdoings" (Lang and Murangira 2009:34). This mythical understanding surrounding disability led many parents, especially fathers to desert their families after conceiving a baby with a disability (Mtetwa 2012). Similarly, the charity model views disability as a personal tragedy. This model avers that persons with disabilities are charity cases, idle, helpless and therefore should be pitied for. According to the charity model, persons with disabilities are people in need of care. This model views disability as a burdensome condition. It also views persons with disabilities as passive and inactive members of society (Oliver 1992).

According to the medical model, disability is understood as a remedial problem that needs medical attention to "fix" or "cure" an individual (Murray and Long 2015). A person with a disability is viewed as a sick person and is required to assume Talcott Parsons' 'sick role'. The medical model views disability from a curative perspective where any engagement with a disabled person should be designed to cure their ailment not empowerment. Choruma (2007) argues that models used by a country in managing disability affairs have direct implications on the welfare and rights of persons with disabilities. Traditional models were criticised for labelling persons with disabilities as charity cases, the cursed and sick (Mtetwa 2012). In the 1980s, Zimbabwe's response to disability issues was largely dominated by the works of Jairos Jiri Association for the Disabled and the Blind (Mtetwa 2012). This association provided charity and rehabilitation services to persons with disabilities with less focus given to environmental changes in order to accommodate persons with impairments. As such, through the Jairos Jiri Association for the Disabled and the Blind, perspectives for community based rehabilitation for PWDs was a far-fetched dream because they were institutionalised and taken care of by the association.

Defining disability simply as a charity case or a medical situation overlooks the many barriers that prevent persons with disabilities from enjoying their rights. This automatically disempowers and marginalises persons with disabilities since they are relegated to people without rights. Traditional models of disability have a negative implication on the design and implementation of disability policies. According to Manatsa (2015), the Disabled Persons Act of 1992 looked at persons with disabilities from a charity model. This involves a situation whereby persons with disabilities are looked upon as people in need of hand-outs, donations and direct care from the non-disabled. This violates their right to participation on an equal basis with other people. As such, the limitations of the traditional models led to the development of more empowering and sustainable models discussed below.

As a response to the deficits of traditional models of disability, various scholars, authors and policy makers advocated for the adoption of newer models of defining disability (Oliver 1990, 1992; Mtetwa 2015). The religious, charity and medical models of disability were superseded by new models that reflect on the social and human rights of persons with disabilities. The social model of disability believes that society disables people with impairments (Rioux & Cabert 2010; Mtetwa 2021). The blame was taken from an impaired person to his or her environment. According to Quinn (2002), disability lies in the environment not in the person. Under this view, society limits the participation of persons with impairments by creating obstacles such as inaccessible buildings, unfriendly transport systems, inaccessible information platforms and bad attitude towards a person with an impairment. For example, during COVID-19, information concerning how the virus spread, associated effects of contracting the virus and how to protect oneself from the virus was made available through the social media with less consideration of people with hearing and visual impairments (Mtetwa 2021; Mtetwa 2014; Manatsa 2015). This shows that the way society is structured infringes the rights of persons with disabilities to accessing information. This was supposed to be solved when that same information was made accessible through braille formats to cater for the visually impaired.

Correspondingly, the human rights model of disability builds on the view that people with disabilities have rights and responsibilities without discrimination. Under the human rights model, persons with disabilities are identified as rights holders and subjects of human rights law on an equal basis with all other persons (Yeo and Moore 2003; Brendan et al 2021). Using this model, a person with an impairment is recognized and respected as a component of natural human diversity on the same basis as race or gender. The model helps to deal with disability-specific prejudices, attitudes and other barriers to the enjoyment of human rights. The human rights model places the responsibility on governments and society for ensuring that the political, legal, social, and physical environments are disability friendly. The model dictates that society must support the maximum realisation and enjoyment of human rights by persons with disabilities. This includes participation in the employment sector, in business and politics as well as social life including marriage and starting a family. This gave a bearing to the development of the United Nations Convention on the Rights of Persons with Disabilities (UNCRPD) and the African Charter on the Rights of Persons with Disabilities. The following section gives an elucidation of the principles of disability rights as espoused in these two global and regional disability policy instruments.

Understanding the UNCRPD and the African Charter

At a global level, the United Nations Convention on the Rights of Persons with Disabilities (UNCRPD) serves as the utmost policy instrument that reflects the rights of persons with disabilities. Similarly, the Protocol to the African Charter on Human and People's Rights on the Rights of Persons with Disabilities (herein referred as the Charter) serves as an African continental tool that obliges member states to promote and protect disability rights. Zimbabwe has ratified these policy instruments and was applauded as the model country for disability rights in Africa and the world (Manatsa 2015), however the slow execution of these laws into practice has proven that ratification alone is not equal to implementation. These two laws (UNCRPD and the Charter) were specifically made to address the rights and responsibilities of persons with disabilities in the world and in Africa, respectively. As such, the authors analysed them to see the degree of compliance by the Zimbabwean government in the domestication of these laws.

The UN Convention on the Rights of Persons with Disabilities (UNCRPD) under article 1 recognizes that "persons with disabilities include those who have long-term physical, mental, intellectual or sensory impairments which in interaction with various barriers may hinder their full and effective participation in society on an equal basis with others" (United Nations Human Rights, 2016:12). The UNCRPD stipulates that the convention is designed "to promote, protect and ensure the full and equal enjoyment of all human rights and fundamental freedoms by all persons with disabilities, and to promote respect for their inherent dignity" (Brendan et al 2021). The convention is guided by a number of principles that include non-discrimination, accessibility and equality of opportunities among other principles. This convention sets parameters to which all member countries should oblige when developing disability laws and programs including Zimbabwe.

Article 4(1a) of the convention stipulates that state parties should adopt all appropriate legislative, administrative and other measures for the implementation of the rights of persons with disabilities. It goes on stating that member countries should take all appropriate measures, including legislation, to modify or abolish existing laws, regulations, customs and practices that constitute discrimination against persons with disabilities. Considerably, the Protocol to the African Charter on Human and People's Rights on the Rights of Persons with Disabilities in Africa is an extension of the United Nations convention, but with a streamlined focus on the African continent. Zimbabwe through the Constitution and the National Disability Policy of 2021 has tried to put this into practice though some areas need to be improved. This is greatly discussed below in the domestication section of the chapter.

The Convention and the Charter represent a shift in approach to persons with disabilities at international and regional policy level respectively. These two human rights treaties provide a normative authority to member states and oblige countries to put in place laws, policies and programmes that ensure the realisation of disability rights within their jurisdictions (Manatsa 2015). It can be noted that governments are increasingly viewing the rights of their citizens in a manner consistent with international and regional human rights codes. In line with the United Nations Universal Declaration of Human Rights of 1948, all people have certain civil, political, economic, social, cultural, and development rights, despite differences between individuals.

Principles Guiding the UNCRPD and the African Charter

The Convention and the Charter successfully put forward a number of principles that guide the implementation of disability rights by member states. These principles are regarded as general requirements for all disability rights and influence the interpretation and implementation of disability programming at national level. Article 3 of the UNCRPD provides eight general principles that include non-discrimination, accessibility, equal opportunity, full and effective participation and inclusion as well as protection during risk situations (African Union 2018). These guiding principles are also reflected in article 3 of the African Charter, although the Charter has two more principles that include respect for the evolving capacities of persons with disabilities and respect for the right of persons with disabilities to preserve their identities.

The principle of non-discrimination as stated under article 5 of the UNCRPD stipulates that persons with disabilities should be treated fairly regardless of race, ethnic group, sex, language or religion. The principle advocates for the promotion of disability rights without favouritism and no person with a disability should be subjected to unfair treatment. On the same note, article 5(1) of the African Charter stipulates that "every person with a disability shall be entitled to the enjoyment of the rights and freedoms without distinction of any kind on any ground including, race, ethnic group, colour, sex, language, religion, political or any other opinion, national and social origin, fortune, birth or any status" (African Union 2018:4). Article 4(2a) of the Charter goes on arguing that states parties shall prohibit discrimination on the basis of disability and guarantee to persons with disabilities equal and effective legal protection against discrimination on all grounds.

Article 9 of the UNCRPD focuses on the right of persons with disabilities to accessibility. The right to access was deemed in the sense of accessing the physical environment and information systems. The convention argues that state parties "shall take appropriate measures to ensure that persons with disabilities access, on an equal basis with others, to the physical environment, to transportation, to information and communications, including information and communications technologies and systems, and to other facilities and services open or provided to the public, both in urban and in rural areas" (UNCRPD, Article 9). This involves the identification and elimination of all obstacles and barriers to accessing buildings, roads, transport, schools, recreational facilities and information and communications systems. On the same note, article 15 of the African Charter stipulates that every person with a disability has the right to barrier free access to the physical environment, transportation, information, including communications technologies and systems, and other facilities and services open or provided to the public. The Charter demands state parties to take reasonable and progressive measures to facilitate full enjoyment of these rights by persons with disabilities both in rural and urban settings. Further, in article 9(d) it stipulates that responsible authorities should provide quality and affordable mobility aids, assistive devices or technologies and forms of live assistance and intermediaries to persons with disabilities.

Having acknowledged the level of marginalisation people with disabilities experienced for the past years, both the convention and the Charter provide for the provision of equal opportunities to persons with disabilities. The UNCRPD in article 5(3) recognizes that in order to promote equality and eliminate discrimination, member countries shall take all appropriate steps to ensure that reasonable accommodation is provided. Article 6(3) of the Charter stipulates that State Parties shall take all appropriate legislative, administrative, budgetary and other measures in order to promote equality for persons with disabilities. Equality of opportunities reveals that persons with disabilities should be able to participate in all sectors of the economy at an equal level with others. Be it in the employment sector, qualified persons with disabilities should be given reasonable accommodation to enjoy those similar rights together with the non-disabled. Reasonable accommodation has been defined in the African Charter as the necessary and appropriate modifications and adjustments where needed in a particular case, to ensure to persons with disabilities the enjoyment or exercise on an equal basis with others of all human and people's rights. The provision of reasonable accommodation gives persons with disabilities an added advantage when competing in the market economy together with others and this guiding principle should be accorded for by all member states.

In Southern Africa, persons with disabilities have been historically subjected to cultural harmful practices such as torture and ritual killings. The Charter argues that harmful practices include behaviours, attitudes and practices based on tradition, culture, religion, superstition or other reasons, which negatively affect the human rights and fundamental freedoms of persons with disabilities. This practice perpetuates the discrimination of persons with disabilities on the ground of their disability. As such, article 11 of the UNCRPD stipulates that member countries shall take all necessary measures to ensure the protection and safety of persons with disabilities in situations of risk, including situations of armed conflict, humanitarian emergencies and the occurrence of natural disasters. Article 10(2a) of the Charter reiterates that state parties shall take appropriate and effective measures to ensure that persons with disabilities, on an equal basis with others are not subjected to torture or cruel, inhuman or degrading treatment or punishment. The convention and the Charter stipulate that persons with disabilities should be protected during risky situations. Situations of risks means any situation that poses grave risk to the general population, including disasters and all forms of armed conflict. Armed conflictual situations are prevalent in Southern Africa especially in Mozambique. These situations expose persons with disabilities to dangers and harmful practices, hence the need to be protected during such times.

Domestication of UNCRPD and the African Charter in Zimbabwe

The UNCRPD and the African Charter as policy instruments embrace a paradigm shift from a social welfarism to a human rights-based approach on disability issues. Persons with disabilities are no longer viewed as objects of charity or as people in need of medical assistance but as individuals with full rights, responsibilities and entitlements. Zimbabwe has recognized the rights of persons with disabilities through its laws, policies and programmes. Reference should be given to three key disability laws in Zimbabwe that are the Disabled Persons Act Chapter 17:01 of 1992, the Constitution of Zimbabwe amendment 20 of 2013 and the National Disability Policy of 2021.

The Government of Zimbabwe amended the Disabled Persons Act (DPA) Chapter 17:01 in 1992, which is the major law that governs disability affairs in the country. The DPA was enacted in 1992 while the UNCRPD and the Charter were adopted in 2006 and 2018 respectively. Thus the DPA is way much older than these two supreme laws. However, despite the disparities in the enactment of such laws, the DPA has some areas where it aligns well with the UNCRPD and the Charter, although more needs to be amended. According to the DPA, a disabled person is a person with a physical, mental or sensory disability, including a visual, hearing or speech functional disability, which give rise to physical, cultural or social barriers inhibiting him or her from participating at an equal level with other members of society in activities, undertakings or fields of employment that are open to other members of society. In the same vein, the UNCRPD and the Charter define persons with disabilities as those who have physical, mental, psycho-social, intellectual, neurological, developmental or other sensory impairments which in interaction with environmental, attitudinal or other barriers hinder their full and effective participation in society on an equal basis with others. Manatsa (2015) maintains that the DPA definition is archaic and fails to identify the fact that disability is not only limited to individual impairments but also to barriers caused by both attitudinal and environmental factors. The Act's definition adopts the traditional models of disability by putting the blame on the individual with an impairment. This needs to be revised and aligned to modern definitions as prescribed by the UNCRPD and the Charter.

With reference to the principle of non-discrimination, the DPA is an overdrive towards inclusion of persons with disabilities. Mwenda (2009) hold that the DPA covers two main areas that prohibits discrimination against persons with disabilities namely access to public premises, services and amenities as well as employment at an equal level with other non-disabled persons. This drive to inclusion and participation influenced Zimbabwean companies and organisations to develop Disability Affirmation and Compulsory Quota Policies whereby a certain percentage was considered for persons with disabilities in their employment criteria. According to SIDA (2022) an estimate of 386 million of the world's working age are people with disabilities and these people have the potential to make a valuable contribution in the workforce, as employees, entrepreneurs or employers of others. The affirmative approach extends to public institutions of higher and tertiary education where universities have a certain section or department that caters for the welfare of persons with disabilities. For example, the University of Zimbabwe has a Disability Resource

Center (DRC) that recognizes the welfare of students with disabilities at the institution.

The Constitution of Zimbabwe recognises the inherent dignity, equality and rights of all citizens including persons with disabilities. These founding principles are well in line with the guiding principles of both the UNCRPD and the Charter. Manatsa (2015) argues that the provision of the founding principles upon which Zimbabwe is built is a commendable move since they have recognised the rights of persons with disabilities among such pertinent values. These founding principles are of utmost significance because they bind the State and all institutions of government at every level. The recognition of the rights of persons with disabilities among the founding values gives an appreciation of the equal worth of all human beings in Zimbabwe. In line with article 1 of the UNCRPD and article 1 of the African Charter which recognize all forms of disabilities including physical, mental, intellectual and or sensory disabilities and persons with multiple disabilities, the constitution also recognizes persons with various forms of disability including those with hearing impairments. According to Mtetwa (2015) the constitution seemingly goes a long way in protecting and promoting the rights of persons with disabilities against any form of violations. This involves the promulgation in section 6(4) that sign language is one of Zimbabwe's official languages just like Shona, Ndebele, Tonga and other local languages. The sole mandate of the UNCRPD and the Charter is to oblige member states to promote the full and effective participation and inclusion of persons with disabilities in society as part of human diversity and humanity. This reveals that the government has moved a step towards the realisation of the rights of people with hearing and listening impairments in Zimbabwe as sign language is now made official nationwide. Section 6(4) obliges the State to promote, advance and create a conducive environment that facilitates the development of all official languages including sign language. However, there is still a need for thorough pragmatic inclusion of sign language practicals from elementary to tertiary levels in Zimbabwe. One can note with concern that many people graduate from high school and tertiary institutions without any basic skills of sign language. Therefore the authors argue that the Zimbabwean government needs to move beyond just spelling out law provisions on paper and start putting these instruments into practice in order to maximise the enjoyment of disability rights by people with impairments.

In Section 22(4), the Constitution provides that the state must take appropriate measures, within the limits of its resources, to ensure that buildings and amenities to which the public has access are disability friendly. This is in line with article 5 and 9 of UNCRPD which emphasises on prohibition of discrimination on the basis of disability. Article 5 states that persons with disabilities are entitled to equal protection and equal benefit of the law, which requires State parties to take appropriate measures to ensure reasonable accommodation is provided. Article 9 states that State parties must ensure that communications and information services, transportation systems, buildings and other structures are designed and constructed so that they can be used, entered or reached by persons with disabilities. Similarly, article 15 of the Charter states that every person with a disability has the right to barrier free access to the physical environment, transportation, information, including communications technologies and systems, and other facilities and services open or provided to the public. It further elucidates that State Parties shall take reasonable and progressive measures to facilitate full enjoyment by persons with disabilities of this right in both rural and urban settings. However, accessibility of the physical environment especially government and other buildings in Zimbabwe is a daunting task since they are not disability friendly, no working ramps and no provision of sign language in staircase lifts. The transport system in Zimbabwe is not easily accessible to persons with disabilities, especially those who use wheelchairs. This critically discriminates against persons with disabilities' right to accessibility.

The Constitution of Zimbabwe has made an official commitment to disability affairs through its promulgation in the founding values and in section 22. This is in line with article 4 of the Charter which reiterates that States Parties shall take appropriate and effective measures, including policy, legislative, administrative, institutional and budgetary steps, to ensure, respect, promote, protect and fulfil the rights and dignity of persons with disabilities, without discrimination on the basis of disability. The move by the constitution in recognizing the rights and welfare of persons with disabilities shows that Zimbabwe is somehow committed to alleviate poverty among persons with disabilities. The Constitution goes a long way to provide for the right to political participation by persons with disabilities. Section 155(b) of the Constitution states that every citizen who is eligible to vote in an election or referendum has an opportunity to cast a vote including persons with disabilities. This is pursuant to article 29 of the UNCRPD which mandates that State parties must take all feasible steps to facilitate and encourage participation of persons with disabilities in government and other civic activities, such as the right to vote, stand for election or participate in political organisations.

The constitution under section 120 stipulates that the senate should comprise eighty senators with section 120(1d) providing that two of them should be selected to represent persons with disabilities. These two senators should be persons with disabilities (Mandipa 2015). This shows the astounding commitment of the constitution and the government of Zimbabwe as a whole to the promotion of the rights and welfare of persons with disabilities. However, there is no direct mention of the protection of persons with disabilities in cases of armed conflict in Zimbabwe. This violates article 11 of the UNCRPD which directly states that in armed conflict or natural disasters States parties are required to take all appropriate additional measures to secure the safety of persons with disabilities. Article 12 of the Charter also stipulates that specific measures should be taken to ensure the protection and safety of persons with disabilities in situations of risk, including situations of armed conflict, forced displacements, humanitarian emergencies and natural disasters. Thus, the authors argue that the government of Zimbabwe should provide a law that directly protects persons with disabilities in situations of risk such as political demonstrations and civil unrest.

Zimbabwe had been working without any specific policy for persons with disabilities all the years. Through the provisions of the Disabled Persons Act of 1992 which set up the Director of Disability Affairs and the National Disability Board, these key personnel were instrumental in the formulation of the National Disability

Policy. The policy is hailed as a milestone in the promotion of human rights for persons with disabilities in the country. It seeks to address the marginalisation and discrimination of Persons with Disabilities, empower them to improve their own quality of life and enable them to contribute towards the national development agenda.

Just like the UNCRPD and the Charter, the National Disability Policy adopts the human rights model of disability whereby the responsibilities and entitlements of persons with disabilities are put into consideration in all facets of life including the public, private and development sectors. Through this policy, the government has called for an end to harmful practices, discrimination, marginalisation and exclusion of persons with disabilities from participating in different sectors of the economy. This is in line with article 11 of the Charter which states that States Parties shall take all appropriate measures and offer appropriate support and assistance to victims of harmful practices, including legal sanctions, educational and advocacy campaigns, to eliminate harmful practices perpetrated on persons with disabilities, including witchcraft, abandonment, concealment, ritual killings or the association of disability with omens. The policy adds that all government departments should mainstream disability issues in their programmes. This shuns the adoption of the charity model when engaging persons with disabilities.

The policy takes a social and human rights bearing in conceptualising disability affairs in Zimbabwe. It argues that institutions should treat persons with disabilities as equals who are capable of productively participating in the building of Zimbabwe. On a positive note, of which it is yet to be applauded for, the policy states that it seeks to inform the process of repealing the outdated Disabled Persons Act (17:01). This means the amended Disabled Persons Act will adopt the developmental models of understanding disability. This will help to strengthen the institutional and legal frameworks that enhance the maximum enjoyment of human rights by persons with disabilities.

Conclusion

Disability rights, like any other human rights, are important in the realisation of an equal and just society. The major achievement is seen in the country's constitution of 2013 which gives government and its partners mandatory responsibilities to implement disability centred policies and programmes. Persons with disabilities face challenges related to accessibility of basic services. In some cases, the ugly head of discrimination continues to be witnessed in various points of interaction in society. Apart from the legal position of repealing some obsolete legal frameworks, more efforts are needed to shift the cultural and social lenses of community on how they view the concept of disability.

Clearly, some disability laws are outdated and need to be repealed to suit the current demands and the changing operating environment. This applies to the Disabled People's Act Chapter 17:01 of 1992. The act has been criticised for taking a social welfaristic model of disability. Through the provisions of the National

Disability Policy of 2021, we are looking forward to having a glimpse of the proposed amended act. It has also been noted that Zimbabwe is good at putting laws on paper while neglecting the implementation part. This seriously affects the maximum realisation and enjoyment of human rights by persons with disabilities. For instance, the constitution provides for the right to accessibility which involves access to public spaces, physical environment including government buildings and transport systems. However, many of such physical environments discourage persons with disabilities from enjoying their rights since many buildings around the country do not have working ramps and lifts for people with physical impairments. The transport system is poorly organised and cannot properly accommodate persons with disabilities.

The promulgation of sign language as an official language in Zimbabwe was supposed to be followed with mandatory teaching of sign language in schools. This can be adopted the same way Zimbabwean education and employment systems adopt Mathematics and English as compulsory modules in schools. This helps to equip the general populace with some basic communication skills in sign language. Since the National Disability Policy is still new and trying to gain ground, we hope that it will go a long way in ensuring a maximum realisation of disability rights in Zimbabwe. There is a need for hands-on pragmatic approach to the implementation of disability laws and legislation in Zimbabwe. Rather than adopting a remedial approach to disability affairs, it is phenomenal to empower persons with disabilities so that they can dictate their own path of life not depending on charity.

The Constitution and the National Disability Policy are fairly aligned to the UNCRPD and the Charter. They make special reference to various types of disability from the definition to speculation of their rights and entitlements. However, there is a need for clear and direct provisions that protect people with disabilities during situations of risk. Unlike the Disabled People's Act that adopts a medical model to disability, the Constitution and the disability policy adopt the human rights model. This is a clear alignment to both the UNCRPD and the Charter. However, there is a lot that needs to be done in order to put the legal provisions into practice. Resources should be mobilised towards the empowerment of persons with disabilities. There is a need for more viable disability grants that should be easily accessible and be in a position to support persons with disabilities in their entrepreneurial endeavours.

References

AFRICAN UNION, (2018) *Protocol to the African Charter on Human and Peoples' Rights on the Rights of Persons with Disabilities in Africa.* [Online]. Available from: https://au.int/sites/default/files/treaties/36440-treaty-protocol_to_the_achpr_on_the_rights_of_persons_with_disabilities_in_africa_e.pdf

BRENDAN J. D, et al., (2021) *Sharing Lived Experiences Framework (SLEF): A Framework for Mental Health Practitioners when Making Disclosure Decisions.* [Online]. Available from: https://www.wypartnership.co.uk/application/files/8716/2091/7399/Sharing_Lived_Experiences_Framework_SLEF_a_framework_for_mental_health_practitioners_when_making_disclosure_decisions.pdf

CHAVHUNDUKA, G., (1993). *Witches and Healing in Southern Africa. Institute of Current World Leaders.* New Hampshire, Hanover.

CHORUMA T., (2007) *The Forgotten Tribe: Persons with Disabilities in Zimbabwe.* Harare, Progressio.

GOVERNMENT OF ZIMBABWE, (1992) *Disabled Persons Act Chapter 17.01.* Harare, Government Printers.

GOVERNMENT OF ZIMBABWE, (2021) *National Disability Policy 2021.* Harare, Government Printers.

LANG, R. and MURANGRIA, A., (2009) Barriers to Inclusion of people with disabilities in the Disability Policy-Making Process. In KUMPUVUORI, J. & SCHEININ, M. H. (eds.). *Disability Rights: A Multidisciplinary Perspectives.* The Centre for Human Rights of Persons with Disabilities, pp. 138-158.

LANG, R., SCHNEIDDER, M. COLE, E. and KETT, M., (2017) *Disability Inclusion in African Regional Policies: Policy review findings from the ESRC/DFID Bridging the Gap Disability and Development in Four African Countries Project.* [Online]. Available from: *https://www.researchgate.net/publication/320757243-*

MANATSA, P., (2015) Are disability laws in Zimbabwe compatible with the provisions of the United Nations Convention on the Rights of Persons with Disabilities (CRPD)? *International Journal of Humanities and Social Science Invention,* 4(4), 25-34.

MTETWA, E., (2010) Understanding the Plight of Persons with Disabilities in Zimbabwe and its Policy Implications: A Literature Review and Analysis. *International Journal of Humanities,* 2(3), 115-123.

MTETWA, E., (2021) The Policy Dimensions of Exclusion: Disability as Charity and not Right in Zimbabwe. *The Indian Journal of Social Work,* 72(3), 73-90.

MTETWA, E., (2012) The Dilemma of Social Difference: Disability and Institutional Discrimination in Zimbabwe. *Australian Journal of Human Rights,* 18(1), 169-199.

MTETWA, E., (2015) *Communities of Practice for Disability Advocacy and Mainstream COPDAM: A situational Analysis of National Policies and their Implications for Disability Mainstreaming.* [Online]. Available from: *http://www.lnfod.org.ls/uploads/1/2/2/5/12251792/final_copdam_baseline_study_2013.pdf*

MTETWA, E., (2014) Disability Policy and Practice in Zimbabwe. In J. Mugumbate. (Ed.). *Development Policy and Practice in Zimbabwe: Making Use of Census Data in Zimbabwe.* IDA Publishers, pp. 165-204.

MURRAY, R. and LONG, D., (2015) *The Implementation of the Findings of the African Commission on Human and Peoples' Rights.* Cambridge, Cambridge University Press.

MWENDWA, T. N., MURANGIRA, A. and LANG, R., (2009) Mainstreaming the Rights of Persons with Disabilities in National Development Frameworks. *Journal of International Development,* 21(5), 662-672.

RIOUX, M. and CABERT, A., (2010) Human rights and disability. *Journal on Developmental Disabilities*, 10(2), 1-14.

SIDA, (2022) *Disability Rights in sub-Saharan Africa.* [Online]. Available from: *https://www.sida.se/English/publications/Publication_database/publications-by-year3/2022/january/disability-as-a-human-rights-issue*

OLIVER, M., (1992) *Post-Positivism, Paradigms and Power: Disabling Research or Researching Disability?* Stockholm, Social Research about Disabilities.

OLIVER, M., (1990) *The Politics of Disablement.* London, Macmillan's Publishers.

QUINN G., DEGENER, T. and BRUCE, A., (2002) *Human Rights and Disability: the Current Use and Future Potential of United Nations Human Rights Instruments in the Context of Disability*. New York, United Nations Publications.

UNITED NATIONS DIVISION OF SOCIAL AND ECONOMIC DEVELOPMENT, (2011) *Including the rights of persons with disabilities in United Nations programming at country level: A Guidance Note for United Nations Country Teams and Implementing Partners*. New York, United Nations.

UNITED NATIONS HUMAN RIGHTS, (2016) *Convention on the Rights of Persons with Disabilities and Optional Protocol*. United Nations. New York, United Nations.

UNICEF, (2022) *UNICEF Disability Inclusion Policy and Strategy 2022-2030*. New York, Disability Section, UNICEF.

YEO, R. and MOORE, K., (2003) Disability and Poverty: the Need for a More Nuanced Understanding of Implications for Development Policy and Practice. *World Development,* 31(3), 571-590.

DOMUNI-PRESS
publishing house of DOMUNI Universitas

« Le livre grandit avec le lecteur »
"The book grows with the reader."

Domuni Universitas

Domuni Universitas was founded in 1999 by French Dominicans. It offers Bachelor, Master and Doctorate degrees by distance learning, as well as "à la carte" (stand-alone) courses and certificates in philosophy, theology, religious sciences, and social sciences (including both state and canonical diplomas). It welcomes several thousand students on its teaching platform, which operates in five languages: French, English, Spanish, Italian, and Arabic. The platform is accompanied by more than three hundred professors and tutors. Anchored in the Order of Preachers, Domuni Universitas benefits from its centuries-old tradition of study and research. Innovative in many ways, Domuni consists of an international network that offers courses to students worldwide.

To find out more about Domuni:

www.domuni.eu

The Publishing House

Domuni-Press disseminates research and publishes works in the academic fields of interest of Domuni Universitas: theology, philosophy, spirituality, history, religions, law and social sciences. Domuni-Press is part of a lively research community located at the heart of the Dominican network. Domuni-Press aims to bring readers closer to their texts by making it possible, via the help of today's digital technology, to have immediate access to them, while ensuring a quality paperback edition. Each work is published in both forms. The key word is simplicity. The subjects are approached with a clear editorial line: academic quality, accessible to all, with the aim of spreading the richness of Christian thought. Six collections are available: theology, philosophy, spirituality, Bible, history, law and social sciences. Domuni-Press has its own online bookshop: www.domunipress.fr. Its books are also available on its main distance selling website: Amazon, Fnac.com, and in more than 900 bookshops and sales outlets around the world.

To find out more about the publishing house:

www.domunipress.fr

EXTRACT FROM THE CATALOGUE

Jean-François ARNOUX,
Et le désert refleurira.

Sabine GINALHAC,
Désir d'enfant. L'éclairage inattendu des récits bibliques.

Pierrette FUZAT,
Un nom au bout de la nuit. Le combat de Jacob.

Patrice SABATER,
La terre en Palestine/Israël.

Marie MONNET,
Emmanuel Levinas. La relation à l'autre.

Apollinaire KIVYAMUNDA,
Maurice Zundel, une biographie spirituelle.

Juliette BORDES,
Viens Colombe. Saint Jean de la Croix.

Joseph MARTY,
Christianisme et Cinéma.

Michel VAN AERDE,
Le père retrouvé

Monique-Lise COHEN, Marie-Thérèse DESOUCHE,
Emmanuel Levinas et la pensée de l'infini.

Claire REGGIO,
Le christianisme des premiers siècles.

Ameer JAJE,
Diaconesses. Les femmes dans l'Église syriaque.

Jean-Paul COUJOU (sous la direction de),
L'État et le pouvoir.

Françoise DUBOST,
L'Évangile des animaux.

Markus JOST,
La Bible à l'école d'Ignace de Loyola et de Menno Simons.

Paul TAVARDON, ocso,
Trappistes en terre sainte. Des moines au cœur de la géopolitique. Latroun, 1890-1946 (T.1).

Paul TAVARDON, ocso,
Trappistes en terre sainte. Des moines au cœur de la géopolitique. Latroun, 1946-1991 (T.2).

Marie MONNET (sous la direction de),
La source théologique du droit.

Nilson Léal DE SA,
La vie fraternelle.

Apollinaire KIVYAMUNDA,
Maurice Zundel. La relation à Dieu.

Lara LOYE,
Fraternités.

Bernadette ESCAFFRE,
Vocations. Quand Dieu appelle.

Raphaël HAAS,
Pleine conscience. Bouddhisme et christianisme en dialogue.

Augustin WILIWOLI,
Axel Honneth. Lutter pour la reconnaissance.

Louis FROUART,
Pascal. Cœur, Corps, Esprit.

Emmanuel BOISSIEU,
Platon. Une manière de vivre.

Emmanuel BOISSIEU,
Kant. Une philosophie de la liberté.

Marie MONNET,
Dieu migrant.

Thérèse HEBBELINCK,
L'Église catholique et les juifs (T.1 et T.2).

Béatrice PAPASOGLOU,
Qu'est-ce que l'homme ?

Augustin WILIWOLI SIBILONI op,
Ce que les philosophes disent du vivre-ensemble.

François MENAGER,
Yves Bonnefoy, poète et philosophe.

Nicole AWAIS,
L'art d'enseigner le fait religieux.

Thérèse M. ANDREVON,
Une théologie à la frontière (T.1 et T2).

Michel VAN AERDE,
Venez vous reposer. Antidotes spirituels au burn-out.

Agnès GODEFROY,
Bien vieillir, dans les pas d'Abraham.

Olivier BELLEIL,
Résolution des conflits dans l'Église primitive.

Anton MILH op & Stephan VAN ERP,
Identité et visibilité. Conflits de générations chez les Dominicains.

Denis LABOURE,
Astrologie et religion au Moyen Age.

Jorel FRANÇOIS,
Voltaire, philosophe de la religion.

Augustin WILIWOLI SIBILONI op,
La reconnaissance. Réparer les blessures.

Jean Baptiste ZEKE,
Loi naturelle et post-humanisme.

Emmanuel BOISSIEU,
Paul Ricœur. Un inconditionnel de l'amour.

Ameer JAJE,
Le chiisme. Clés historiques et théologiques.

Jean-René PEGGARY,
L'aube d'une pensée américaine. L'individu chez H. D. Thoreau.

Jean-François ARNOUX,
Comme un feu dévorant. Flammèches d'une lecture incarnée de la Bible.

Olivier BELLEIL,
L'autre dans l'islam coranique.

Sœur Agnès DE LA CROIX,
Miroir juif des évangiles.

Jean-Michel COSSE,
Au centre de l'âme.

Jean-Paul BALDAZZA,
Antoine. Un saint d'Orient et d'Occident.

Ameer JAJE,
Marie dans l'islam.

Olivier PERRU,
Le corps malade.

Jesmond MICALLEF,
Trinitarian Ontology.

Abel TOE,
Pauvreté et développement au Burkina-Faso.

Jude Thaddeus MBI AKEM,
Le développement en Afrique.

Claude LICHTERT,
Lire la Bible ensemble.

Jorel FRANÇOIS,
Voltaire, philosophe contre le fanatisme.

Bruno CALLEBAUT,
Les Évangiles. Leurs origines, leurs exégèses.

Claude LICHTERT,
La parole pour sortir de soi. Dieu et les humains aujourd'hui : parcours biblique.

Heriberto CABRERA REYES,
Effondrement, apocalypse ou renaissance ? Théologie en temps de crise.

Patrick MONJOU,
Comment prêcher à la fin du Moyen Âge ? (T. 1 et T. 2).

Robert PLÉTY,
À la découverte du Rabbi de Nazareth (T. 1).

Robert PLÉTY,
À la rencontre du Rabbi de Nazareth (T. 2).

Jules KATSURANA,
Guide pour la Prévention de la violence sexiste.

Jacques FOURNIER,
La Trinité, mystère d'amour.

Louis D'HÉROUVILLE,
Marie-Madeleine, femme pascale.

Olivier PERRU,
Martin-Stanislas Gillet (1875-1951). La peur de l'effort intellectuel.

Paul-Marcel LEMAIRE,
Vivre l'Évangile.

John Jack LYNCH,
Judith, Sarah and Esther. Jewish heroines.

Paul NYAGA,
Moral Consistency with Lonergan's Thought.

François FAURE,
Emmanuel Mounier : La personne est son engagement (T. 1).

François FAURE,
Emmanuel Mounier : Montrer, sans démontrer (T. 2).

Olivier-Thomas VENARD, Gregory TATUM,
Conversations sur Paul. « Supportez-vous les uns les autres ».

Isaac MUTELO,
Muslim Organisations in South Africa. Political Role Post-1948.

Stephen Musisi KASOZI,
Issues of Constitutionalism. A case study of Uganda.

Pierre Dalin DOMERSON,
La gestion des biens de l'Eglise. Enjeu pastoral.

Philippe ANDRÈS,
Notre-Dame de Rocamadour. Du Moyen Âge à nos jours.

Oliver BARRETT,
Ecological Crisis. In Catholic Social Teaching.

Augustin WILIWOLI SIBILONI,
Négociation pacifique des conflits sociaux.

Alfred DIBAN KI,
Ubuntu et vie chrétienne.

Claude VALENTIN,
99 Questions sur l'Humanitaire.

Philippe MONTOISY,
Le chien militaire et la Première Guerre mondiale.

Alice NEPVEU-BARRIEUX,
La marine dans l'Ancien Testament.
Représentations et enjeux.

Marie MONNET,
En chemin.

Christophe-Marie, O.P. MOGHA NGAMANAPO MUDAKA,
L'éducation en crise.
Analyse philosophique.

Caroline FERRER,
Saint Jérôme dans la collection Fesch en Corse.